Personal Financial Literacy

Jeff Madura

Mike Casey

Sherry J. Roberts

Prentice Hall

Boston   San Francisco   New York
London   Toronto   Sydney   Tokyo   Singapore   Madrid
Mexico City   Munich   Paris   Cape Town   Hong Kong   Montreal

To my wife Diane for all of her encouragement during this project.
—Mike Casey

To my parents, John and Jean Roberts, for teaching me how to be a lifelong learner.
To Terris, Abigail, Ariadne, and Meghan, this textbook is for your future.
—Sherry J. Roberts

Editor in Chief: Donna Battista
Assistant Editor: Kerri McQueen
Development Editor: Peter Lacey
Managing Editor: Jeff Holcomb
Senior Production Supervisor: Meredith Gertz
Director of Media: Susan Schoenberg
MyFinanceLab Content Lead: Miguel Leonarte
Media Project Managers: Arti Sharma and Holly Wallace Bastier
Media Producer: Nicole Sackin
Senior Manufacturing Buyer: Carol Melville
Senior Media Buyer: Ginny Michaud
Senior Author Support/Technology Specialist: Joe Vetere
Electronic Production Specialist: Dawn M. Stratchko
Permissions Supervisor: Charles Morris
Permissions Editor: Wendy Guarino
Manager, Rights and Permissions: Zina Arabia
Manager, Research Development: Elaine Soares
Image Permission Coordinator: Jan Marc Quisumbing
Image Researcher: Kathy Ringrose
Project Management, Composition, Illustrations, and Text Design: Gillian Hall, The Aardvark Group
Copy Editor: Kathleen Cantwell, C4 Technologies
Proofreader: Holly McLean-Aldis
Indexer: Jack Lewis
Design Manager: Linda Knowles
Cover Designer: Susan Paradise
Cover illustration: © Doug Rugh/Images.com/Corbis

The Career Clusters icons in Chapter 5 are being used with the permission of the States' Career Clusters Initiative, 2009, www.careerclusters.org.

Library of Congress Cataloging-in-Publication Data
Madura, Jeff.
   Personal financial literacy / Jeff Madura, K. Michael Casey, Sherry J. Roberts.
      p. cm.
   Also issued as multi-volume publication.
   Includes bibliographical references and index.
   ISBN 978-0-321-54775-0 (alk. paper) -- ISBN 978-0-13-607641-4 (annotated instructor's edition : alk. paper)
   1. Finance, Personal--United States. I. Casey, K. Michael. II. Roberts, Sherry J. III. Title.
   HG179.M2522 2010
   332.02400973--dc22   2009003031

Prentice Hall
is an imprint of

www.pearsonhighered.com

ISBN-13: 978-0-321-54775-0
ISBN-10: 0-321-54775-6
5 6 7 8 9 10—CRK—13 12 11

To the Student,

We all make personal financial decisions every day of our lives. Many of those decisions have a lasting impact that we may fail to see. For example, if you began saving $1,000 a year when you were 16 and could earn 10 percent a year, you could accumulate over $1.16 millon by the time you turned 66. If you waited until you were 26 to begin the same investment, you would only accumulate about $440,000. Waiting a mere 10 years could cost you $700,000! This is just one example of how an understanding of personal finance can have a tremendous impact on your future.

Our primary goal with this text is to provide you with some basic personal finance tools and knowledge that will enable you to build the life you want. The text is organized into four units that group topical areas together.

Unit 1, on financial responsibility and decision-making, focuses on the creation of a financial plan, goal setting, and budgeting. This unit will encourage you to begin thinking about your goals and provides you with the tools to begin achieving those goals.

Unit 2 focuses on income and careers. Did you know that your choice of career is a financial decision? In addition, we discuss taxes, benefit packages, and how certain trends in the economy could impact you. For example, what should you do individually in response to expected changes in Social Security?

Unit 3 focuses on spending and credit. How do you establish and maintain good credit? What are the benefits of good credit? Should you apply for credit cards? Given the recent mortgage crisis and subsequent foreclosures, these topics are critical to everyone.

Finally, Unit 4 focuses on saving and investing, including discussions of various investment vehicles and the time value of money. Retirement and estate planning are also explored, since an early start can virtually guarantee financial security in your later years.

Personal financial knowledge can provide you with power over your future. It is our sincere hope that you will learn and apply this material to your everyday life. We believe that if you choose to do so, you will discover a world of possibilities and options that will contribute to your future happiness.

Jeff Madura
Mike Casey
Sherry J. Roberts

Real-World Applications

From start to finish, *Personal Financial Literacy* is filled with examples, stories, and applications designed to grab the attention of today's high schooler.

Chapter-Opening Scenarios

These engaging introductory stories set the stage and are revisited throughout the chapter to illustrate the issue being addressed and its relevance to students.

Terris walked into his new apartment and sat down. After completing a prestigious music program in New York, the day he had been working toward for years was finally here. In his hands was his first paycheck from his first real job! At long last, he could begin to live the life of his dreams.

Immediately he began to think about the purchases he had been putting off for so long—a new car, a laptop, some nice clothes. Maybe he could buy season tickets for baseball or a new stereo system. Or perhaps he could finally make good on his promise to his friend Martin to take

Learning Objectives

Correlated to the main chapter heading, these clearly stated goals help students connect classroom learning to their own lives.

Learning Objectives

Explain the steps involved in creating a budget.

Explain the steps involved in creating a personal balance sheet.

Analyze the importance of budgeting in your financial plan.

Professor FIN

This cartoon representation of an instructor relates funny and interesting facts about the world of personal finance.

Professor FIN

Facts about the "graying of America":

- Because of healthier lifestyles, Americans have added 25 years to their life spans over the last several decades. In 2005, there were 36 million Americans over the age of 65. By 2020, this number is expected to be closer to 55 million.

- One million Americans turn age 60 every month!

Finance ONLINE

Meets Phase 3 of the NCLB requirement for technology by guiding students to Web-based personal finance tools and resources.

Finance ONLINE

If you want to compare the buying power of $20 or any other amount from one year to another, visit **www.bls.gov** and click the link to the inflation calculator. It is fun and informative to see how inflation can affect your money!

Personal Financial Literacy provides extensive, immediate opportunities to reinforce concepts, assess mastery, and demonstrate relevance to both real life and other curriculum areas.

Key Terms

Taken from each chapter's learning objectives, these terms are prominently listed right at the start of the chapter. To bring learning full circle, they're also included in the end-of-chapter sections along with additional vocabulary.

> ### Key Terms
>
> Bond
> Budget
> Investment
> Market value
> Mutual fund
> Personal balance sheet
> Real estate
> Stock

MATH for Personal Finance

Reinforces the basic math skills students need to navigate the real world of personal finance. This feature meets Phase 1 of NCLB requirements.

> ### MATH for Personal Finance
>
> Lakisha's car is worth about $6,000 and she still owes $1,200 on it. She has an outstanding credit card balance of $450.
>
> **What is her net worth?**
>
> Solution: Lakisha's net worth is $6,000 − $1,200 − $450 = $4,350.

CHECK Your Financial IQ

"How am I doing?" Lets students self-assess their mastery of key concepts and each chapter's Learning Objectives.

> ☑ CHECK Your Financial IQ
> What are the steps involved in creating a budget?

Teamwork

Ideas for group activities, related to the concepts and content, allow students to practice topics just covered.

> ### Teamwork
>
> In teams, research the Great Depression. Develop a skit, poster, PowerPoint presentation, or newsletter that traces the history of the Great Depression.
>
> You might know an older adult who lived through the Great Depression or was born near the end of it. You could interview that person to learn firsthand information about how it was living during this period. You might look up information about teenagers during the Great Depression.

Student Workbook

In addition to practice features found within the text, look here for additional practice and assessment opportunities, including vocabulary checks, math checks, and open-response questions. Sample pages from the *Student Workbook* appear at the end of this Preface. The workbook is available for purchase. See page vii.

> Name: _____
> Date: _____
>
> **CHAPTER 4**
>
> Budgets and Balance Sheets:
> Your Personal Financial Statements
>
> OPEN RESPONSE #2
>
> *Please answer all parts of the question in the space provided.*
> **Prompt:** Below is Peter's weekly and monthly budget:
>
> **Peter's Budget**
>
> | Cash Inflows | Typical Week | Typical Monthly Total |
> |---|---|---|
> | Disposable Income (after tax) | $125 | $550 |
> | Allowance (from parents) | $50 | $220 |

"You Do It" icons in the text indicate that students can apply the concept being discussed using the workbook activity indicated.

You
Do It

Activity #1

Assessment

Personal Financial Literacy combines a rich array of end-of-chapter questions and problems with a robust *Student Workbook* for multiple opportunities to assess subject knowledge. These tools also give students multiple opportunities to put their critical thinking, math, cross-disciplinary, ethical reasoning, and team-building skills to the test.

What Are the Connections?

End-of-chapter activities illustrate links between personal finance concepts and other curriculum areas, including math, technology, science, and language arts. Weekly writing prompts meet Phase 1 of the NCLB language arts requirement.

Teamwork

Provides ideas for group activities to assess comprehension and application.

What Are Your Finance Math Skills?

Students gauge their knowledge through real-life scenarios that allow for assessment of both chapter content mastery and math skills.

What Do You Know?

End-of-chapter activities pick up the pace by encouraging higher-level critical thinking skills.

w!se End-of-Chapter Problems

Working In Support of Education (W!SE) is an educational nonprofit dedicated to providing educational support services nationwide to build financial literacy. These end-of-chapter problems were developed by W!SE and are modeled after the types of problems found on the *W!SE Financial Literacy Certification Exam*.

Student Workbook

Provides additional assessment opportunities, including vocabulary checks, math checks, open-response questions, and personal finance activities. The workbook is available for purchase. See page vii.

The *Personal Financial Literacy* program combines critical content and student-friendly delivery with the flexibility and support tools you need.

Student Text

Choose from a comprehensive 15-chapter, single volume (0321547756) or four separate units:

1. Financial Responsibility & Decision Making (0136087906)
2. Income & Careers (0136087914)
3. Spending & Credit (0136087922)
4. Saving & Investing (0136087930)

Student Supplements

Student Workbook (0136087566)

This workbook features open-response questions, additional vocabulary review exercises, and personal finance activity worksheets.

Math Workbook (0136095186)

This workbook provides additional math-focused practice and assessment opportunities, from basic math drills to more complex math for personal finance.

Personal Finance Journal (0136076424)

This 30-day journal allows students to track their daily spending down to the smallest purchase.

MyFinLitLab™ (www.MyFinLitLab.com)

MyFinLitLab™ is a powerful online homework, tutorial, and assessment system that accompanies the comprehensive version of the text and is available for purchase with any unit or as a stand-alone item.

With MyFinLitLab™, teachers can create, edit, and assign online homework and tests using content developed from end-of-chapter and Math Workbook material that is marked with the MyFinLitLab™ logo. Teachers can also import TestGen questions for added flexibility. All student work is tracked in the MyFinLitLab™ gradebook.

Students can use MyFinLitLab™ for self-study, even if teachers don't set up a course. Students can take preloaded sample tests and receive personalized study plans based on the test results. Study plans diagnose weaknesses and link students directly to tutorial exercises covering topics they need to practice.

To Access MyFinLitLab™

Access to MyFinLitLab™ is included with the purchase of the single-volume student edition. Access for teachers and students is as follows:

Teachers

- All purchasers will automatically receive a pin code card (0130343919) that will allow access for up to 2 teachers and up to 50 students.

- Teacher access for previewers or adopters can be obtained by registering at www.PearsonSchool.com/Access_Request. Using section 2, select the title of the text, then complete and submit the brief registration form. All teacher requests will be verified.
- Registered teachers automatically receive access for the following year's class via e-mail (occurs each May for up to 6 years).

Students
- Student access is available to adopters through the teacher.

To Purchase MyFinLitLab™

Teachers may purchase class registration kits in packages of 10 or 25 student redemptions. Each package includes teacher access codes.

- Class Registration Kit: 10 Student Access Codes (0136117597)
- Class Registration Kit: 25 Student Access Codes (0136117589)
- Student access is for 12 months from date of access code redemption.

For questions concerning access, please contact your local Pearson sales representative or e-mail PHwebaccess@pearsoned.com.

Companion Web Site (PearsonSchool.com/PersonalFinance)

This open-access Companion Website features the glossary, flash cards, and student workbook activity templates, and Web sites from the book.

Teacher Supplements

All teacher supplements and resources for this book are available electronically on the Instructor Resource Center. Upon adoption or to preview, please go to **PearsonSchool.com/Advanced** and select "Online Teacher Supplements." You will be required to complete a one-time registration before you are e-mailed access information to download materials.

The following items are available to qualified adopters:

Annotated Instructor Edition (0136076416)

The *Annotated Instructor Edition* of the single-volume text includes answers and solutions to all "Check Your Financial IQ" questions and end-of-chapter questions and problems.

Teacher's Resource Binder (0136087558)

The *Teacher's Resource Binder* includes the following items:

- **Test Item File** with multiple-choice, matching, true/false, and short answer questions
- **Teacher Guide** with lesson plans, tips on teaching the chapter, Internet resources, information on differentiated learning, and additional activities
- **Transparency Masters** with lecture notes
- **Annotated Editions** of the *Student Workbook* and *Math Workbook* with solutions to all questions and problems

Instructor's Resource CD-ROM (0136087418)

Take advantage of time-saving PowerPoint® files, which include all figures from the text, lecture notes, and electronic versions of all resources found in the Teacher Resource Binder. In addition, the Test Item File is available in easy-to-use TestGen®. TestGen® enables instructors to view, edit, and add questions; transfer questions to tests; and print different forms of tests.

w!se | **Financial Literacy** CERTIFICATION

Working in Support of Education (W!SE)

Pearson Education is proud to partner with **W!SE**—Working in Support of Education. **W!SE** is an educational 501(c)3 nonprofit dedicated to providing educational support services nationwide, building financial literacy, fostering business and social entrepreneurship, and preparing students for college and the global workplace.

The **W!SE** family of innovative programs positively affects the lives of students and improves the quality of education. **W!SE** inspires students to dream and prepare for their future, equips them with the tools and life skills they need to achieve their full potential, and encourages them to make good choices.

Extensive partnerships with schools and the private sector and a reputation for sustainable programs with measurable results have made **W!SE** a leader in the educational community.

Pearson has partnered with **W!SE** to provide students with questions developed by **W!SE** and which follow the **W!SE** standards and methodology used in the Financial Literacy Certification Test. Look for the **W!SE** logo at the end of each chapter to find the materials developed by **W!SE**.

Financial Literacy Certification Program

Most students who drop out of college do so not because of academic failure but because of personal debt, and the fastest growing group of people filing personal bankruptcy is in the 18 to 25 age range.

W!SE's Financial Literacy Certification Program addresses the urgent need for financial literacy and education. The program provides high school students with access to financial education and the opportunity to earn certification in financial literacy. Participating schools teach personal finance and administer **W!SE**'s standardized Financial Literacy Certification (CFL) Test. Teachers have access to training, educational resources, pretests, and online practice tests. Students who pass the CFL Test are Certified Financially Literate, earning their CFL. Developed in 2003, the program has expanded nationally and has been widely recognized for its success, including the 2007 U.S. Treasury Department's John Sherman Award for Excellence in Financial Education.

W!SE programs reach more than 20,000 students each year.

About the Authors

Jeff Madura

Jeff Madura is the SunTrust Bank Professor of Finance at Florida Atlantic University. He has written several textbooks, including *Financial Markets and Institutions*. His research on international finance has been published in numerous journals, including *Journal of Financial and Quantitative Analysis*; *Journal of Money, Credit and Banking*; *Journal of Financial Research*; *Financial Review*; *Journal of Multinational Financial Management*; and *Global Finance Journal*. He has received awards for excellence in teaching and research and has served as a consultant for international banks, securities firms, and other multinational corporations. He has served as a director for the Southern Finance Association and Eastern Finance Association, and also served as president of the Southern Finance Association.

Mike Casey

Mike Casey is the McCastlain Professor of Finance and Chair of the department of Economics, Finance, Insurance and Risk Management (EFIRM) at the University of Central Arkansas. He has a doctorate in finance from Louisiana Tech University and has served as a media consultant for Active Learning Technologies, Inc. He has published over 70 refereed journal publications in such journals as *The Financial Review*, *The Journal of Computer Information Systems*, *The Review of Business Information Systems*, *Real Estate Review*, *The Journal of Property Investment and Finance*, *The Journal of Real Estate Finance and Economics*, the *Quarterly Review of Economics and Finance*, and the *Journal of Lending and Credit Risk Management*. Dr. Casey is also a Registered Investment Advisor Representative for Mustard Seed Financial, LLC, a fee-only financial planning firm.

Sherry J. Roberts

Sherry J. Roberts has been teaching for 23 years. She taught 14 of those years as a business education teacher at the secondary level. Dr. Roberts currently teaches at Middle Tennessee State University in the Jennings A. Jones College of Business. Her presentations include international, national, regional, and state levels on the subjects of instructional technology and business education. As a consultant for Roberts Educational Consultants, Dr. Roberts provided professional development in instructional technology, writing portfolios, open response, and business education. She has also been an instructor with the University of Central Arkansas Insurance Education Institute and Personal Finance Institute. Her doctorate is from the University of Louisville in Curriculum and Instruction.

Acknowledgments

The authors extend their thanks to the many people who have offered their support and guidance throughout this project.

Thanks to Donna Battista, Kerri McQueen, and Peter Lacey for all your hard work during the development of the book; and to Meredith Gertz and Gillian Hall for putting our words into a beautiful book. You've been a wonderful team to work with. Mike Casey would like to thank Sherry Roberts for having such a great idea and pushing him to collaborate, and Sherry Roberts would like to thank Mike Casey for listening to her idea and helping to transform that idea into a book.

We would like to thank the following educators who have generously shared their constructive criticism on every chapter and feature:

Tim Ballas, *Marion Technical Institute, Florida*

Gary Benson, *Seward High School, Alaska*

Matt Bergman, *Cocalico High School, Pennsylvania*

Jennifer Birkmeier, *Blaine High School, Minnesota*

Sandi Bullington, *Neosho High School, Missouri*

Nettie Carson, *Mullins, Alabama State Department of Education, Alabama*

Amy Collette, *David Crockett High School, Tennessee*

Mary Davis, *Marian Catholic High School, Pennsylvania*

Renee Dickson, *Mcguffey High School, Pennsylvania*

Shok Dylan, *Bronx School of Law and Finance, New York*

Monica Edwards, *Greene County High School, Mississippi*

Marilyn Erwin, *Pickens County High School, Alabama*

Lori Fordyce, *St. Joseph Central, Missouri*

Marlene Grabbe, *Marion Technical Institute, Florida*

Jon Greenwalt, *New York State Education Department, New York*

Linda Hayes, *Northampton High School, Pennsylvania*

Melanie D. Herring, *Fike High School, North Carolina*

Joel Hilbrink, *Ninilchik High School, Alaska*

Todd Howsare, *Dunedin High School, Florida*

Elaine Hutson, *Union High School, Missouri*

Chakita Jackson, *Hazelwood West High School, Missouri*

Brenda A. Jenkins, *Fredericktown High School, Missouri*

Frank Lane, *Salisbury High School, Pennsylvania*

Linda Leeking, *Warwick School District, Pennsylvania*

Linda Love, *Villa Maria Academy, Pennsylvania*

Lana Main, *Brandon Valley High School, South Dakota*

Audrey Marshall, *Auburn High School, Alabama*

Larry Mark McGee, *West Johnston High School, North Carolina*

Barbara McQueen, P.D. Jackson, *Olin High School, Alabama*

Kenneth Mengani, *Franklin K. Lane High School, New York*

Judy Mitchell, *Thomas More Prep, Marian, Kansas*

Michele Moore, *Monrovia High School, Indiana*

Trey Ondrus, *Siegel High School, Tennessee*

Linda Ralston, *Nikiski Middle/High School, Alaska*

Barbara Ramsdell, *Elk River High School, Minnesota*

Kay Roberts, *Red Spring High School, North Carolina*

Amy Rosenkrans, *MD Council on Economic Education, Maryland*

Bonnie Sibert, *Nebraska Department of Education, Nebraska*

Heidi Stirm, *Melba High School, Idaho*

Carl Sundell, *Hunter High School, Utah*

Thomas Svehla, *Oak Park High School, Missouri*

Deb Tettenborn, *Abraham Lincoln High School, Iowa*

Marla Thompson, *North Platte High School, Nebraska*

James Timmons, *Heide Trask High School, North Carolina*

Eileen Tims, *Memorial Senior High School, Texas*

Margaret A. Wanger, *Interboro High School, Pennsylvania*

Patricia Wheatley, *Turkeyfoot Valley Area High School, Pennsylvania*

—Jeff Madura, Mike Casey, and Sherry J. Roberts

Credits

Page Number	Description and Credit
2, 5, 20, 21, 36, 37, 43, 45, 52, 60, 68, 78, 90, 93, 98, 105, 112, 113, 115, 120, 130, 131, 132, 167, 168, 190, 191, 212, 213, 222, 232, 242, 252, 262, 275, 276	Photos: © 2009 iStockphoto.com
3, 7, 22, 69, 76, 91, 253	Photos: © 2009 Jupiterimages Corporation
4, 15, 26, 54, 70, 92, 132, 163, 181, 203	Cartoons: © 2007 ZITS Partnership Distributed by King Features Syndicate.
11	Screenshot: Reproduced with permission of Yahoo! Inc. © 2008 Yahoo! Inc. YAHOO! and the YAHOO! Logo are registered trademarks of Yahoo! Inc.
28, 93, 103	Photos: © 2009 JUPITERIMAGES/ClipArt.com
38	Cartoon: © 2005 ZITS Partnership Distributed by King Features Syndicate.
53	Photo: © 2009 RubberBall Productions/PunchStock
56	Photo attributed to http://www.flickr.com/photos/76046205@N00/119753144/. Reproduced under Flickr's Creative Commons License Deed.
57	Photo: © 2009 WebStockPro
58	Screenshot: Reprinted by permission of Forbes Magazine © 2008 Forbes LLC
70, 72, 73, 75, 78	Icons: © 2008, States' Career Clusters Initiative. All Rights Reserved.
131, 233, 256	Photos: © 2009 Getty Images
154, 172	Photos: © 2009 Corbis Images
169	Figure 10.1: © 2009 Digital Federal Credit Union. Printed with permission.
	Photo: © 2009 Shutterstock Images/Anthony Cottrell
170	Finance Online: © 2009 Capital One. Printed with permission.
178	Photos: The Kelley Blue Book trademark and photos are used with permission of Kelley Blue Book Co., Inc.
192, 215	Photos attributed to http://www.flickr.com/photos/thetruthabout/2666475768/. Reproduced under Flickr's Creative Commons License Deed.
198	Finance Online: © 2009 CreditCards.com. Printed with permission.
200	Finance Online: © 2009 Google. Printed with permission.
201	Photo: © 2009 Gregory F. Maxwell. Reproduced under the terms of the GNU Free Documentation License, Version 1.2 published by the Free Software Foundation.
214, 234	Cartoons: © 2004 ZITS Partnership Distributed by King Features Syndicate.
241	Figure 13.4: Printed by permission from Financial Planning Toolkit (www.finance.cch.com)
254, 276	Cartoons: © 2008 ZITS Partnership Distributed by King Features Syndicate.
	Professor Fin artwork courtesy of Jason Consalvo.

Personal Financial Literacy

The following pages are taken directly from the *Student Workbook*.

In addition to practice features found within the text, look here for additional practice and assessment opportunities, including vocabulary checks, math checks, and open response questions.

The workbook is available for purchase. See page vii.

Jeff Madura
Mike Casey
Sherry J. Roberts

CHAPTER 4

Budgets and Balance Sheets:
Your Personal Financial Statements

VOCABULARY CHECK

1. Samantha decided to sell her ATV so she could have extra cash for books when she began vocational school after graduation. She bought the ATV for $2,300 but sold it for $1,200. This lower price is the _____ of the ATV.

2. XYZ Company has decided to raise money by issuing debt in $1,000 increments that are known as _____ .

3. Terris needs to forecast his future cash inflow and outflow. To help him do this he must create a _____ that will help with his financial planning.

4. Meghan's grandfather left a portion of his farm to her in his will. Upon his death, Meghan will own _____ and can count this as an asset.

5. Georgia takes a look at her budget. She sees a difference in what she forecast would happen and what is really happening. This difference is known as _____ .

6. Antwone needs to keep track of how much money he is worth. One tool that he could use to help make this decision is a _____ .

7. Jonathan's car was having brake problems. He needed cash fast to help pay for repairs. He had set aside some money in _____ that should be enough to cover the repairs.

8. David's parents invested in a _____ as part of their Section 529 College Savings Plan for his higher education.

9. Terris wanted to get a loan but needed to lists his assets. He already knew the value of his violin but needed to include his car, furniture, entertainment system, and other _____ .

10. Jonathan's credit card debt is a _____ , while his student loan for school is a _____ .

11. Terris purchased a violin that would grow in value over time. Terris decided this would be a good _____ in his future as a professional musician.

12. When Joley's dad decided to start a business, he sold _____ to investors as part ownership in the business.

13. Jonathan owes $2,000 on his credit card. This is listed as a _____ on his balance sheet.

14. When Terris calculates his assets and subtracts his liabilities, the difference is his _____ .

Bond

Budget

Current liability

Forecast error

Household asset

Investment

Liability

Liquid asset

Long-term liability

Market value

Mutual fund

Net worth

Personal balance sheet

Real estate

Stock

CHAPTER 4

Budgets and Balance Sheets:
Your Personal Financial Statements

CHECK YOUR KNOWLEDGE

Asset or Liability? You be the judge. In the blank beside each word place an **A** if it is an asset or an **L** if it is a liability. Remember, assets are things you own or possess and liabilities are debts that you owe.

_____ Car

_____ Car note

_____ Dirt bike

_____ IBM stock

_____ Savings account

_____ Mutual fund

_____ A loan from your parents

_____ Credit card bill

_____ Xbox

_____ Clothing

_____ Cash

_____ $20 you owe a friend

_____ Past due amount for lunch

_____ Guitar

Multiple Choice Questions *Circle the correct answer for each of the following.*

1. Which of the following is not a tool for monitoring your finances?
   a. personal balance sheet
   b. budget
   c. liability
   d. cash flow statement

2. One way to increase savings is to _____ cash inflows.
   a. increase
   b. decrease
   c. spend
   d. monitor

3. A scholarship would be an example of a cash _____.
   a. outflow
   b. inflow
   c. decrease
   d. statement

4. Which of the following is not an asset?
   a. car
   b. stock
   c. credit card bill
   d. jewelry

5. Shares of ownership in a company are represented by _____.
   a. bonds
   b. stocks
   c. assets
   d. liabilities

6. Your net worth is calculated by summing up the value of your _____ and subtracting your liabilities.
   a. stocks
   b. cars
   c. assets
   d. debts

7. Which of the following is more likely to be a long-term liability?
   a. house payment
   b. credit card bill
   c. electric bill
   d. water bill

8. If you buy land that increases in value your _____ will increase as long as your debt remains the same or declines.
   a. net worth
   b. liabilities
   c. budget
   d. cash flows

9. If your total debt is $4,500 and the value of your assets is $9,100 then your debt-to-asset ratio is equal to _____.
   a. 2.02 percent
   b. 49.40 percent
   c. 57.05 percent
   d. 50.60 percent

10. Which of the following is a type of college savings plan created by the government to encourage people to save for their children's and grandchildren's education?
    a. bond savings alternatives
    b. stock plans
    c. Section 529 plans
    d. IRS college funds

SCANS Foundation Skills: Basic

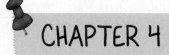

CHAPTER 4

Budgets and Balance Sheets:
Your Personal Financial Statements

MATH CHECK UP

Instructions: *In the space provided, answer each of the following math problems. Be sure to show your work in the space provided.*

1. Tammy owns a laptop computer she paid $1,200 for about two years ago. Today, she thinks she could sell it for about $700. She also has a car worth $2,900 on which she still owes $800 and that will be paid off next year. How much is her net worth?

2. Valerie's monthly income is $450 and her monthly outflows are $425. How much money could Valerie save in the next eight months without changing her income or spending patterns?

3. Jamal wants to save at least 8 percent of his income every month for a year. Assume he gets a $100 allowance every month from his grandfather and he makes an average of $320 a month working part time after school. How much will he save in one year?

4. Lakita's dad was teaching her about the stock market. He has 100 shares of Company A stock valued at $45 a share and 250 shares of Company B stock valued at $22 a share. How much is his stock worth?

5. Jill estimated she would spend $50 a month on clothing. However, at the end of the year she discovered she actually spent $711 on clothing that year. What was her forecast error for that budget item?

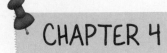

CHAPTER 4

Budgets and Balance Sheets:
Your Personal Financial Statements

OPEN RESPONSE #1: Planning a Budget

Please answer all parts of the question in the space provided.

Prompt: Samantha wants to move into an apartment when she begins school in the fall. Right now she has a job where she makes $250 a week working 20 hours and will be able to keep this job once she begins school. Her parents have decided to put $500 a month in for extras that she might need once she begins school. Although Samantha is very excited about moving into an apartment, she wants your advice on where to begin preparing for her move. She wants to put together a budget but has no idea where to begin.

1. Explain to Samantha how to set up her budget.

2. Once Samantha has a budget, what should she consider when determining if moving out when she is beginning school is a good idea or not. Give specific reasons why this might be a good or bad idea.

Scoring Guide

4 Student gives correct answers for parts 1 and 2. All explanations are clear and complete. There is evidence of clear understanding of the concept.

3 Student gives correct answers for parts 1 and 2. Explanations are correct, but possibly unclear. There is less evidence of clear understanding.

2 Student answers 1 (1 or 2) part of the questions completely correct. There is some evidence of understanding.

1 Student gives only parts of correct answers. There is little evidence of understanding.

0 Response is totally incorrect or irrelevant (does not add any new information to the question).

_____

_____

_____

_____

_____

_____

_____

_____

_____

Name: _____

Date: _____

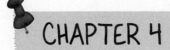

CHAPTER 4

Budgets and Balance Sheets:
Your Personal Financial Statements

OPEN RESPONSE #2: Cash Inflow and Cash Outflow

Please answer all parts of the question in the space provided.

Prompt: Below is Peter's weekly and monthly budget:

Peter's Budget

Cash Inflows	Typical Week	Typical Monthly Total
Disposable Income (after tax)	$125	$550
Allowance (from parents)	$50	$220
Total Cash Inflows	$175	$770
Cash Outflows		
Recreation	$60	$250
Gas (for parents' car)	$40	$180
Clothing	$10	$50
Cell Phone (with text messaging)	$12	$50
Other	$20	$100
Total Cash Outflows	$142	$630
Net Cash Flows	+$33	+$140

1. Peter wants to buy a used car. His father has agreed to put in half the cost of the car up to $2,500. What advice can you give Peter to help him save for the car he wants?

2. Once Peter purchases his car, how will this affect his cash outflow? What will he need to do to adjust his budget after the purchase of his car?

Scoring Guide

4 Student gives correct answers for parts 1 and 2. All explanations are clear and complete. There is evidence of clear understanding of the concept.

3 Student gives correct answers for parts 1 and 2. Explanations are correct, but possibly unclear. There is less evidence of clear understanding.

2 Student answers 1 (1 or 2) part of the questions completely correct. There is some evidence of understanding.

1 Student gives only parts of correct answers. There is little evidence of understanding.

0 Response is totally incorrect or irrelevant (does not add any new information to the question).

CHAPTER 4

Budgets and Balance Sheets:
Your Personal Financial Statements

ACTIVITY #1: Personal Cash Flow Statement

Personal Cash Flow Statement

Cash Inflows	Actual Amounts Last Week	Expected Amounts This Week
Disposable Income from Job (after tax)		
Allowance		
Special Event Monies (birthday money, graduation money, etc.)		
Other		
Total Cash Inflows		

Cash Outflows	Actual Amounts Last Week	Expected Amounts This Week
Car Payment		
Car Expenses (insurance, maintenance, and gas)		
Cell Phone		
Food (eating out and at home)		
Clothing		
Entertainment (movies, dates, etc.)		
Extra (makeup, hair products, etc.)		
Other		
Total Cash Outflows		
Net Cash Flow		

Instructions:

1. Determine your cash inflow for last week. This could be from a job you have, from an allowance, or from any other source. Put this under the first column of *Cash Inflows*.

2. Think about what you spent last week. Look at the different titles under *Cash Outflows*. Put the totals for each outflow that you have under the first column of *Cash Outflows*.

3. Under the second column of *Cash Inflows*, place the estimated amounts you expect to receive this week. Remember to include expected income from all possible sources.

4. Under the second column of *Cash Outflows*, place the estimated amounts you expect to spend for each item. There may be an item you will not have an amount for during this week. You might have an item for which you had no spending last week but for which you expect to have some this week. For example, last week there was no school dance but this week you have a school dance. Maybe you will spend more this week than last week.

SCANS Foundation Skills: Basic, Thinking, and Personal
SCANS Workplace Skills: Resources, Information, and Systems

CHAPTER 4

Budgets and Balance Sheets:
Your Personal Financial Statements

ACTIVITY #2: Creating an Annual Budget

Annual Budget

Cash Inflows	Typical Month	One Year's Cash Flow
Disposable Income (after tax)		
Allowance		
Special Event Monies (birthday money, graduation money, etc.)		
Other		
Total Cash Inflows		
Cash Outflows	**Typical Month**	**One Year's Cash Flow**
Car Payment		
Car Expenses (insurance, maintenance, and gas)		
Cell Phone		
Food (eating out and at home)		
Clothing		
Entertainment (movies, dates, etc.)		
Extra (makeup, hair products, etc.)		
Other		
Total Cash Outflows		
Net Cash Flow		

Instructions:

1. Look at your Personal Cash Flow Statement (Activity #1). You can see how much your expected net cash flow will be as you go through the month. Next, think about the whole

year. Some months you might spend more (the holidays, spring break, vacation during the summer, dances, birthdays of friends and family, and so on).

2. The first column of this budget activity identifies what your expected cash inflows and outflows will be for a typical month. Using the figures you have in your personal cash flow statement for one week, determine the cash flow for one month. Put these figures in the appropriate column on the chart given.

3. To calculate your cash flow for a year, multiply each of the figures in the first column by 12. For example, if your income is $400 per month, then $400 × 12 = $4,800. So you would put $4,800 in the *Year* column for income.

SCANS Foundation Skills: Basic, Thinking, and Personal
SCANS Workplace Skills: Resources, Information, and Systems

CHAPTER 4

Budgets and Balance Sheets:
Your Personal Financial Statements

ACTIVITY #3: Creating a Personal Balance Sheet

Instructions:

1. Determine the value of your assets. You can do this by looking at how much money (cash) you have in your "piggy bank," checking account, and savings account. You also know the value of any other assets you might have, such as computer equipment, entertainment systems, gaming units, car, ATV, musical instruments, and so on. Put these under the *Assets* column.

2. Now you must determine if you have any liabilities. You may have a credit card or money you owe to a parent or the bank. List these next under *Liabilities*.

3. Total each section (*Assets* and *Liabilities*). To calculate your *Net Worth*, subtract your assets from your liabilities. For example, if your total assets are $1,200 and your total liabilities are $600, then your net worth would equal $600 ($1,200 – $600 = $600).

Personal Balance Sheet

Assets		Totals
Cash		
Car (and/or other vehicle)		
Entertainment System		
Computer Equipment		
Other (list)		
Total Assets		
Liabilities		
Credit Card Balance		
Outstanding Loans (bank, parents, etc.)		
Other (list)		
Total Liabilities		
Net Worth		

SCANS Foundation Skills: Basic and Thinking
SCANS Workplace Skills: Resources, Information, and Systems

Contents in Brief

Detailed Contents

Unit 2 Income & Careers 67

Chapter 5 Careers and Education 68

Chapter 6 Paying Taxes 90

Chapter 7 Insuring Your Health and Your Life 112

Personal Financial Literacy

CHAPTER 1

Learning Objectives

Define personal finance and personal financial planning.

Analyze the benefits of good financial decision making.

Examine the goals for which people make financial plans.

Identify sources of financial planning information.

Key Terms

Bankruptcy

Liquid asset

Opportunity cost

Personal finance

Personal financial planning

Overview of Personal Finance

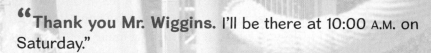

"Thank you Mr. Wiggins. I'll be there at 10:00 A.M. on Saturday."

Lindsey put down her cell phone and smiled. She had landed her first job, and it was at the mall. A thousand questions popped into her head. How much money would she make every week? Should she loan Alicia that $20 to help her buy those new jeans? How much of her earnings would her mom expect her to save for college? How long would it take her to save enough money to buy that sleek new phone? Now that she had a job, maybe she could apply for and get a credit card? Then she wondered about how much money she'd need for her planned trip to the water park this Saturday with Alicia and Deanna—before realizing that she'd have to cancel that date in order to go to work.

In an instant, Lindsey's excitement about her new job had faded. She and her friends had been planning the water park outing for weeks. They were going to be very irritated with her. But she knew she couldn't miss her first Saturday of work.

She also knew that having a job and a little more money was going to make her life easier—and more fun—in a lot of ways. It would just take a little more planning and adjusting to fit everything in.

Lindsey's financial decisions—decisions about money—are just beginning. Yet even the decisions she makes today can affect her future. For that reason, Lindsey needs to learn how to make better financial decisions. So do you. Becoming knowledgeable about the many financial issues that can affect an individual—that is, about **personal finance**—should be a goal for everyone. All people can improve every aspect of their lives, including their personal lives, by learning about personal finance and making good financial decisions.

The thought process used in financial decision making will vary from person to person and situation to situation. Yet all good decision makers will use the same basic tools. The purpose of this text is to help you understand how the decisions you make are actually financial decisions and to provide the knowledge, skills, and tools necessary to make good choices.

The choice is yours. Do you want to live paycheck to paycheck like some of the people you know? Do you want bill collectors hounding you? Or do you want to have the peace of mind that comes with financial security? Manage your cash wisely and you can have the latter. Good planning and money management not only gives you peace of mind, but it also allows you to have all those things you think you want—in due time. Along with a little self-discipline, the techniques and tools you will learn about in this book can change your life.

WHAT IS PERSONAL FINANCIAL PLANNING?

Personal financial planning is the process of planning every aspect of your personal finances. This process includes planning your spending, your borrowing or financing, and your saving and investing in order to achieve the highest quality of life possible. Who doesn't want that? Everyone does!

The Vocabulary of Personal Finance

Keep in mind that any time you learn a new subject such as personal finance, you also will be learning a new language or vocabulary. Mechanics, plumbers, and business people all have vocabularies that are unique to their skills or trades. Personal finance is no different. Your ability to understand these concepts and tools hinges on your studying the terms and phrases that have unique meanings in the context of personal finance.

Cash is a liquid asset.

Steps to Personal Financial Planning

Every one of you needs to create your own personal financial plan. This plan will be a detailed road map that outlines your financial goals and the spending, financing, and saving and investing steps that will allow you to achieve those goals. The more detailed you get, the better the plan will be. A good plan will include creating a budget as well as plans for managing your liquid assets. Your **liquid assets** are those things you might have that can be very rapidly converted to cash without a risk of significant loss. An example of a liquid asset is a savings account at a bank. A good financial plan will also include plans for managing your borrowing and a plan to make sure you have enough insurance to protect your assets (houses, cars, and other assets). Additionally, a personal financial plan includes developing a plan for investing and your ultimate retirement.

Perhaps one of the most critical decisions you will face in your life is the decision regarding the type of career you want to pursue. After all, much of your life will be spent on the job, so shouldn't you spend some time thinking about finding the right job fit for your personality? Equally as important as finding a job suited to your personality is finding one that has a pay and employee benefit package that allows you to afford the things you need. What type of training or education will you need for that job? Figure 1.1 lists the various education requirements and expected salaries for a number of the fastest growing jobs. In general, the more education you have, the higher your salary. Lindsey's mom understands that, which is why she's going to require Lindsey to save some of her new income for education. Lindsey might not appreciate that now. But she probably will when she gets to enjoy the higher income her education will help make possible.

Don't forget that the United States and perhaps your state and local governments will take a cut of your paycheck in taxes. So, we need to spend some time focusing on paying taxes and how tax planning contributes to your overall financial health. The overall health of the economy also factors in when discussing employment prospects and taxation.

In today's financial world, people face many opportunities to make purchases and investments with borrowed money. Understanding the concepts of credit and borrowing are central to maintaining both short-term and long-term financial health. Credit and borrowing are powerful tools. Used wisely, they have the potential to make increased wealth possible. Used improperly, they can lead to financial disaster. The danger is not remote. Sadly, many hardworking people suffer serious problems with credit—simply because they do not plan. Many of you may know someone who has had a vehicle repossessed or even lost a house because he or she failed to make payments on time. Once something like this happens it makes it extremely difficult to buy anything on credit again for several years. Your credit is something that should be built and protected so that when you need it for a major purchase you can get the best financing deal.

If you are like most people, you will have some financial goals that are far in the future. Reaching them will involve saving money. And, learning how to invest that money wisely can speed your progress toward that goal. Indeed, at this point in your life, time is on your side. Considering the number of years you have to work with, even small monthly contributions

Figure 1.1 Fastest-Growing Occupations, 2000–2010

Among the factors you should consider when choosing a career are the opportunities available and the level of training necessary to achieve your career goals.

Occupation	Number (in 1000s)	Change (percent)	Quartile Rank by 2000 Median Annual Earnings[1]	Most Significant Source of Education or Training
Computer software engineers, applications	380	100	1	Bachelor's degree
Computer support specialists	490	97	2	Associate degree
Computer software engineers, systems software	284	90	1	Bachelor's degree
Network and computer systems administrators	187	82	1	Bachelor's degree
Network systems and data communications analysts	92	77	1	Bachelor's degree
Desktop publishers	25	67	2	Postsecondary vocational award
Database administrators	70	66	1	Bachelor's degree
Personal and home care aides	258	62	4	Short-term on-the-job training
Computer systems analysts	258	60	1	Bachelor's degree
Medical assistants	187	57	3	Moderate-term on-the-job training
Social and human service assistants	147	54	3	Moderate-term on-the-job training
Physician assistants	31	53	1	Bachelor's degree
Medical records and health information technicians	66	49	3	Associate degree
Computer and information systems managers	150	48	1	Bachelor's or higher degree, plus work experience
Home health aides	291	47	4	Short-term on-the-job training
Physical therapist aides	17	46	3	Short-term on-the-job training
Occupational therapist aides	4	45	3	Short-term on-the-job training
Physical therapist assistants	20	45	2	Associate degree
Audiologists	6	45	1	Master's degree
Fitness trainers and aerobics instructors	64	40	3	Postsecondary vocational award
Computer and information scientists, research	11	40	1	Doctoral degree
Veterinary assistants and laboratory animal caretakers	22	40	4	Short-term on-the-job training
Occupational therapist assistants	7	40	2	Associate degree
Veterinary technologists and technicians	19	39	3	Associate degree
Speech-language pathologists	34	39	1	Master's degree
Mental health and substance abuse social workers	33	39	2	Master's degree
Dental assistants	92	37	2	Moderate-term on-the-job training
Dental hygienists	54	37	1	Associate degree
Special education teachers, preschool, kindergarten, and elementary school	86	37	1	Bachelor's degree
Pharmacy technicians	69	36	3	Moderate-term on-the-job training

[1]The quartile rankings of Occupational Employment Statistics annual earnings data are presented in the following categories: 1=very high ($39,700 and over), 2=high ($25,760 to $39,660), 3=low ($18,500 to $25,760), and 4=very low (up to $18,490).

Source: Bureau of Labor Statistics, U.S. Department of Labor.

to your savings can result in the buildup of vast sums of money. In fact, if you begin now and have some discipline, most of you should be able to amass more than $1 million by the time you retire. This is possible with a monthly commitment that is lower than what many ordinary people pay each month on their car loan.

The Need for Personal Financial Planning

You Do It

Activity #1

While people in the United States are on average among the wealthiest people in the world, many Americans pay little or no attention to their personal finances. They rely on credit cards and other forms of debt to the point where the debt and financial problems begin to control their existence. Consider these facts:

- More than 30 percent of high school students use a credit card and more than 80 percent of undergraduate college students have at least one credit card.

- More than 2 million people filed for personal **bankruptcy** in 2005. Bankruptcy is a legal process in which a court takes over some of the finances of a person who is unable to pay his or her bills. Another 600,000 people filed for personal bankruptcy in 2006.

- The level of savings in the United States has recently been negative. In other words, people are spending more than they earn.

- About half of all people surveyed who are working full-time in the United States report that they live paycheck to paycheck. That is, they have no money available for paying bills or meeting their needs aside from what they receive in their paychecks.

- About 40 percent of people who work full-time do not save money for retirement. Those people who do save money for retirement tend to save very little.

In other words, people just do not prepare well for the future. With health care costs going up, anticipated problems with Social Security, and other uncertainties about the future that will impact everyone, it makes sense to learn everything you can about personal finance. This knowledge will mean you are in control of your destiny. Why let someone else dictate what you can afford to do in the future?

Poor financial planning can prevent you from achieving your dreams. It can even put you at risk for serious financial problems.

 CHECK Your Financial IQ

What is personal financial planning?

 ## BENEFITS OF GOOD FINANCIAL DECISION MAKING

An early knowledge of personal finance can help you accomplish your goals. In fact, it can help you define your goals. What type of career are you interested in pursuing? Just like Lindsey, you may wonder how much money certain jobs pay. Should you go to college? Should you buy a car? Should you work part-time or focus all of your efforts on school and try to get a scholarship? Should you really apply for that credit card? What are the pros and cons of that decision?

An understanding of personal finance helps you make informed decisions about your personal situation. For example, every time you decide to buy a DVD (or anything else) you incur an **opportunity cost**. In other words, you give up the opportunity to do something else with that money. Rather than buying the DVD, you could have used the money to go to the movies, buy a pizza, or put gas in your car. You could have also put the money in savings. When you begin to view every purchase in terms of its opportunity cost, you may begin to change your spending habits.

Consider the money you spend on sodas every year. If every day you buy one soda that costs $1.25, you end up spending $456.25[1] on sodas during the year. You could have spent that money on something else. Or you could have saved and invested some of that money. Think about the fact that you could begin to save $100 a month at age 16 and accumulate over $1 million by the time you turn age 56 if you were able to earn a 12 percent annual return.

Learning about financial decision making may help you to begin thinking in these terms. Money does not buy happiness but financial security certainly makes life easier. Good financial decisions lead to flexibility and allow you to achieve your true desires in due time without fear of not being able to make the payments.

You Do It
Activity #2

 CHECK Your Financial IQ

What do you stand to gain from your knowledge of personal finance?

MATH for Personal Finance

Jacob earns $8 an hour at the pizza place and he is scheduled to work four hours this afternoon. However, Tara called and wanted to know if he could go to a movie.

Assuming the movie will cost Jacob $10, what is his opportunity cost of going to the movie?

Solution: Jacob will forego earning $8 an hour × 4 hours = $32. He will also spend $10 that he would not spend if he were working. Therefore, his opportunity cost of going to the movie is equal to $32 + $10 = $42.

WHAT YOU ARE PLANNING FOR?

Every person is different. Everyone has his or her own personal goals. These can range from starting a business to taking a dream vacation. The possibilities are endless. Brainstorm a bit here and see what personal goals you have that might require saving some money. Remember Lindsey? She wants a new phone. What do you want? You will see that some of your goals will be short-term in nature, and others may require years to accomplish. A phone should be a short-term goal. Saving enough money to buy a house is obviously a much longer-term goal. With good planning, you can identify and begin working toward short-term, medium-term, and long-term goals—all at the same time.

Education

One of the major decisions that you will be required to make very soon is whether to pursue a college degree or some other type of post-high school education. Refer to Figure 1.2 and note that there is a significant relationship between the number of years of education and your earnings potential. At this point in your life, you should begin to explore various career options and determine the education required to pursue each option. While you should always focus on a career that holds your interest, it is also important to investigate the expected payoffs. Education is costly both

[1]$1.25 × 365 days = $456.25 per year in total cost.

in time and money. You should spend some time planning your career choice and then engaging in financial planning to determine how to pay for that education.

Emergencies/Rainy Day Fund

Most people will have an emergency need for funds at some time in their lives. Unexpected events, such as car breakdowns, occur often. Good financial planning will help you establish an emergency fund that will help you weather any future financial crisis. Financial planning forces you to think about and plan for those unexpected expenses or the possibility of an interruption in wages as the result of illness or job change. If you begin to

Figure 1.2 Comparison of Income among Education Levels

Education can be quite costly, but in general it will pay for itself in a relatively short time.

Education	Median Level of Annual Income
Master's degree	$55,300
Bachelor's degree	46,300
Associate degree	35,400
Some college, no degree	32,400
High school graduate	28,800
Some high school, no degree	21,400

Source: Bureau of Labor Statistics, U.S. Department of Labor

plan for the unexpected now, you can be sure that there is enough money set aside to cover those expenses.

Buying a Car

Do you want to own a car someday? Will your parents provide it? Or will you have to pay for it with your own money? When do you want to buy it? At age 16? At age 18? While a Maserati might be out of reach financially, a good used $5,000 vehicle is probably possible if you take the right steps. If you can set a specific goal, good financial planning can help you determine whether you can eventually afford the car. It can also help you identify the steps you need to take to achieve ownership.

Buying a Home

Some of you may already be thinking about your dream home. Some of you may want to travel the world and just rent a place to live for a time in an exotic location. Regardless of your desire, you can begin planning financially to achieve your goals. You can actually begin saving now for the down payment on your first home. What better time to accumulate wealth than when you are young?

Why worry about something today that may be years down the road? The earlier you begin the less money you have to set aside on a regular basis. If you plan carefully, you can set aside money for long-term goals while still having money left over for more short-term desires. The key is planning.

And remember: It gets increasingly more difficult to save money when you have to pay rent and buy groceries. Take advantage of your freedom and your youth now.

Having a Family

Families are expensive. To have a child and put that child through college is estimated to cost more than $250,000 over the child's life from birth to age 22. That is quite a bit of money. Should you begin planning for some of those expenses now? What about a car at age 16 for the children you might have? Are your children going to public school or private school? These are all decisions that may be impacted by your wealth. A good financial plan can allow you to have the financial flexibility to make these choices instead of having them made for you.

Retirement

At this stage of your life it is difficult to think about retirement. However, do you know someone who retired at age 40 or 45 and now does exactly what he or she wants to do? Contrast that with someone you know who hates his or her job and is still working at age 70. While many people may choose to work well into their 60s or 70s because they enjoy working, many people do it because they have no other options. Financial planning can give you those options. You can begin to build your wealth at an early age. This may allow you to retire at age 40 or 45. While you may decide to continue working, it is nice to have the option to retire.

Charitable Giving

A number of people have a strong desire to donate some of their money to worthy causes, and charitable giving is an important component of many financial plans. Some people may prefer to accumulate wealth and provide a large sum to a specific charity. Others may give smaller amounts on a regular basis. Knowledge of financial planning can help you achieve whatever goals you may have in this area. Check out Professor Fin for a look at some recent top philanthropic gifts.

Professor FIN

Charitable giving does not happen with everyday people only. For example, members of the "Billionaire Club" have provided funding for health care, research, and much more. Carlos Slim Helu, a Mexican businessman and at one time the world's second richest person, established a $450 million philanthropic foundation. Bill and Melinda Gates have established their own foundation, and Warren Buffet, another of the world's richest people, has pledged to turn over much of his fortune to the Gates Foundation.

✓ **CHECK Your Financial IQ**

What three categories of goals you should you plan for?

SOURCES OF INFORMATION

Finance ONLINE

When you are young, it may seem difficult or even frightening to think about some aspects of financial planning. Goals may seem too numerous or out of reach. The stakes of good and bad decisions may seem high. Fortunately, there are many resources available to help you make good choices. And remember—time is on your side.

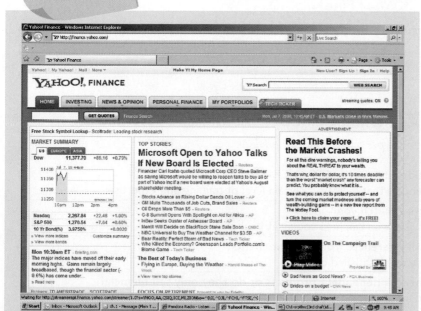

Source: finance.yahoo.com

The Internet

The Internet can be a wonderful source of information about a number of financial aspects of your life. You can use the Internet to research prices of major purchases or look up investment performance data. There are a number of Web sites that provide payment calculators or information on wealth building. However, the Internet also poses some dangers. You need skill and care to evaluate the quality of information you find there. And you must always be cautious about advice from sources that are selling a service. The Internet has its share of unethical people trying to defraud you and increase their wealth at your expense.

Judging the Advice of Financial Planners/Advisors and Financial Information

Finance ONLINE

As you learn more about personal finance, some of you may become interested in pursuing a financial planning career. Financial advisors are in demand because many people do not understand financial planning and are at a loss when trying to make the best financial decision. Good financial planners need a great deal of training and education. They may even decide to gain a certification. However, the good news is that you can get a degree in financial planning and begin to help people immediately while making a good income. More information about Certified Financial Planners can be found at **www.cfp.net**. Other information concerning careers in finance can be found at **www.careers-in-finance.com/fpskill.htm**.

Understanding personal financial planning will help you make good decisions about how to spend money, finance purchases such as cars and houses, and save and invest your money. However, many of you may want to turn some of these decisions over to professionals who understand all the tax laws and can monitor your investments more closely.

Lindsey's Uncle Joe may want to manage her money for her, but is he competent? He acts goofy at every family function and Lindsey's mom told her that Uncle Joe filed for bankruptcy 10 years ago. Should she trust him with her money? Oddly enough, many people select financial advisors and entrust their future to people whom they know even less about than their Uncle Joe. Many people spend more time picking out music to download than they spend choosing a financial advisor. Understanding financial planning will help you determine whether an advisor is giving you advice that is in your best interest. Figure 1.3 contains a list of things to consider when selecting a good financial advisor.

Again, the Internet is a good source of information about financial planners. Stick with planners who have reputable credentials such as a CFP® or Certified Financial Planner designation, since credentials indicate a certain level of knowledge about financial planning. Remember that no matter who you hire to help you with your finances, you are responsible for monitoring your own investments. Be cautious. Never rush into a financial decision. If someone tries to rush a decision, it is rarely good for you.

☑ CHECK Your Financial IQ

Who is responsible for judging the quality of financial advice you receive?

Figure 1.3 Questions to Ask When Selecting a Financial Advisor

It is vital to use great care in evaluating a personal financial advisor.

1 **Do they have a certification such as the CFP or CPA?**
These are important credentials that indicate a certain level of training and expertise.

2 **Does their area of expertise match your needs?**
Obviously you want an advisor who can help you meet your own goals.

3 **Can they provide you with references from current clients?**
A good advisor should have many satisfied clients.

4 **Are they able to recommend independent products or do they only sell financial products that generate commissions or referral fees?**
Some advisors only sell products that bring financial benefits to *them*.

5 **Do they make you feel comfortable?**
The relationship between you and your advisor should not be uneasy or tense.

Chapter Review

Summary

- Personal financial planning is the process of planning your spending, financing, and saving and investing to create your best possible financial future. Your financial planning decisions allow you to develop a financial plan, which involves a set of decisions on how you plan to manage your spending, financing, and investing.

- You will find that an early knowledge of personal finance can help you avoid common financial pitfalls and accomplish your goals, whatever they are. You will see that most goals have a financial component.

- There are many good reasons to plan for your financial future, but some common goals include getting an education, preparing for emergencies, buying a car or home, having a family, retiring, and donating to charity.

- There are many resources available to help you make your financial decisions. One resource is the Internet. Other resources include financial planners or advisors. Financial planners or advisors can help you with all aspects of your financial decisions including monitoring your investments and keeping you posted on tax law.

Key Terms

Bankruptcy

Liquid asset

Opportunity cost

Personal finance

Personal financial planning

What Do You Know?

myFinLitlab

1. (a) Define personal financial planning.

   (b) Why is learning about personal financial planning important?

2. (a) Define opportunity cost.

   (b) Give an example of opportunity cost.

3. (a) Name some factors that might affect your current financial position.

   (b) How would you expect the earning of a college degree to affect your financial plans?

4. (a) What does the high rate of bankruptcy suggest about the average person's understanding of personal finance?

   (b) What is the significance of the generally low rate at which people save for retirement?

5. (a) How do your goals affect decision making for your financial plan?

   (b) Explain how you might be able to work toward short-term, medium-term, and long-term goals at the same time.

6. (a) Why plan for the future?

   (b) Why might you need to revise your financial plan?

7. (a) How can financial planning help you plan for your education future?

   (b) Why is it worth investing significantly in education?

8. (a) List some information available on the Internet that might be useful for financial planning.

   (b) Describe one way you might use some of this information for financial planning purposes.

9. (a) What does certification tell you about a financial planner?

   (b) Why do you think you must be responsible for your own financial plan, no matter who you get to help you?

10. (a) What type of person needs to engage in personal financial planning?

    (b) Does having wealth reduce a person's need for financial planning? Explain.

What Are Your Finance Math Skills?   myFinLitlab

The first three questions correlate to *Math for Personal Finance* features located throughout the chapter.

1. Ryan worked 40 hours during the first week of his summer job and made $9 an hour. His paycheck was for $332.46. How much did his employer withhold from his paycheck?

2. Justin's boss said work was optional this afternoon, so Justin decided to skip work and go swimming with his friends. Normally he would have worked three hours. Assuming he makes $11 an hour and the swimming trip will cost him $8 in gas, what is the opportunity cost of Justin's decision to go swimming?

3. Mary Beth would like to buy a more fuel efficient vehicle instead of driving her mom's gas guzzler. Assuming she can find a car that gets 32 miles to the gallon (mpg) and her mom's car only gets 16 mpg, how much will she save if she usually drives about 3,000 miles a year and the average price of gasoline is $3.75 a gallon?

4. Assume you drink eight sodas per week and they cost $1.59 each. How much money can you accumulate over the course of the year if you opt to save the money instead?

5. If you worked an extra two hours a week during your junior year in high school and you average bringing home $9 an hour, how much money could you accumulate over that 52-week period?

6. What is the opportunity cost of going to the football game on Friday night instead of working at the mall when you make $7.50 an hour and usually work six hours? Admission to the game is free for students, but you usually spend about $5 on snacks while you are there.

7. Assume you wanted to save $2,000 to buy a used car 18 months from now. How much money do you need to save every week to accomplish your goal?

8. If you decide to study four hours more a week during your junior year (32 weeks) with the expectation of getting a $2,000 scholarship to college, how much is your study time worth per hour?

What Would You Do?

Read the comic strip. Is what Pearce (the red-headed character) did by calling in sick right or wrong (ethical or unethical)? Many employers pay their employees even when they are sick, but sometimes if you call in sick you will not receive pay for that day. What happens at work when Pearce calls in sick? Does someone else have to do his work? Since he called in sick, is it right for him to go out to the mall to visit friends?

1. If you were Pearce's employer, what would you do if you found out that he had called in sick but was not really sick?

2. If you were Pearce's coworker, what would you think about Pearce's decision?

3. How might Pearce's action affect the business where he works?

What Are the Connections?
Math, Language Arts, and Technology

a. Prepare a list of financial decisions you are likely to make over the next 5 years and then the next 10 years. For example, think of what you hope to purchase over that time, or how much progress you hope to make toward specific goals. Be specific about anticipated dollar costs for each decision. If spreadsheet software is available, develop a chart that shows what you can do to begin preparing for these decisions. If you do not have access to a computer, use paper and pencil to prepare the chart.

b. Prepare a personal goal statement that explains how you plan to carry out the steps of your financial plan for the next 5–10 years.

Teamwork

In a team, develop a presentation explaining to teens why it is important for them to begin personal financial planning. You may create a brochure, write a newsletter, produce a skit, or present a video presentation. Be creative but make sure you stress information discussed in this chapter and the importance of personal financial planning. You might include information you have researched in the library or on the Internet.

w!se | Financial Literacy CERTIFICATION

TEST PREP QUESTIONS

myFinLitlab

1. The *best* definition of personal financial planning is
   a. a process of mapping decisions for spending, borrowing, and saving and investing in order to achieve financial goals.
   b. an investment schedule established by a financial advisor to help a person pay a debt.
   c. the process of determining how much a person can afford to pay for a house based on the person's income.
   d. the comparison between the cost of education and a person's projected income.

2. Which is a true statement about Americans saving for retirement?
   a. Most Americans save more money than they need for retirement.
   b. Americans do not need to save for retirement since Social Security will cover expenses during retirement years.
   c. Less than half of Americans have a retirement account.
   d. The average American saves 9 percent of annual income for retirement.

3. Which is a true statement about the relationship between education and a person's earning power?
   a. The age a person starts to work determines earning power more than the person's education.
   b. The average person with an associate's degree can expect to earn 20 percent more than a high school graduate earns each year.
   c. A person with a master's degree can expect an annual income that is double that of a person with a bachelor's degree.
   d. A college education does not influence a person's earning power during the first five years of employment.

4. Which person's goal is correctly matched with a sound financial plan to achieve the goal?
   a. Buying a new computer for college in the fall: depositing 25 percent or more of weekly take-home pay in a bank savings account.
   b. Having a down payment for a house in 10 years: saving percent of take-home pay in a checking account each month.
   c. Having enough money to retire in 25 years: buying all of the things needed now and beginning to invest in 15 years.
   d. Buying a new cell phone in two months: making the purchase on credit and paying the minimum balance each month.

5. Money in an emergency fund should be used to pay for
   a. items that suddenly go on sale.
   b. necessary expenses when a person loses a job or is unable to work because of illness or injury.
   c. large expenses such as a house or college education.
   d. long-term investments such as stocks.

6. The following statement about financial advice on the Internet is true.
   a. If the information has been posted to the Internet, it is reliable information.
   b. If the information comes from a company that is selling financial products, it is sound, objective information.
   c. There are a number of valuable sources of information on the Internet that can be used for financial planning.
   d. The Internet protects individuals against the loss of money by not allowing unethical financial advisors to post their information.

7. When a person decides to use the services of a certified financial planner, the person will
   a. no longer need to check on how her money is invested.
   b. make a steady profit on the money invested by the planner.
   c. need to make all investments with the same planner.
   d. check in regularly with the planner to review investment decisions.

8. A person decides to bike to school rather than drive his car. The opportunity cost related to this decision is
   a. the money that is saved by not buying as much gas for the car.
   b. the exercise that riding the bike provides.
   c. the time that might be saved by driving the car.
   d. the shorter route from home to school that the bike can take.

Financial Responsibility & Decision Making

CHAPTER 2

Learning Objectives

Describe the purpose of a financial plan.

Identify the key components of a financial plan.

Key Terms

Asset
Budgeting
Equity
Income
Interest
Liability
Liquidity
Net worth

The Financial Plan

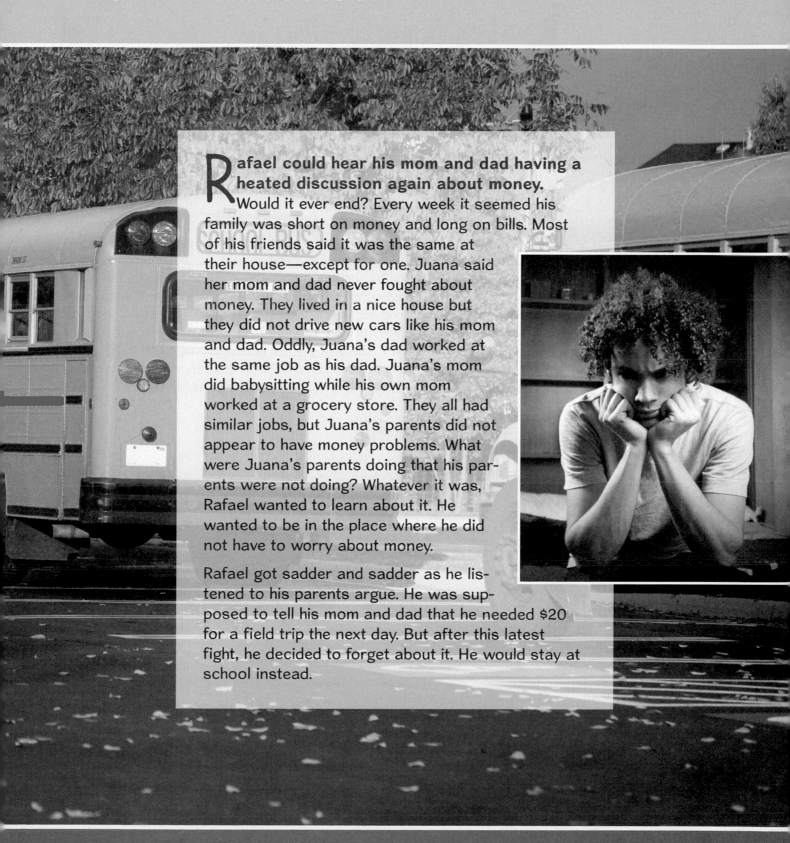

Rafael could hear his mom and dad having a heated discussion again about money. Would it ever end? Every week it seemed his family was short on money and long on bills. Most of his friends said it was the same at their house—except for one. Juana said her mom and dad never fought about money. They lived in a nice house but they did not drive new cars like his mom and dad. Oddly, Juana's dad worked at the same job as his dad. Juana's mom did babysitting while his own mom worked at a grocery store. They all had similar jobs, but Juana's parents did not appear to have money problems. What were Juana's parents doing that his parents were not doing? Whatever it was, Rafael wanted to learn about it. He wanted to be in the place where he did not have to worry about money.

Rafael got sadder and sadder as he listened to his parents argue. He was supposed to tell his mom and dad that he needed $20 for a field trip the next day. But after this latest fight, he decided to forget about it. He would stay at school instead.

Rafael was dreaming about something that his friend Juana's parents apparently had: financial stability. For most people, however, financial stability does not happen by accident or through good fortune. It requires careful planning and effort. In this chapter, you will study the steps to making a personal financial plan, which can serve as the basis for financial success in your life.

WHAT IS A FINANCIAL PLAN?

As Rafael thought more about why Juana's family seemed to have more money than his family, he became more and more curious. What were they doing that his family was not doing? One big difference was that Juana's family had a financial plan in place and stuck to it. They didn't have to argue over every financial decision. They just followed their plan.

A **personal financial plan** involves specifying financial goals and describing in detail the spending, financing, and investing plans needed to reach those goals. A good financial plan is like a builder's blueprint: It spells out every aspect of how to accumulate and grow wealth and provide for emergencies. It helps ensure that as you move forward in your life, you are making steady progress toward your financial goals.

As shown in Figure 2.1, a solid financial plan addresses seven key components. Each of these areas is a critical piece of your personal financial plan, and each component requires you to make a set of personal decisions. However, when you are finished, you will have a comprehensive road map to help you achieve your dreams. You are now going to spend some time understanding each area. Later, you will have the chance to apply what you have learned when you create your own personal financial plan.

✓ CHECK Your Financial IQ

What is the purpose and function of a financial plan?

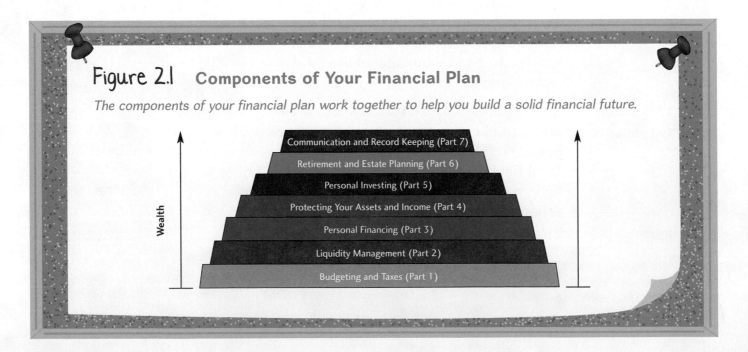

Figure 2.1 **Components of Your Financial Plan**

The components of your financial plan work together to help you build a solid financial future.

Wealth →

- Communication and Record Keeping (Part 7)
- Retirement and Estate Planning (Part 6)
- Personal Investing (Part 5)
- Protecting Your Assets and Income (Part 4)
- Personal Financing (Part 3)
- Liquidity Management (Part 2)
- Budgeting and Taxes (Part 1)

Making a budget is a basic part of personal financial planning.

Professor FIN

The first step in building a financial plan is understanding its different parts. You will now explore the seven components and how they can help you achieve financial security.

Did you know that the following is estimated of teens ages 12–17:

- 47.4 percent have a savings account
- 11.6 percent have a checking account
- 15 percent have an ATM card
- 3.5 percent have a credit card in their own name

Source: PR Newswire, January 7, 2008

COMPONENT ONE: A Plan for Your Budgeting and Taxes

Budget planning, or **budgeting**, is the process of forecasting future expenses and income. In other words, it involves asking how much you plan to spend next week or month, and what is the expected source of that money. The purpose of a budget is to plan your spending and saving, given your income level, so that you can meet your needs and wants.

Creating a budget involves four steps as follows:

1. Establishing your net worth
2. Establishing your income
3. Identifying your expenses
4. Considering the impact of taxes

Step 1: Establishing Your Net Worth

The first step in budget planning is to determine where you are right now financially. Do you have money in the bank? Do you owe people money? Do you have a job? What are your expenses? Answering these questions can help you to get an accurate picture of your current financial position This, in turn, will help you recognize how far you are from your goals—and help you set budget priorities.

The formula for determining your net worth is as follows:

Net Worth = Assets − Liabilities

Think about it like this. What if Rafael's dad owned a car worth $5,000? That car is called an asset. **Assets** are anything we own, such as cars or motorcycles. Your parents might own their house or a farm. Those are all assets. Your baseball card collection is also an asset.

For now, let's look at Rafael's dad's car that is valued at $5,000. He still owes the bank $2,000 on the car loan. That remaining debt is called a liability. **Liabilities** are what we owe, or our debt. If this car were the only asset and the only liability that Rafael's dad had, his **net worth** would equal $3,000, or the difference between the value of the asset (car) and how much he still owes on the car.

Asset	=	Car worth	$5,000
Liability	=	Amount owed on the car	− $2,000
Net Worth	=	Car value minus amount owed	$3,000

MATH for Personal Finance

Emily's car is worth approximately $5,300 according to *Kelley Blue Book*, yet she still owes $1,600 on her loan. She also has $800 in a savings account.

What is Emily's net worth?

Solution: Emily's assets are a car worth $5,300 and $800 in savings for a total of $6,100. Her liabilities are the $1,600 loan. Therefore, her net worth is $6,100 − $1,600 = $4,500.

Sometimes you will hear people refer to a person's equity in a car or a home or other asset. **Equity** means ownership. In the example above, Rafael's dad has $3,000 equity in the car. If he paid off the remaining $2,000, his equity would be $5,000.

As you save money, you will accumulate more assets (including cash) and increase your net worth. You will also have the chance to reduce your liabilities, which will also increase your net worth. In other words, you can increase your net worth by increasing your assets or decreasing your liabilities. Check out Figure 2.2. What color will the car be when Rafael's dad pays off the loan? How much will his net worth be at that time assuming the car is still worth $5,000?

Step 2: Establishing Your Income

A key factor in shaping a budget is understanding your income. **Income** is the money coming in through wages earned, allowance, or other sources. Having an income is the major means by which a person saves money, builds wealth, acquires assets, and fulfills wants and needs. How much income you have will determine many of the details in your budget.

A person's income often depends on decisions he or she makes about education and career choice. In general, more education or specialized training translates into more income. Think about the people you know. Who makes a good income? What jobs do they do? You will probably list a number of professions, some that require a college degree, such as medical professionals and teachers. Others, such as electricians, mechanics, and

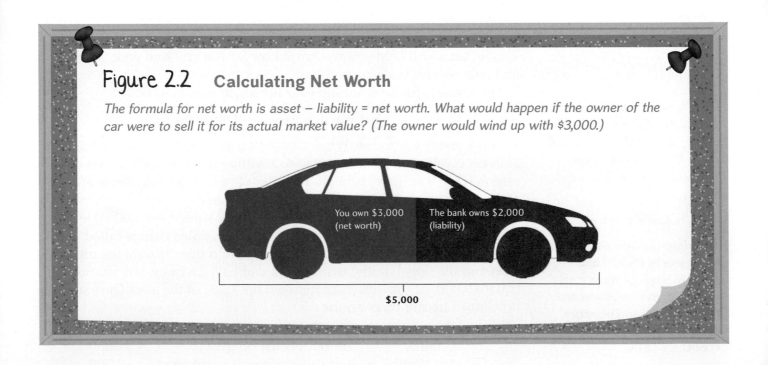

Figure 2.2 Calculating Net Worth

The formula for net worth is asset – liability = net worth. What would happen if the owner of the car were to sell it for its actual market value? (The owner would wind up with $3,000.)

You own $3,000 (net worth)

The bank owns $2,000 (liability)

$5,000

plumbers received very specialized training. In almost every case, you will find that higher income comes with higher levels of education and/or training.

Step 3: Identifying Your Expenses

Your expenses are also important in your budget. When you create your budget, you will estimate how much money you are spending every month. Typical expenses might be clothing or entertainment. Some of you might even have a car payment and related expenses. Refer to the chart in Figure 2.3 for typical household expenditures.

You will need to have accurate estimates of your expenses to determine how much you can save. Remember that saving for the future requires sacrificing spending today. If you spend $20 on a DVD today, that is money you can't save. Think about the fact that if you manage to save $20 a week for 52 weeks a year, you would accumulate over $1,000.

$$\$20 \times 52 \text{ weeks} = \$1,040 \text{ total savings.}$$

Step 4: Considering the Impacts of Taxes

Income taxes—money owed to government on earned income—may also impact your budget. In general, the more money you make, the higher the share of your income you will pay in income taxes. As your income level increases, you will want to begin to include tax planning in your financial plan. For example, you may want to save some of your income in ways that help you put off or avoid taxes. Examples include certain retirement or college savings plans. Tax laws change constantly, and many of your financial decisions will have tax impacts that you will want to consider.

Figure 2.3   How We Spend Our Money

The average person has many demands on his or her budget. What areas seem to be subject to individual control and decision making?

According to the U.S. Department of Labor, consumers had the following spending patterns in 2006:

Food	12.6%
Housing	33.8%
Apparel and service	3.9%
Transportation	17.6%
Health care	5.7%
Entertainment	4.9%
Personal insurance and pensions	10.9%
Other	10.6%

Source: www.bls.gov/news.release/cesan.nr0.htm

You Do It

Activity #1

COMPONENT TWO: A Plan for Managing Your Liquidity

Did you ever go to the store to buy something only to realize that you didn't have enough money? You had a liquidity problem. In other words, you did not have enough liquid assets to cover that purchase. Liquid assets include cash and assets that can be quickly and easily turned into cash. Your level of **liquidity**, then, refers to how much readily available cash you have on hand for meeting immediate wants and needs. Note that your liquidity is very different from your net worth. You may have a number of valuable assets. But if they are not liquid, they will be of little use to you when facing a short-term financial need.

For example, what if your car breaks down or you need new tires? Or, what if, like Rafael, you need $20 to pay for a field trip? The fact that you own a car worth $5,000 will do little to help you solve such problems. These types of expenses require liquid assets. A good financial plan will help you manage your liquidity so that you don't get caught off guard by an unexpected expense.

Money management and credit management decisions are both involved in liquidity management. **Money management** involves making decisions about how much cash or liquid assets to keep in reserve and how much to invest in less liquid assets, such as **real estate** (buildings and land). If you find out you don't have enough money to cover your immediate needs then you need more liquidity. You may have the money invested but not easily and quickly accessible. Money management helps you determine how much money to keep liquid to avoid cash shortfalls.

One way to determine how much money Rafael might need for the year is to keep track of last year's needs and set aside enough cash to cover that amount, plus some additional money. For example, if Rafael needed $500 last year to cover field trips, school supplies, and the cost of playing a sport or traveling with the band, then that amount is a good start. After planning for some additional, unforeseen expenses, Rafael may determine he needs approximately $1,000 readily available to satisfy his liquidity needs. Money management would involve putting that money in a short-term investment that would allow easy access and not penalize him for withdrawal.

Credit management involves making decisions about getting credit and using credit. Credit is commonly used to cover immediate cash shortfalls, so it increases liquidity. But credit, and particularly credit cards, can be very costly. When you use credit (borrow money) the lender charges interest on the money you borrow. Think about **interest** as rent on the money. Some lenders charge higher rent (interest) on money than others. In general, it is not wise to rely on credit cards if you will not be able to pay back the borrowed money quickly. A financial plan should contain a credit management plan. This might involve details such as limiting the number of credit cards you have and the amount of credit you can use at any one time. Figure 2.4 shows an illustration of liquidity management.

COMPONENT THREE: A Plan for Your Financing

Major purchases such as cars, houses, and paying for college, typically require borrowing money for long periods of time. Most of the time you do not have time to accumulate enough wealth to pay cash for a house. However, it is common to pay a portion of the cost of a house or car and to take a loan for—or **finance**—the remaining amount. For example, you may save $1,000 for a down payment on a $4,000 car and finance the remaining $3,000. Figure 2.5 illustrates the financing process you might go through to buy this car.

This type of borrowing differs from the temporary, short-term borrowing that credit cards are often used for. Longer-term financing is usually available at a lower cost to the borrower than can be found with credit cards. Still, use of long-term financing requires great caution. For example, if you cannot pay back the $3,000 you borrowed for that car, the lender may take the car back from you. You lose the car—and the $1,000 you already paid toward it.

There are a number of factors that will determine how much you can borrow and the payment terms. **Payment terms** include the specific information about the interest rate the lender will charge you and the time period for paying back the loan. Remember lenders make their money by charging you rent (interest) on the money they loan.

MATH for Personal Finance

Ruston plans on buying a car that is priced at $3,500. He has saved $1,000 for a down payment and his grandparents have agreed to contribute another $500 toward the purchase.

How much of the vehicle will Ruston need to finance?

Solution: Ruston can put a total of $1,500 down on the car and finance the remainder which is $3,500 − $1,500 = $2,000.

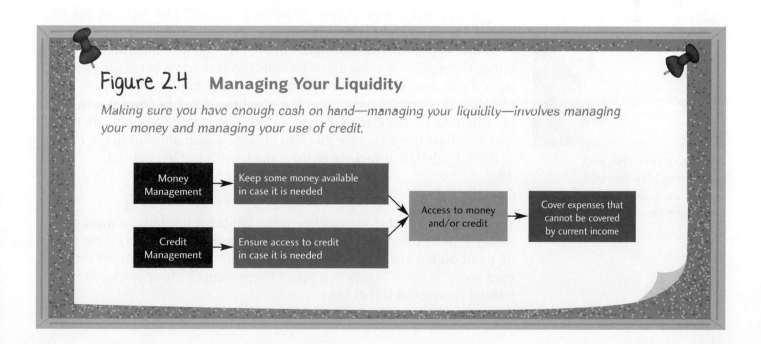

Figure 2.4   Managing Your Liquidity

Making sure you have enough cash on hand—managing your liquidity—involves managing your money and managing your use of credit.

Money Management → Keep some money available in case it is needed

Credit Management → Ensure access to credit in case it is needed

→ Access to money and/or credit → Cover expenses that cannot be covered by current income

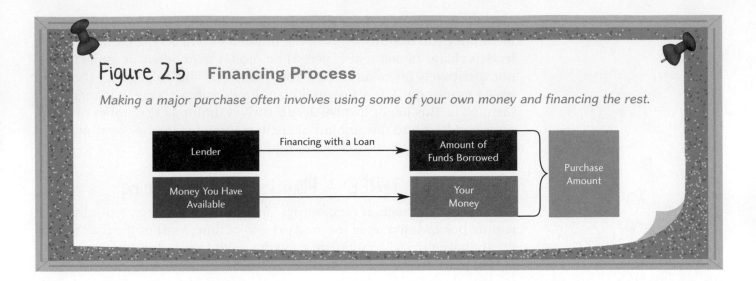

Figure 2.5 **Financing Process**

Making a major purchase often involves using some of your own money and financing the rest.

However, some lenders will loan you more money than you should borrow. Remember that every time you borrow money you have a payment schedule that requires you to make timely payments. Most of the time these payments are monthly. If Rafael's parents are having liquidity problems, what does that indicate about their monthly payment obligations? It's very possible that Rafael's parents have borrowed too much money and do not have enough flexibility in their budget to provide for emergencies. A comprehensive financing plan would prevent that from happening.

COMPONENT FOUR: A Plan for Managing Your Risk

As you accumulate assets, you need to devise a plan to protect those assets. For example, if you buy a car, what happens if that car is stolen or rammed in a parking lot by another car? Unless you have insurance on that car you will suffer the loss of that asset yourself. You are assuming all the **risk**—the possibility of a financial loss. Risk is related to the likelihood of loss. If there is a greater chance of your suffering a financial loss then the risk is higher. For that reason many people purchase insurance.

Insurance planning is a component of your financial plan that determines the types and amounts of insurance you need. What other assets should you have insured? People typically insure houses, boats, cars, and other major assets. However, you also need insurance to cover you in case of other unexpected events, such as an illness or injury. Many of your parents also have life insurance that will provide a cash amount in the event of their death. Life insurance protects the loved ones left behind.

COMPONENT FIVE: A Plan for Your Investing

You know you need to accumulate some funds for liquidity to meet day-to-day expenses and to pay for sudden unexpected events. Any other funds that you do not spend should be invested with the expectation of earning even more money. Common types of investments include stocks, bonds, mutual funds, and real estate.

Managing your risk and preventing loss through insurance is key to your long-term financial security.

Who do you think is more likely to be investing? Rafael's parents or Juana's parents? Since money for investment tends to be money remaining after paying necessary bills, you might suspect Juana's parents are more likely to be investing. As a result, they are likely to have even more money available to meet their wants and needs.

People invest money so they can make more money. But you should always remember that different types of investments have different levels of risk. Riskier investments can produce great returns—but they may also experience significant losses. That is, a risky $1,000 investment may earn $200, $300, or more in a good year. But it may also lose money—or even lose all of its value.

COMPONENT SIX: A Plan for Your Retirement

How many of you know people who are retired? Have you noticed that some people retire earlier than others? People who retire early are often people who began planning for retirement while they were young. Retirement planning involves determining how much to save for retirement every year and how to invest that money. The government provides several ways to save for retirement that allow you to accumulate wealth without paying taxes until you retire. By putting off paying taxes until later, you increase the amount invested. This, in turn, may increase the amount of money the investment earns.

COMPONENT SEVEN: A Plan for Communicating and Keeping Records

Communicating your financial plan to your family is critical. Sometimes you may hear someone quarreling over money and you will learn that the dispute could have been avoided with clear communication.

Equally as important as making personal financial decisions and communicating that decision is keeping good records. You will need these records when you file your taxes and when you calculate your net worth. Your heirs may also need them at some point. Good financial records can be a motivational tool. You will find that if you actually write your goals down and periodically refer to them, you will be much more likely to achieve them.

Rafael doesn't want his financial situation to end up like that of his parents. He can start by identifying his goals and writing them down. Then he can begin to identify steps he can take to achieve those goals.

You Do It

Activity #2

 **CHECK Your Financial IQ**

What are the components of your financial plan?

Summary

- Financial planning involves specifying financial goals and describing in detail the spending, financing, and investing plans needed to reach those goals. Your plan will be like a blueprint for your financial future.

- A good financial plan contains seven key components: (1) budgeting, which requires an understanding of concepts such as net worth, income, expenses, and taxes; (2) managing liquidity, including management of money and credit; (3) financing large purchases; (4) managing your risk, through the use of insurance; (5) investing your money; (6) planning for retirement and transferring wealth; and (7) communicating and keeping records.

Key Terms and Vocabulary

Asset	Liquidity
Budgeting	Money management
Credit management	Net worth
Equity	Payment terms
Finance	Personal financial plan
Income	Real estate
Interest	Risk
Liability	

What Do You Know?

myFinLitlab

1. (a) What are the components of a financial plan?

2. (a) Define budget planning.

   (b) What elements must be assessed in budget planning?

3. (a) How is your net worth calculated?

   (b) Why is knowing your net worth important?

4. (a) What factors influence income?

   (b) Why is an accurate estimate of expenses important in budget planning?

   (c) How do tax laws affect the budgeting process?

5. (a) What is liquidity?

   (b) What two factors are considered in managing liquidity?

   (c) How are they used?

6. (a) What factors determine how much you can borrow?

   (b) Can you rely on a lender to lend you the appropriate amount of money? Explain.

7. (a) What is the purpose of insurance?

   (b) Explain how owning a car or house exposes you to financial risk.

8. (a) What is the primary objective of investing?

   (b) Why would you not invest all the money you have available?

9. (a) How do your financial goals fit into your financial plan?

   (b) Why should goals be realistic?

10. (a) Why is it important to communicate your financial plans?

What Are Your Finance Math Skills?

 myFinLitlab

The first three questions correlate to *Math for Personal Finance* features located throughout the chapter.

1. Maria has a car that she could sell for about $7,000 according to her uncle who is a used car dealer. However, she still owes $2,200 on her car loan. She also has $1,100 in her checking account and $300 in cash. What is Emily's net worth?

2. Assume you make $10 an hour and work 20 hours a week. In addition, you receive $1,200 a year in income from a trust fund. What is your total annual income?

3. Kedra would like to buy a vehicle that is priced at $4,100. Assume she has saved 20 percent of the purchase price for a down payment. How much money does she need to finance?

4. Assume you work 12 hours per week and make $7.50 per hour. How much is your annual income?

5. You have a car worth $3,200. You owe $1,400 on the loan. You also owe $320 on a credit card. How much are your total liabilities?

6. Assume you took $2,500 in cash out of your savings account and bought a car worth $2,500. How much did your net worth change?

7. If you intend to begin saving 25 percent of your income and you bring home $50 a week, how much will you save in one year?

8. What is the value of your total assets if you have a car worth $4,000, you owe $1,500 on the car loan, and you have a baseball card collection valued at $750?

What Would You Do?

Danielle has been invited to her friend's house for an afternoon pool party. It is going to be a great time, and all her friends are planning to go—if they can get a ride. Danielle is the only one who has access to a car at the moment. The trouble is, the car she has access to belongs to her parents. Danielle just got her driver's license, and her parents have not yet changed insurance coverage on their SUV so that she is covered in the event she has an accident while she's behind the wheel.

Danielle's friends have been pushing her to take the SUV. After all, they point out, she has a key to the vehicle. And her parents aren't supposed to be home until after the pool party is over, so they will never know. It's only a couple of miles across town. What, they say, could go wrong?

What risk would Danielle be taking to drive the SUV without the proper insurance coverage?

1. What are the possible costs to Danielle if she makes the wrong choice?

2. What would you do in this situation?

What Are the Connections?
Language Arts, Math, and Technology

Many of you will continue your education after high school graduation. Research three post-secondary (college/university, technical college, vocational school) or training programs that you might want to attend following high school. Collect data for each of these that includes the following:

- Tuition for one year (dollars per hour or per semester) or training costs

- Other expected fees, such as housing and cafeteria costs

- Estimated costs of getting to and from each facility (home to campus/training site)

If you have access to spreadsheet software, design a spreadsheet of the information showing the comparisons of the costs for each. If not, use paper and pencil to design the spreadsheet.

Then write a paper about your findings. This paper should include any graphs, charts, or tables that will help you show comparisons between education/training programs. When you make the comparisons, keep in mind the possible benefits of one type of education/training program over another. Explain why additional education/training after high school is necessary or important. As part of your paper, answer the following questions:

a. Why is it important to research colleges/universities or training programs of your choice at an early age?

b. What does planning for these expenses have to do with financial planning?

c. How can you communicate with your parents or high school counselor your plans for further education upon high school graduation?

Teamwork Service-Learning Activity

Prepare a group presentation on the steps of a financial plan. Create a brochure or newsletter that shows the steps of making a financial plan. Imagine this brochure or newsletter might be used for a PTO meeting at your school, placed in the guidance counselor's office, or sent home with school announcements for students to share with their parents. Work together in a team to find information from the text and on the Internet that you might use to help explain the need for and steps of making a financial plan. Remember that it is important not only to explain or describe the steps but also to explain why it is important for young people to have a financial plan in place.

In your brochure or newsletter, be sure to give examples of information that are needed for each step. For example, what does a budget look like or what taxes should be included? Include any graphics that might be helpful in the explanation of the steps. These might include pictures, graphs/charts, or tables.

1. A financial plan is created like a
   a. map of the world.
   b. blueprint for building a house.
   c. bank account statement.
   d. receipt for an item purchased with a credit card.

2. A person increases his net worth by
   a. buying a new car with a 10 percent down payment from savings and a 90 percent loan.
   b. making purchases with a credit or debit card.
   c. increasing assets and decreasing liabilities.
   d. transferring money from a savings account to a checking account.

3. A person has a house worth $100,000, a mortgage of $90,000, savings of $5,000, a car valued at $10,000, a $7,000 car loan, and $3,000 in credit card debt. This person's net worth is
   a. $115,000.
   b. $100,000.
   c. $15,000.
   d. $5,000.

4. A financial plan does not include
   a. managing risk.
   b. retirement planning.
   c. bankruptcy.
   d. investing.

5. A person increases liquidity when he
   a. buys more items on credit and fewer items with cash.
   b. uses money saved to buy an asset like a car.
   c. has 10 percent of each paycheck deposited into a retirement account.
   d. makes weekly deposits in a bank savings account.

6. "Good credit management" means
   a. making purchases with credit or debit cards.
   b. using credit to make purchases that cost more than $1,000 and paying the minimum required each month.
   c. using credit to make purchases when the buyer knows she can quickly pay the amount owed.
   d. making most purchases on credit in order to track money spent.

7. Why is insurance a method of managing risk?
   a. Insurance protects assets from being lost or damaged.
   b. Insurance limits a person's financial loss if an asset is lost, stolen, or damaged.
   c. A person's liabilities are reduced when insured assets are lost or stolen.
   d. A person's budgeted monthly expenses are covered by insurance.

8. A 21-year-old college graduate starting her first full time job wants to buy a home by age 30. Why should she include this goal in her financial plan?

a. She can apply for a mortgage now while she is young and rates are low.

b. She is more likely to achieve her goal if she starts saving and investing now in order to have the down payment needed to buy the house.

c. She can start buying things for her house while she is living with her parents and having limited expenses.

d. She can buy the house as soon as she finds the one she likes.

CHAPTER 3

Key Terms

Cash inflow

Cash outflow

Expense

Fixed expense

Variable expense

Financial Decision Making

Alicia's senior year was so busy with one school event, ball game, and function after another. In fact, her activity schedule probably was a little too hectic. Her grades were beginning to slip and her parents were not happy. In fact, Alicia and her parents were arguing all the time now.

Until recently, Alicia had been planning to stay at home and attend the local university in the fall. But now, she was rethinking those plans. In fact, after a recent, especially bad argument with her mother, Alicia promised herself that as soon as she graduated from high school, she would get an apartment of her own. Then, she could do whatever she wanted to do, whenever she wanted to do it. Excited by this idea, Alicia began to gather some information.

First, she considered her income. She earned about $300 a month waiting tables—not enough to live on, but if she were willing to work Friday and Saturday nights, she could make another $80 per weekend night. Of course, this would mean giving up many social activities.

Alicia then thought about getting loans to help with college expenses. If she borrowed money, she could work a little less *and* still go out on the weekends. Sure, it would be a pain to have to pay back the loans in a few years. But by that time she would have a good job, and anyway it was a long time in the future.

The next day Alicia shared her thoughts with her friend, Tiffany. Tiffany's face lit up. "Let's move in together and split the costs!" Tiffany said. "I can't wait to get away from my parents, too."

Tiffany said her uncle could give them full-time jobs at his hardware store. "I was sort of thinking about going to college," said Tiffany. "But my uncle said he'd pay me $10 an hour—that's $350 a week! If I can make that kind of money, college can wait!"

At first, Alicia thought Tiffany's ideas sounded great. But the more she thought about it the more doubts she had. First, Tiffany was not the most reliable person Alicia knew. She was not sure about sharing an apartment with her. While $350 a week sounded great, Alicia knew that taxes would reduce that amount by a bit. A nice apartment might cost $800 a month or more. Then there was telephone, cable, electricity, gas, food, a car . . . and putting off college—was that a good decision?

Alicia has a lot to think about. Should she move out? If so, how should she pay for it? Should she work more? Take out a loan? Get a roommate? Put off college so she can earn more money today?

This dilemma facing Alicia is not unusual. In some form or another, we all face these kinds of questions and the questions do not end. For the rest of our lives, we will face choices about our cash inflow and outflow. Having a solid method for making financial decisions and answering these questions can have a big impact on our lives.

At the heart of Alicia's dilemma are questions about cash flow. She faces choices about **cash inflow**—money that she receives from different sources—and **cash outflow**—money that she may spend.

Think about the key components of a financial plan. Each component of your plan also reflects decisions about how you get or use cash. For example, budgeting decisions determine how much of your income you spend on products and services—and how much you have left over. How much you have left over is related to your plans to manage liquidity—how much cash you have available, and how much you rely on credit to meet your wants and needs. Your available cash is also related to what and how much you finance, how much you invest, and so on. The central role of cash in your financial plan is illustrated in Figure 3.1.

Like Alicia, you will face many questions as you build your financial plan and make other financial decisions in life. Some of these questions are outlined in Figure 3.2.

These questions can be difficult to answer and they can have effects that you might not anticipate or recognize for a long time. For example,

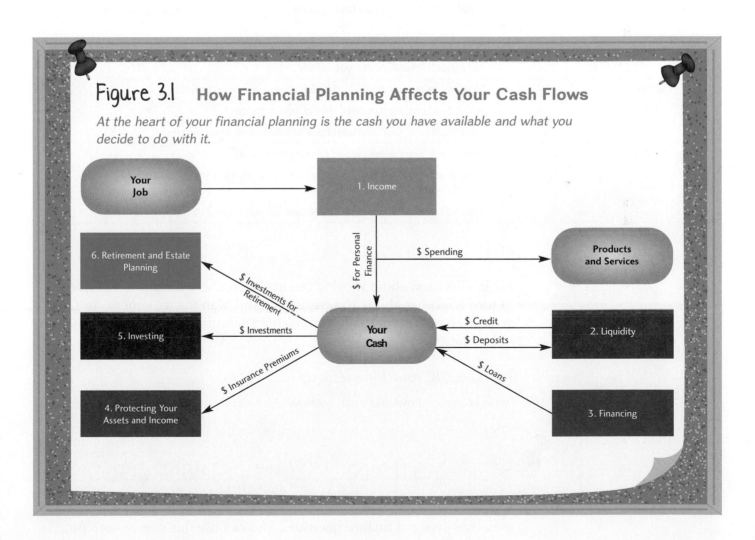

Figure 3.1 How Financial Planning Affects Your Cash Flows

At the heart of your financial planning is the cash you have available and what you decide to do with it.

Your Job → 1. Income

1. Income → $ Spending → Products and Services

$ For Personal Finance

Your Cash → $ Spending → Products and Services

6. Retirement and Estate Planning ← $ Investments for Retirement

5. Investing ← $ Investments

4. Protecting Your Assets and Income ← $ Insurance Premiums

Your Cash ← $ Credit — 2. Liquidity

Your Cash → $ Deposits → 2. Liquidity

Your Cash ← $ Loans — 3. Financing

Figure 3.2 Examples of Decisions Made in Each Component of a Financial Plan

At each stage of creating your financial plan, you will face a number of challenging decisions.

A Plan for:	Types of Decisions
1. Managing your income	What expenses should you anticipate?
	How much money should you attempt to save each month?
	How much money must you save each month toward a specific purchase?
	What debt payments must you make each month?
2. Managing your liquidity	How much money should you maintain in your checking account?
	How much money should you maintain in your savings account?
	Should you use credit cards as a means of borrowing money?
3. Financing	How much money can you borrow to purchase a car?
	Should you borrow money to purchase a car or should you lease a car?
	How much money can you borrow to purchase a home?
	What type of mortgage loan should you obtain to finance the purchase of a house?
4. Protecting your assets and income	What type of insurance do you need?
	How much insurance do you need?
5. Investing	How much money should you allocate toward investments?
	What types of investments should you consider?
	How much risk can you tolerate when investing your money?
6. Your retirement and estate	How much money will you need for retirement?
	How much money must you save each year so that you can retire in a specific year?
	How will you allocate your estate among your heirs?

Alicia's decision about moving out may affect her education, which could in turn affect her ability to save, invest, and plan for retirement. You can see that the effects of that decision could send ripples throughout the rest of her life.

✓ CHECK Your Financial IQ

What is cash inflow and cash outflow?

STEP-BY-STEP DECISION MAKING PROCESS

Fortunately, people such as Alicia—and you—can learn a process for facing these key personal finance questions. You can use this step-by-step process

as you develop each component of your financial plan. Indeed, you can use it whenever you face difficult choices about finances.

STEP 1: Establish Your Financial Goals

You have read several times that planning can help you achieve your goals. But what are your goals? What do you want to accomplish in the future? Needless to say, you cannot reach a goal if you do not know what it is. Establishing clear goals is essential to any successful plan.

Understand that there are many different types of goals. People may have more than one of them. For example, you may have a goal of making a particular purchase and of getting out of debt. Like Alicia, you may want to move into your own apartment or get a college education. How about a car? Maybe you would like to pay off debt or finish college debt free. Some of you may want to start your own plumbing business or catering company. Maybe you would like to have $200,000 in total wealth by age 40 or you might be interested in helping a charity buy a new facility.

You can categorize your financial goals in terms of when you hope to accomplish them as follows:

- **Short-term goals** are those you plan to accomplish within the next year.
- **Middle-term goals** are those you aim to meet within the next one to five years.
- **Long-term goals** will take more than five years to accomplish.

A short-term goal might be to save enough money to buy an MP3 player in a few weeks. A middle-term goal may be to save enough to buy a nice used car next year. A long-term goal might be to save enough money for the down payment on a house in the next 10 years. As your goals become more involved, you will need a more specific and ambitious financial plan. Refer to Figure 3.3 to look at a sample of Alicia's goals.

Figure 3.3   Alicia's Goals

Setting goals—and discriminating between short-term, middle-term, and long-term goals— is the first step in achieving them.

Short-term	Middle-term	Long-term
Buy MP3 Player	Graduate from college	Accumulate $20,000 for a down payment on a house in 10 years
Increase income by $80 a week	Buy a better vehicle next year	Earn a graduate degree
Save money for a deposit on rent and utilities	Accumulate $5,000 in savings in the next five years	Accumulate $100,000 in savings by age 40
Save $1,200 this year for college		
Complete senior year with a 3.0 GPA		

It is essential that you set realistic goals. Goals must be achievable. It does not do any good to set a goal that you can never reach. If you focus on unrealistic goals, you will likely become discouraged when you do not achieve them. On the other hand, establishing an achievable goal encourages you when you accomplish it or as you see that you are making progress toward it. For example, what if Alicia wanted to save $1,200 a year for her college education? If she is successful in the first three months and has accumulated $300, she will feel encouraged to continue saving. If she said she wanted to save $12,000 a year for her college education, she would likely be very disappointed at the end of three months and probably abandon her goal.

Remember—you will set a number of goals for your financial life. In particular, you will want to set goals for each of the components of your financial plan.

STEP 2: Evaluate Your Current Financial Position

Imagine you are traveling in an unfamiliar city. You know you want to get to the museum. You have located it on a map. But how do you get there? In which direction should you travel? Before you can chart your course on a map, you must identify your starting point.

The same principle is true for your personal finances. You need an accurate picture of your current personal and financial situation. Only then can you plan effectively. For example, your decisions about how much money to spend next month, how much to save, and how often to use your credit card depend to a large extent on your current situation. A person with low debt and a lot of assets will make different decisions about spending and saving than a person with a lot of debt and no assets. Single people with no dependents make different decisions than married people with children. People make different decisions at age 18 than at age 50.

Since financial goals are tied to your income, you can see that they are also tied to your level of education and your choice of career. Simply put, having a good, solid income allows you to set more and loftier goals.

For this reason, Alicia is right to be concerned about Tiffany's plans to delay college. This decision may be right for some people at some times. It may even allow these two young women to reach their short-term goals (and even some middle-term goals) more quickly. But Alicia is correct to consider the impact of this decision on her long-term financial well-being.

Now let's take a look at the next leg of the journey. You may know where you are and where you want to be, but you also need to know what roads to take to get there. In Alicia's case, she can map out her current financial condition and what she hopes to achieve. Then, she can begin to figure out how she might reach her goal by making accurate forecasts. A **forecast** is a projection about what will happen in the future. For business and personal finance, forecasts typically involve making projections about cash flows—money you have coming in (inflow) and going out (outflow). Obviously, when we are evaluating our financial position, it is helpful to make projections about the future.

For individuals, cash inflow is referred to as **income**. You can get income from some external source, such as a job, allowance from your parents, or

You Do It

Activity #1

MATH for Personal Finance

Dewanna needs to save $1,500 by August to pay for her tuition. She only has 12 weeks remaining before school starts, and her boss is letting her work 20 hours per week. She brings home about $9 an hour after taxes are withdrawn from her check.

Is it possible for her to save the $1,500?

Solution: Yes, it is possible. She makes $9 an hour × 20 hours per week = $180 per week × 12 weeks = $2,160 she will make prior to school starting.

You may not know when your next variable expense will occur. But you can plan to be ready when misfortune strikes.

a scholarship. You may also get income from savings or investments—for example, interest earned on a savings account.

Most people also have cash outflows to consider. We refer to these as expenses. An **expense** is anything on which we spend money. Examples include the phone bill and car payments. Some expenses we are obligated to pay every month and may be fixed. For example, rent of $600 a month would be a **fixed expense**. Fixed expenses, by definition, remain the same from period to period. Other expenses may be variable, or change from one period to the next. Your phone bill is an example of a **variable expense**. Each bill differs depending on how many minutes you use in the billing period.

Think about Alicia. She already makes $300 a month waiting tables. That is, she makes $3,600 per year. She wants to forecast the impact of an increase in the number of Friday and Saturday nights she works. Assuming $80 in tips for each night worked, Alicia should make an extra $8,320 next year (104 Friday and Saturday nights per year × $80 each = $8,320). This forecast can help Alicia determine how much spending money she will have for the year. She can forecast an $11,920 cash inflow from waiting tables and collecting the money.

However, waiting tables is not cost free to Alicia. In order to do her job, occasionally she has to make some cash outflows. These outflows are her expenses. Alicia's expenses include the purchase of her uniforms for work and the cost of getting them dry-cleaned. The difference between her cash inflow (money from waiting tables) and her cash outflow (job expenses) is her profit. Refer to Figure 3.4 to look at Alicia's forecast if she moves out.

STEP 3: Identify and Evaluate Options for Accomplishing Your Goals

There may be multiple roads that reach the same destination. The same is true for financial goals. Often there are several ways to achieve a goal.

Alicia realizes this. Her goal is to move out of her house while attending college. That is, she wants to create a budget in which she can afford the rent and additional expenses. Toward this end, she is considering adding hours to her work schedule. She is also thinking about taking a loan to help pay for college expenses. She has discussed the idea of having a room-mate so that renting an apartment would be less costly. She has even considered the possibility of postponing college in order to pursue full-time work.

There are probably other options Alicia could consider. For example, she might seek some financial aid to help lower the costs to her parents. She might consider getting education at a less costly school—perhaps a community college. Refer to Figure 3.5 to look at Alicia's options.

Each of these plans may have had the potential to help Alicia reach her goal of moving out of the house after graduation. Of course, each option probably has its drawbacks and shortcomings. Refer to Figure 3.6 for a look at the pros and cons.

You need to take a similar approach to all aspects of your financial plan. This can be tricky: Sometimes one decision has a major impact on your

Figure 3.4   Alicia's Cash Flow Forecast (Income-Expense) Assuming She Moves Out

Look at Alicia's forecast. As you can see, Alicia's expected expenses if she moves out exceed her expected income.

Annual expected cash inflow (income)

Current Job	$300 per month × 12 months	$3,600
Work additional weekends	$80 night × 104 nights	$8,320
	Total cash inflow (income)	**$11,920**

Annual expected cash outflow (expenses)

Rent	½ of $800 per month	$4,800
Utilities	½ of expected $300 per month	$1,800
Food	$300 per month × 12 months	$3,600
Auto expenses (insurance, gas, etc.)		$3,600
Additional expenses, including uniforms and dry-cleaning	$50 per month × 12	$600
Entertainment	$100 per month × 12	$1,200
	Total cash outflow (expenses)	**$15,600**

financial plan. For example, if Alicia takes out student loans in order to get through college, it will have an impact on the financing component of her financial plan and affect her for many years.

You Do It

Activity #2

STEP 4: Pick the Best Plan

After you develop multiple ways to achieve a goal, you need to decide which option is more realistic and works for you. Two people who seem to be in identical situations may still opt for two different plans. Your toler-

Figure 3.5   Alicia's Options

Alicia has identified several options, all of which might enable her to achieve certain goals.

Option 1	Move into an apartment. Alicia realizes this will only be possible if she has at least two roommates and works more than just weekends or takes out college loans.
Option 2	Continue to live at home with her parents while going to college.
Option 3	Work full time and postpone college.

Figure 3.6 Pros and Cons of Alicia's Options

In general, each option will offer certain benefits—"pros"—and drawbacks—"cons." You must identify and evaluate both in order to make good decisions.

	Pros	Cons
Option 1	More freedom to make her own decisions	Very expensive
Option 2	Cheapest alternative while in college	Less freedom to make her own decisions
Option 3	More freedom to make her own decisions	Postpones education that could lead to higher income—has a high opportunity cost (lost future income) and may harm progress toward long-term goals

There is an element of risk in all financial decisions. Knowing your tolerance for risk can help you make the choices that are right for you.

ance for risk and your self-discipline often determine which particular plan offers the best option for achieving a specific goal. **Risk** is often defined as the likelihood of loss. Think about different tolerances for risk in terms of a football game. Your school may be playing last year's state champs in the opening game. Some of your team members are dreading the game because they realize the risk that they will lose is very high. These players have a low risk tolerance. However, some other team members welcome the risk. They are excited about the game because even though the risk is high, the potential reward is huge. They realize that if they are able to beat the state champs, they will achieve much recognition. Neither of these two attitudes is right or wrong. Each indicates different tolerances for risk.

You can apply the same thought process to your financial decision making and financial plan. Some of you will choose plans that have a higher level of risk of loss but also have a higher potential payoff. Others will pick plans with lower risk that are more certain to accomplish the ultimate goal. Alicia may choose a different plan than Tiffany would choose to achieve the same goal. Both options may be good for each individual.

What if two people want to get a college degree? Refer to Figure 3.7 for a summary of how Alicia and one of her other friends, Rafael, might choose different paths or plans to achieve their goal.

STEP 5: Periodically Evaluate Your Plan

After you pick a plan, you need to monitor your progress because sometimes your plans may falter or get off track. Unless you are monitoring your progress toward your goals, it is likely that you will not notice a problem and make any needed adjustments.

Let's say Alicia has opted to work six Friday and Saturday nights each month to earn enough money to fund her budget and pay rent on an apartment. After several weeks of doing this, she notices that she does not make $80 every night. In fact, the average amount she makes for weekend shifts is really closer to $60. Alicia needs to reconsider her forecasts—and reconsider whether her goals are feasible. She may have to make some adjustments in her plan in order to make it work.

Figure 3.7   Different Paths to Same Goal

Different people may find different ways to accomplish the same goal.

Alicia	Raphael
Step 1: Establish Goal	
• get a four-year college degree from University X	• get a four-year college degree from University X
Step 2: Evaluate Your Current Financial Position	
• has a job and savings she can use for spending money • is likely to receive scholarships • is eligible for loans • has option of living at home rent-free	• has no job or resources • is unlikely to earn scholarships, but is eligible for government grants and loans • must pay for dorm room or apartment to attend University X
Step 3: Identify and Evaluate Different Ways to Accomplish Your Goals	
• could get apartment—with roommates and increased work schedule • could borrow money and work less • could live at home and work less	• could get job • could live at home and attend lower-cost, nearby community college for first two years, then transfer to University X • could attend four-year school *if* he gets a roommate and takes out loans
Step 4: Pick the Best Plan	
• live at home and cut back work schedule • use combination of savings, earnings, and scholarship money to graduate debt-free	• get a part-time job and save money • use grants to begin education at community college while living at home • use savings and perhaps loans for final two years at University X

MATH for Personal Finance

Lesia's original financial plan required that she save $100 a month for two years in order to have $2,400 for the down payment on a car. However, after one year she has only managed to save $1,000.

What will Lesia need to do in order to accomplish her original goal?

Solution: Lesia needs to save another $1,400 to reach her original goal or $2,400 − $1,000 she has saved = $1,400. To accomplish that goal in 12 months she will need to save $1,400 / 12 = $116.67 per month. She will have to increase her savings to $116.67 per month to accumulate the original $2,400 by the end of next year.

You Do It

Activity 3

STEP 6: Revise Your Financial Plan as Necessary

What happens when you determine your plan is unachievable or too restrictive? Revise it. But remember: Any revision to one part of your financial plan may impact other aspects of your plan.

 CHECK Your Financial IQ

What are the steps of financial decision making?

Summary

- Financial decisions—and financial planning—begin with questions about cash flows. Each component of your financial plan reflects or is affected by your decisions about cash inflow and cash outflow.

- There are six steps that are critical for making financial decisions and creating your personal financial plan. (1) establish your financial goals; (2) evaluate your current financial position; (3) identify and evaluate different ways to accomplish your goals; (4) pick the best plan; (5) evaluate your plan periodically; and (6) revise your financial plan as necessary.

Key Terms and Vocabulary

Cash inflow	Long-term goal
Cash outflow	Middle-term goal
Expense	Risk
Fixed expense	Short-term goal
Forecast	Variable expense
Income	

What Do You Know?

myFinLitlab

1. (a) Explain how cash inflow and outflow affects the components of your financial plan.

2. (a) What are the three different types of financial goals?

   (b) What key quality must all financial goals have?

3. (a) What is the role of forecasting in financial planning?

   (b) How does forecasting relate to one's decision about education?

4. (a) Why is it necessary to identify your current financial position before making further financial plans?

   (b) Explain why a person's current financial position might affect his or her financial plans.

5. (a) Explain how speeding progress toward a short-term goal might slow progress toward a long-term goal.

6. (a) Identify at least three different possible sources of income.

7. (a) Using the metaphor of a roadmap, to what feature do different options for reaching financial goals compare?

   (b) What are the benefits of picking multiple options for achieving financial goals?

8. (a) What is the difference between a high and a low tolerance for risk?

   (b) Explain how risk and an individual's tolerance for it can affect planning.

9. (a) What must you do when you revise one part of your financial plan?

   (b) Why might you need to revise your financial plan?

What Are Your Finance Math Skills?

myFinLitlab.

The first three questions correlate to *Math for Personal Finance* features located throughout the chapter.

1. Echo wants to put a $1,000 down payment on a car 10 weeks from now. She works about 10 hours per week at her current job. She brings home about $8 an hour after taxes are withdrawn from her check. Is it possible for her to save the $1,000?

2. Caleb expects to work an average of 12 hours a week during next semester. Assuming he makes $9.50 an hour and works the entire 17 week semester, what is his forecast for income next year?

3. Connor intended to save $150 a month for the next 18 months to purchase a fishing boat. However, after 10 months he has only managed to save $1,200. What will Connor need to do in order to accomplish his original goal?

4. Assume your phone bill averages $45 a month and you have a car payment that is $140 per month. You also spend about $20 a week on food. How much are your monthly expenses?

5. You make $50 a week and you want to buy a car with an expected payment of $200 a month. Is that a feasible goal?

6. Can you afford to buy a $50 video game every month if you make $40 a week and spend an average of $150 a month on food and gasoline?

7. How much is your monthly cash inflow if you earn $80 a week but about 20 percent is withdrawn from your check for taxes?

8. If you want to increase your income next year by $1,000 how many additional hours will you need to work per month if you make $7 an hour?

What Would You Do?

Dennis has decided on a car to purchase. He has a financial plan that he put together in his economics class. During that class, Dennis decided that a car purchase would need to wait until he had enough in his savings account for a good down payment.

Gregory, Dennis' friend, is going to sell his car so that he can go to trade school after high school. Dennis has always liked Gregory's car. He knows it is in good condition because Gregory is planning to become a mechanic after trade school and always works on his car.

Dennis is faced with a problem. He does not have the money in his savings to pay what Gregory is asking. He is also thinking of his financial plan. Is this really the time to purchase a car, even a great car like Gregory's? If he purchases the car, he will have to ask his parents for a loan to help him pay for it.

1. If you were in Dennis' place, what would you do?

2. Where could Dennis go to get a loan? What considerations should he make when thinking about a loan?

3. Should Dennis follow his financial plan or revise it? What should he do to help him make this decision?

What Are the Connections? Science and Technology

Think about a purchase you want to make, or an event you want to attend in the next few months. This might be an MP3 player, a new audio system for your car, or a day at a spa that includes a new hair style, nails (manicure and pedicure), and a massage. It might be tickets to see your favorite group or team. How will you make a decision about what to purchase? How will you pay for it? What steps do you need to take to help you make this decision?

Develop a flowchart that shows what steps you will take in your decision making process. You could use poster board to display your flowchart or you could use a software program to help you design your flowchart. Be sure to think about all the decisions and events that will be needed to get to the "finish line"—that final purchase or event you want to attend. Include steps for evaluating progress along the way—with options for responding depending on your progress toward your goal.

Teamwork Service-Learning Activity

As a team, develop a public service announcement (PSA) about the steps involved in good financial decision making. A PSA is an audio or video presentation that brings awareness to the public. This one should tell the importance of financial planning for teens. Think about what you have learned in this chapter.

For your PSA, you should work together to write and perform a simple skit or presentation that helps others understand the process you have read about in Chapter 3. You can present your PSA live or in audio or video format.

1. The best description of cash inflow is money
   a. received from different sources, such as salary and interest earned on bank accounts.
   b. spent for items that must be included in a budget, such as rent and utilities.
   c. invested in financial products, such as stocks and bonds.
   d. left after paying for items included in a financial plan.

2. A person's cash outflow includes
   a. liquid assets a person has accumulated.
   b. money spent by a company to pay a person's salary.
   c. payments by a person to a retirement account.
   d. the difference between the asking price of two houses for sale in the same neighborhood.

3. Which is the correct order for making financial decisions?
   a. Put goals in writing, rethink goals if necessary, have a plan of action, set specific goals.
   b. Be realistic about goals, put goals in writing, implement goals, have specific goals.
   c. Set specific goals, put goals in writing, have a plan of action, rethink goals if necessary.
   d. Have a plan of action, set specific goals, implement goals, put goals in writing.

4. Which is a true statement about goals?
   a. A person should only work on one goal at a time.
   b. Intermediate goals are those that can be accomplished in one to five years.
   c. A person should accomplish short-term goals before starting on any other goals.
   d. A short-term goal should be tied to a long-term goal.

5. Which one of the following does *not* show a correct match?
   a. Cash inflow: scholarship award
   b. Cash inflow: interest paid on a loan
   c. Cash outflow: insurance premiums
   d. Cash outflow: tuition

6. A high school student starts a lawn mowing business. His riding lawn mower cost $1,000; gas for the season is $2,000. He spends $500 for gas driving to and from jobs, $300 for supplies and repairs, and $200 for a trimmer. Each of his 20 customers pays $40 a week for a 20-week season. What is the outcome of this business venture?
   a. He makes a $12,000 profit.
   b. He makes a $4,000 profit.
   c. He has an $8,000 total cash inflow.
   d. He has a $4,000 total cash inflow.

7. A financial plan should
   a. be followed as it is written until the goals set in the plan are achieved.
   b. be evaluated periodically and revised as needed.
   c. only be revised when a person's job changes.
   d. remain the same unless a person changes financial goals.

8. Which of the following is a correct statement?
   a. If cash inflow exceeds cash outflow, a person has a surplus to save or invest.
   b. An expense is considered a cash inflow.
   c. Fixed expenses should be paid before variable expenses.
   d. Cash outflow can be reduced by buying everything on credit.

CHAPTER 4

Learning Objectives

Explain the steps involved in creating a budget.

Explain the steps involved in creating a personal balance sheet.

Analyze the importance of budgeting in your financial plan.

Key Terms

Bond

Budget

Investment

Market value

Mutual fund

Personal balance sheet

Real estate

Stock

Budgets and Balance Sheets
Your Personal Financial Statements

Terris walked into his new apartment and sat down. After completing a prestigious music program in New York, the day he had been working toward for years was finally here. In his hands was his first paycheck from his first real job! At long last, he could begin to live the life of his dreams.

Immediately he began to think about the purchases he had been putting off for so long—a new car, a laptop, some nice clothes. Maybe he could buy season tickets for baseball or a new stereo system. Or perhaps he could finally make good on his promise to his friend Martin to take that road trip to Chicago. Now he had the income to afford these things—or, at least, to pay off his credit card bills.

Just as he was getting excited, Terris seemed to hear a small voice in his head. It was his grandfather. "Use your head, Terris," he could almost hear him say. "Be sure to put something away for a rainy day!"

Terris sighed. He realized he probably could not afford to get all the things he wanted right away. He also knew he had to think about more than just spending his new paycheck. At the same time, he was ready to treat himself. He had worked hard to get to this point, and he felt he deserved to enjoy the rewards.

Terris's situation is one in which you may find yourself one day. He is anxious to begin living his life as a working adult. But what he needs to do, he realizes, is to sit down, look at where he is financially—and where he wants to go. In other words, Terris needs to make a budget and a personal balance sheet.

CREATING A BUDGET

Creating a budget is a key part of your financial plan. A **budget** is a forecast of future cash inflows and outflows. Once you have identified your personal goals, you need some specific plans about how to reach those goals. Your household budget provides that guidance. It gives you a detailed roadmap to your financial future.

Think about Terris's goals. He wants to pay off his credit cards, save some money for a rainy day, and treat himself to a few things he wants. Can he accomplish all those goals? If he plans well and doesn't attempt to do all of them at once he can achieve his goals. A budget will be his detailed plan of action for the next several years.

You Do It

Activity #1

STEP I: Create a Personal Cash Flow Statement

The first step in the budgeting process is to identify your current cash inflows and outflows. The primary cash inflow for most people is their salary, hourly wages, or any money they earn. However, some people may have income from savings accounts or other similar sources. Others may receive an allowance of some type. In addition, if you receive money from a scholarship, that is income, too. Any money that you have coming in is a cash inflow.

On the other hand, your cash outflows are any money that you have going out. Expenses such as car payments or insurance premiums are cash outflows. At some point you may begin paying rent and utilities or your cell phone bill. These are all cash outflows. Cash outflows are typically impacted by family size, age, and your personal spending habits.

Your personal cash flow statement records cash inflows and outflows. This allows you to track where your money comes from and where it goes easily. Check out Figure 4.1 to see where Terris's money has gone in the past two months.

Figure 4.1 Terris's Personal Cash Flow Statement

A personal cash flow statement compares cash inflows to cash outflows and is the first step in creating a budget.

Cash Inflows	January	February
Disposable (after-tax) income	$2,500	$2,500
Interest on deposits	0	0
Income from investments	0	0
Total Cash Inflows	**$2,500**	**$2,500**

Cash Outflows	January	February
Rent	$600	$600
Cable TV	50	50
Electricity and water	60	60
Telephone	60	60
Groceries	300	300
Health care insurance and expenses	130	430
Clothing	100	100
Car expenses (insurance, maintenance, and gas)	200	500
Recreation	600	600
Total Cash Outflows	**$2,100**	**$2,700**
Net Cash Flows	**+$400**	**−$200**

You Do It
Activity #2

STEP 2: Turn Your Cash Flow Statement into a Budget

The next step is to turn your personal cash flow statement into a budget. To take this step you must forecast your net cash flows for a period of time into the future. A good budget should cover anticipated cash inflows and outflows for several months to a year or more.

As you take this step, it's important to think about how your cash flows might change from month to month. Will you spend more money at certain times of the year, or are your cash flows similar from month to month? What about the holiday seasons? Be sure that you consider expected but irregular expenses. Examples include activity fees for school functions or money for your spring break activities. A yearly vacation is another example of an expense that will not show up in the typical month.

Indeed, many people find that expenses occur unexpectedly. Car breakdowns or medical emergencies are unpredictable—but, unfortunately, nearly certain to strike at some point. What happens when you are at college and you unexpectedly need to return home for a weekend? Who will pay for the gas? At other times an opportunity may arise for you to take a ski trip or go to a concert with friends. A good budget will force you to set

Who will pay for gas? Good planning can make it possible for you to meet unexpected expenses.

aside money to take care of unexpected expenses and to take advantage of unexpected opportunities.

Taking your personal cash flow statement and turning it into a budget for an entire year involves some guesswork and estimating. Obviously, you cannot plan the precise cost of events or expenses that have not occurred yet. Don't worry. You can always go back and adjust the budget as you get more information. This annual budget can help you identify times when you can save money and times when you will have more outflows than inflows.

Look at Figure 4.2. When should Terris be saving?

Working with and Improving Your Budget

By now you can see that a budget is a great planning tool. A budget can help you save money for major purchases, unexpected expenses, or unexpected opportunities. After all, you don't want to be broke when someone offers you a month's stay in Europe if you will just buy the plane ticket.

Indeed, one of the primary benefits of your budget is that it will help you anticipate future cash shortfalls. For example, think about Terris's situation. He is earning a good, steady income now. But he also needs to be

Figure 4.2 Terris's Annual Budget

An annual budget projects inflows and outflows for an entire year and should help ensure that you have adequate net cash flows.

Cash Inflows	Typical Month	This Year's Cash Flows (equal to the typical monthly cash flows × 12)
Disposable (after-tax) income	$2,500	$30,000
Interest on deposits	0	0
Income from investments	0	0
Total Cash Inflows	**$2,500**	**$30,000**
Cash Outflows	Typical Month	This Year's Cash Flows
Rent	$600	$7,200
Cable TV	50	600
Electricity and water	60	720
Telephone	60	720
Groceries	300	3,600
Health care insurance and expenses	130	1,560
Clothing	100	1,200
Car expenses (insurance, maintenance, and gas)	200	2,400
Recreation	500	6,000
Charitable giving	100	1,200
Total Cash Outflows	**$2,100**	**$25,200**
Net Cash Flows	**+$400**	**$4,800 (difference between cash inflows and outflows)**

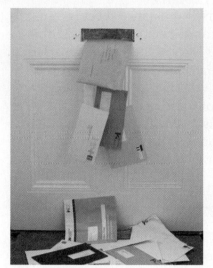

As you gather new information —and perhaps identify new expenses—you should adjust your budget.

thinking about some significant expenses. For example, in Figure 4.1 you can see that Terris spent only $200 on his car in the last month. But his car is old, and it's due for its annual inspection. He knows there are several things wrong that he'll need to fix—at the cost of several hundred dollars. Where will the money come from? A budget will help him plan for those expected outflows and save money to cover the unexpected outflows that happen as well.

Sure, it may be tempting for him to satisfy all his desires at once—perhaps by continuing to overuse his credit card. However, this is a risky path that leads many people into financial disaster. With a good budget, Terris can meet his wants and needs without a costly and unwise dependence on credit.

Assessing the Accuracy of the Budget

One of the things you need to do is periodically evaluate your forecasts and compare those with the actual cash flows. It's a good idea to look at last month's forecasts or the last three months' forecasts and compare those with actual numbers.

The best way to know exactly how you spend your money is to keep an expense journal. Write down every nickel you spend during the course of a week or a month. It might really surprise you where your money is going. Sometimes you will find that you underestimated your cash outflows or were too optimistic regarding your cash inflows. The difference between what you forecast to happen and what actually happens is known as **forecast error**. After you look at your forecast error, you may find that you need to adjust your spending. If you continue to come up short of money at the end of each month, you need to increase your income or decrease your outflow. Let's look at Terris's summary data for the last three months in Figure 4.3. Should he take any action?

Terris obviously needs to revisit his budget. His forecasts are not matching up with reality. He needs to increase his income or decrease his outflow. Review the details in Figure 4.1. What are some ways Terris could reduce his outflows?

Figure 4.3 Terris's Actual versus Forecast Cash Flows (Three-Month Period)

It is easy to make forecasting errors, and you should be thorough in checking that your actual and forecast cash flows match.

	Forecast	Actual
Cash Inflows	$7,500	$7,500
Cash Outflows	6,300	7,400
Net Cash Flows	1,200	100

✓ CHECK Your Financial IQ

What are the steps involved in creating a budget?

PERSONAL BALANCE SHEET

A budget helps ensure that you have a positive net cash flow. But what will you do with the cash you have left over? One of the tools you can use to help you make that decision is a personal balance sheet. While the budget tracks our cash flows over time, the **personal balance sheet** tells us our financial position at a point in time. The personal balance sheet is a summary of our assets (what we own such as a car or cash in the bank), our liabilities (money we owe such as a personal loan we need to pay back or a car loan), and our net worth (assets minus liabilities). Your net worth is what people track to determine your overall wealth. The Forbes list of wealthiest Americans reports the net worth of these individuals.

Having a good picture of your net worth is essential for financial planning. Knowing where you stand will help you decide how to manage your liquidity, your credit and borrowing, your investments, and more.

Assets

Assets are items of value that a person owns and they can be classified in several ways. Typical asset categories are liquid assets, household assets, and investments. While many of you may not have assets in all of these categories, at some point in the future you will if you apply the tools learned in this text.

Liquid Assets

Liquid assets are financial assets that are either cash or can be quickly and easily converted to cash without significant loss of value. What does this mean? Every asset can be converted to cash, but some may require that you drop the price to sell it quickly. A house, for example, may be worth a lot of money, but it may take months to sell it at its full value. However, liquid assets can be turned into cash in a hurry without dropping the price. Liquid assets include money in checking and savings accounts.

Liquid assets are necessary for covering unexpected emergency expenses. When we talk about money management we are referring to liquid assets.

While the key quality of liquid access is quick availability, it's also important that liquid assets be making money—that is, earning interest. For this reason, it's common to keep liquid assets in an interest-bearing checking or savings account.

Household Assets

Another type of asset is **household assets**. These include those assets typically owned by a household—for example, cars, houses, and furniture. In

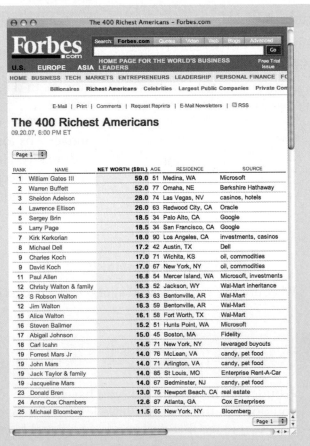

general, household assets will make up a larger proportion of a person's balance sheet than liquid assets.

When you create your personal balance sheet you will need to evaluate the true market value of your household assets realistically. The **market value** of something is what it would be worth if you sold it today. While you may have paid $12,000 for a car two years ago, it may only be worth $6,000 today. You should list the value of the car as $6,000 in this case. A guide to car market values can be found on a number of Web sites, such as Kelley Blue Book (www.kbb.com). House values may be harder to find, but you can estimate those based on what similar houses have sold for in your neighborhood recently. Various Internet sites, such as Ebay, may be the best source of values for your other possessions.

Investments

Investments are the third major category of assets. An **investment** is something you acquire with the ultimate goal of making money. That is, an investment is something you buy that you believe will actually increase in value over time. Some of the more common investment assets are stocks, bonds, and real estate. Some people invest in collectibles but they are much harder to evaluate and require very specialized knowledge.

Bonds are basically certificates that function like IOUs—promises to repay a certain amount of money at some future time. For example, a company or government decides to issue a series of bonds valued at $1,000 each. An investor agrees to buy one of these bonds by giving $1,000 to the bond issuer. In return, the bond issuer agrees to pay interest to the owner of the bond, and also to repay the original $1,000 at some point in the future. So, when you buy the bond, you are essentially loaning the issuer money. The issuer will pay you interest until the maturity date and at that time they will pay back the $1,000. People buy bonds with the expectation of receiving interest income while they hold the bond and getting their money back when the bond matures. In fact, bond issuers are not always able to pay interest or even to return the original investment. For this reason, investing in bonds involves some risk.

Perhaps some of you have Series EE savings bonds issued by the United States government. This type of bond is somewhat different from the bonds described above. Savings bonds do not pay interest while you hold the bond. Instead, they merely accrue interest and increase in value.

Stocks are certificates that represent fractional ownership of a firm. For example, you could start a business and sell ownership fractions to 100 dif-

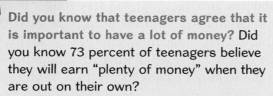

Professor FIN

Did you know that teenagers agree that it is important to have a lot of money? Did you know 73 percent of teenagers believe they will earn "plenty of money" when they are out on their own?

One recent survey found that teenagers believe that they will earn an average annual income of $145,500. Of this group, boys think they will earn $173,000, while girls estimate their salary at $114,200 per year.

Reality check:

- Just five percent of the U.S. population earns a six-figure salary.
- Approximately $40,000 is the national average wage.

Source: "Optimistic Teens May Need Financial Reality Check, Schwab Survey Shows." PR Newswire (March 27, 2007): NA. General OneFile. Gale. Middle Tennessee State University. 10 Apr. 2008 <http://find.galegroup.com/itx/start.do?prodId=ITOF>.

Emily owns 50 shares of Company Y's stock that is currently selling for $170 a share. She also owns 65 shares of Company Z's stock worth about $47 a share.

What is the total value of her stock holdings?

Solution:

Company Y
50 × $170 = $8,500

Company Z
65 × $47 = $3,055
Total = $11,555

ferent people. Each share of ownership would represent one percent of the business and would be called a share of stock. Most firms have millions of shares outstanding, so one share of stock is usually a very small fraction of ownership in that company. People buy stocks with the expectation that the company will do well and the value of the stock will increase. As with bonds, however, there is some risk. It's possible that the value of the stock will decline or even disappear entirely.

Mutual funds are created so investors can pool their money in order to invest in a larger variety of financial assets, such as stocks and bonds from many different companies. Mutual funds are managed by professional portfolio managers who decide which stocks and/or bonds to purchase. Therefore, individual investors who buy shares in the fund do not have to be experts in stock or bond selection. Most mutual funds require a minimum investment that typically ranges between $500 and $3,000. With mutual funds, the risk of loss is generally spread across many different investments. So, even if one or two of the fund's stock or bond investments collapse, the fund itself may decline only a little. This can help protect an investor from a severe drop in the value of an investment. Still, mutual fund investments can and sometimes do lose their value.

Mutual funds can be used for a variety of purposes. One such use is a Section 529 College Savings Plan. Parents, grandparents, or other relatives can open 529 plans for their children and make contributions designed to be used for education. The plans help investors avoid some taxes on the earnings and withdrawals from the plans. Mutual funds are commonly used as investments for 529s.

Real estate includes homes, rental property, farms, and other land. Rental property includes houses or commercial property that is rented out to others. Some people buy timberland or farms with the expectation that it will generate revenue over time and also increase in value.

Liabilities

Liabilities represent the amount of debt a person owes. These debts can be split into two categories: current liabilities and long-term liabilities.

Current liabilities are debts that must be paid off within one year. Credit card balances are the most common form of current liability for individuals. When you charge something on your credit card, you will be billed for those charges during the next billing cycle. In other words, when used properly, a credit card acts like a short-term loan that should be paid off every month. When you pay that credit card bill, you are eliminating that current liability.

Long-term liabilities are debts that will take longer than one year to pay off. Student loans, car loans, and home mortgages are common examples of long-term liabilities. Each payment you make contains an interest component and some amount that will reduce the initial liability (principal). After making all the required payments on time, the long-term liability is eliminated.

Note that many people use credit cards in a way that creates a long-term liability. They make purchases with their cards that they cannot pay off quickly. As a result, they pay interest on their debt and reduce their liability by only a very small portion every month. In general, using credit cards to create a long-term liability is a bad move. The interest rates charged on

Making purchases with credit cards that you cannot pay off quickly is a bad move.

MATH for Personal Finance

Lakisha's car is worth about $6,000 and she still owes $1,200 on it. She has an outstanding credit card balance of $450.

What is her net worth?

Solution: Lakisha's net worth is $6,000 − $1,200 − $450 = $4,350.

most credit cards far exceeds the interest rate individuals could get at a bank or credit union for long-term financing. It is much better to pursue other kinds of financing, such as bank loans, for long-term liabilities.

Net Worth

Net worth is the difference between your assets and your liabilities.

Net worth = Value of your total assets − the sum of your total liabilities

To put it another way, if you sold all of your assets today and paid off your debt (liabilities), the remaining amount would be your net worth. Some people find that they have a negative net worth and may be on the verge of bankruptcy.

Figuring your net worth is an easy way to measure your wealth. It makes it easy to track your wealth over time. The way you figure your net worth is with a personal balance sheet. You can see an example in Figure 4.4. How much is Terris worth?

Changes in Your Personal Balance Sheet

Your personal balance sheet changes as you acquire new assets and/or new liabilities. If you spend all your income on living expenses, your balance sheet will remain the same. However, if you run up your credit card debt and do not pay off the balance at the end of the month, your net worth will decline. If you save some money, your net worth will increase. You can increase your net worth in two ways. One way requires that the value of your assets increases by more than the value of your liabilities. For example, you may buy stock that increases in value. As long as you maintain the same level of debt, your net worth will increase. The other way is to pay down debt on your assets that hold their value.

Figure 4.4 Terris's Personal Balance Sheet

A personal balance sheet gives you a quick assessment of where you stand financially at a specific point in time.

Assets		
Cash		$3,200
Car		4,000
Musical instruments		5,500
Furniture		1,200
Total Assets		**$13,900**
Current Liabilities		
Student loan	$2,500	
Credit card balance	3,000	
Total Current Liabilities		**$5,500**
Net Worth ($13,900 − $5,500)		**$8,400**

Analysis of Your Personal Balance Sheet

What do lenders look at before they make a loan? They want to see if you can make the payments. One of the tools they use is your personal balance sheet. Loan officers often use a debt-to-asset ratio to determine whether you have borrowed too much money. For this reason alone, you should pay careful attention to your personal balance sheet. Keeping it in good shape can influence the options you have for making financial decisions and constructing a healthy

You Do It
Activity #3

financial plan. Look again at Figure 4.4. You can see that Terris's debt-to-asset ratio is $5,500/$13,900 = 39.5 percent. Remember, this particular ratio is often used by lenders to determine whether you have enough wealth to repay debt. According to a lender, lower is always better.

☑ **CHECK Your Financial IQ**

What are the steps in creating a personal balance sheet?

BUDGETING AND YOUR FINANCIAL PLAN

You Do It
Activity #4

Your cash flows obviously feed into your personal balance sheet. If your cash inflows exceed your cash outflows, you will either increase assets or reduce liabilities. This will show up on your balance sheet in the form of increased net worth (see Figure 4.5). The personal balance sheet is basically a scorecard. It tells you how much your level of wealth is changing, and it gives you information you can use when building your financial plan.

Budgeting helps in financial planning because it forces you to evaluate your current financial condition and also helps you answer the following questions:

- How can I improve my net cash flows in the near term?
- How can I improve my net cash flows in the long term?
- What decisions should I make about using credit, borrowing, and investing?

An evaluation of your budget might identify places where you can reduce outflows or places where you can increase cash inflows. Either of these actions will help create wealth.

☑ **CHECK Your Financial IQ**

What is the importance of budgeting to your financial plan?

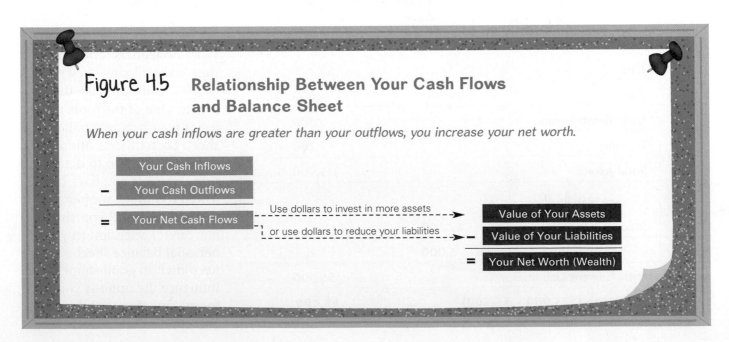

Figure 4.5 **Relationship Between Your Cash Flows and Balance Sheet**

When your cash inflows are greater than your outflows, you increase your net worth.

Chapter Review

Summary

- The budgeting process allows you to monitor and control cash inflows and outflows. By examining the difference between your forecast and your actual cash inflows and outflows, you can anticipate future problems and make adjustments in your budget that will help you reach your financial goals.

- Your personal balance sheet tells you your financial position at a point in time. It is a summary of your assets, your liabilities, and your net worth. Assets can be listed as liquid assets, household assets, and investments. Liabilities represent the amount of debt you owe and can be split into two categories: current liabilities and long-term liabilities.

- Budgeting can help you manage your cash flows to increase your net worth, which you can use in building a financial plan.

Key Terms and Vocabulary

Bond	Liability	Personal balance
Budget	Liquid asset	sheet
Current liability	Long-term liability	Real estate
Forecast error	Market value	Stock
Household asset	Mutual fund	
Investment	Net worth	

What Do You Know?

1. (a) What is the purpose of a budget?

   (b) How can a budget help when you are anticipating cash shortages or a cash surplus?

2. (a) How do you assess the accuracy of your budget?

   (b) How can finding forecasting errors improve your budget?

3. (a) Describe the process of creating an annual budget.

4. (a) Suppose you want to change your budget to increase your savings. Explain what you could do.

5. (a) What is the purpose of a personal balance sheet?

   (b) How can a personal balance sheet help you when you are making financial decisions?

6. (a) Briefly define and give examples of each category of asset.

   (b) Why do you think stocks are not considered liquid assets?

7. (a) What are bonds?

   (b) What are stocks?

(c) What are mutual funds?

(d) Describe how each of these provides a return on your investment.

8. (a) Give an example of a current liability and a long-term liability.

(b) What's an example of how a current liability can be converted into a long-term liability?

9. (a) Explain how net worth is a measure of wealth.

10. (a) Describe how your net worth increases.

(b) Will the purchase of additional assets always increase your net worth? Why or why not?

What Are Your Finance Math Skills?

The first three questions correlate to Math for Personal Finance features located throughout the chapter.

1. Let's assume your net worth is currently $2,650. What happens to it if you get a $1,000 gift from your grandparents?

2. In the previous problem, what happens to your net worth if you spend $250 of the gift and save the remainder?

3. According to your budget forecast you will have expenses of $1,200 next month and income of $800. How much do you have available to save?

4. What is the value of Stephanie's stock holdings if she owns 20 shares of a company that are worth $112 each?

5. What is the value of your total assets if you own stocks worth $3,700, have $578 in a savings account, and own a motorcycle valued at $2,100?

6. Michael has $3,100 in his savings account, $400 in his checking account, and owns a truck worth $2,300. How much does he have in liquid assets?

7. Kevin's grandfather left him 100 shares of Apple Computer, Inc. and 40 shares of Ford Motor Company. How much is his stock worth, assuming Apple sells for $182 a share and Ford sells for $6.85 a share?

8. Jawanda's car is worth about $4,000 and she owes $1,500 on it. She also has a sound system valued at $500 and $350 in her checking account. What is her net worth?

What Would You Do?

Dani is applying for a loan so that she can purchase a new car. On her application, she is asked to write down the value of the assets she owns. She does not have many items of value—except for a custom-made guitar her parents bought for her when she was in high school. She does not know the value of the instrument; but she knows it originally cost $2,000—and that fine instruments often increase in value. She also knows that the greater the value of the instrument, the better her chances are to be approved for a loan. She is tempted to put down the value of the guitar at $5,000.

1. If you were in Dani's place, what would you do?
2. What might happen if Dani gives an inflated value for the guitar?
3. How might Dani solve this problem?

What Are the Connections? Math and Technology

Record your expenses for one month. What did you purchase? How many times did you buy gas? Did you eat out? What extra purchases or expenses did you have this month? Were any of those expenses unexpected?

Make a spreadsheet that lists all the expenses you had for the month. Continue to design the spreadsheet to show expenses that have occurred and plan for those you might have for the next two months. How much money will you need to cover the expenses for the next two months? Have you planned for unexpected expenses? How can you plan for the unexpected?

Teamwork

In a team, develop a budget for a Volunteer Day luncheon and ceremony. Your Volunteer Day will be designed to thank the parents/community who have helped at your school throughout the year. The budget needs to include the following:

- Funds for printing handouts about the Volunteer Day
- Lunch for 25 people
- Certificates or small thank-you gifts for the school volunteers
- Any other items you think might be needed to make the day a success

Write a proposal to the administration of your school requesting that your organization be allowed to have a Volunteer Day. Be sure you include in your proposal the date of the event, how you are going to get the word out about the day, and the importance of having such a day. Include your budget with your proposal.

w!se | **Financial Literacy** CERTIFICATION

TEST PREP QUESTIONS

1. Creating a cash flow statement is a good way for a person to determine how much money the person
   a. receives from various sources over the course of a month.
   b. has left at the end of the year to buy holiday presents.

   c. actually spent on food this year.

   d. needs to pay for medical expenses each month this year.

2. Which is a true statement about a budget?

   a. A budget should remain the same from month to month.

   b. A person's budget should be the same as other people with the same income.

   c. When a person spends more than he has budgeted, he should reduce his cash inflow.

   d. A budget should include both fixed and variable expenses.

3. A personal balance sheet

   a. shows how much is available each month to pay for necessities.

   b. shows how much money a person has available for savings.

   c. is used to determine if a person's budget is realistic.

   d. is a picture of a person's financial well-being at a point in time.

4. Which asset is correctly matched with its description?

   a. House: liquid asset.

   b. Car: household asset.

   c. Mutual fund: liquid asset.

   d. Checking account: investment asset.

5. The purpose of investing money is to

   a. increase a person's net worth each month.

   b. qualify for a low interest rate bank mortgage.

   c. pay for car loans, credit card balances and other monthly debt.

   d. have an asset that will increase in value over time.

6. When a person applies for a loan, the lender will review the person's balance sheet in order to find out if he

   a. has enough assets to cover both current liabilities as well as the debt created by the new loan.

   b. is following his monthly budget.

   c. has made good investments in stocks and bonds over the time he has been employed.

   d. will be able to pay back the loan within three years.

7. How does a person determine her net worth?

   a. Subtract investments from cash inflow.

   b. Add interest earned on investments to salary.

   c. Subtract liabilities from assets.

   d. Add cash outflow to savings.

8. Which of the following shows, in the correct order, the steps a person should take to organize his financial life?

   a. Create a financial plan, determine net worth, establish financial goals.

   b. Create a personal cash flow statement, create a budget, develop a personal balance sheet.

   c. Establish financial goals, create a personal balance sheet, create a personal cash flow statement.

   d. Determine net worth, create a personal cash flow statement, create a budget.

UNIT 2

Income & Careers

CHAPTER 5

Learning Objectives

Explain the process for deciding a career path.

Describe different sources of information to research careers.

Explain how one can gain the skills needed for a career choice.

Describe the process of applying for a job.

Key Terms

Accreditation

Apprenticeship

Certification

Compensation

Internship

Résumé

Careers and Education

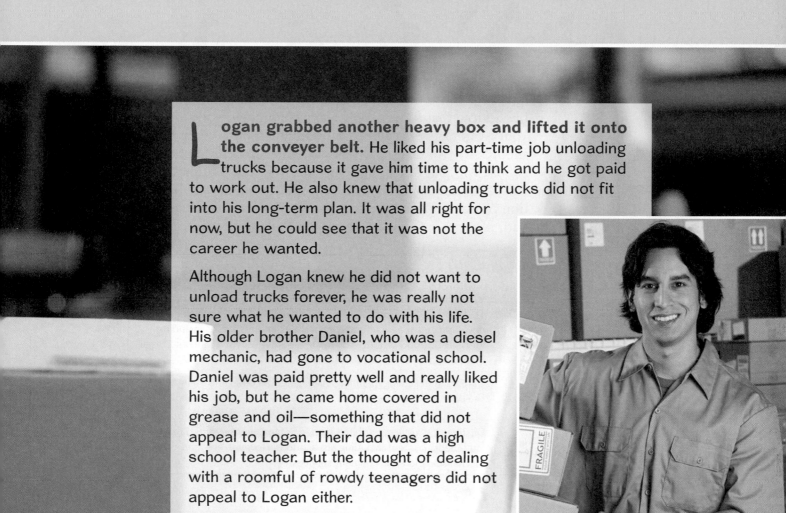

Logan grabbed another heavy box and lifted it onto the conveyer belt. He liked his part-time job unloading trucks because it gave him time to think and he got paid to work out. He also knew that unloading trucks did not fit into his long-term plan. It was all right for now, but he could see that it was not the career he wanted.

Although Logan knew he did not want to unload trucks forever, he was really not sure what he wanted to do with his life. His older brother Daniel, who was a diesel mechanic, had gone to vocational school. Daniel was paid pretty well and really liked his job, but he came home covered in grease and oil—something that did not appeal to Logan. Their dad was a high school teacher. But the thought of dealing with a roomful of rowdy teenagers did not appeal to Logan either.

Logan knew that he wanted a job in a cleaner environment than where Daniel worked and one that paid good money and did not involve teaching. Beyond that, he had few firm ideas. He made a mental note to visit with the high school counselor about his options. He would be a senior next year and was feeling a little uneasy about what to do with the rest of his life.

Like Logan, you may be trying to decide on a career path. You have probably noticed that some people really enjoy their work and others don't. Your working life occupies a substantial amount of your time; so you should strive to find a job that you enjoy. In addition, the career you choose will play a major role in your financial future because your choice will affect how much income you earn. It may dictate how much education or training you need to get—and pay for. Deciding on the best career path requires some research and careful consideration.

Professor FIN

Here and throughout this chapter is information about major career clusters. You can use this information to help you investigate different careers.

Agriculture, Food & Natural Resources — The production, processing, marketing, distribution, financing, and development of agricultural commodities and resources including food, fiber, wood products, natural resources, horticulture, and other plant and animal products/resources.

Architecture & Construction — Careers in designing, planning, managing, building, and maintaining the built environment.

Arts, A/V Technology & Communications — Designing, producing, exhibiting, performing, writing, and publishing multimedia content including visual and performing arts and design, journalism, and entertainment services.

Source: www.careerclusters.org

Finance ONLINE

For information on the fastest growing occupations and occupations projected to have the largest increases in employment between 2006 and 2016 see the *Occupational Outlook Handbook*—**www.bls.gov/oco/home.htm**.

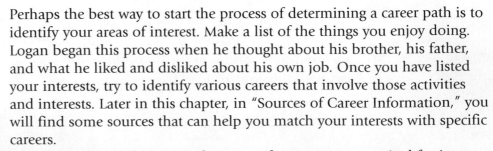

DETERMINING A CAREER PATH

Perhaps the best way to start the process of determining a career path is to identify your areas of interest. Make a list of the things you enjoy doing. Logan began this process when he thought about his brother, his father, and what he liked and disliked about his own job. Once you have listed your interests, try to identify various careers that involve those activities and interests. Later in this chapter, in "Sources of Career Information," you will find some sources that can help you match your interests with specific careers.

Another way to determine the types of careers you are suited for is to take a personality test. Your career counselor may be able to provide a personality test that will help you find a career that matches your personality. You may have already taken a similar test during a class on career choices.

After you identify some possible career choices, you can begin the process of screening those choices. You should consider each possible career choice in relation to the following factors: level of education or skill needed, job availability, and compensation level. Figure 5.1 shows some occupations where jobs are being created at the fastest rate for the period

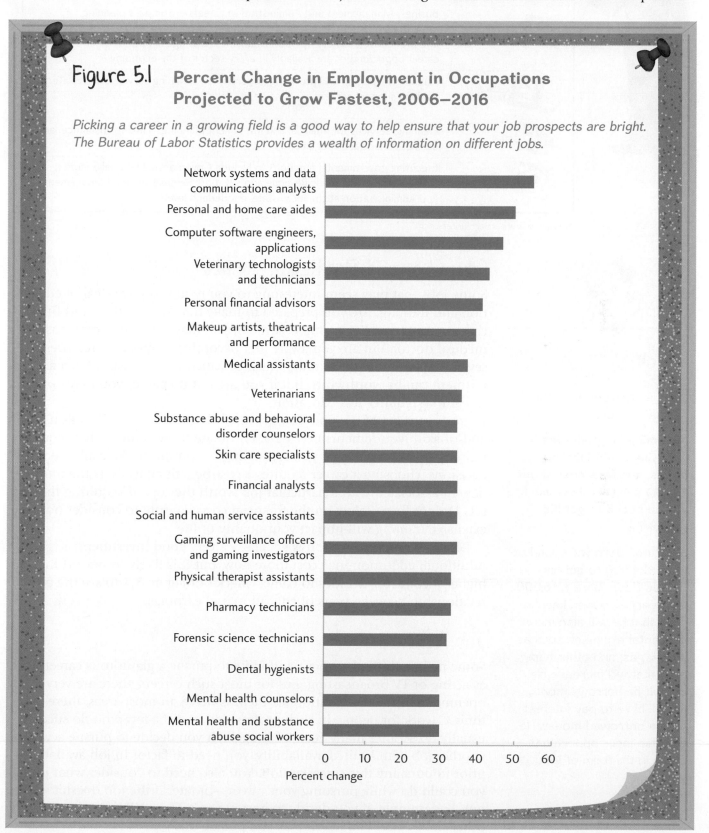

Figure 5.1 Percent Change in Employment in Occupations Projected to Grow Fastest, 2006–2016

Picking a career in a growing field is a good way to help ensure that your job prospects are bright. The Bureau of Labor Statistics provides a wealth of information on different jobs.

2006 through 2016. As people like you and Logan begin thinking about career choices, it's a good idea to consider options where job growth is expected.

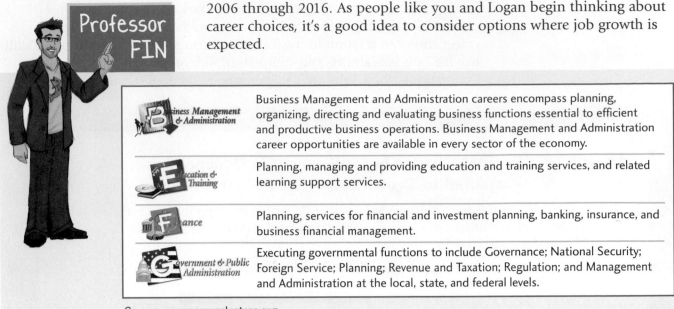

	Business Management and Administration careers encompass planning, organizing, directing and evaluating business functions essential to efficient and productive business operations. Business Management and Administration career opportunities are available in every sector of the economy.
	Planning, managing and providing education and training services, and related learning support services.
	Planning, services for financial and investment planning, banking, insurance, and business financial management.
	Executing governmental functions to include Governance; National Security; Foreign Service; Planning; Revenue and Taxation; Regulation; and Management and Administration at the local, state, and federal levels.

Source: www.careerclusters.org

MATH for Personal Finance

Jorn is considering getting a college degree.

Assuming he graduates in four years and tuition, books, and fees cost about $6,000 per year, how much will he spend to get his degree?

Solution: Jorn will spend at least $24,000 to get his degree (four years × $6,000 per year). However, keep in mind that he will also incur incidental expenses such as meals, gas, and other supplies that will increase his cost. If he borrows money, he will have to pay interest on the borrowed money. He will also incur opportunity costs in the form of lost wages.

Education and Skill Requirements

Some jobs that may seem interesting to you require a great deal of education and training. Are you prepared to make that kind of time and financial commitment? For example, some of you may consider a career as a medical doctor. But are you aware that becoming a physician requires seven years or more of training, much of which is very costly? Such a commitment can be worthwhile, but if you are not prepared, you may opt for a career that requires less education.

From your list of possible careers, carefully consider the education and/or skill requirements necessary. Eliminate those options that require training that exceeds what you are willing to commit to. Like all major life decisions, choosing a career requires a cost/benefit analysis. Is the ultimate benefit associated with a particular job worth the cost of acquiring the skill set? Do not focus solely on the financial costs. Be sure to consider how the extensive training will impact your quality of life.

Remember that education is generally a very good investment. Additional education may cost more now, but it is likely to pay off in a higher income for decades to come. Check out Figure 5.2 to see the general relationship between years of education and earnings.

Job Availability

Some people think that they would like to pursue a glamorous career, such as acting or TV broadcasting. But for most such careers, there are very few openings and the competition for them is fierce. In most areas, there is limited work for people in such professions, and the few who do succeed usually do so after many years of struggle. If you decide to pursue acting or another job with limited availability, you need to factor in job availability prior to pursuing this career option. You also need to consider what job you could do while pursuing your career—or later if the job doesn't work out. For example, if you decide to become an NFL or NBA player, what other skills could you develop as you pursue this job?

Figure 5.2 Comparison of Income among Education Levels

Generally, education is costly, but it is an excellent investment that pays off in a reasonable time.

Education	Median Level of Annual Income
Master's degree	$55,300
Bachelor's degree	46,300
Associate degree	35,400
Some college, no degree	32,400
High school graduate	28,800
Some high school, no degree	21,400

Source: Bureau of Labor Statistics, U.S. Department of Labor.

Additionally, some jobs may not be in high demand in the region where you would like to live. In that case, you may have to relocate. Moving involves substantial costs and it may take you some time to recover that investment. While some companies pay all or at least a portion of relocation expenses for employees, not every company offers this benefit. Finding a new place to live, hiring a moving company, getting the utilities turned on, and the organizing hassles are not without cost.

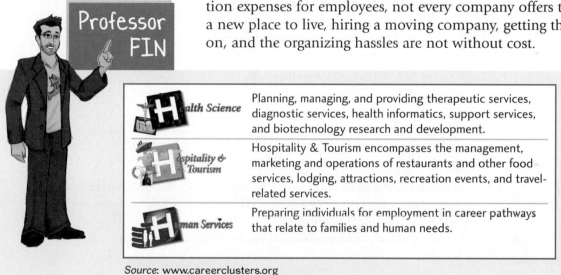

Health Science — Planning, managing, and providing therapeutic services, diagnostic services, health informatics, support services, and biotechnology research and development.

Hospitality & Tourism — Hospitality & Tourism encompasses the management, marketing and operations of restaurants and other food services, lodging, attractions, recreation events, and travel-related services.

Human Services — Preparing individuals for employment in career pathways that relate to families and human needs.

Source: www.careerclusters.org

Compensation

When considering careers, most people want to know how much money they will make—what their **compensation** will be. While your list may contain a number of jobs that would be a lot of fun, many of them may not pay well. Keep in mind that you will need a minimum level of income in order to cover your expenses. You may also want to increase your net worth over time—by building up your savings, buying a home, and so on. A job that does not pay well may not allow you to cover expenses or increase your net worth. Just as Logan considered money when thinking about his future, compensation should be an important consideration of your career choice, too. Choosing a career for money alone may not be wise. But neither is ignoring how your income may affect your life.

You Do It

Activity #1

Finance
ONLINE

According to **www.bls.gov**, during the 2006–2016 period, approximately 15.7 million new wage and salary jobs will be generated by service-providing industries.

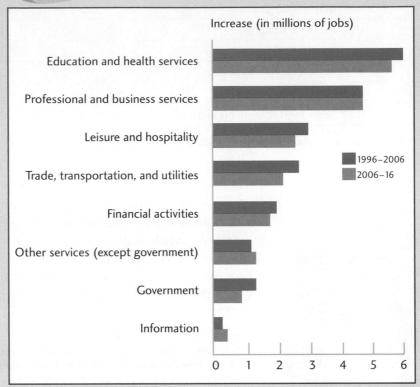

Increase (in millions of jobs)

| Education and health services |
| Professional and business services |
| Leisure and hospitality |
| Trade, transportation, and utilities |
| Financial activities |
| Other services (except government) |
| Government |
| Information |

■ 1996–2006
■ 2006–16

0 1 2 3 4 5 6

Source: Bureau of Labor Statistics, www.bls.gov/oco/images/ocotjc04.jpg

Since the early 1980s, goods-producing industries have seen little or no growth (increase in the number of jobs). A decline of 3.3 percent is expected during the 2006–2016 period. This decline varies within the goods-producing industries.

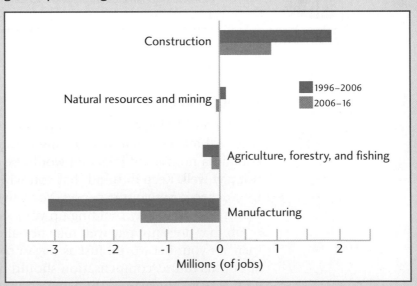

Construction

Natural resources and mining

■ 1996–2006
■ 2006–16

Agriculture, forestry, and fishing

Manufacturing

-3   -2   -1   0   1   2

Millions (of jobs)

Source: Bureau of Labor Statistics, www.bls.gov/oco/images/ocotjc05.jpg

MATH for
Personal
Finance

Latrell is comparing two job opportunities. One job will pay $12 an hour and he will work 40 hours a week. The other one pays an annual salary of $22,000 and he will work 45 hours a week.

Which job pays more?

Solution: The first job will pay an annual amount of $12 × 40 hours a week × 52 weeks a year = $24,960. The second job pays $22,000 a year and requires Latrell to work five extra hours per week.

If you want to know how much money certain professions pay, visit www.careerjournal.com and search on a job title. You can learn the salary range of many jobs you might be interested in pursuing. The United States government also publishes pay information at **www.bls.gov**.

 CHECK Your Financial IQ

What are the steps in developing a career path?

SOURCES OF CAREER INFORMATION

You just read about Web sites that list the pay of certain professions. Indeed, the Internet is an outstanding source of up-to-date career information. Web sites such as **www.careers.org** provide you with different career options, possible compensation levels for these careers, and the skill sets needed for careers in several fields, such as finance, management, construction, health, agriculture, and broadcasting. Other Web sites, such as **www.careerbuilder.com**, list the most frequently available jobs so you can evaluate those careers that are currently in high demand. Pay close attention to the number of applicants for these jobs. It is easier to get a job when the applicant pool is small. This analysis is one way to gauge the supply of qualified applicants with a particular skill set. You can also easily search for specifics on virtually every career option available to you.

Another outstanding source of information on careers is the *Occupational Outlook Handbook*. It is published by the federal government and can be found at **www.bls.gov**. Look for the link under "Occupations."

The Web, of course, is only one source of information. There are many other options available that you can use to find information about interesting jobs.

Information Technology	Building Linkages in IT Occupations Framework: For Entry Level, Technical, and Professional Careers Related to the Design, Development, Support and Management of Hardware, Software, Multimedia, and Systems Integration Services.
Law, Public Safety, Corrections & Security	Planning, managing, and providing legal, public safety, protective services and homeland security, including professional and technical support services.
Manufacturing	Planning, managing, and performing the processing of materials into intermediate or final products and related professional and technical support activities such as production planning and control, maintenance and manufacturing/process engineering.

Source: www.careerclusters.org

Books on Careers

There are many books that will help you identify career options and the necessary skills required to pursue those careers successfully. It may be useful to study a book that simply provides a broad overview of jobs so that you can narrow your search. At that point, you may want to locate a book with much greater detail and focus on a specific job—for example, mechanical engineering, carpentry, or nursing.

Keep in mind that the job market changes quickly. Books that are only a few years old may be useless—or actually misleading. Make sure the information you get from a book—or from any source—is up-to-date.

Field Trips and Speakers

During your high school years, many of you will have opportunities to take field trips that will help you identify careers of interest. Your school may also have visiting speakers who will provide valuable information on what they do for a living. Make use of these opportunities to investigate various career options.

Job Experience

Even a part-time high school job can help you learn about what you might like—and not like—in a job.

Think about Logan's experience unloading trucks. You may also have worked part-time jobs that allowed you to learn something about working for a living. As a result of these experiences, some of you may have eliminated certain career options, and others may have identified possible job choices. At the very least, you may have learned some broad lessons about what you do and do not like about a job. For example, you may have found that you prefer moving around to sitting at a desk or working at a workstation. You may enjoy dealing with the public—or prefer not to. These insights can be valuable.

Internships

One way to gain additional information about a particular career or job is through an **internship**—a temporary, short-term position designed to provide exposure to and training in a particular job. Often, companies will hire interns to perform various office tasks such as making copies or delivering documents. While this type of work may seem mundane, it's a good way to gain knowledge about certain types of careers. Even an unpaid internship can provide you with valuable experience and enough information to know whether a particular career interests you.

Contacts

Make use of your network of friends. Perhaps some of them have a relative who works in a career you are considering. Logan learned quite a bit about his career likes and dislikes by observing his brother and father. You may be able to visit with someone's parents or grandparents to learn firsthand what they do for a living. Most people will be happy to answer any questions you might have about their jobs.

 CHECK Your Financial IQ

What are two ways to get career information?

Once you narrow the search on the types of careers that truly interest you, you should spend some time investigating the training and education you will need to be able to land that dream job. Figure 5.3 contains a list of various high-demand career choices, the education needed to get these jobs, and the expected wages.

Training Programs

For some careers, you must obtain specific, specialized training before entering the field. Training requirements vary widely by profession. For some jobs, you may need to earn a certificate or receive a license. In some

Figure 5.3   The Future Job Market

Here are a few more jobs that are expected to grow quickly in the years ahead, along with information about average income and the training required to find work in the field.

Job	Anticipated Increase in Employment	Median Annual Wages (2006)	Education and Training
Education administrators	23.5%	$37,740	Bachelor's degree or higher plus work experience
Personal financial advisor	41%	$66,120	Bachelor's degree
Applications computer software engineer	44.6%	$79,790	Bachelor's degree
Environmental scientists and specialists	25.1%	$56,100	Master's degree
Forensic science technicians	30.7%	$45,330	Bachelor's degree
Social and human services assistants	33.6%	$25,580	Some college, on-the-job training
Court reporter	24.5%	$45,610	Postsecondary vocational training
Preschool teachers	26.3%	$22,680	Postsecondary vocational training
Curator	23.3%	$46,300	Master's degree
Multimedia artists and animators	25.8%	$51,350	Bachelor's degree
Personal and home health care aides	50.6%	$17,700	High school and some college; on-the-job training
Registered nurse	23.5%	$57,280	Associate degree
Physical therapist	27.1%	$66,200	Master's degree
Rock splitters, quarry workers	25%	$27,100	High school and some college; on-the-job training
Dental assistant	29.2%	$30,220	High school and some college; on-the-job training
Skin care specialist	34.3%	$26,170	Postsecondary vocational training
Ambulance driver and attendant	21.7%	$20,370	High school and some college; on-the-job training
Landscaping and groundskeeping	20.5%	$21,260	High school; on-the-job training

Source: Bureau of Labor Statistics, Occupational Projections and Training Data, 2008–2009: www.bls.gov/emp/optd

In some trades, people train on the job as apprentices.

cases, you may be able to receive formal training while you are working. Such on-the-job training programs are sometimes called **apprenticeships**. In other cases, you may not be allowed to work in your chosen career until you have completed training. Apprenticeships are common for skilled trades such as plumbing, electrical contracting, heating and air-conditioning, and welding. Many of theses skilled workers go into business for themselves after serving lengthy apprenticeships.

Additional information on the amount and type of training needed for various jobs is available on Web sites such as CareerOneStop (**www.acinet.org**) and the Bureau of Labor Statistics (**www.bls.gov**). Don't forget to utilize the *Occupational Outlook Handbook* published by the Bureau of Labor Statistics.

Be careful about training recommendations and information provided elsewhere on the Internet. Some Web sites sell training or try to get you to use their educational materials. At the extreme end, there are companies that promise to provide acting or modeling skills as well as contacts within the industry. Most of these companies are preying on individuals who have big dreams. Some of them actually can deliver what they promise, but most cannot.

You should also be cautious about training that promises certifications. A **certification** is an official document or record stating that a person has met some standard for training or knowledge. Some certifications offered online are recognized as meaningful in the field. Others are merely the product of a good color laser printer and worth less than the paper they are printed on. Make sure that any training you pursue is in a field with job demand and provides valid, real-world certifications if any are offered.

Education

Colleges and universities provide training in the form of education leading to a degree. Web sites such as **www.collegeboard.com** can provide you with career profiles by college major. This type of information can be useful in trying to determine whether to get a degree in something as specific as accounting or geology, or whether to pursue a broader liberal arts degree. You will find that many companies hire successful college graduates

Professor FIN

Marketing	Planning, managing, and performing marketing activities to reach organizational objectives.
Science, Technology, Engineering & Mathematics	Planning, managing, and providing scientific research and professional and technical services (e.g., physical science, social science, engineering) including laboratory and testing services, and research and development services.
Transportation, Distribution & Logistics	Planning, management, and movement of people, materials, and goods by road, pipeline, air, rail and water and related professional and technical support services such as transportation infrastructure planning and management, logistics services, mobile equipment and facility maintenance.

Source: www.careerclusters.org

Jill is thinking about getting an MBA. She will give up making $38,000 a year for the two years it takes to complete the MBA. She will also pay $35,000 in total costs to get the degree. Assume she will make $75,000 a year after she gets her MBA.

How long will it take her to recover her investment?

Solution: Jill will be investing a total of $38,000 in lost annual wages × two years = $76,000 plus the $35,000 cost for a total of $111,000. However, she will earn $37,000 more per year after getting her MBA ($75,000 − $38,000 = $37,000). Therefore, it will take her three years to recover her investment, or $111,000 / $37,000 per year increase in salary = three years.

You Do It

Activity #2

of any major since completion of the degree signals a person's ability to stick to a task and continue to learn. Many employers find these qualities as important as any particular skills, at least for entry-level jobs.

University reputations vary significantly and some may have a better reputation for certain degrees. Some jobs will require that your degree is from an accredited or certified program. **Accreditation** is an official recognition that a school or program meets a certain standard. Make sure you investigate the various types of accreditations that a university has and match those with the job market or career field you are interested in pursuing. That is, is the program accredited by the organizations that future employers will require? These accreditations are especially important in the field of nursing, some technical areas such as automotive or mechanical, and trade areas.

Learn as much as you can about the universities you are interested in attending. What are their graduation rates? How many years does it take to graduate? What percentage of recent graduates passed their certifications, if applicable? Do firms visit the campus to recruit employees? It is always useful to learn as much as you can about the universities you are considering.

Expanding Your Education

Graduate degrees, such as a master's degree, law degree, or doctoral degree provide you with the additional specialized knowledge and skills that should qualify you for a better job. However, there are costs associated with pursuing a graduate degree.

To begin, it can cost a lot of money to get a graduate degree. For that reason, you need to weigh these costs against the benefits to determine whether a graduate degree is right for you. Tuition, fees, books, room and board, and the opportunity cost can add up to a substantial amount of money. Recall, opportunity cost is the cost of what you give up when you take particular action. For a full-time graduate program, the opportunity cost is the loss of income from a full-time job and the potential loss of social and recreational time for the time it takes you to complete the program. Is it worth it? In many cases, it will be. Only you can make that decision.

In most cases, an advanced or graduate degree enhances your employability. Many positions require a graduate degree as the minimum qualification to apply. Sometimes it is useful to get your graduate degree in a different field from your undergraduate degree. For example, engineers often find it useful to get a graduate business degree as they move into management positions within their engineering firms.

Some of you may opt to pursue a doctoral degree. You should evaluate the university carefully, since doctoral program reputations vary substantially. If you hope to teach at the college level, for example, where you get your Ph.D. may be significant. Some programs may have a local or regional reputation, others may be known nationally, and still others may have a solid international reputation. Pick the program that most closely aligns with your goals.

CHECK Your Financial IQ

What are some ways people get training for different careers?

Most jobs require you to fill out a job application such as the one shown in Figure 5.4. Job applications provide your prospective employer with rel-

Figure 5.4 Sample Job Application

For many jobs, filling out an application is the first step in the job-seeking process.

Sample Job Application

Fill out this sample application using your personal information. Include all applicable information and addresses.

PLEASE NOTE: Complete all parts of the application. If your application is incomplete, or does not clearly show the experience and/or training required, your application may not be accepted. If you have no information to enter in a section, please write N/A.

Name and Address	
Name (First, MI, Last)	Social Security Number
Mailing Address	
City, State, and Zip Code	
Home Phone	Message Phone
E-mail Address	May we use e-mail to contact you? Yes ☐ No ☐

Additional Information
Have you been an employee of this organization in the past?   Yes ☐   No ☐
I certify that I am in compliance with the provisions of the Selective Service Act (Draft Registration). **   Yes ☐   No ☐
I certify that I am a U.S. citizen, permanent resident, or a foreign national with authorization to work in the United States. **   Yes ☐   No ☐
Have you ever been convicted of, or entered a plea of guilty, no contest, or had a withheld judgment to a felony? **   Yes ☐ No ☐   If Yes, please explain:
** These questions must be answered in order to be considered for employment

Education (Schools attended or special training received)			
School	From	To	Did you graduate?
Location		Type of degree or diploma	
School	From	To	Did you graduate?
Location		Type of degree or diploma	

evant information about your previous work history that helps when he's making a decision about whether to hire you. Keep that in mind as you work during the summer. Your next employer may contact your previous employer and ask him or her how punctual you were and if you were a good worker.

Figure 5.4 Sample Job Application (continued)

Work History				
Job Title	From	To	Hrs/Week	Employer
Address	Phone	Supervisor		May we contact this employer? Yes ☐ No ☐
Reason for leaving?				

Work History				
Job Title	From	To	Hrs/Week	Employer
Address	Phone	Supervisor		May we contact this employer? Yes ☐ No ☐
Reason for leaving?				

Work History				
Job Title	From	To	Hrs/Week	Employer
Address	Phone	Supervisor		May we contact this employer? Yes ☐ No ☐
Reason for leaving?				

How did you find out about this position?				
Current Employee ☐	Career Fair ☐	State website ☐	Company Newsletter ☐	Job Service ☐
Monster.com ☐	Newspaper Ad ☐	Other Internet Source ☐	Prof. Organization website ☐	Radio/TV Ad ☐
	Recruiter ☐	University/College ☐	None of the above ☐	

Job Type/Shift				
Full Time ☐	Part Time ☐	Permanent ☐	Temporary ☐	6 Month ☐
9 Month ☐	Seasonal ☐	Limited Service ☐	Shift ☐	Night ☐

Signature	Date
I certify that all answers and statements on this application are true and complete to the best of my knowledge. I understand that should an investigation disclose untruthful or misleading answers, my application may be rejected, my name removed from consideration, or my employment with this company terminated.	

You
Do It
Activity #3

Résumé

Many jobs will require you to provide a **résumé**, which gives prospective employers a snapshot of your qualifications. Typically, your résumé will include your personal background information, including education and previous work history. Additionally, you should provide a list of your skills, such as computer training or language ability. Check out Logan's résumé in Figure 5.5.

You can choose from different styles of résumés, depending on the strength of your background. For example, résumés that emphasize skills rather than work experience may be a good choice for someone with a limited work history. The Internet is a good source of information about how to structure an effective résumé that best highlights your skills.

You
Do It
Activity #4

Cover Letter

Generally, the more education and training you have the more information is required during a job application. For example, many professional jobs require a cover letter, a résumé, and multiple interviews. The length of some interviews can be several days and require you to travel out of state to a specific site. Figure 5.6 contains a sample cover letter that Logan may use if he chooses to earn a college degree and is applying for a job.

Internet Job Searches and Applications

Many companies have moved to electronic applications or pick applicants from employment sites such as MonsterTRAK. Check out **www.MonsterTrak.com** to learn what jobs are in demand. Learn the process of posting your own contact information.

Professor FIN

The following are some keywords to use in your job application or résumé. They reflect the kinds of qualities employers are looking for. Many more lists can be found on the Internet to help you be more successful in your job search.

Keywords

- ability to plan
- ability to train
- accurate
- adaptable
- aggressive worker
- competitive
- creative
- customer oriented
- ethical
- follow instructions

- follow through
- high energy
- industrious
- innovative
- leadership
- multitasking
- open minded
- oral communication
- organizational skills
- problem solving
- results oriented
- safety conscious
- self-accountable
- self-managing
- setting priorities
- takes initiative
- team player

Source: Business Communication, page 555, Mary Ellen Guffey

Figure 5.5 Sample Résumé for Logan

There are a variety of ways to format a résumé. This résumé is a functional résumé that focuses on Logan's skills rather than his employment history, which might be short at this point in his life.

Logan Bolin (555)123-4567
987 East Street, MainTown, CA 90210 lgmaintown@speeddial.com

OBJECTIVE	To obtain a position in sales using my experience working with people and handling my own business.
SALES SKILLS	Successfully serviced 30 lawn care customers yearly, handling all yard work needed
	Prepared brochure to advertise lawn care business
	Built business to current client list in one year
COMMUNICATION AND COMPUTER SKILLS	Earned top honors in Business Communication class
	Developed Word, Excel, PowerPoint, and Internet skills
	Received award for Outstanding Computer Student of the Year
ORGANIZATIONAL SKILLS	Developed work schedule for lawn care of 30 customers
	Scheduled FBLA Week for local chapter
	Organized time for homework, extracurricular activities, and lawn care business
EDUCATION	MainTown High School, MainTown, CA
	Business Academy
	Graduation, 2007
EMPLOYMENT	2008–present, Bolin Lawn Care
	Summer, 2007, March of Dimes Headquarters volunteer, MainTown, CA

Personal References Provided Upon Request

Example of Personal References Page for Logan

Logan Bolin
REFERENCES

Mr. Kevin Carsey	Ms. Shirley Rogers	Ms. Tena Crews
1143 Linoper Drive	Work Supervisor	NW Division Director
MainTown, CA 90210	MainTown High School	March of Dimes
(123)555-1111	1 Champion Drive	987 Bumble Bee Circle
	MainTown, CA 90210	MainTown, CA 90210

Become comfortable with the process. Young people like you and Logan may ultimately change jobs 10 or 20 times during your lifetime and could likely change careers several times.

 CHECK Your Financial IQ

What are two ways to apply for a job?

Figure 5.6 Sample cover letter for Logan

The cover letter is Logan's introduction to the potential employer. It's his chance to highlight his strengths and to persuade the would-be employer that he should be called for an interview. Such letters should be prepared carefully.

Ms. Janie Baney
WWW Landscaping Company
53 July Road
MainTown, CA 90210

Dear Ms. Baney,

Your advertisement for a sales position, which appeared May 28 in Section C of the *MainTown Chronicle*, caught my attention because my education and training fits your needs. The advertisement states that the job involves outside landscaping sales for individual homes and businesses.

As a small business owner for the past five years, I have dealt with a variety of landscaping tasks for individual homeowners. I have also worked with other small businesses in designing and maintaining their landscapes. Budgeting, planning, and organizing are skills that are needed for the job you advertise. I can bring these skills to your company.

I would like to discuss my qualifications with you and answer any questions you have about my enclosed résumé. The best way to reach me is to call my cell phone at (555)123-4567 during business hours. I look forward to putting my skills to work for WWW Landscaping Company.

Sincerely,

Logan Bolin

Chapter Review

Summary

- Your career path is a choice you make. It can change throughout your life until you retire. Each time you look at a new career, you will need to review the education/skills needed, its availability, and the compensation expected.

- There are several sources available to research jobs and careers. You may have opportunities to take field trips or listen to speakers to gather information about a career, or you may gather information by networking with family, friends, and others. Job experience will also help you make decisions about your career choice. The Internet provides many sources to help you in your career decision making process. You can go online to find out about various careers or you can take a personality test or interest inventory to help you make your decision.

- Remember that additional training or education may be required for your career choice or when changing to a different career. As you expand your education and training, benefits will increase, but there could also be additional costs to you. You need to weigh the costs and the benefits; this will allow you to see if a change is worth your effort.

- Applying for a job may involve filling out applications, writing and posting a résumé, writing cover letters, and using online services. It is a process that most young people will go through many times in their lives.

Key Terms and Vocabulary

Accreditation	Certification	Internship
Apprenticeship	Compensation	Résumé

What Do You Know?

myFinLitlab.

1. (a) How does your choice of career affect your financial future?

   (b) What else, besides the financial impact of your choice, should you consider when choosing a career?

2. (a) Why is it important to know the educational or training requirements when deciding upon a career?

   (b) Where can one find information about education or training requirements for a job?

3. (a) Why is it critical to know the compensation for a job?

   (b) What sources can you use to find information about compensation for different careers?

4. (a) What does it mean to say that education is a good investment?

   (b) What would be a good reason to avoid a career that requires a lot of education?

5. (a) What kinds of occupations typically require apprenticeships?

   (b) What do you think is the purpose behind this kind of training program?

6. (a) What is a certification?

   (b) Why is it important that possible employers recognize the value of any certification you might seek?

7. (a) What kinds of credentials do colleges provide?

   (b) Is it worthwhile to seek a college degree if the degree is not in a specific field or part of a specific training program?

8. (a) What is the purpose of a résumé?

   (b) What factors might influence the type of résumé you select?

9. (a) What are three items that may be needed in the application process?

   (b) Why is it especially important for younger people to get familiar with the job-seeking process?

What Are Your Finance Math Skills?

 myFinLitlab

The first three questions correlate to *Math for Personal Finance* features located throughout the chapter.

1. Asa wants to get his degree in engineering. He estimates it will take him five years to complete the degree and that he will spend about $8,000 a year for tuition, fees, books, and room and board. How much will it cost Asa to get his degree?

2. Doug has been offered two different jobs. One company has offered him $31,000 a year and will furnish a vehicle with a company gas card. The other job will pay him $20 an hour and he will work 40 hours a week. Doug believes the vehicle allowance will save him about $7,000 a year that he would otherwise have to spend on transportation. Which job pays the most?

3. Miss McClure is thinking about getting her master's degree in education. She estimates that she will spend about $6,000 a year for three years to get her degree. Her plans are to take evening classes so she can keep her current teaching job. However, when she finishes her degree she will get a $4,000 a year raise. How long will it take her to recover her investment?

4. Tiffany makes $8 an hour and works 15 hours a week. Tosha makes $9.50 an hour and works 50 hours per month. Who will make more money this year?

5. Anton is seeking an advanced degree that requires an investment of $70,000 and a three-year commitment during which he will lose $20,000 a year in income. Even without considering the interest lost on the investment and lost earnings, how long will it take him to recover his investment if he makes $10,000 more per year after completing the degree?

6. If Josh spends $4,000 a year on tuition and fees, $1,200 a year on books, and foregoes earning $10,000 a year, how much will his four-year degree cost?

7. If you study an extra 10 hours a week for a year (52 weeks) and you earn a four-year scholarship valued at $50,000, what is your hourly return on your investment in study time?

8. Assume you spend $3,500 a year for the first two years attending a junior college and then you spend $6,000 a year for the remaining two years at the local college. Your friend spends $5,000 a year for four years at another local school. Compare the costs of both options.

What Would You Do?

Maurice is looking for a job as a salesman. As he prepares his résumé, he is discouraged at his lack of experience and education. He is confident of his abilities and is certain that he has the ability to sell. But he is concerned that no employer will give him a chance if they look at his background.

It occurs to him that if he exaggerates just a little about some of his accomplishments, he has a better chance of getting called to an interview. Then he can let his personality and charm take over.

Maurice has asked you to serve as a reference in his job search. You agree that he would make an excellent salesman, but you are not in favor of vouching for his background if you are called about it.

1. Is Maurice doing the right thing?

2. Who is hurt if Maurice gets a job based on false information?

3. How might your involvement with Maurice's plan hurt you?

What Are the Connections? Language Arts and History

Conduct a survey of four adults to find out about their careers, training, career switches, and work experiences. Put this information in a table. Put this table in a research paper explaining what you were researching, how you conducted your survey, your findings, and the conclusions you draw from this data. In your conclusions you might compare what the adults told you about their careers with what you hope for in your future career.

Teamwork

In teams, choose one of the career clusters (the 16 clusters given by Professor Fin throughout this chapter). Research all the information you can find about the cluster. Find out what course work you might need for a job in this cluster, what jobs might be considered in this cluster, salary ranges in this cluster, what education or training is necessary for this cluster, and any other interesting facts.

   Create a newsletter to be placed in the counselor's office about the cluster you have researched. Make the newsletter interesting, with graphics, pictures, and facts so that your fellow students will want to learn more.

---

w!se | Financial Literacy CERTIFICATION

TEST PREP QUESTIONS

1. Which of the following is a true statement about the United States job market?
   a. There has been growth in all sectors of the job market every year since 2002.
   b. The manufacturing industries have seen little or no job growth for more than 20 years.
   c. Service-related industries are not expected to produce new jobs for at least another 10 years.
   d. The job market basically remains the same from year to year.

2. A career that requires a college degree, is expected to grow in employment in the coming years, and provides its employees with a high income is
   a. personal and home care aides.
   b. applications computer software engineers.
   c. dental assistants.
   d. education administrators.

3. If a college or university offers a nationally accredited nursing program, it most likely means that
   a. anyone who graduates from the program will get a job as a nurse.
   b. anyone in the United States who wants to be a nurse can go to that college or university.
   c. the program has been cited by a nationally recognized nursing professional organization as meeting certain standards.
   d. the program will award graduates with a nationally recognized nursing license.

4. Which of the following is a true statement?
   a. A certification is recognition that a person has acquired a certain level of knowledge or training in a particular area of study.
   b. Certification programs are regulated by the United States Department of Education.
   c. Certification programs award their certificates to everyone who enrolls in and completes their programs.
   d. A certification is a license that permits a person to practice a certain profession such as accounting or physical therapy in one or more states.

5. As a first step in selecting a career path, a person should
   a. find out which careers pay the highest salaries.
   b. determine which career areas are interesting.
   c. look online for inexpensive certification programs.
   d. find out what majors are offered at the local college in the person's geographic area.

6. The *Occupational Outlook Handbook* is a good source for finding information about
   a. colleges that offer specific career programs.
   b. the availability of jobs in different cities.
   c. the areas that will need more employees in the coming years.
   d. the amount of money a person can expect to earn over a lifetime.

7. A person finds out that with a bachelor's degree he can expect to earn $55,000 a year as a financial researcher. If he spends two years (full-time) getting an MBA, it will cost him $25,000 a year for his education; however, he can expect to then earn a minimum of $90,000 a year as a financial analyst. If he decides to take the additional education route, to make up for the financial cost of postponing his career it will take him
   a. less than two years.
   b. slightly more than two years.
   c. almost five years.
   d. more than ten years.

8. In deciding whether to pursue additional education and training for a job, a person decides to do a cost/benefit analysis. This is a good idea because it will help her to
   a. decide whether the benefits she believes she will have in a certain job and career are worth the financial and quality of life costs associated with gaining the necessary skills and education.
   b. determine how many years it will take before she can enjoy the benefits of retirement.
   c. compare the costs of different educational programs and different colleges to the benefit of beginning a career without any additional education.
   d. determine whether the benefits package a company offers will cover the cost of the education required for the job.

9. A person's résumé should *not* include
   a. knowledge of various computer programs.
   b. career objectives.
   c. current salary.
   d. prior work experience.

10. Why do many employers say that a cover letter is as important as the résumé that it accompanies?
    a. The cover letter can be much longer than the résumé and provide details that do not belong in the résumé.
    b. The cover letter gives the writer a chance to explain why she believes that her skills and knowledge make her the ideal person for the position.
    c. Once a good cover letter is written, it can be copied in large quantities and easily sent with the résumé.
    d. A handwritten cover letter is a chance to show a potential employer a person's best handwriting.

CHAPTER 6

Learning Objectives

Describe the basic principles of taxation and the major categories of taxes.

Explain payroll taxes.

Describe the purpose and process of filing tax returns.

Explain how taxes affect your financial plan.

Key Terms

Adjusted gross income

Capital gain

Gross income

Itemized deduction

Payroll tax

Standard deduction

Tax

Tax return

Paying Taxes

Ryan's boss handed him his check and thanked him for a good work week. "You have picked up everything really fast, Ryan. I appreciate your hard work." Ryan nodded, grateful for the praise. "Thank you, sir. I've enjoyed it so far." This was Ryan's first "real" job. He'd made some money cutting lawns and raking leaves, but this was his first actual paycheck. He resisted the urge to tear open the envelope and look at his check.

Ryan was home before he finally allowed himself to look at the paycheck. Disappointment covered his face. The check was too small! He glanced at the total amount again. It read $147.76, but he knew he had worked 20 hours and was supposed to be making $8 an hour. He had been counting on getting $160—in fact he needed $150 by Monday to pay the deposit for the upcoming senior class trip. What had happened? It had to be a mistake.

Then, Ryan looked at the pay stub attached to the check. He saw $160 in a box labeled "gross pay." What was gross pay? And what were FICA, net pay, and all the other little boxes on his pay stub? When would he get the rest of his money?

Ryan is learning a valuable lesson—one that virtually all working people in this country have learned: There is a difference between what workers earn and what they actually get to keep and use—that is, their **take-home pay**. The total amount of money Ryan actually earned (his hourly wage multiplied by the hours he worked) is called his **gross pay**. The amount he actually takes home is called his **net pay**. The reason for the difference between the two is taxes. Learning about the taxes the government imposes on your income, how those taxes are paid, and what you can do to plan for them, is a key step in your financial education and in building your financial plan.

 ## TAX BASICS

A **tax** is money collected by a government from its citizens for the purpose of operating the government. Businesses also pay taxes. The government levies taxes on many different things. For example, most Americans pay a tax on the income they earn and on the property they own. They also pay a tax when they buy certain things—gas, tobacco, and in some states, other consumer items. Why do people pay these taxes? Tax revenue is the government's income. The government uses the taxes it collects to fund governmental services and programs. Tax revenue pays for our national defense, fire and police protection, road construction and maintenance, and schools. It pays the Social Security payments many of our parents and grandparents rely on. It helps provide medical care for the elderly and the poor. Virtually any public program you can think of is funded by tax receipts.

Sales Taxes

People pay taxes in different ways and on a variety of different things. For example, many of us pay **sales taxes** when we make a purchase at a store. That is, some of the price we pay for the item we buy is, in fact, a tax. The merchant collects this money and then sends it to the government.

The federal government does not impose a sales tax, but many state governments do. In some cases, local governments, such as city governments, may be able to charge sales taxes.

MATH for Personal Finance

Ryan's take-home or net pay was $147.76 and his gross pay was $160.00. Assume the FICA withholdings are 7.65 percent.

How much did Ryan pay in FICA from this check?

Solution: Ryan paid 7.65 percent of the $160 or $12.24 in FICA from this check.

This aircraft carrier cost hundreds of millions of dollars to build and operate each year. The money for this and other government projects comes from tax revenue.

Real Estate Taxes

Sometimes, the government sends us a bill for the taxes we owe. Taxes on real estate are often handled this way. Governments calculate real estate taxes based on the value of the property. For example, property owners may pay a certain amount in property tax for each $1,000 worth of property they own. The government sends the property owner a bill for this tax.

Real estate taxes are primarily used to fund local schools. Many of you have probably heard discussions about increases on property tax rates to help provide better school facilities.

Real estate taxes vary significantly from state to state and county to county. Always check the local tax rates before moving to a new location. That new job with a big raise might not generate a higher standard of living if you have to pay much of it in taxes.

Payroll Taxes

Many people pay taxes each and every time they get paid. Like Ryan, a portion of what they earn is withheld from their paycheck by their employer. The employer then sends this money to the government. The taxes that are collected in this way are known as **payroll taxes**, which can include federal and state income taxes and social security (or FICA) withholdings. You will read about them shortly. Refer to Figure 6.1 for a look at Ryan's pay stub. As you can see, his employer withheld FICA taxes only from Ryan's check.

Note that many workers are self-employed or earn significant income from investments. Such people do not get a regular paycheck for this

Professor FIN

The four Rs of taxes are: Revenue, Redistribution, Repricing, and Representation. They help explain the purpose of taxation. The first R is the main purpose of taxes: to raise the revenue the government uses for roads, schools, hospitals, and other services the government provides. The second R refers to the taking of wealth from one part of society—the wealthy—and redistributing it to another part. The third R refers to the way taxes can sometimes be used to make some items more expensive and thus discourage their use. Taxes on cigarettes illustrate this point. The fourth R harkens to the saying "no taxation without representation," and it reflects the principle that people expect government to serve their needs in return for their financial support.

The Boston Tea Party is a famous example of people protesting taxation without representation.

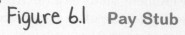

Figure 6.1   Pay Stub

Ryan's pay stub includes information about what he has earned, what he is taking home, and why. Some stubs provide summary information for the entire year.

Dave's Auto Shop	Check No. 200
Payroll Account	Date: January 27, 2009

Pay to the order of   Ryan Jones $147.76

********** One-Hundred, Forty-Seven Dollars and 76/100s ***********

Memo   January payroll   Dave Davie

Detach below before depositing, and save for your records:

Employee: Jones, R.	**Gross Earnings**		$160.00
Pay Period: 01/27/09	**Deductions:**		
	Federal Income Tax	$0	
	State Income Tax	0	
	Social Security	12.24 ◄	
	Medicare/Medicaid	0	
	Insurance	0	
	Retirement Savings Plan	0	
	Charity	0	
	Health/Child Care Flex Plan	0	12.24
	Net Pay		**$147.76** ◄

Ryan's net pay is his gross pay of $160 minus the $12.24 of
FICA taxes withheld, for a total of $147.76.

Ryan's paycheck is too small for withholding federal, state,
or local taxes, but FICA taxes of $12.24 have been withheld.

You
Do It

Activity #1

income and do not have taxes withheld from it. Instead, they must make regular estimated tax payments to the federal and state governments. It is possible (though somewhat unlikely) that a young person such as Ryan should have been paying estimated taxes for the income he earned cutting lawns and doing other odd jobs. Failure to pay estimated taxes can lead to a penalty. If you earn income from such sources, you should visit **www.irs.gov** and your state's department of revenue to see if you need to file estimated taxes. Your state's department of revenue can give you information about requirements in your state.

The Internal Revenue Service

While the tax rules for each state and local government vary widely, all of us are subject to federal tax laws. We shall focus on those.

Did you know that the Internal Revenue Service (IRS) has a Web site? Here you can find information about the most requested forms, individuals, businesses, charities, tax professionals, and more. Go to **www.irs.gov** to look at all the information that can be found. You might even find the answer to questions you have about taxes.

The **Internal Revenue Service (IRS)** is the government body that carries out the federal tax system. It is a branch of the United States Treasury Department. The United States Congress makes our tax laws, but the IRS enforces the laws and collects the taxes.

Each year in which you earn an income over a certain amount, you are required to file a federal tax return with the IRS. (The minimum amount of earnings required before a person must file a return varies based on several factors. Check the IRS Web site at **www.irs.gov** to learn if you must file a return.) Generally, a tax return consists of a form called 1040 or 1040EZ, plus any supporting documents. Figure 6.2 shows a sample of the 2-page Form 1040EZ.

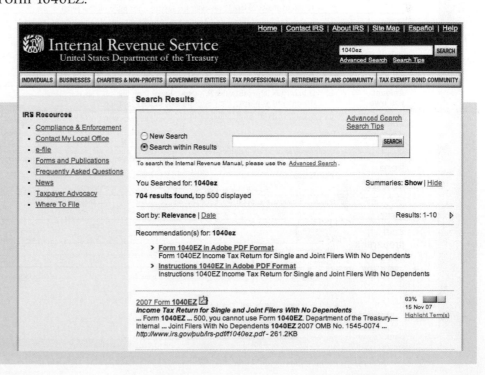

Have you seen the 1040EZ form and all the other forms available on the IRS Web site? Visit **www.irs.gov**. There you will find online forms that you can simply fill out and submit.

Figure 6.2 Form 1040EZ

The easiest way to file a tax return is with the form 1040EZ, although taxpayers who choose this form cannot itemize deductions.

Department of the Treasury—Internal Revenue Service

Form 1040EZ

Income Tax Return for Single and Joint Filers With No Dependents **2007**

OMB No. 1545-0074

Label (See page 8.)
Use the IRS label. Otherwise, please print or type.

Presidential Election Campaign (page 9)

Your first name and initial	Last name
Ryan	Jones
If a joint return, spouse's first name and initial	Last name

Your social security number

Spouse's social security number

Home address (number and street). If you have a P.O. box, see page 9. | Apt. no.

111 Doodle Street

City, town or post office, state, and ZIP code. If you have a foreign address, see page 9.

Anytown, USA 11121

▲ You **must** enter your SSN(s) above. ▲

Checking a box below will not change your tax or refund.

Check here if you, or your spouse if a joint return, want $3 to go to this fund . . . . . ▶ [X] **You**   [ ] **Spouse**

Income

Attach Form(s) W-2 here.

Enclose, but do not attach, any payment.

1	Wages, salaries, and tips. This should be shown in box 1 of your Form(s) W-2. Attach your Form(s) W-2.		1	6400	00
2	Taxable interest. If the total is over $1,500, you cannot use Form 1040EZ.		2		
3	Unemployment compensation and Alaska Permanent Fund dividends (see page 10).		3		
4	Add lines 1, 2, and 3. This is your **adjusted gross income.**		4	6400	00
5	If someone can claim you (or your spouse if a joint return) as a dependent, check the applicable box(es) below and enter the amount from the worksheet on back. [X] **You** [ ] **Spouse** If no one can claim you (or your spouse if a joint return), enter $8,750 if **single;** $17,500 if **married filing jointly.** See back for explanation.		5	5350	00
6	Subtract line 5 from line 4. If line 5 is larger than line 4, enter -0-. This is your **taxable income.** ▶		6	1050	00

Payments and tax

7	Federal income tax withheld from box 2 of your Form(s) W-2.	7	0	
8a	**Earned income credit (EIC).**	8a	0	
b	Nontaxable combat pay election.	8b		
9	Add lines 7 and 8a. These are your **total payments.** ▶	9	0	
10	**Tax.** Use the amount on **line 6 above** to find your tax in the tax table on pages 18–26 of the booklet. Then, enter the tax from the table on this line.	10	105	00

Refund

Have it directly deposited! See page 15 and fill in 11b, 11c, and 11d or Form 8888.

11a	If line 9 is larger than line 10, subtract line 10 from line 9. This is your **refund.** If Form 8888 is attached, check here ▶ [ ]	11a	0	
▶ **b**	Routing number	▶ c Type: [ ] Checking [ ] Savings		
▶ **d**	Account number			

Amount you owe

12	If line 10 is larger than line 9, subtract line 9 from line 10. This is the **amount you owe.** For details on how to pay, see page 16. ▶	12	105	00

Third party designee

Do you want to allow another person to discuss this return with the IRS (see page 16)? [ ] **Yes.** Complete the following. [ ] **No**

Designee's name ▶ | Phone no. ▶ (   ) | Personal identification number (PIN) ▶

Sign here

Joint return? See page 6.
Keep a copy for your records.

Under penalties of perjury, I declare that I have examined this return, and to the best of my knowledge and belief, it is true, correct, and accurately lists all amounts and sources of income I received during the tax year. Declaration of preparer (other than the taxpayer) is based on all information of which the preparer has any knowledge.

Your signature	Date	Your occupation	Daytime phone number ( )
Spouse's signature. If a joint return, **both** must sign.	Date	Spouse's occupation	

Paid preparer's use only

Preparer's signature ▶	Date	Check if self-employed [ ]	Preparer's SSN or PTIN
Firm's name (or yours if self-employed), address, and ZIP code ▶		EIN	
		Phone no. ( )	

For Disclosure, Privacy Act, and Paperwork Reduction Act Notice, see page 32.

Cat. No. 11329W

Form **1040EZ** (2007)

Figure 6.2   Form 1040EZ (continued)

Form 1040EZ (2007)   Page **2**

Use this form if

- Your filing status is single or married filing jointly. If you are not sure about your filing status, see page 6.
- You (and your spouse if married filing jointly) were under age 65 and not blind at the end of 2007. If you were born on January 1, 1943, you are considered to be age 65 at the end of 2007.
- You do not claim any dependents. For information on dependents, see Pub. 501.
- Your taxable income (line 6) is less than $100,000.
- You do not claim any adjustments to income. For information on adjustments to income, use TeleTax topics 451–453 and 455–458 (see page 30).
- The only tax credit you can claim is the earned income credit. You do not need a qualifying child to claim it. For information on credits, use TeleTax topics 601, 602, 607, 608, and 610 (see page 30).
- You had only wages, salaries, tips, taxable scholarship or fellowship grants, unemployment compensation, or Alaska Permanent Fund dividends, and your taxable interest was not over $1,500. But if you earned tips, including allocated tips, that are not included in box 5 and box 7 of your Form W-2, you may not be able to use Form 1040EZ (see page 9). If you are planning to use Form 1040EZ for a child who received Alaska Permanent Fund dividends, see page 10.
- You did not receive any advance earned income credit payments. If you cannot use this form, use TeleTax topic 352 (see page 30).

Filling in your return

For tips on how to avoid common mistakes, see page 27.

If you received a scholarship or fellowship grant or tax-exempt interest income, such as on municipal bonds, see the booklet before filling in the form. Also, see the booklet if you received a Form 1099-INT showing federal income tax withheld or if federal income tax was withheld from your unemployment compensation or Alaska Permanent Fund dividends.

Remember, you must report all wages, salaries, and tips even if you do not get a Form W-2 from your employer. You must also report all your taxable interest, including interest from banks, savings and loans, credit unions, etc., even if you do not get a Form 1099-INT.

Worksheet for dependents who checked one or both boxes on line 5

(keep a copy for your records)

Use this worksheet to figure the amount to enter on line 5 if someone can claim you (or your spouse if married filing jointly) as a dependent, even if that person chooses not to do so. To find out if someone can claim you as a dependent, see Pub. 501.

A. Amount, if any, from line 1 on front . _____	
 + 300.00 Enter total ▶	**A.** 6700.00
B. Minimum standard deduction	**B.** 850.00
C. Enter the **larger** of line A or line B here	**C.** 6700.00
D. Maximum standard deduction. If **single,** enter $5,350; if **married filing jointly,** enter $10,700	**D.** 5350.00
E. Enter the **smaller** of line C or line D here. This is your standard deduction	**E.** 5350.00
F. Exemption amount.	
• If single, enter -0-.	
• If married filing jointly and—	
—both you and your spouse can be claimed as dependents, enter -0-.	**F.** 0
—only one of you can be claimed as a dependent, enter $3,400.	
G. Add lines E and F. Enter the total here and on line 5 on the front . . .	**G.** 5350.00

If you did not check any boxes on line 5, enter on line 5 the amount shown below that applies to you.

- Single, enter $8,750. This is the total of your standard deduction ($5,350) and your exemption ($3,400).
- Married filing jointly, enter $17,500. This is the total of your standard deduction ($10,700), your exemption ($3,400), and your spouse's exemption ($3,400).

Mailing return

Mail your return by **April 15, 2008.** Use the envelope that came with your booklet. If you do not have that envelope or if you moved during the year, see the back cover for the address to use.

Form **1040EZ** (2007)

The purpose of a **tax return** is to report to the IRS all the information relative to your income taxes. This includes how much you earned from all income sources and how much you paid to the IRS through withholding and estimated payments. As part of your tax return, you must figure exactly what tax you should have paid for the tax year. If your withholding or estimated payments were greater than this amount, you will receive a refund from the government. If your withholding or estimated payments were too low, you must pay the difference to the IRS.

Taxes are figured based on your earnings in the calendar year—January to December. When the year is over, you have until April 15th to file your return. For example, by April 15, 2010, you will be required to file your tax return for your income in the calendar year 2009.

Over the years, the United States tax code has become very complex. Tax laws provide taxpayers a variety of ways to lower their tax bills. You will read about some of these ways shortly. In fact, there are many careers that involve helping individuals and corporations to take advantage of tax laws to pay the lowest possible tax. Many attorneys and accountants make good incomes by becoming tax experts and helping people with tax issues. Therefore, in this chapter, we will only cover some very simple tax concepts.

✓ CHECK Your Financial IQ

What is the major purpose of taxes?

UNDERSTANDING PAYROLL TAXES

Again, payroll taxes include Social Security and Medicare taxes, and personal income taxes (state and federal). Medicare and Social Security taxes are also known as FICA, which is short for Federal Insurance Contributions Act. (Note that in some cases, FICA may be listed as OADSI (Old Age, Disability, and Survivors Insurance.) **Personal income taxes** include federal income taxes and in those states that have them, state income taxes. We will discuss each one of these in turn.

Social Security and Medicare

Take a look at Ryan's pay stub in Figure 6.1. What types of taxes did his employer withhold from his check? For most Americans, earned income, which includes wages and salary, is subject to FICA taxes. Your employer withholds FICA taxes from your paychecks and sends this amount to the government. Some of this money funds **Social Security**, which provides payments to eligible retirees and disabled people. The rest goes to **Medicare**, which provides health care coverage to mostly older Americans and some younger disabled people.

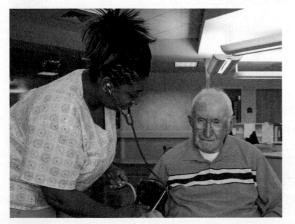

Millions of older Americans rely on Medicare for much of their health care coverage. This program is paid for in part by payroll taxes.

If you work for an employer, your portion of the Social Security tax is equal to 6.20 percent of your salary—up to a specific income level. For example, in 2008, taxpayers paid the 6.20 percent tax only on the first $102,000 of earned income. This amount is linked to inflation and

increases slightly every year. For any income you earn above the maximum, you will not have to pay the 6.20 percent tax for Social Security.

Medicare is a government health insurance program that covers people who are age 65 and older and some people who are disabled and less than 65 years old. Of the FICA amount listed on Ryan's pay stub, 1.45 percent went to Medicare. There is no cap on the amount of earnings subject to this tax.

For both Social Security and Medicare, your employer matches your contributions and sends the total amount to the government. Note: Self-employed people do not enjoy this employer match. In fact, they must pay both halves of the FICA tax themselves. This amounts to an extra tax on self-employed income. They may pay double what a person on a payroll pays.

Personal Income Taxes

In addition to the FICA and Medicare taxes, your income is also subject to personal income taxes, or taxes imposed on the income you earn. It is this income that you report on your tax return. Refer to Figure 6.3 for the IRS table of individual tax rates.

As mentioned earlier, the tax code is extremely complex, and as your income increases and you begin to invest and plan for retirement, you may find it necessary to use the services of a tax professional. For simple returns, many people use tax preparation software. These programs guide you through preparing your tax returns and include all the necessary forms.

In addition to federal income taxes, many of you will pay a state income tax. The amount can be a significant factor when deciding where to live. Refer to Figure 6.4 for a listing of states with the highest and lowest tax rates.

Also, some cities collect income taxes. Pay careful attention to where you live. Taxes and cost of living are factors that need to be factored into the overall equation.

✓ CHECK Your Financial IQ

What are the payroll taxes?

FILING TAXES

Refer to Figure 6.2 for an example of the simplest tax return, the 1040EZ. As you can see, a tax return form allows you to record several different categories of information. These include filing status, exemptions, gross income, adjusted gross income, tax and credits, and other categories. Understanding these categories will help you understand how our tax system works. We will address each one of these items in a little more detail.

Filing Status

Taxpayers are required to specify a filing status when they submit their income tax return. They must choose one of the following options:

- Single
- Married filing jointly

- Married filing separately
- Head of household
- Qualifying widow(er) with dependent child

Generally, the tax rules and rates differ depending on which status you choose. It is important to read all of the documentation that comes with the tax forms so that you can choose the filing status that is most appropriate for you. Usually, a married couple will combine their income and file a joint return. However, in some specific cases, it may be better for a married couple to file separate returns. Usually, a single person who has a child

Figure 6.3 Individual Tax Rates for 2007

Two key factors affect what federal income taxes you must pay: your filing status and your total income. Generally, the more you make, the higher tax rate you pay.

If your taxable income is over	But not over	The tax is
Schedule X — Single		
$0	$7,825	10% of the amount over $0
$7,825	$31,850	$782.50 plus 15% of the amount over 7,825
$31,850	$77,100	$4,386.25 plus 25% of the amount over 31,850
$77,100	$160,850	$15,698.75 plus 28% of the amount over 77,100
$160,850	$349,700	$39,148.75 plus 33% of the amount over 160,850
$349,700	no limit	$101,469.25 plus 35% of the amount over 349,700
Schedule Y-1 — Married Filing Jointly or Qualifying Widow(er)		
$0	$15,650	10% of the amount over $0
$15,650	$63,700	$1,565.00 plus 15% of the amount over 15,650
$63,700	$128,500	$8,772.50 plus 25% of the amount over 63,700
$128,500	$195,850	$24,972.50 plus 28% of the amount over 128,500
$195,850	$349,700	$43,830.50 plus 33% of the amount over 195,850
$349,700	no limit	$94,601.00 plus 35% of the amount over 349,700
Schedule Y-2 — Married Filing Separately		
$0	$7,825	10% of the amount over $0
$7,825	$31,850	$782.50 plus 15% of the amount over 7,825
$31,850	$64,250	$4,386.25 plus 25% of the amount over 31,850
$64,250	$97,925	$12,486.25 plus 28% of the amount over 64,250
$97,925	$174,850	$21,915.25 plus 33% of the amount over 97,925
$174,850	no limit	$47,300.50 plus 35% of the amount over 174,850
Schedule Z — Head of Household		
$0	$11,200	10% of the amount over $0
$11,200	$42,650	$1,120.00 plus 15% of the amount over 11,200
$42,650	$110,100	$5,837.50 plus 25% of the amount over 42,650
$110,100	$178,350	$22,700.00 plus 28% of the amount over 110,100
$178,350	$349,700	$41,810.00 plus 33% of the amount over 178,350
$349,700	no limit	$98,355.50 plus 35% of the amount over 349,700

Figure 6.4 Tax Rates by State

Tax rates vary greatly from one state to the other, and this can be a significant factor in your financial planning.

State	Tax Rate Low	High	Brackets	Income Brackets Low	High	Personal Exemptions Single	Married	Child	Federal Tax Deduction
ALABAMA	2.0 – 5.0		3	500(b) –	3,000(b)	1,500	3,000	300	*
ALASKA	No State Income Tax								
ARIZONA	2.59 – 4.54		5	10,000(b) –	150,000(b)	2,100	4,200	2,300	
ARKANSAS (a)	1.0 – 7.0(e)		6	3,699(b) –	31,000(b)	23(c)	46(c)	23(c)	
CALIFORNIA (a)	1.0 – 9.3(w)		6	6,827(b) –	44,815(b)	94(c)	188(c)	294(c)	
COLORADO	4.63		1	----------Flat rate---------		-------None------			
CONNECTICUT	3.0 – 5.0		2	10,000(b) –	10,000(b)	12,750(f)	24,500(f)	0	
DELAWARE	2.2 – 5.95		6	5,000 –	60,000	110(c)	220(c)	110(c)	
FLORIDA	No State Income Tax								
GEORGIA	1.0 – 6.0		6	750(g) –	7,000(g)	2,700	5,400	3,000	
HAWAII	1.4 – 8.25		9	2,400(b) –	48,000(b)	1,040	2,080	1,040	
IDAHO (a)	1.6 – 7.8		8	1,237(h) –	24,736(h)	3,500(d)	7,000(d)	3,500(d)	
ILLINOIS	3.0		1	----------Flat rate---------		2,000	4,000	2,000	
INDIANA	3.4		1	----------Flat rate---------		1,000	2,000	1,000	
IOWA (a)	0.36 – 8.98		9	1,379 –	62,055	40(c)	80(c)	40(c)	*
KANSAS	3.5 – 6.45		3	15,000(b) –	30,000(b)	2,250	4,500	2,250	
KENTUCKY	2.0 – 6.0		6	3,000 –	75,000	20(c)	40(c)	20(c)	
LOUISIANA	2.0 – 6.0		3	12,500(b) –	25,000(h)	4,500(i)	9,000(i)	1,000(i)	*
MAINE (a)	2.0 – 8.5		4	4,849(b) –	19,450(b)	2,850	5,700	2,850	
MARYLAND	2.0 – 5.5		7	1,000 –	500,000	2,400	4,800	2,400	
MASSACHUSETTS (a)	5.3		1	----------Flat rate---------		4,125	8,250	1,000	
MICHIGAN (a)	4.35		1	----------Flat rate---------		3,300	6,600	3,300	
MINNESOTA (a)	5.35 – 7.85		3	21,800(j) –	71,591(j)	3,500(d)	7,000(d)	3,500(d)	
MISSISSIPPI	3.0 – 5.0		3	5,000 –	10,000	6,000	12,000	1,500	
MISSOURI	1.5 – 6.0		10	1,000 –	9,000	2,100	4,200	1,200	* (r)
MONTANA (a)	1.0 – 6.9		7	2,500 –	14,900	2,040	4,080	2,040	* (r)
NEBRASKA (a)	2.56 – 6.84		4	2,400(k) –	27,001(k)	113(c)	226(c)	113(c)	
NEVADA	No State Income Tax								
NEW HAMPSHIRE	State Income Tax is Limited to Dividends and Interest Income Only.								
NEW JERSEY	1.4 – 8.97		6	20,000(l) –	500,000(l)	1,000	2,000	1,500	
NEW MEXICO	1.7 – 5.3		4	5,500(m) –	16,000(m)	3,500(d)	7,000(d)	3,500(d)	
NEW YORK	4.0 – 6.85		5	8,000(b) –	20,000(b)	0	0	1,000	
NORTH CAROLINA (n)	6.0 – 7.75		3	12,750(n) –	60,000(n)	2,000	4,000	2,000	
NORTH DAKOTA (a)	2.1 – 5.54(o)		5	31,850(o) –	349,701(o)	3,500(d)	7,000(d)	3,500(d)	
OHIO (a)	0.618 – 6.24		9	5,000 –	200,000	1,450(p)	2,900(p)	1,450(p)	
OKLAHOMA	0.5 – 5.5(q)		7	1,000(q) –	8,701(q)	1,000	2,000	1,000	
OREGON (a)	5.0 – 9.0		3	2,900(b) –	7,300(b)	169(c)	338(c)	169(c)	* (r)
PENNSYLVANIA	3.07		1	----------Flat rate---------		-------None------			
RHODE ISLAND	25.0% Federal Tax Liability(s)			------		------			
SOUTH CAROLINA (a)	0 – 7.0		6	2,670 –	13,350	3,500(d)	7,000(d)	3,500(d)	
SOUTH DAKOTA	No State Income Tax								
TENNESSEE	State Income Tax is Limited to Dividends and Interest Income Only.								
TEXAS	No State Income Tax								
UTAH	5.0		1	-----Flat rate-----		(t)	(t)	(t)	
VERMONT (a)	3.6 – 9.5		5	32,550(u) –	357,700(u)	3,500(d)	7,000(d)	3,500(d)	
VIRGINIA	2.0 – 5.75		4	3,000 –	17,000	930	1,860	930	
WASHINGTON	No State Income Tax								
WEST VIRGINIA	3.0 – 6.5		5	10,000 –	60,000	2,000	4,000	2,000	
WISCONSIN (a)	4.6 – 6.75		4	9,700(v) –	145,460(v)	700	1,400	700	
WYOMING	No State Income Tax								
DIST. OF COLUMBIA	4.0 – 8.5		3	10,000 –	40,000	1,675	3,350	1,675	

Source: www.taxadmin.org/fta/rate/ind_inc.html

would be better off filing as "head of household" rather than as single.

Until you reach the age of 18, most of you will be considered dependents by the IRS. As such, you can be claimed on your parent's or guardian's tax return as a dependent—someone who is dependent upon someone else for financial support. By claiming you as a dependent, your parent or guardian is able to lower what he or she owes in taxes. Note, however: Even though you may be a dependent and appear as such on someone else's tax return, you will still be required to file your own tax return if you earned enough income.

Gross Income or Total Income

You Do It

Activity #2

The first step in calculating the federal tax you owe is to determine your gross income. **Gross income** or total income consists of the total amount of a person's income from (almost) any source. Take Ryan, for instance. The primary source of income for Ryan is the wages he earns at his job. At the end of the year, his employer will send him a document called a W-2 form that details how much money Ryan made. See Figure 6.5 for a look at Ryan's W-2 form.

Figure 6.5   W-2 Form

The W-2 form is a year-end summary of all relevant income and tax withholding information. You will receive one from your employer shortly after the end of the year.

22222	a Employee's social security number XXX-XXX-XXX	OMB No. 1545-0008		
b Employer identification number (EIN) XX-XXXXXXX			1 Wages, tips, other compensation 6400.00	2 Federal income tax withheld XXXXXXXXX
c Employer's name, address, and ZIP code Dave's Auto Shop 555 Main Street Anytown, USA 11121			3 Social security wages XXXXXXXXX	4 Social security tax withheld 96.80
			5 Medicare wages and tips XXXXXXXXX	6 Medicare tax withheld 92.80
			7 Social security tips	8 Allocated tips
d Control number XX			9 Advance EIC payment	10 Dependent care benefits
e Employee's first name and initial Last name Suff. Ryan Jones 111 Doodle Street Anytown, USA 11121			11 Nonqualified plans	12a Code
			13 Statutory employee ☐ Retirement plan ☐ Third-party sick pay ☐	12b Code
			14 Other	12c Code
				12d Code
f Employee's address and ZIP code				

15 State Employer's state ID number	16 State wages, tips, etc.	17 State income tax	18 Local wages, tips, etc.	19 Local income tax	20 Locality name
MAI	6400.00				

Form **W-2** Wage and Tax Statement   **2008**   Department of the Treasury—Internal Revenue Service

Copy 1—For State, City, or Local Tax Department

Source: www.irs.gov/pub/irs-pdf/fw2.pdf

Last year Colt's salary was $32,000 but he also received $1,200 in dividend income and lost $400 on the sale of one stock and gained $650 on the sale of another stock.

What was Colt's gross income?

Solution: Colt's gross income was $32,000 + $1,200 − $400 + $650 = $33,450.

Other forms of income in addition to wages and salary include interest income, dividend income, and capital gains from the sale of assets. **Capital gains** occur when you sell an asset for more than what you paid for it. For example, suppose you bought 20 shares of stock for $1,000 and later sold the shares for $2,200. The $1,200 difference is a capital gain, and it counts as gross income. Capital gains are taxed, but typically at a lower rate than other forms of income.

Gross income also includes income from tips, rental properties, and business income. Game show winnings and any scholarship amounts that exceed the cost of tuition and books are also considered part of gross income.

Some types of income are not included in gross income and therefore are not taxed. These include insurance reimbursements, child support payments received, moving expenses paid by an employer, and veteran's and welfare benefits.

This discussion highlights the need to keep detailed financial records. At tax time you are often required to provide a lot of information. It can be hard to remember how much you paid for a stock five years ago. Nevertheless, accuracy is important. Filing an incorrect tax return can lead to serious penalties.

Adjusted Gross Income

The next step in filling out a tax return is to figure your adjusted gross income, or AGI. **Adjusted gross income** is figured by taking the total income and subtracting certain allowable amounts. These can include contributions to certain retirement accounts, alimony payments, interest paid on student loans, and other special circumstances. Again, IRS rules detail exactly what can be subtracted from your total income to figure your AGI.

Professor FIN

Did you ever watch a game show and think to yourself "Boy, would I like to win all that money or prizes." Or maybe you think it would be great to win the lottery. As good as it sounds, all winnings, including cash and the value of any items you win, are considered as income, and you will have to pay taxes on them. These winnings are reported on a 1099-MISC.

For example, if you have over $600 in winnings in one year, this will be taxed as income. It does not matter if these winnings are in cash or in the form of items such as cars or vacations. How much you will have to pay in taxes varies with what you have won, what your state will ask for, and how much the IRS will collect. Most say a good rule of thumb is to save 50 percent of what you receive as a cash prize to be paid in taxes.

Remember Richard Hatch, who won $1 million on the television reality show *Survivor*? He learned the hard way what can happen if you forget to pay the taxes on your winnings. He was found guilty of tax evasion.

Expect around 50 percent of what you win as a cash prize to be taken up in taxes.

For example, you may reduce your gross income by as much as $2,500 if you paid that amount in student loan interest. Your adjusted gross income will always be less than or equal to your total income.

Deductions and Exemptions

You may be able to claim various deductions and exemptions that will reduce the amount of your AGI that is subject to income taxes. This, of course, will lower the amount of tax you pay.

The **standard deduction** is a fixed amount all people are allowed to deduct from their AGI to reduce their tax liability. The amount of the standard deduction varies according to your filing status and whether you are over the age of 65.

Many taxpayers also have the option of taking so-called itemized deductions in place of the standard deduction. **Itemized deductions** are specific expenses that, under tax law, can be deducted from income to reduce the amount of income subject to income tax. Congress has approved certain items as tax deductible in order to encourage certain behaviors. For example, Congress wants to encourage home ownership. So, it allows the homeowner to deduct the interest paid on a mortgage loan. Homeowners can also deduct the real estate taxes they pay. (On the other hand, in most cases, money paid on rent is not deductible.) Congress wants to encourage people to give money to charities. So, it has made charitable gifts deductible. There are several other deductions that are allowed when you itemize. They include certain large medical expenses if they meet certain guidelines.

Is it smarter to take the standard deduction or to itemize deductions? This depends on the person. If the value of the itemized deductions you are entitled to is small, you will want to take the standard deduction. If the value of the itemized deductions is larger than the standard deduction, you will want to itemize. The goal, of course, is to have the smallest possible tax liability.

Refund or Payment

Activity #3

Accurate completion of your tax return will show you whether you need to pay additional income taxes that year, or whether you overpaid and will receive a refund. In some cases, low income families will receive more money back in the form of an Earned Income Credit than was withheld from their paycheck. However, in most cases, you will not receive an income tax refund unless you pay taxes during that year.

 CHECK Your Financial IQ

When does a person file his or her taxes?

Taxes can have a big impact on major financial decisions, such as when and where to buy a home.

As you can see, the tax system is complex. Each person's situation is different. But all people face the same basic situation: They want to take steps to lower their tax liability to the lowest possible level for their income. That way, they get to keep more of their own money rather than paying it to the government in taxes. This is just good financial sense.

Taking full advantage of the many ways to reduce your taxable income takes planning. And, the older you get and the more money you make, the more critical this planning becomes.

Still, even now you can see how you might factor in tax planning in your short-term future. For example, tax issues may affect your decision to buy a house or rent an apartment. It might affect how much money you put each year into a tax-advantaged retirement account and other investments. Making these decisions will be covered in greater detail later.

As your life unfolds, you will find many other opportunities to use tax planning to your advantage. Tax planning may influence the way you save money for a college education for children you might have. It might affect when you decide to retire. Indeed, it is essential that you consider the tax implications of your financial life at all stages. Since circumstances vary widely from person to person, many people find that getting expert tax advice is an excellent investment.

Think about Ryan. What are some of the things Ryan will eventually need to consider that are tax related? For starters, Ryan needs to think about where he works and lives. Remember, in some places he will pay city, state, and federal income taxes and also real estate and personal property taxes.

CHECK Your Financial IQ

Why are taxes an important part of your financial plan?

Summary

- Taxes are monies the government collects from citizens for the purpose of operating the government. The government collects taxes in a variety of ways and forms: sales taxes, real estate taxes, and payroll taxes. The government also collects taxes from businesses. The Internal Revenue Service (IRS) is the governmental body that carries out the federal tax system.

- Payroll taxes include personal income taxes (state and federal) and Social Security and Medicare taxes. Social Security and Medicare taxes are also known as FICA. Many workers have these taxes withheld from their gross pay.

- Filing taxes involves reporting your earnings for the year on a tax return that is sent to the IRS and to any appropriate state or local tax collection agency. There are several different categories of information needed for your tax return. They include the following: filing status, gross income, adjusted gross income, deductions, and exemptions.

- Tax planning is another important step in your financial plan. Taking full advantage of the many ways to reduce your taxable income takes planning. The older you get and the more money you make, the more critical this planning becomes.

Key Terms and Vocabulary

Adjusted gross income	Itemized deduction	Standard deduction
Capital gain	Medicare	Take-home pay
Gross income	Net pay	Tax
Gross pay	Payroll tax	Tax return
Internal Revenue Service (IRS)	Personal income tax	
	Sales tax	
	Social Security	

What Do You Know?

myFinLitlab

1. (a) What is the difference between gross pay and net pay?

   (b) Why is it important to know the difference?

2. (a) Who pays taxes?

   (b) What kind of tax are you paying when you pay $1.05 for a $1 item at a convenience store?

3. (a) What agency administers the federal tax laws?

   (b) What is the purpose of a tax return?

   (c) What factors make tax rules so complicated?

4. (a) What are the two programs funded by FICA?

(b) What is one way that FICA taxes differ from the federal income tax?

5. (a) Briefly describe how your filing status is determined.

(b) Give an example of how one person might be eligible for more than one filing status.

6. (a) List some types of income that are included in gross income.

(b) What are some types of payments you might receive that would not be included in gross income?

(c) In Ryan's case, what explains the difference between his gross income and his net income?

7. (a) What is the difference between gross and adjusted gross income?

(b) Which figure can never be lower than the other?

8. (a) What is a standard deduction?

(b) Why would a person choose a standard deduction over itemized deductions?

9. (a) Why does the federal government allow certain itemized deductions?

(b) Who is likely to pay lower taxes for the same level of income: A homeowner who pays $1,000 per month on a mortgage loan or a renter who pays $1,000 a month in rent?

10. (a) Why is it important to understand the tax consequences of your financial decisions?

(b) How might hiring a tax advisor be a good investment?

What Are Your Finance Math Skills? myFinLitlab

The first three questions correlate to *Math for Personal Finance* features located throughout the chapter.

1. Josh's gross pay was $320.00 this week. How much in FICA will be withheld from his check?

2. Amber's starting salary with her new job will be $35,500 a year. How much will she pay to the Social Security system for her first year?

3. What is Corbin's gross income for 2009 if his salary is $21,050 and he receives $420 in interest income for the year?

4. Washburn's employer withheld $4,245 from his paycheck for federal taxes. After calculating his tax liability, he discovers he will only have to pay $3,211 this year. Will he get a tax refund and, if so, how much?

5. Cecelia bought a stock five years ago for $3,400. She sold it this year for $4,100. How much capital gain will she be required to pay taxes on?

6. Franklin made $165,000 for the tax year 2008. How much did he pay in FICA taxes?

7. Zachary has a taxable income of $70,000. How much did he pay in Medicare tax this year?

8. Joseph's standard deduction filing single is $5,350 for 2007. However, he paid $6,200 in mortgage interest and contributed $1,100 to charity. Should Joseph itemize or take his standard deduction? Explain your answer.

What Would You Do?

The IRS allows for the deduction of expenses incurred in traveling to a job interview. Fritz, Erica, and their two children have used this deduction to fund their vacations for the last eight years. Each year, several months prior to their vacation, Fritz and Erica begin reviewing the want ads in newspapers in the city or cities they plan to visit. They each apply for several jobs for which they are qualified. Any applications that result in interviews are scheduled during their vacation. They are careful to deduct only those expenses allowed under the IRS Tax Code, such as mileage, meals (not the children's), and hotel and motel expenses (not the children's). This plan has resulted in between $300 and $500 in allowable tax deductions each year. Fritz and Erica have determined that in most cases, they would not accept the jobs if offered; however, if the perfect offer were to appear, they would give it serious consideration.

1. Discuss whether you think Fritz and Erica are being ethical in using the IRS Code to fund part of the expenses of their family vacation.

2. How might the behavior of Fritz and Erica affect you and other tax-payers?

3. Do you see other areas of the tax code discussed in this chapter that could be subject to abuse?

What Are the Connections?

Math, Language Arts, and Technology

Research the various taxes in your area. These might include city tax, county tax, food tax, property tax, and so on. Make a chart that reflects the various taxes in your area. Be sure to include examples of each of the types of taxes, who pays them, and when they would be paid (for example, at the time of purchase or end-of-year).

Write an article for your school newspaper explaining these taxes to your fellow students and how many taxes they are already paying. Also, provide information on the types of taxes your fellow students can expect to pay when they purchase a car or other major purchases. Keep in mind that licenses and fees are types of taxes.

Teamwork Service-Learning Activity

As a team, write an informative presentation explaining the Four Rs of Taxes for the children of the local elementary school (see page 93). Your presentation might be in the form of a rap, song, skit or play, or role-play. Your team might even come up with a video of their presentation that could be used with Parent Teacher Organizations in your school district.

w!se | **Financial Literacy**
CERTIFICATION

TEST PREP QUESTIONS

myFinLitlab

1. Another name for take-home pay is
   a. gross pay.
   b. salary.
   c. net pay.
   d. income.

2. Which of the following statements about taxes is true?
   a. Only the federal government has the right to tax a person's income.
   b. Any taxes collected by the government are returned to the person when she files her income tax return.
   c. Taxes are the major source of revenue for the government.
   d. Taxes can only be taken out of a person's income when she has a full-time job.

3. From the following, select the tax that is matched with its correct explanation:
   a. Payroll tax: money deducted from a person's salary that is sent to the government by the employer.
   b. Real estate tax: money paid to the government to use for building federally subsidized housing.
   c. Sales tax: a percentage of money that the federal government deducts from the cost of new purchases.
   d. Income tax: money that an employer pays out of company profits to the federal government for each person employed.

4. If a person is self-employed and earns $70,000 annually, the person
   a. does not have to pay federal income tax because his salary is too low.
   b. must pay estimated income taxes every quarter.
   c. is only responsible for paying FICA tax to cover Social Security.
   d. will not have to pay any local or state taxes.

5. The purpose of the IRS is to
   a. pass laws to determine what will be taxed.
   b. enforce tax laws and carry out the federal tax system.
   c. prepare tax returns for businesses and individuals.
   d. cut federal taxes and distribute taxes that have been collected to local and state governments.

6. A person completes her federal 1040EZ form and sees that she paid quarterly estimated taxes of $12,000. But the calculations show that she should have only paid $9,500 in taxes. What will happen if she sends the IRS this completed form with the necessary supporting documents?
   a. Nothing, because she completed the short form, the 1040EZ, instead of the long form, the 1040.
   b. The IRS will deduct the over payment of $2,500 from next year's taxes.
   c. She will receive a federal tax refund of $2,500.
   d. The IRS will make sure that her employer deducts the correct amount of taxes in the next year.

7. Juanita and Jessica work at the same company. Each is married and earns $75,000 per year. Juanita is paying more in taxes than Jessica. What two factors can help to explain why this is true?
   a. Juanita does not have any children and does not itemize deductions; Jessica itemizes deductions and has three children.
   b. Jessica earns an additional $15,000 from a part-time job and rents her house; Juanita owns her house and does not earn any additional income.
   c. Juanita contributes the maximum she is allowed by law to her pension plan and Jessica does not contribute more than the minimum that her employer will match to her pension plan.
   d. Jessica files her return as a single person and lets her husband claim their three children as exemptions on his taxes when he files as head of household.

8. Which of the following statements about adjusted gross income is true?
   a. It will always be higher than a person's gross income.
   b. It is the amount used to determine what a person actually has to pay in taxes.
   c. It will decrease when a person takes a deduction for real estate taxes, contributions to charities, and interest on a mortgage.
   d. It is the amount used to determine if a person gets a refund for paying Social Security taxes.

9. Which of the following statements about taxes and financial planning is true?
   a. It makes sense for everyone to use the services of a tax professional in order to avoid paying additional taxes.
   b. It is not really possible to reduce the taxes a person has to pay. Therefore, people need to save more money to pay annual taxes.
   c. Using a tax planner does not really make sense until a person is earning more than $85,000 a year.
   d. It is possible for a person to reduce her tax liability by adjusting her financial plan.

10. A person looks over his pay stub and sees that in addition to paying state and federal personal income taxes, he is paying other personal taxes such as Social Security and Medicare. He is only age 20, so he is

sure that his employer has made a mistake since Social Security and Medicare are for old people, and the money should be returned to him. Is he right?

a. No. The money he is contributing to Social Security and Medicare is paying the benefits for today's older people.

b. No. If he pays Social Security and Medicare taxes now he can start collecting benefits now.

c. Yes. Only people within 20 years of retiring are expected to pay Social Security and Medicare taxes.

d. Yes. He needs to let his employer know that he does not want to pay into the Social Security and Medicare benefits program in the future.

11. Which is a valid statement about a dependent?

a. A teenager who is living at home and earns $5,500 does not have to pay taxes on that money because his parents will claim him as a dependent on their taxes.

b. If a person is single but has two children he cannot count the children as dependents when he files his tax return.

c. Declaring someone as a dependent on a tax return increases the taxes that have to be paid by the person filing the return.

d. For each dependent a person has, she is able to take a deduction from the amount of taxes she owes when filing her tax return.

12. A 28-year-old earns $54,000 from his job as an illustrator. He also earned another $23,000 doing work for private clients. In May of this year he got married. His wife, also an illustrator, earned $47,000. They bought a house in June. He has always done his own taxes—filing the 1040EZ and taking the standard deductions. What advice should he follow for this year?

a. He should file as a single person, take the standard deductions, and do his own taxes.

b. He should file a joint return, take the standard deductions, and use an online computer program to complete the 1040EZ tax form.

c. Because of all of the changes in his life, he should pay a tax professional to complete his taxes and figure out the most beneficial filing status and tax form for him to use.

d. Given the changes in his life, he should do exactly what he has done in the past; however, this year he should claim his wife as a dependent.

13. A person wins $25,000 on a game show and a trip to Costa Rica worth $5,700. Does he have any tax obligation from these winnings?

a. No. The prize is not considered earned income.

b. Yes. However, he only has to pay taxes on the $25,000 since the trip is considered a gift.

c. Yes. All of these winnings become part of his gross income.

d. Yes. However, he will be able to deduct the cost of the trip next year when he returns from Costa Rica.

CHAPTER 7

Learning Objectives

Explain why health insurance is important.

Describe different features of health insurance.

Explain the need for life insurance.

Describe the ways people obtain insurance.

Key Terms

Coinsurance

Deductible

Group plan

Health insurance

Insurance

Life insurance

Preexisting condition

Premium

Insuring Your Health and Your Life

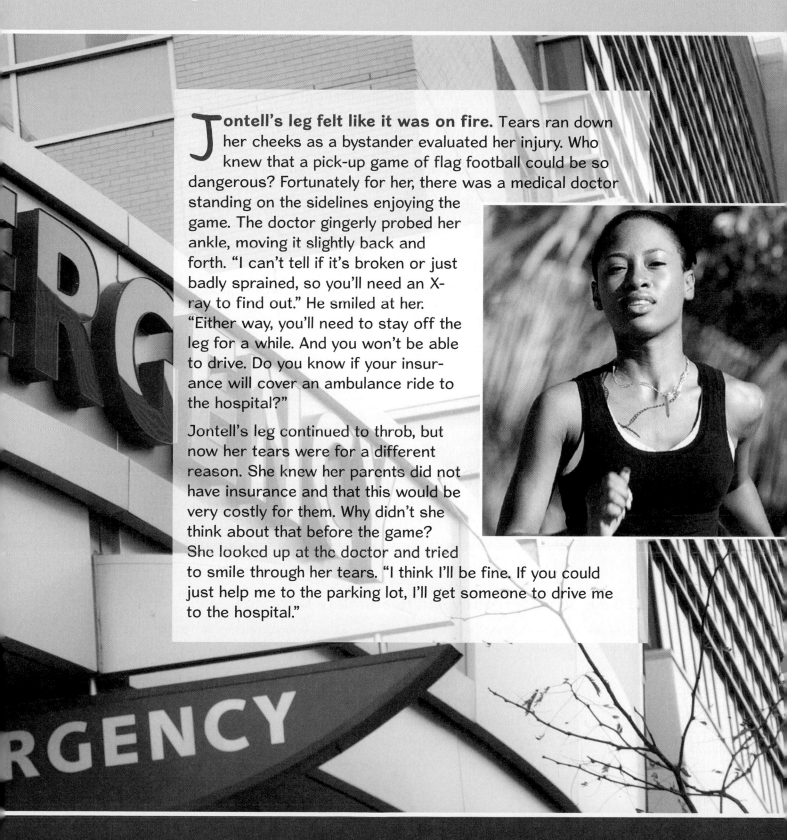

Jontell's leg felt like it was on fire. Tears ran down her cheeks as a bystander evaluated her injury. Who knew that a pick-up game of flag football could be so dangerous? Fortunately for her, there was a medical doctor standing on the sidelines enjoying the game. The doctor gingerly probed her ankle, moving it slightly back and forth. "I can't tell if it's broken or just badly sprained, so you'll need an X-ray to find out." He smiled at her. "Either way, you'll need to stay off the leg for a while. And you won't be able to drive. Do you know if your insurance will cover an ambulance ride to the hospital?"

Jontell's leg continued to throb, but now her tears were for a different reason. She knew her parents did not have insurance and that this would be very costly for them. Why didn't she think about that before the game? She looked up at the doctor and tried to smile through her tears. "I think I'll be fine. If you could just help me to the parking lot, I'll get someone to drive me to the hospital."

Unfortunately, Jontell's situation is a common one. Many people do not have insurance to protect them from loss in the event of an injury or other health problem. Yet insurance is an important component of your financial plan. A person obtains **insurance** by paying money to an insurance company, which agrees to reimburse that person in the event of certain types of financial loss. In this chapter, we will explore two essential types of insurance: health insurance and life insurance.

THE IMPORTANCE OF HEALTH INSURANCE

Health insurance provides payment to people who suffer a financial loss as a result of illness or injury. Individuals covered by health insurance limit their potential liabilities and ensure that they will receive adequate medical care. Remember that any time you owe someone money, you have a **liability**. Since medical care tends to be very expensive, adequate health insurance is an important component of your financial plan. People without health insurance could find their net worth quickly eliminated with one major health problem.

Sources of Health Insurance

Health insurance is available in many forms. Some people get their coverage from private companies, which make money by selling health insurance policies. Generally, this is the most expensive way to obtain insurance. Instead, many people get coverage as a company benefit. Employers often pick up some or most of the cost. See Figure 7.1.

The federal government has two health care plans, Medicare and Medicaid, that are available to some individuals. **Medicare** is a government-sponsored health insurance plan that is funded largely by taxes that most working people pay. It provides benefits to individ-

> **Professor FIN**
>
> To learn more about Medicare go to **www.medicare.gov**. At the site, look at the choices for Medicare plans. You can also go to "Search Tools" and click "Participating Physician Directory," enter your Zip code, and select a specialty to find out how many physicians in your area are listed in the directory. Click "Plan Choices" and access "Medigap (Supplemental Insurance)."

Figure 7.1   Employer-Provided Health Care Coverage

Employers are a major source of health care coverage, although employees must frequently make significant monthly contributions to the cost of this care.

	Private Employers	State and Local Government Employers
Percentage Employers Offering Coverage	71%	87%
Average Monthly Cost to Employee (single coverage)	$81	$38
Average Monthly Cost to Employee (family coverage)	$313	$196

Sources: www.bls.gov/news.release/pdf/ebs2.pdf www.bls.gov/ncs/ebs/sp/ebsm0007.pdf

uals who are at least age 65 and qualify for Social Security, or to individuals who are disabled. Medicare consists of two components, part A and part B. Part A is hospital insurance, which recipients receive at no cost to them. Part B covers doctor visits and other care provided outside a hospital, and recipients must pay some premium for this coverage. (In the world of insurance, **premium** means regular payments in return for insurance coverage.)

Medicaid is a government-sponsored program that provides health insurance for low-income individuals. The program is administered on a state-by-state basis, so eligibility may differ for people from different states. The coverage is designed for the elderly, blind, disabled, and needy families with dependent children.

Of course, too many people, including Jontell, have no health care coverage. Her parents do not have insurance. Perhaps their employers offer no coverage or they cannot afford it. As a result, Jontell may have to wait until college to get health care coverage. (College students can often buy a relatively inexpensive plan that provides limited coverage.) In the meantime, Jontell's parents could face several thousands of dollars worth of expense for her care.

Professor FIN

Did you know that insurance fraud loss is estimated to be $27.6 billion per year? The following types of fraud lead the way:

- Automobile fraud at $12.3 billion
- Business and commercial fraud at $1.8 billion
- Homeowner fraud at $1.8 billion
- Life/disability fraud at $1.5 billion

Source: www.insurancefraud.com/

Health Care Costs

Health insurance has received a lot of attention recently because it has become very expensive (see Figure 7.2). Many employers are cutting back or dropping health insurance as a benefit for their employees. As the nation's population continues to age, you will hear more about health care costs and health insurance, since older people tend to have a greater need for health care. People are living longer and they require health care coverage for longer periods of time. In addition, a lot of new expensive technologies have emerged in the health care field. Fraudulent claims have also driven the cost of health insurance higher. Fraud occurs when someone submits false information in order to get a financial benefit.

Even though health insurance costs have increased significantly, having health insurance is a critical risk-reduction tool of your financial plan. Even minor accidents and injuries can do severe harm to your financial future. The bill for the kind of care Jontell will likely need can easily reach into the thousands. A severe injury or illness can lead to bills in the hundreds of thousands of dollars. Indeed, in 2005, health care spending by Americans averaged nearly $7,000 for each man, woman, and child. Spending is expected to rise sharply in the years ahead. One recent study found that health care costs were a factor in about half of all bankruptcies. Your decision is not whether to purchase health insurance but instead what type of plan to get and how much coverage to obtain.

In spite of the fact that health insurance is a key piece of a financial plan, many people find it too costly. A 2007 report published by the United

Even when you're young and healthy, you may find yourself in need of costly medical care —and health insurance.

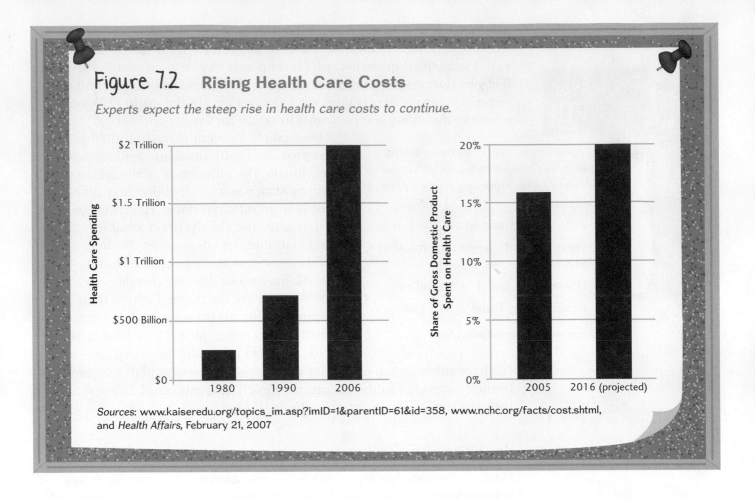

Figure 7.2 Rising Health Care Costs

Experts expect the steep rise in health care costs to continue.

Sources: www.kaiseredu.org/topics_im.asp?imID=1&parentID=61&id=358, www.nchc.org/facts/cost.shtml, and *Health Affairs*, February 21, 2007

States Census found that 47 million Americans—almost 16 percent of the population—had no health insurance. (You can go to **www.census.gov** and click "Health Insurance" to read the latest census information.)

 CHECK Your Financial IQ

Why is health insurance a critical part of your financial plan?

HEALTH INSURANCE FEATURES AND TERMS

Insurance plans come in many forms and provide a range of coverage and services. However, different policies have different features, which can greatly affect the cost and the level of service you receive. When talking about health care plans, it's important that you know about the features and terms commonly used.

Indemnity Plans versus Managed Care

Health care plans are usually classified as indemnity plans or managed care plans. Indemnity plans allow participants to seek health care from any qualified medical provider. Managed care plans limit participants to a specific list of providers. Regardless of the option available, you should be aware of the following issues.

Did you know that the high cost of health care in the United States has caused many people to look overseas for treatment? This is called "Medical Tourism." Simply put, many people are traveling overseas to get lower-cost medical care in foreign countries.

Although many think medical tourism is new, it actually began thousands of years ago with the Greeks. They would take pilgrimages to the small territory in the Saronic Gulf called Epidauria. Epidauria, the original medical tourism spot, was the sanctuary of the healing god, Asklepios.

In more recent times, Americans have sought healing spa treatments. One such treatment can be found in Hot Springs, Arkansas. For more than 200 years, health seekers both rich and poor have used the waters there to heal illnesses and promote relaxation. Other springs can be found in Georgia. Can you name the American president who frequented the hot springs at Georgia? The answer is Franklin Roosevelt.

COMPARING COSTS

Prices at Bangkok's Bumrungrad hospital versus average costs at private hospitals in the United States*

Prostate surgery: $5,000–$7,000 versus $35,000–$40,000

Comprehensive checkup: $400 versus $2,000

Spinal surgery: $6,000–$8,000 versus $50,000–$70,000

Open-heart bypass surgery: $10,000 versus $60,000–$80,000

Root canal: $320 versus $900–$1,000

Hip replacement: $9,000 versus $40,000–$50,000

Private hospital room per day: $150 versus up to $1,000

Airfares: Under $1,000 to more than $3000 round-trip economy class from the United States to Bangkok.

*Information from Bumrungrad International; southeastern U.S. average.

Family Coverage

The person who buys a health insurance policy or subscribes to it through an employer is known as the **policyholder**. Additionally, many health insurance plans provide coverage for immediate family members, such as a spouse and dependent children. However, children may become ineligible for coverage once they reach a certain age or status—for example, when they finish high school unless they enroll in college. The loss of your existing family coverage, if you have it, is important to consider as you make your plans.

Group Plans

Group plans are insurance plans that cover a large group of individuals, such as all the employees of a particular company or local government. Within a group plan, an individual's high risk or loss is spread across the entire pool of group members. So, even though some group members may develop costly health problems or have much higher health risks, they have equal access to health care as those who enjoy perfect health. They also pay the same amount for coverage. By contrast, an individual or family that is not part of a group plan may pay much more for coverage if there is any history of illness or significant health risk. For example, an adult who was treated for cancer several years ago may have trouble finding an affordable individual or family policy.

Location Restrictions

Some United States insurance companies will cover medical care delivered inside the United States only. Others will provide coverage in foreign countries. If you travel abroad, it is a good idea to consider purchasing short-term health insurance for the duration of your trip.

Preexisting Conditions

Insurance policies may exclude coverage for **preexisting conditions**, or health conditions that existed before your policy was granted. For example, if Jontell decides to purchase health insurance, she would probably find that her recent injury will not be covered under her new policy.

Cancellation Options

Some health insurance plans allow the insurance company to cancel the policy at any time. Others guarantee coverage as long as you pay your insurance premiums on time. Having a policy that cannot be canceled can be tremendously important in the event of serious or long-term illness. It ensures that you will have the coverage you need—when you need it most.

Deductibles

Some insurance policies begin paying claims only after the policyholder has paid a certain amount of money. This amount of money is known as a **deductible**. For example, your policy may have a $500 annual deductible, which means you will pay the first $500 worth of medical expenses in any given year. After you have paid that amount, your insurance company will begin to pay for some of the covered expenses. The deductible removes some of the financial burden from the insurance company. As a result, you will find that the higher the deductible, the lower your cost for insurance. Policies exist that have very high deductibles—many thousands of dollars—and comparatively low premiums. In effect, these policies trade lower insurance costs for higher risk of out-of-pocket expenses.

Coverage Limits

Many policies limit the total amount they will pay for certain procedures. Some policies may exclude some procedures completely—for example, voluntary surgeries to correct eyesight or improve appearance. Typically, experimental treatments are not covered. Many policies limit the number of days of hospital care they will pay for or the frequency of certain treatments. If you have a bill that exceeds your policy's coverage limits, you have to pay the difference.

Policies differ on coverage for prescription drugs. Some policies cover them, others do not. Some cover only certain drugs or provide only partial payment for unapproved drugs.

MATH for Personal Finance

Michael needs laser eye surgery to correct his vision. After a visit to the ophthalmologist, he learns that the surgery will cost about $4,500 but that the procedure is not covered.

How much will Michael be required to pay for the surgery?

Solution: Michael will be responsible for the entire cost of the surgery ($4,500) because it is not a covered procedure.

Jontell needs surgery on her foot. Assume that she has insurance and the surgery cost $5,000 and she has a $500 deductible. She also has 20 percent co-pay.

How much will Jontell have to pay for the surgery?

Solution: Jontell will have to pay the $500 deductible and then 20 percent of the remaining amount. Therefore, she will pay $500 + .20($5,000 − $500) = $1,400.

You Do It

Activity #1

Coinsurance

Coinsurance is the term for the share of costs for covered services that the insured person is required to pay out of his or her pocket. Coinsurance is often called a co-pay. For example, many policies have a $20 co-pay for a doctor's visit. That is, when you visit a doctor, you pay $20 and the insurance company pays the rest. Usually, co-pay amounts apply to most medical services. In many cases, you will be required to pay 20 percent of the cost of the treatment.

Provider Networks

Managed health care plans limit your choice of health care provider to a specific list of physicians and other medical professionals. Getting care from someone outside of this network may not be covered or may require a higher co-pay.

The two most common types of provider networks are Health Maintenance Organizations (HMOs) and Preferred Provider Organizations (PPOs). HMOs are based on negotiated agreements with specific doctors to provide health care. Individuals choose a primary care physician from an approved list and must be referred for any additional specialized care. That primary care doctor may approve and arrange for care from a specialist— and set limits on the number of times the patient may visit. PPOs function similarly, but they generally provide a larger network of providers. In return for this greater flexibility, PPOs typically cost more than HMOs. Refer to Figure 7.3 for a comparison of the different types of private health insurance plans. Remember, some policies limit a policyholder's ability to see a specialist.

Auto Policies

Your automobile insurance will contain limited accident coverage. It may pay a portion of your medical costs associated with a vehicle accident.

✓ CHECK Your Financial IQ

Why is it important to understand the different features and terms used in health care plans?

Figure 7.3 Comparison of Private Health Insurance Plans

The different terms and features of different managed care plans can be bewildering.

Type of Private Health Plan	Premium	Selection of Physician
Indemnity Plan	High	Flexibility to select physician or specialist
Managed care: HMOs	Relatively low	Primary care physician refers patients to specialist
Managed care: PPOs	Low, but usually higher than HMOs	There is a greater number of physicians to choose from in PPOs than in HMOs

Jontell's injury prompted her to begin thinking about insurance needs. She understood the importance of having health insurance, but she wondered about life insurance. What, exactly, was it? Did she have any? Did she need any? If so, how much should she buy?

Life insurance provides a payment to a specific person or persons when the policyholder dies. The person who receives the payment is known as a **beneficiary**. For example, a $100,000 life insurance policy in your name would pay your beneficiary $100,000 if you died. (Life insurance payments are not subject to income taxes.) Much like health insurance, people buy life insurance from a company. These policyholders pay periodic premiums. Many employers also provide fully or partially paid life insurance coverage for their employees as a benefit.

Life insurance helps protect a family from financial disaster in the event of a loss of income.

Role of Life Insurance

Life insurance is a component of your financial plan. Whether you need life insurance and how much to purchase depends on your financial goals. The most common financial goal or reason for buying life insurance is to make sure that those who depend on you have financial support in the event of your death. In most cases, life insurance is more critical for someone who provides income for the household. That is, it helps ensure that a breadwinner's death does not eliminate all cash coming into the household. In Jontell's case, she may not need much life insurance. Does anyone depend on her income to live?

The primary consideration for Jontell is whether she wants to provide some support for her parents in the event of her death. Sometimes, people carry a bit of life insurance to cover the costs incurred when they die. After all, "final expenses"—a funeral, cemetery plot, headstone, and so on can total several thousand dollars. Additionally, some people decide that it is wise to get a policy when they are young and healthy, because life insurance can be costly or difficult to obtain as people get older—and perhaps experience serious illness.

For these reasons, Jontell may want to think about her life insurance options. So, she will need to learn a little about the main types of life insurance.

MATH for Personal Finance

The premiums to Janice's $200,000 whole life policy total $1,300 a year. A term insurance policy for $200,000 might cost Janice $400 in premiums. Janice bought the term policy and invested the difference, earning a rate of 8 percent.

How much money could she "make" in a year?

Solution: Janice would have $900 to invest. $900 × .08 = $72.

Types of Life Insurance

Life insurance comes in several different forms. They include term insurance, whole life insurance, and universal life insurance. These forms differ in how long they provide coverage, how much they cost, and whether or not they provide any sort of benefit besides a payment at death.

Whole life insurance, sometimes referred to as permanent insurance, provides coverage for as long as the policyholder continues to pay the premium. These types of policies also build up savings for the policyholder over time. That is, part of what you pay in premiums goes into an account that grows. As this account builds a "cash value," you may be able to borrow against it or even take cash out. At some point, the cash value of the policy may be used to pay your premiums until your death. Whole life

insurance policies can serve as a source of liquidity and as a kind of investment in your financial plan.

Term insurance is life insurance provided over a specific period of time. This period usually ranges between 5 and 20 years. Unlike whole life insurance, a term insurance policy builds no savings and does not serve as an investment. For these reasons, it generally has lower premiums.

Let's say a single mother with young children purchases a $100,000 benefit 20-year term life policy with her children named as beneficiaries. She would pay premiums to the insurance company. If the mother were to die during the 20-year term, the policy would pay the $100,000 benefit to her children. If she did not die during the 20-year term, the policy would simply expire. There would be no savings, and no more coverage.

Universal life insurance provides coverage for a specified term and builds savings for the policyholder. Therefore, it is a combination of term insurance and whole life insurance. Universal life allows more flexibility than other types of life insurance. You can add units of term coverage for periods of time and also alter your payments during your life. You may increase the size of your payment, and the additional amount will be invested. You may have choices about how that money is invested.

You Do It

Activity #2

✓ **CHECK Your Financial IQ**

What is the main purpose for buying life insurance?

GETTING INSURANCE

In recent times, most Americans have relied on their employers for access to health insurance. Employers often provide access to term life insurance, too. In many cases, employers pay some or even all the premiums for health or life insurance. They may also provide coverage to family members of the employee.

The availability of employer-provided coverage is significant for a number of reasons. For one thing, insurance is costly. Employer-provided benefits of this sort can represent a significant amount of money—and a large share of an employee's overall compensation.

Additionally, employer-provided plans generally provide coverage to employees and their families that they may have trouble getting on their own. Remember, people who have had health problems in the past may find it difficult or very expensive to buy individual health or life insurance. After all, insurers are not anxious to take on high risks. But if they become part of an employer's group plan, they will pay no more than any other employee of that company.

There are also laws that help ensure that a person who leaves a job can continue to get access to health coverage—even if he or she has developed a serious health problem. The Health Insurance Portability and Accounting Act (**HIPAA**) ensures that workers can continue their health insurance coverage even if they switch jobs. This act prohibits insurance companies from denying new employees access to coverage based on their health or preexisting conditions. In addition, the Consolidated Omnibus Budget Reconciliation Act (**COBRA**), allows you to continue health insurance coverage for up to 18 months after your employment ends. You will, of course, be required to pay the premiums that your previous employer was paying for your coverage. COBRA and HIPAA make sure that people switching jobs have a way to maintain health insurance coverage during and after the switch. Finally, some companies even offer employees a chance to get health coverage after retirement.

Clearly, access to employer provided health and life insurance can be a valuable benefit. But the trend in recent years is not favorable for employees of tomorrow. Health care costs are soaring in the United States. Each year, fewer and fewer employers offer health benefits to their employees. Those who offer coverage are asking employees to pay a growing share of the premiums. The availability of health benefits looms as a major challenge facing workers of tomorrow. It is certainly a factor you will need to consider when thinking about future jobs and careers.

Employers often provide a host of other insurance-related benefits. One important type is **disability insurance**, which provides regular payments to replace lost income in the event injury or illness makes it impossible to work. Other common employer-provided benefits include dental insurance, vision insurance, and other supplemental insurance policies designed to cover specific diseases such as cancer or heart disease.

There may come a time when you have to purchase health and life insurance on your own. For example, you may lose employer health coverage for a time when you switch jobs and your 18-month COBRA period has expired. Or you may decide that you want additional life insurance besides that provided by your employer. You may also decide you want to have a policy in place if you lose your job. And, if your employer does not offer it, or if you are self-employed, you may want to buy disability insurance. In many cases, unions, trade associations, and guilds may offer members the opportunity to purchase these insurance coverages at a reduced rate.

Insurance is like any other product you purchase. There are various kinds of coverage and prices. The Internet can help you learn about the many different types of products and services. Some Web sites will help you find a company that will provide the coverage you desire for the best price. You may want to visit an insurance agent to discuss options. In any case, it is always best to shop around and compare products. Choosing insurance coverage is a major financial decision and should be made with as much information as possible about your options. Remember that health, life, and disability insurance costs also vary according to your age and health history. To receive accurate quotes, companies will ask you to fill out personal information regarding your and your family's health history. You may even need to get a physical exam before receiving coverage.

Note also that when you buy a life insurance policy, you need to be aware of the financial strength of the company. After all, you are counting on that company being able to pay a large amount of money at some unknown time in the future. There are a number of companies that rate the strength of insurers. Be sure you check the ratings of the companies you are considering, and avoid those with low ratings.

✓ CHECK Your Financial IQ

What has been the most common means of obtaining health insurance in recent years?

Summary

- Insurance is the promise of payment to be made in the event of some kind of loss. Health insurance provides payment to policyholders who suffer a loss as a result of illness or injury. Health insurance is available in different forms: government programs, such as Medicare or Medicaid, or private companies, which make money by selling health insurance policies. Employers can offer health insurance through a group plan for their employees as a benefit.

- Insurance plans come in many forms and provide a range of coverage and services. Some issues to be aware of when considering insurance programs include the following: family coverage, location, preexisting conditions, cancellation options, deductibles, coverage limits, coinsurance, provider networks, referral limits, prescription coverage, and student policies.

- Life insurance is a component of your financial plan. The most common financial goal or reason for buying life insurance is to make sure your dependents have financial support in the event of your death. There are several options available, including term insurance, whole life insurance, and universal life insurance.

- Employers are a main source of insurance, but an individual may purchase health or life insurance. Insurance is like any other product: It is essential that you purchase it only after thoroughly investigating the options.

Key Terms and Vocabulary

Beneficiary	Liability
COBRA	Life insurance
Coinsurance	Medicaid
Deductible	Medicare
Disability insurance	Policyholder
Fraud	Preexisting condition
Group plan	Premium
Health insurance	Term insurance
HIPAA	Universal life insurance
Insurance	Whole life insurance

What Do You Know?

myFinLitlab

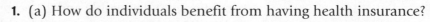

1. (a) How do individuals benefit from having health insurance?

   (b) Why is health insurance likely to become a bigger and more complex issue in the future?

2. (a) What are the sources from which an individual can obtain health insurance?

   (b) Why do you think the government provides insurance to older and poorer Americans?

3. (a) What is a group plan?

   (b) What are the advantages of group plans?

   (c) Why do you think insurance companies are willing to offer coverage to large groups that may include people with high risks?

4. (a) What is a deductible?

   (b) What kind of person might be a good candidate for a high-deductible health insurance policy?

5. (a) What is the purpose of life insurance?

   (b) If a young person had to choose between buying health insurance and life insurance, which might he or she choose, and why?

6. (a) What is the difference between term insurance, whole life insurance, and universal life insurance?

   (b) Which might be the best choice for a young parent living on a tight budget? Explain.

7. (a) What benefit does whole life insurance provide that term insurance does not?

8. (a) What is disability insurance?

   (b) Why might younger individuals consider purchasing disability insurance?

9. (a) What are two types of health insurance that might be offered by an employer?

10. (a) Why might someone purchase insurance on their own?

    (b) Why is research so important when choosing insurance coverage?

What Are Your Finance Math Skills?   myFinLitlab.

The first three questions correlate to the *Math for Personal Finance* features located throughout the chapter.

1. The insurance policy provided by Darrell's company has a $1,000 deductible and a 20 percent co-pay. How much will he have to pay for elbow surgery that will cost $9,000?

2. Gracie's insurance premiums are $131 per month. This year she also paid a $500 deductible and 20 percent of $3,200 for a minor accident. How much was her total health care expense this year?

3. Candice paid $2,000 for her whole life insurance policy this year. A term insurance policy with the same coverage would cost her about

$700 a year. Assuming she decides to buy the term policy and invest the difference, earning a rate of 6 percent, how much money could she "make" in a year?

4. Jaden carried her receipt for the doctor visit to the cashier. The amount billed was $112 and she has $20 co-pay. How much will Jaden be required to pay?

5. Kevin was paying $250 a month for his health insurance coverage that had a $200 deductible. He dropped that coverage for a $50-a-month policy that had a $5,000 deductible. Assuming Kevin had no health care costs, how long would it take Kevin to save enough with his high-deductible plan to pay for a possible $5,000 out-of-pocket expense?

6. Jamarcus's employer pays 80 percent of his medical insurance. If the insurance costs Jamarcus $20 a week, how much is his employer paying?

7. Michelle listed her three children as equal beneficiaries on her life insurance policy. If she has a $400,000 policy, how much will each receive in the event of her death?

8. Brittany needs to buy some term life insurance. She has evaluated two 20-year fixed premium policies. One policy will cost $30 a month for $100,000 in coverage. The other will cost $40 a month for $150,000 in coverage. Which policy is a better deal?

What Would You Do?

Ethan is 18 and a recent high school graduate. His part-time employer through high school now wants him to work full time. He really enjoys the work and decides to go for it. The only problem is the job does not offer health insurance benefits. Ethan goes online to look for a health insurance company that offers benefits he can afford. Many of the companies ask the same questions. As he is filling out the information for quotes, he is uncertain how to respond to one of the questions. All the companies want to know if he smokes. Ethan does not smoke every day, but he does like to have a cigarette or two when he is out with his friends on weekends. Ethan is not sure why the insurance companies want to know this information. He thinks that smoking only one or two evenings a week is not bad. What could it hurt? Still, he is unclear what he should say when asked this question.

1. What should Ethan do? Should he tell the companies that he smokes occasionally? Explain your answer.

2. Is someone who smokes only on the weekends when out with friends a "smoker"?

3. Why do you think insurance companies want to know if a person smokes?

4. Is there an ethics issue if Ethan tells the companies he does not smoke? What does Ethan stand to lose if he tells the companies that he does not smoke?

What Are the Connections?
Technology, Language Arts, and Math

Research the possible costs of health insurance. If you have access to the Internet, go to **ehealthinsurance.com**. If not, contact a local insurance agent for a quote.

1. Obtain health insurance estimates for yourself by providing your birth date and some personal information. How do the resulting plans differ? Which plan do you find most attractive? Why?

2. Now obtain dental insurance estimates by providing some personal information. Which plan do you find most attractive? Why?

3. If you have access to spreadsheet software, design a spreadsheet of the data you have obtained. If not, use paper and pencil to design the spreadsheet. Prepare a presentation of the data that helps to explain your decision for health and dental insurance.

Teamwork Service-Learning Activity

In a team, use the Internet to research health care insurance fraud. Develop a newsletter providing information about insurance fraud. Your newsletter might include information on the costs of insurance fraud to others, how insurance fraud makes health care costs rise, tips on reporting insurance fraud, and the consequences of being suspected of insurance fraud. Your newsletter could also be a Web page, multimedia presentation, or other form of getting the word out about this important subject.

---

w!se | **Financial Literacy CERTIFICATION**

TEST PREP QUESTIONS

myFinLitlab

1. The reason that a person buys health or life insurance is to
   a. make sure that he will earn an income if he becomes ill or injured.
   b. limit the amount of financial loss if there is an illness, injury, or loss of life.
   c. have protection from being sued if another person is injured while visiting his home.
   d. guarantee that the person will not suffer any loss in a natural disaster such as an earthquake or hurricane.

2. Usually the least expensive way for a person to obtain health insurance is by
   a. enrolling in an employer-provided health care plan.
   b. purchasing the insurance through a private company.
   c. using the services of the local hospital emergency room.
   d. enrolling in Medicare.

3. A young, healthy, athletic woman receives her monthly insurance premium notice. Her premium has increased to $350 a month. She decides to drop her insurance, reasoning that she can better spend her

money on a gym membership and yoga classes to relieve the stress in her back. She decides that dropping this health insurance will also enable her to start saving money in an IRA. This is a

a. good idea because she will be getting what she needs to keep her from getting sick or injured.
b. good idea because if she is really sick or injured, she will just go to the nearest hospital emergency room.
c. bad idea because one bad illness or even a small injury can wipe out all of her savings.
d. bad idea because most companies will not hire a person who does not have her own insurance.

4. Which insurance term is *not* correctly matched with its description?
   a. Indemnity insurance plan: permits the policyholder to obtain treatment from any health care provider.
   b. Group insurance plan: covers a large number of people and reduces the premium cost to any one person by spreading risk across many people.
   c. Managed care: restricts a person to use only participating providers of health care; those who belong to the health care plan.
   d. Family coverage: the policyholder pays a lower premium in order to obtain coverage for all members of the family as long as they live at home.

5. A person submitted his claim for reimbursement of medical expenses to his insurance company and his claim was denied. Recently he switched insurance coverage. His former insurance company always paid for the injections he received to calm down the arthritis in his knee. What is the most likely reason that the new insurance would not pay for his treatment?
   a. They consider his knee problem to be a preexisting condition and will not cover any claims for this problem until he goes two years without making a claim for his knee problems.
   b. He has not paid his coinsurance to the doctor for the services that were performed.
   c. Since this is his first claim of the year, he has not met his annual deductible so the claim was rejected.
   d. He has a family coverage plan and his daughter recently had to go to the doctor with a knee injury from playing soccer and her claim used up the family's coverage.

6. A person with insurance coverage ends up in the hospital with a broken wrist suffered while playing football with a group of friends. After an X-ray, MRI, doctor visit, orthopedist visit, and cast he leaves the hospital with a bill for $9,000. He has a $2,000 annual deductible and this is his first visit to a doctor in this calendar year. He also has a 20 percent co-pay. The amount that he is responsible for paying is
   a. $3,400.
   b. nothing since he did not need to stay overnight in the hospital.
   c. only the $2,000 annual deductible.
   d. $1,800.

7. A person decides that she needs braces to correct her teeth. Her orthodontist agrees and tells her that it will take about 18 months to correct her teeth completely and the work will cost $7,500. Her insurance company says that this is cosmetic work and therefore it is not covered by her plan. If she goes ahead with this dental work, she will have to pay
   a. $1,500, the coinsurance.
   b. $7,500, the full amount.
   c. $2,000, the annual deductible.
   d. $2,000, the annual deductible for the first year and $1,000, half the annual deductible for the final six months.

8. Rebecca and Eduardo have medical insurance through their employers; Rebecca's coverage is through an HMO and Eduardo's is through a PPO. Which of the following is a true statement about the probable difference in coverage each will receive?
   a. Rebecca's monthly premiums will probably be higher than Eduardo's.
   b. Eduardo will probably have a larger provider network from which to choose doctors.
   c. Eduardo will be able to go to any doctor he chooses.
   d. Rebecca will be able to go to any specialist she chooses.

9. Even though Preferred Provider Organizations (PPOs) usually charge a higher premium for insurance coverage than Health Maintenance Organizations (HMOs), people are often willing to pay the difference because they know that the
   a. HMO doctors are usually new doctors without much experience.
   b. HMO only covers the first visit to a doctor; after that, the person has to pay out-of-pocket.
   c. PPO usually has a greater number of doctors from which the person can select a primary care doctor and specialists.
   d. PPO covers the cost of as many doctors' visits as necessary to treat a condition.

10. The purpose of life insurance is to
   a. provide funds to help a person's beneficiaries maintain a certain standard of living should the policyholder die.
   b. pay for large purchases such as a home or college education while the person is alive.
   c. cover the cost of nursing care and other expenses not covered by a person's health insurance.
   d. provide financial support for a policyholder's parents should they need to go into a nursing home.

11. Since it is true that a term life insurance policy expires at the end of the term and there are no accumulated savings, why would a single 38-year-old father of three children under the age of five decide to buy a 20-year term policy instead of a whole life policy?
   a. He will be ready to retire in 20 years and then his children can support him.
   b. Compared to whole life insurance, he can buy much more coverage for his children in case of his death for a relatively low price.

c. Term life insurance will cover the cost of paying for college for his three children even if he is still alive.

d. Term life insurance is designed for single people and single parents; whole life insurance is designed for married couples.

12. A young, healthy single person without dependents decides that she is going to buy a whole life policy that is offered where she works. Since she is engaged and is hoping to have children within five years, she thinks that buying this insurance is a good move. Is this a wise financial decision?

a. No. She should just buy five-year term insurance now.

b. Yes. She is young and healthy and she will get a good rate on the insurance and will have it when her family may really need it.

c. Yes. This is a way to make sure that she will be able to pay for her children's education when they reach college age.

d. No. She would be spending money on something she may not need for years.

13. A person is trying to decide between buying term life insurance and whole life insurance when someone suggests that he consider buying a universal life policy. What is an advantage of universal life that attracts many people to this financial product?

a. It is considered the most flexible type of life insurance because it combines the ability to accumulate savings and extend the policy's term.

b. It is less expensive than other forms of life insurance.

c. It pays the insured person the full face value of the policy even if the person lives beyond the term of the policy.

d. It can help a person pay off other debts by cashing in the policy for its full face value after five years.

14. A person had breast cancer while employed by a company. She was treated and has been cancer free for eight years. She has a wonderful offer for a top position at a new company but she is worried that she will not be able to get health insurance coverage. Should she worry?

a. Yes. Because she has a preexisting condition, the new company's insurance plan can refuse to cover her.

b. No. Workers are protected by law from being denied insurance if they switch jobs even if they have a preexisting condition.

c. Yes. The new company's insurance plan is only required to cover her for 18 months.

d. No. She can buy her own insurance from a private company even though it will be very expensive.

15. What is a true statement about insurance?

a. Health, life, and disability insurance premiums are the same for everyone who is less than age 65.

b. As the cost of insurance has risen, more companies are cutting back on employee coverage or requiring employees to pay a larger share of the premiums.

c. A person who is self-employed is not able to purchase disability or health insurance.

d. When a person receives information from one company on how much she will have to pay for insurance, she can anticipate that other insurance companies will charge her almost identical rates.

CHAPTER 8

Learning Objectives

Explain how economic factors impact financial decisions.

Analyze how demographic changes will impact your future.

Analyze how events in the national and global economy might affect you.

Key Terms

Business cycle
Consumer price index
Depression
Economics
Economy
Global economy
Gross domestic product
Inflation
Recession

The Economy and You

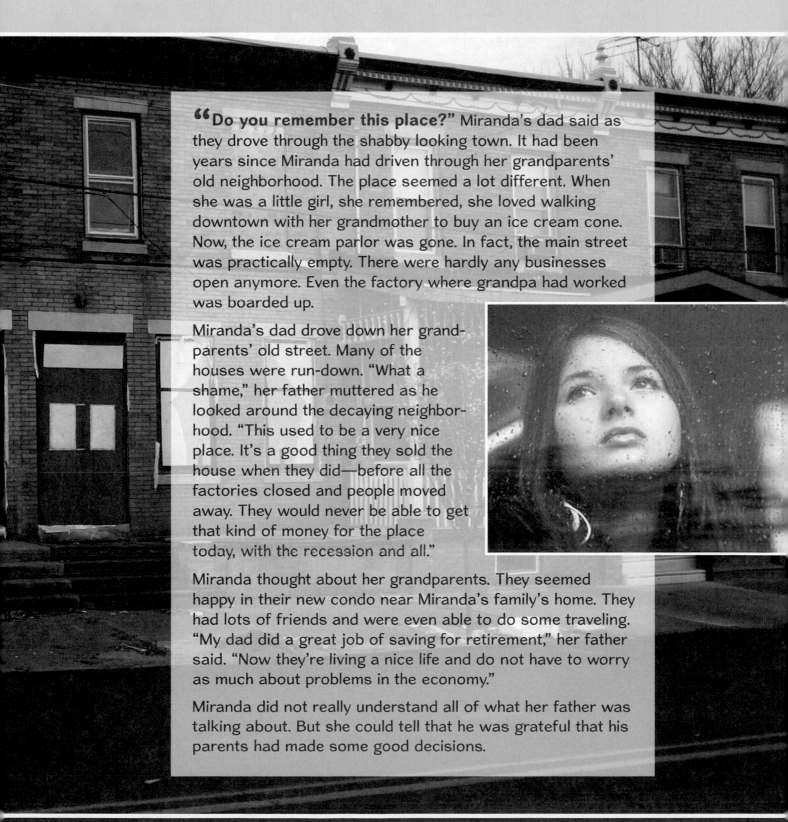

"Do you remember this place?" Miranda's dad said as they drove through the shabby looking town. It had been years since Miranda had driven through her grandparents' old neighborhood. The place seemed a lot different. When she was a little girl, she remembered, she loved walking downtown with her grandmother to buy an ice cream cone. Now, the ice cream parlor was gone. In fact, the main street was practically empty. There were hardly any businesses open anymore. Even the factory where grandpa had worked was boarded up.

Miranda's dad drove down her grandparents' old street. Many of the houses were run-down. "What a shame," her father muttered as he looked around the decaying neighborhood. "This used to be a very nice place. It's a good thing they sold the house when they did—before all the factories closed and people moved away. They would never be able to get that kind of money for the place today, with the recession and all."

Miranda thought about her grandparents. They seemed happy in their new condo near Miranda's family's home. They had lots of friends and were even able to do some traveling. "My dad did a great job of saving for retirement," her father said. "Now they're living a nice life and do not have to worry as much about problems in the economy."

Miranda did not really understand all of what her father was talking about. But she could tell that he was grateful that his parents had made some good decisions.

Miranda may not have understood everything her father said. But she and her family provide a great lesson in the way the economy can affect us. In this chapter, we will look at how global events can impact our financial planning.

ECONOMICS AND YOUR FINANCIAL PLAN

Economics is often defined as the study of choices: Economists assume that people cannot simply have everything they need and want. They must decide what they will seek, how they will seek it—and what they will do without. Economists seek to understand ways that these decisions are made, the factors that influence them, and the impact those decisions have on others.

Each of you makes economic decisions every day. In fact, almost every decision we make could be viewed as an economic decision. How much did you spend on lunch today? What options did you pass up when you made that decision? Will you go to a movie this weekend? Or will you save your money in order to buy the more costly concert tickets? Larger decisions might involve what kind of education or job training you seek, or whether to start a new business.

In economics, we study choices made by individuals. We also study the decisions of businesses and governments, and the world as a whole. The system in which all these different people and groups interact is called the **economy**.

While economics is not the main subject of this text, it is not hard to see how it might affect your financial life. As you have read, building a financial plan involves making choices. In addition, the choices or actions of others can have a big effect on you. In Miranda's grandparent's case, they made good decisions to save well for retirement and to sell their home at a time when they could get a good price for it. These good decisions helped protect them from the effects of events over which they had no control— the closing of factories and the start of an economic downturn.

We will now look at several broad economic issues and concepts that are likely to shape your economic world. Understanding or at least being aware of these issues and concepts can help you formulate your plans and make your decisions.

Broad trends in the economy can have a powerful impact on the economic well-being of a particular community.

Bear in mind that economics is broken into two categories: macroeconomics and microeconomics. **Macroeconomics** deals with broad issues that impact the economy as a whole. **Microeconomics** focuses on the study of individual choices or decisions made by smaller units, such as a firm. While most of the issues we discuss in this chapter are macroeconomic issues, we will present them so that you can think about how they impact you on a micro level. Our goal is to provide a simple overview of economic issues; therefore, we will leave the more detailed study of supply and demand issues and the related graphic analysis to be covered in your economics course.

 CHECK Your Financial IQ

What does the study of economics have to do with your financial plan?

DEMOGRAPHIC FACTORS

Demographics is the study of human populations. Demographers look at groups of people and their unique combination of features such as race, education, gender, and age. Understanding demographics can help us predict certain needs in advance. For example, if the number of grade school age students is increasing in a certain community, we can predict that high school enrollments will increase in the near future. That community may need to plan to build more classroom space or otherwise plan to meet the need.

We can also examine demographic trends in the whole country's population. For example, two important demographic trends that will impact everyone in the United States are the "graying of America" and increased immigration. A related challenge is the future of the Social Security system.

The Graying of America

The "graying of America" refers to the fact that the number of older people in the United States is increasing at a faster rate than that of other age groups. Why is this happening? One reason is the so-called "baby boom." The **baby boom** was a period of very high birthrates that occurred between 1946 and 1964. Families started after World War II produced children in large numbers. In fact, people born during that time—baby boomers—make up about one-third of the United States labor force today. The leading edge of this group is beginning to reach retirement age. What does this mean to you?

For one thing, boomers are beginning to leave their jobs, which will open up opportunities in numerous fields. While many companies will offer options to retain some of these older workers, many boomers will opt to retire. In fact, the United States workforce grew by about 30 percent during the 1970s and is expected to level off by 2010. This population shift will open positions and create opportunities for rapid advancement in almost every field.

The pending retirement of the baby boomers will also have other effects. After all, older people have a unique set of needs and wants. What types of

goods and services will this group demand? Jobs in health care and other services that serve older people will be in high demand. Historically, many retired people relocate to warmer locations. Will housing choices change for this gray population? Are there opportunities to start your own company or enter an industry that is in position to take advantage of these trends? Do you need to be concerned about how the behavior of retirees might affect housing prices where you live? Think about how these coming changes will reshape your community and create new opportunities and challenges.

You Do It
Activity #1

Immigration

In recent decades, immigration changes have also produced some important demographic changes in the United States. Hispanic Americans are a rapidly growing share of the population. In many parts of the country, this group already forms the majority. How does this impact you? Jobs that cater to the needs of Hispanic Americans will be in high demand. If you don't already speak Spanish, you might decide to learn the language in order to create more opportunities for your career advancement.

These are just two examples of demographic trends that will reshape the United States in the years ahead. All students should consider the impact of coming shifts on career decisions.

Professor FIN

Facts about the "graying of America":

- Because of healthier lifestyles, Americans have added 25 years to their life spans over the last several decades. In 2005, there were 36 million Americans over the age of 65. By 2020, this number is expected to be closer to 55 million.

- One million Americans turn age 60 every month!

Social Security

When you receive a paycheck from your employer, you will find that FICA taxes are deducted from your total earnings. These taxes are withheld to pay for the Social Security system. Many retirees rely on Social Security payments for at least part of their living expenses when they stop working.

When the United States government first established Social Security, there were a lot of people paying into the system and very few drawing money out. As recently as 1950, there were more than 16 workers paying FICA taxes for every one person receiving Social Security benefits. Today, that ratio is about 3.3 workers paying taxes for every one person drawing retirement. In Figure 8.1, you can see that in about 25 years, there will be just over two workers for every one person drawing Social Security.

Now remember the demographic discussion. Seventy-six million baby boomers will retire within the next 20 years. Who will pay for their

Professor FIN

Historians sometimes come up with names to describe major demographic groups or trends. Here are a few examples:

- Silent Generation—born between 1925 and 1945
- Baby Boomers—born between 1946 and 1964
- Generation X—born between 1964 and 1981
- Generation XY Cusp (MTV Generation)—born between 1975 and 1986
- Generation Y (Echo Boomers or Millennials)—born between 1981 and 2001
- Generation Z (Homelanders or Vista Generation)—born after 2001

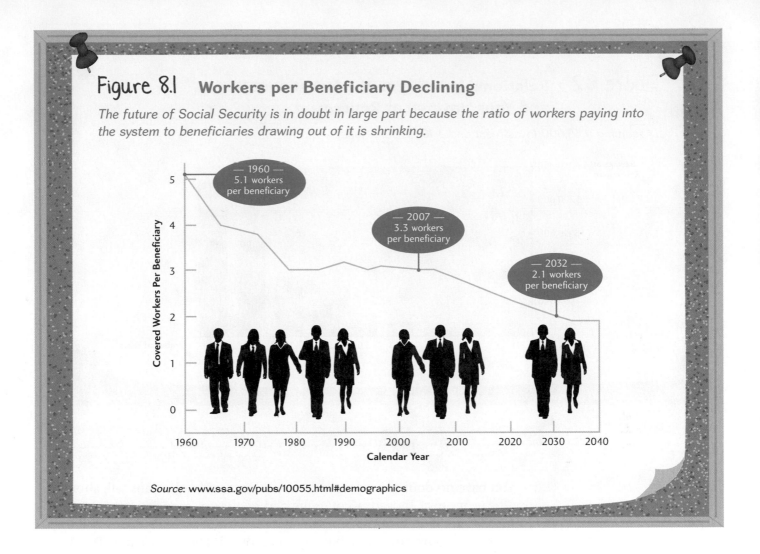

Figure 8.1 **Workers per Beneficiary Declining**

The future of Social Security is in doubt in large part because the ratio of workers paying into the system to beneficiaries drawing out of it is shrinking.

— 1960 —
5.1 workers
per beneficiary

— 2007 —
3.3 workers
per beneficiary

— 2032 —
2.1 workers
per beneficiary

Source: www.ssa.gov/pubs/10055.html#demographics

MATH for Personal Finance

Assume that by 2040 there are 110 million workers in the labor force and 61 million retirees drawing Social Security.

How many workers will be paying in per retiree in 2040?

Solution: 110 / 61 = 1.8 workers per retiree.

retirement? Many of you will see that your FICA tax may increase to cover these promised benefits. You also may see benefits reduced for future retirees—you. What does that mean to your financial plan? You should count on being responsible for a greater share—perhaps even all—of your own retirement.

In fact, wise people have always saved money above and beyond what they could expect from Social Security. Think again about Miranda's grandparents. They saved money during their working years, and as a result they are now enjoying a good quality of life. As a young person, time is clearly on your side. You can enjoy a comfortable retirement if you plan for it. Remember, the financial plan is a road map to achieving your goals in life. If you want to retire with plenty of money with which to do what you want, map out your path. In Figure 8.2, you can see a how even a small investment can help you accumulate a large sum of money for your retirement.

☑ **CHECK Your Financial IQ**

What are some demographic trends that may affect your financial future?

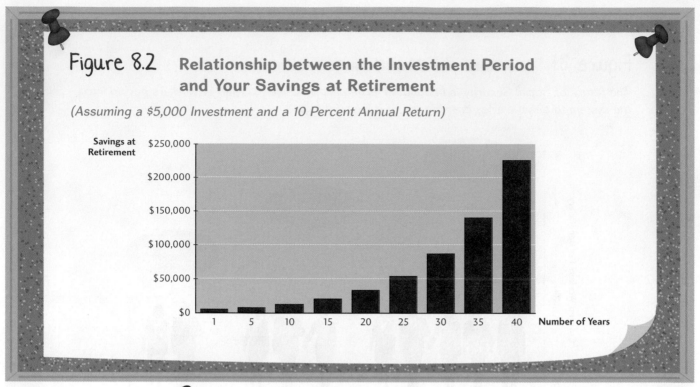

Figure 8.2 Relationship between the Investment Period and Your Savings at Retirement

(Assuming a $5,000 Investment and a 10 Percent Annual Return)

Savings at Retirement — Number of Years

FACTORS IN THE LARGER ECONOMY

You have no doubt heard news commentators and politicians talk about "the economy." Indeed, all of us are part of a larger economic system, which may at one time or another be doing well—or not so well. The overall trends in the economy can have a big impact on our financial decisions. That is why it is important to have a basic understanding of how the economy generally behaves, and about significant factors that can shape its future.

Business Cycles

One of the ways we measure national economic activity is by keeping track of the total dollar amount of all final goods and services purchased in a given year. This dollar amount is known as the **gross domestic product**, or GDP. Looking at the GDP and how it changes over time helps us see how strong the economy is. Refer to Figure 8.3 to see how the economy has grown over the past several decades. Note that "real" GDP factors in inflation.

When GDP is higher from one year to the next, it means businesses and individuals are selling more goods and services and the economy is growing. People, in general, are earning higher incomes. When GDP is lower, it means fewer goods and services are being sold and the economy is shrinking. A period of time in which the economy is shrinking is known as a **recession**. A **depression** is a severe recession. During these times, the risk of job loss is much higher as many businesses are forced to lay off workers.

Historically, the economy goes through alternating periods of shrinking and growth, or expansion. This pattern is known as the **business cycle**. The business cycle, shown in Figure 8.4, is one full period of economic growth followed by a period of recession. Recessions are characterized by fewer goods being sold and higher levels of unemployment.

MATH for Personal Finance

Factory X in the United States pays 200 workers a total of $7 million each year to produce 1.5 million widgets. Foreign factory Y employs 150 workers at a total cost of $750,000 to produce 750,000 widgets.

How do the costs per widget of the American and foreign factory compare?

Solution: The cost per widget in the United States is $7 million/1.5 million, or $4.67 per widget. The cost per widget overseas is $750,000/750,000, or $1 per widget.

Figure 8.3 Current-Dollar and "Real" Gross Domestic Product

	Annual			**Annual**	
	GDP in billions of current dollars	GDP in billions of chained 2000 dollars		GDP in billions of current dollars	GDP in billions of chained 2000 dollars
1970	1,038.5	3,771.9	1990	5,803.1	7,112.5
1971	1,127.1	3,898.6	1991	5,995.9	7,100.5
1972	1,238.3	4,105.0	1992	6,337.7	7,336.6
1973	1,382.7	4,341.5	1993	6,657.4	7,532.7
1974	1,500.0	4,319.6	1994	7,072.2	7,835.5
1975	1,638.3	4,311.2	1995	7,397.7	8,031.7
1976	1,825.3	4,540.9	1996	7,816.9	8,328.9
1977	2,030.9	4,750.5	1997	8,304.3	8,703.5
1978	2,294.7	5,015.0	1998	8,747.0	9,066.9
1979	2,563.3	5,173.4	1999	9,268.4	9,470.3
1980	2,789.5	5,161.7	2000	9,817.0	9,817.0
1981	3,128.4	5,291.7	2001	10,128.0	9,890.7
1982	3,255.0	5,189.3	2002	10,469.6	10,048.8
1983	3,536.7	5,423.8	2003	10,960.8	10,301.0
1984	3,933.2	5,813.6	2004	11,685.9	10,675.8
1985	4,220.3	6,053.7	2005	12,433.9	11,003.4
1986	4,462.8	6,263.6	2006	13,194.7	11,319.4
1987	4,739.5	6,475.1	2007	13,841.3	11,566.8
1988	5,103.8	6,742.7			6/26/2008
1989	5,484.4	6,981.4			

Source: www.bea.gov/national/xls/gdplev.xls

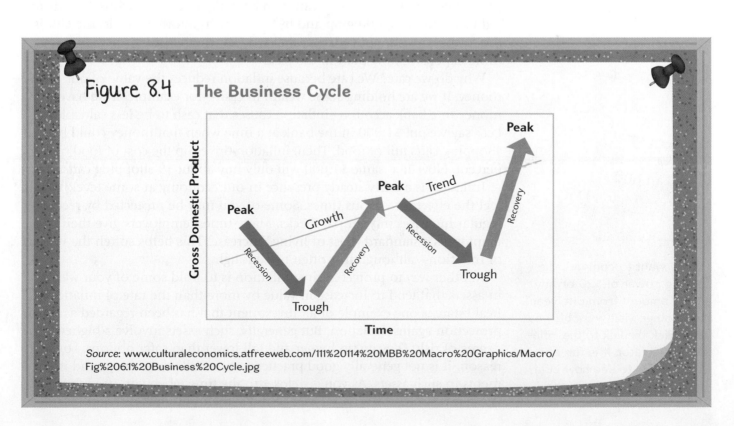

Figure 8.4 The Business Cycle

Source: www.culturaleconomics.atfreeweb.com/111%20114%20MBB%20Macro%20Graphics/Macro/Fig%206.1%20Business%20Cycle.jpg

So how does the business cycle affect you? It is important to know that the cycle exists and that good times are always followed by bad times—which are followed again by good times. With regard to financial planning, you need to prepare during good times for the next recession. Set aside an emergency fund that will enable you to continue to pay your bills in the event of a layoff. Store up some reserves during the good economic times and live off these reserves if the economy negatively impacts your finances.

Understanding the business cycle can also help you make basic life decisions. Miranda's grandparents may have had the business cycle in mind when they sold their house during good times. And, if you were thinking of making a career change, you might consider the state of the economy. After all, it is generally much harder to find a new job during a recession than during a time of expansion. Even if you find a job, you may be first in line to be let go if the economy worsens.

Inflation and Purchasing Power

Inflation is defined as a sustained increase in the general level of prices. In other words, during a time of inflation, most things get more expensive. When inflation occurs, the purchasing power of your money goes down. Many of you may be seeing some indication of inflation. Has the price of movie tickets increased in the past few years? What about eating in a restaurant? One way of looking at inflation is to say that $20 will not buy as much today as it bought a few years ago.

The way economists measure inflation is to look up prices on a set of about 300 goods and services that most people consume during the year. Clothing, groceries, and electronic goods are all part of this "market basket" of goods. Haircuts, medical care, education, and other expenditures are also included. This price data is then used to construct the **consumer price index**, or CPI. The CPI can then be compared to previous periods to tell us if prices are going up and by how much. In other words, the CPI is the formal measure of inflation that tells us whether things overall are more expensive now than in the past.

Why do we care? We care because inflation reduces the value of our money. If we are holding some wealth in cash—for example, if we have money in a bank account—inflation causes that cash to be less valuable. Let's say we put $1,000 in the bank at a time when that money could buy 20 shopping carts full of food. Then, inflation drives up the cost of food by 5 percent. Now, that same $1,000 will only buy about 19 shopping carts full.

Inflation is a fairly steady presence in our economy at some level. We all feel the effects at various times. Some of you may be protected by receiving regular increases in your paychecks. Many times, employers give their employees a standard "cost of living" increase. This helps soften the impact of inflation—although it is often not enough.

Another way to protect against inflation is to hold some of your wealth in assets that tend to increase in value by more than the rate of inflation. Real estate is one example of an investment that has been regarded as good protection against inflation. But generally, such assets involve a higher degree of risk. They go up higher and fall lower than safer options. For that reason, it is not generally good practice to place all your savings and investments in such assets. As you get closer to the time when you need to rely on those investments, it may be wise to move them into less risky options.

Finance ONLINE

If you want to compare the buying power of $20 or any other amount from one year to another, visit **www.bls.gov** and click the link to the inflation calculator. It is fun and informative to see how inflation can affect your money!

Think again about Miranda and her grandparents. Miranda's dad was a little worried about the effect of inflation on the older couple. As retirees, the grandparents no longer enjoyed a worker's income or consistent income increases. They had to rely on their savings to meet their needs and wants for the rest of their lives. If the costs of goods and services rose quickly—that is, if inflation were high—then the purchasing power of their savings would shrink at a faster rate.

Fortunately, Miranda's grandparents had managed to sell their old home—real estate—before its price fell. And they had invested their money wisely. As a result, they had built up enough savings to live comfortably, even though they had a reduced income and even if inflation reduced the value of their savings. Their story underlines the rewards of good planning—while also pointing out some of the risks that must be considered.

Globalization

There was a time not too long ago when the people and businesses in the United States relied very little on businesses and consumers in other countries. Miranda's grandfather, for example, worked in a factory that made goods in this country and sold them to people in this country. The factory competed only with other American factories to build the best product at the lowest price.

Today, we live in a **global economy**, in which economies of all the world's countries interact and depend on each other. You have heard it said many times, and it is true: The world is shrinking. Look at the typical products you buy. Where are they made? Check the label to see where they are manufactured. You will see places such as China, Indonesia, Turkey, and Mexico. You will find few items that are made solely in the United States. In fact, a large and growing share of what we buy and sell is imported or exported. Refer to Figure 8.5 for an eye-opener. All of this is evidence of our global economy, but how does it impact you?

Whether you go to work for a multinational corporation or the corner grocery store, the global nature of today's economy will affect you. You will deal with imported products or be involved in exporting products to other countries. You will compete for customers and jobs with people from countries around the world. You will shop for products on the Internet from all over the planet. If you have problems with your computer and call a helpline for technical support, you will likely speak to someone in a country such as India.

Miranda's grandfather's company was affected by globalization. Just as he was getting ready to retire, his company began losing sales to a company overseas that made the same product. The workers in that overseas factory earned much less money than Miranda's grandfather. And, the factory was not regulated by the same costly pollution controls that American factories must have. As a result, the overseas company could make and sell products for less than the American company was able to sell them. Consumers began buying more of the foreign-made goods because they cost less. Soon, other foreign companies were making the same product—also for less money than the American company. The American company could not compete. Soon after Miranda's grandfather retired, the company closed its American factories. It opened new ones overseas. The lower-skilled factory workers lost their jobs. The higher-skilled managers kept theirs.

You Do It
Activity #2

Figure 8.5 Top U.S. Trade Partners

Ranked by 2007 U.S. Total Export Value for Goods (in millions of U.S. dollars)

| | | Exports | | | | | | Imports | | | | | |
Rank	Country	2006	2007	% Change	Through May 2007	Through May 2008	% Change	2006	2007	% Change	Through May 2007	Through May 2008	% Change
1	Canada	230,656	248,888	7.9%	100,157	112,637	12.5%	302,438	317,057	4.8%	129,035	144,196	11.7%
2	Mexico	133,979	136,092	1.6%	55,025	60,631	10.2%	198,253	210,714	6.3%	82,981	90,644	9.2%
3	China	55,186	65,236	18.2%	24,646	30,278	22.9%	287,774	321,443	11.7%	120,935	126,311	4.4%
4	Japan	59,613	62,703	5.2%	26,043	28,019	7.6%	148,181	145,463	−1.8%	59,785	61,587	3.0%
5	UK	45,410	50,229	10.6%	21,906	24,064	9.9%	53,513	56,858	6.3%	22,329	24,001	7.5%
6	Germany	41,319	49,651	20.2%	19,914	22,889	14.9%	89,082	94,164	5.7%	37,757	41,682	10.4%
7	Korea	32,442	34,645	6.8%	13,948	14,928	7.0%	45,804	47,562	3.8%	20,353	20,407	0.3%
8	Netherlands	31,129	32,963	5.9%	14,164	16,867	19.1%	17,342	18,403	6.1%	6,458	8,257	27.9%
9	France	24,217	27,413	13.2%	11,568	12,619	9.1%	37,040	41,553	12.2%	16,351	18,106	10.7%
10	Taiwan	23,047	26,309	14.2%	10,039	11,691	16.5%	38,212	38,278	0.2%	15,186	15,080	−0.7%

Source: ita.doc.gov/td/industry/otea/ttp/Top_Trade_Partners.pdf

What does this mean to you? You will need to develop the ability to adapt to a rapidly changing work force and business environment. You will need to recognize what types of skills are in demand, and you must be willing to learn new skills as the environment changes. You may change jobs based on that information, or you may make new or different investments based on that information. Some jobs, such as plumbers, electricians, and mechanics will be difficult, if not impossible, to "outsource," or replace with a foreign source. Most health-care-related jobs will also be difficult to outsource—although the high cost of medical care is causing more and more Americans to seek care overseas.

As you create your financial plan for your life, remember that new issues will continue to emerge that will either create new opportunities or cause you to revise your plan. A number of these issues will be economic issues. Demographic trends will make some jobs in high demand and make others obsolete. The way our leaders address the Social Security problem may affect the way you save for retirement. If inflation increases to a high level, you will need to protect your wealth by holding inflation-resistant assets. The phase of the business cycle might impact you when you decide to go to graduate school. Do you see the common theme? Educate yourself on economic issues and how they might directly impact your future.

✓ CHECK Your Financial IQ

What are some broad economic factors that might affect your financial future?

Summary

- Economics is often defined as the study of choices. Building a financial plan involves making choices. Understanding or being aware of broad economic issues and concepts can help you formulate your plans and make better financial decisions.

- Demographics is the study of human populations. It allows us to examine trends in the whole country's population. Understanding demographics can help you predict certain needs in advance and make informed career choices. Two important demographic trends that will impact everyone in the United States are the graying of America and increased immigration. Demographic trends also play an important role when looking at Social Security and planning for retirement.

- Economic activity can be measured by the gross domestic product (GDP). A period of time in which the economy is shrinking is known as a recession. A depression is a severe recession. The economy goes through alternating periods of shrinking and growth, or expansion, known as the business cycle. Knowing about and understanding the business cycle can help you make basic life decisions. You should also consider inflation and globalization when looking at your financial plan.

Key Terms and Vocabulary

Baby boom
Business cycle
Consumer price index
Demographics
Depression

Economics
Economy
Global economy
Gross domestic product
Inflation

Macroeconomics
Microeconomics
Recession

What Do You Know?

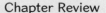

1. (a) What is the definition of economics?

   (b) How do economic factors impact financial decisions?

2. (a) What is demographics?

   (b) What is the significance of the baby boom to young people today?

3. (a) What do demographic trends suggest about the future of Social Security?

   (b) How might a young person use this knowledge when building a financial plan?

4. (a) How is immigration changing the United States today?

   (b) How might a young person use this knowledge in choosing a career?

5. (a) What does the gross domestic product measure?

   (b) What would it mean if the gross domestic product went down from one year to the next?

6. (a) How would you describe the trend of the gross domestic product in recent decades?

   (b) How does the business cycle affect your financial planning?

   (c) Based on your understanding of the business cycle, what should you be prepared for during good economic times?

7. (a) What is the difference between a recession and a depression?

8. (a) What is happening to prices during inflationary times?

   (b) Why might people with a fixed income be especially concerned about inflation?

9. (a) What do we mean when we say we live in a global economy?

   (b) How might globalization affect your education or career plans?

What Are Your Finance Math Skills?

 myFinLitlab.

The first three questions correlate to *Math for Personal Finance* features located throughout the chapter.

1. Jayce is thinking about going to technical school and getting a two-year degree that will qualify him for a $38,000 a year job. He could go to work today and make $14,000 a year. How long will it take Jayce to recover his investment if he goes to college? Assume he will not work at all while in college and that he will spend $4,000 a year on tuition and books.

2. If by 2023 there are 102 million workers in the labor force and 48 million retirees drawing Social Security, how many workers will be paying in per retiree in 2023?

3. A textile factory in the United States pays 300 workers a total of $9 million each year to produce 4.5 million shirts. A foreign factory employs 225 workers at a total cost of $1,050,000 to produce 2,500,000 shirts. How do the labor costs per shirt of the American and foreign factory compare?

4. Last year the consumer price index indicated that inflation was 3 percent. Assuming new cars increased in price by the rate of inflation, how much did a $30,000 car increase in price?

5. If housing prices fall by 4 percent, how much will the value of a $200,000 home decline in price?

6. If job growth in your state is projected to be 2 percent and you have 11,000,000 workers, how many new jobs will be created?

7. Jordan's raise last year was 3 percent of her salary, but inflation numbers released yesterday indicated that inflation was 3 percent last year. How much did Jordan's purchasing power increase?

8. Zeke learned that he could make another $2,000 a year if he was fluent in Spanish. If he intends to learn the language and work another 10 years at that job, how much is learning Spanish worth to him?

What Would You Do?

You are shopping for a new pair of shoes. You find a pair that you really like and that you can afford. But you notice that they are made by a company that has been in the news recently. The company shut down all of its manufacturing plants in the United States and opened new ones overseas. Also, some people have accused the company of hiring workers at very low wages and making them work in unclean surroundings.

You feel a little bad about buying shoes from that company. At the same time, you do not feel it is your responsibility to resist the trends of globalization.

1. What alternative do ordinary consumers have to buying lower-priced shoes made in other countries?

2. What alternative does the American shoemaker have to opening plants in foreign countries?

3. Do you think it is possible for a company to compete for long if its products cost more than those made elsewhere? Explain your answer.

What Are the Connections?
Technology, Language Arts, and History

Research information about each of the generations: Baby boomers, Generation X, Generation Y, and the generations after these. Who are these people? What are the differences of each of these groups? What is the name of the group after "Generation Y?" How does this group differ from the previous three groups?

Develop a chart that shows your family and where each member fits into the generation groups. This can include anyone living in your house, or friends of all ages. Include the following in your chart:

1. The age of the family members or friend(s) (year that family members or friend(s) were born).

2. The economic condition(s) that were prevalent when that generation was born.

3. Something unique about the times of that generation (music, art, books, news, and so on). This could include some fun facts you find about that time period.

4. Something that members of each generation have in common.

Teamwork

In teams, research the Great Depression. Develop a skit, poster, PowerPoint presentation, or newsletter that traces the history of the Great Depression.

You might know an older adult who lived through the Great Depression or was born near the end of it. You could interview that person to learn firsthand information about how it was living during this period. You might look up information about teenagers during the Great Depression.

---

w!se | **Financial Literacy**
CERTIFICATION

TEST PREP QUESTIONS

myFinLitlab.

1. The best definition of economics is that it is the study of
   a. unlimited wants versus limited resources.
   b. how societies govern their people.
   c. communism versus capitalism.
   d. how the stock market has developed in America.

2. Which decision illustrates the idea that a person's financial decisions are influenced by the overall economy?
   a. A person decides to use her lunch break to work out at a gym and eat lunch at her desk rather than going out to lunch with three friends.
   b. A person switches the language she is studying in college from French to Spanish after she reads a newspaper article about how the population of the United States is changing.
   c. A person decides to read a book instead of going to the movies after she reads a review of the movie she was planning to see.
   d. A person who buys a new M car every three years switches to a B car after comparing the prices and features of each car.

3. The demographic trend that helps explain why there has been an increase in demand for health care workers is
   a. that Generation X is not saving for the future.
   b. declining immigration.
   c. the graying of America.
   d. the declining American birthrate.

4. National economic trends
   a. should have little or no impact on individual financial planning.
   b. should only impact individuals once they are in the workforce for more than 10 years.

    c. are the same as long-term financial goals set by individuals.

    d. should impact individual financial planning.

5. If gross domestic product (GDP) is going up, it is a sign that

    a. economic trends are turning down.

    b. the economy is in a period of inflation.

    c. the economy is gaining strength.

    d. individual consumers are making more money.

6. During a recession, it is noticeable that

    a. people are buying less and there are higher levels of unemployment.

    b. more than 20 percent of the United States population is living below the poverty level.

    c. the gross domestic product (GDP) is rising.

    d. businesses are expanding and people have more money to spend on leisure-time activities.

7. As a result of globalization

    a. there are more jobs in America for unskilled workers.

    b. it is easier for American companies to compete with foreign companies for a larger share of the marketplace.

    c. more goods sold in America are produced in other parts of the world.

    d. more American goods are sold in China than Chinese goods are sold in the United States.

8. A person is collecting his pension and is very happy that his plan has a "cost of living" increase each year. This feature helps the person from feeling the full impact of

    a. inflation.

    b. globalization.

    c. taxation.

    d. depression.

9. How do economists measure inflation?

    a. They survey consumers and ask if they are able to buy the same number of goods today as they were a year ago.

    b. They compare the cost of today's imports from China and the Middle East to goods made in the United States.

    c. They survey employers to determine how much they are paying in salaries and for raw materials today.

    d. They compare the costs of a standard group of goods and services bought today to how much those goods cost a year ago.

10. Which of the following is a true statement about inflation?

    a. Inflation only affects senior citizens who are living on fixed incomes.

    b. Some investments are able to grow at a rate greater than the rate of inflation; these investments, however, may carry greater risk.

    c. A young person is wise to invest all of her money in real estate since it grows at a rate greater than the rate of inflation.

    d. People who are fully employed and receive annual raises are not impacted by the effects of inflation.

11. If a person earned $50,000 last year and again earns $50,000 this year, but the rate of inflation is 4 percent, this year's buying power when compared to last year's
    a. is $48,000.
    b. is $50,000.
    c. is $52,000.
    d. cannot be determined from the information given.

12. What is the business cycle?
    a. It is a period of economic growth followed by a period in which the economy is shrinking.
    b. It is a 20-year period during which prices for goods and services rise and then fall back to a set level.
    c. It is the annual change that takes place in the course of a business's activities from highs during holiday seasons to lows during the winter season.
    d. It is the time that it takes a business to emerge from a recession or fall back into a depression.

13. Because of globalization, an individual may have to decide whether to
    a. sell a house during a recession.
    b. take a job with an annual salary of $50,000 or a job with an annual salary of $45,000 with a guaranteed cost of living increase.
    c. invest in a company that drills for oil off the coast of Alaska.
    d. buy a pair of jeans made in America at three times the cost of jeans made in China.

UNIT

3

Spending
& Credit

CHAPTER 9

Learning Objectives

Explain the concept of consumer credit, including major types and its benefits and drawbacks.

Describe the keys to building and maintaining healthy credit.

Identify ways to protect your identity.

Key Terms

Credit
Credit bureau
Credit report
Credit score
Identify theft
Installment credit
Interest
Noninstallment credit
Principal
Revolving open-ended credit

Obtaining and Protecting Your Credit

As she sat in the sales office, Nancy opened her checkbook and peered sadly again at the balance. She knew the figure was not going to change, but she wanted it to! The car she had chosen cost more than she had in her account. It was perfect, it was a very good deal, and she needed a vehicle for college. Yet in spite of the fact that she had been saving money for three years, she was still a little short.

Should she try to borrow the difference? The salesman seemed to think it was a good idea. In fact, when he told her what she might expect for a monthly payment, Nancy was thrilled. "But don't hold me to that number," he cautioned. "First, I need to check a few things with the business manager."

The more Nancy thought about the loan, the better the idea seemed. "It *is* a great deal, and a great car," she said to herself. "And I can manage a small monthly loan payment."

Just then the salesman returned and interrupted her thoughts. "Well, I've got good news and bad news, Nancy."

"What's the bad news?" she asked.

"With your credit history, we're not going to be able to get you a low-cost loan of the type I was thinking about. We can probably arrange a loan, but it will cost you more than the number I gave you earlier."

Nancy was puzzled. "What could be wrong with my credit history?" she wondered. "I didn't even know I had one."

What is credit? **Credit** is money that a lender makes available to a borrower with the understanding that the borrower will repay the money in the future. Often, borrowers also agree to pay lenders something called interest. **Interest** is the price one pays for the right to use another party's money. Think of interest as a rental fee paid for using someone else's money. Understanding how credit works—for you and against you—can help you build a strong financial plan.

Businesses offer credit to customers as a way of encouraging them to make purchases they might otherwise not be able to make at that time.

MATH for Personal Finance

Barbara borrowed $2,300 to buy some furniture and is paying 15 percent interest a year for the loan. The terms of the loan do not require her to pay off any of the loan balance during the first year. She only has to make interest payments.

How much interest will she pay the first year if she does not reduce the principal of the loan?

Solution: Barbara will pay $2,300 \times .15 = \$345$ in interest the first year.

THE BASICS OF CREDIT FOR CONSUMERS

Like Nancy, you will almost certainly need or want to use credit at some point in your life. One day you will want to purchase something, such as a house, a car, or a college education, for which it is difficult to save the entire amount. Used properly, credit can make it possible for you to purchase these things. Used unwisely, credit can wreak havoc in your financial life. Therefore, it is essential that you know about the major types of credit, the advantages and disadvantages of each, and about the laws that protect your right to get credit.

Types of Credit

Credit for consumers such as Nancy and you come in many forms. But all of these fall into one of three categories: noninstallment, installment, or revolving open-end credit.

Noninstallment credit is credit that is extended for a short term, such as 30 days or less. The consumer borrows the money at the time of purchase and pays off the entire amount within a short time. Noninstallment credit is typically issued by department stores, furniture stores, or other businesses selling items that cost several hundred dollars. Its purpose is to encourage immediate purchases of specific items. You may see an advertisement that says "30 days, same as cash," which describes a noninstallment credit arrangement. The ad means that the store is willing to lend you the purchase price for 30 days. If you pay it off within that time, the purchase price is the same as if you had paid cash.

This type of credit may be useful to a person who is expecting to receive money soon enough to repay the amount borrowed. An example might be a person expecting an income-tax refund. Most noninstallment credit will not incur interest charges if paid within the allotted time period.

Installment credit is also used for specific purchases but allows the borrower more time to repay the money. "Installment loans" typically require the borrower to make monthly payments. Part of each payment goes to reduce the **principal**—the total amount of money outstanding on the loan. Monthly payments also include interest charges. That is, the lender charges interest each month on the unpaid principal. So, if you have an unpaid principal of $100, the lender will charge you an agreed-upon percentage of that $100 in interest.

Installment loans may span a few years and are typically used for purchases such as lawn tractors, furniture, boats, and other big-ticket items.

You Do It

Activity #1

MATH for Personal Finance

Harlan used his credit card—a form of short-term credit—to charge three tanks of gas this month.

If his charges were $43.12, $51.87, and $38.35, how much should he pay at the end of the month?

Solution: Harlan should pay the bill in full: $43.12 + $51.87 + $38.35 = $133.34.

Note that using installment credit does make the purchase of these items more costly. Refer to Figure 9.1, which shows how much interest you might pay over the life of a typical loan.

Revolving open-end credit, such as credit cards, allows consumers to borrow up to some preset maximum amount, such as $1,000 or $10,000. This **credit limit** is established based on the borrower's income level, debt level, and overall credit record. Consumers can use revolving credit to make one purchase or many. They can repay the entire amount borrowed at the end of the month or spread payments over a longer time. As they pay off money borrowed in the past, they can continue to use credit to make additional purchases as long as they do not exceed their credit limit.

Advantages of Using Credit

Should Nancy use credit to buy her car? There are obvious advantages and disadvantages. First, consider the advantages.

As you have read, credit helps you make large purchases sooner than you would if you had to save the entire purchase price in advance. Nancy has been saving for quite some time, yet she still does not have enough to buy her car outright. With credit, Nancy just may be able to purchase that car she wants and needs.

Using credit also simplifies your finances by eliminating the need to carry cash or checks. For example, you can use credit to buy your gasoline and pay for an entire month's purchases in a single monthly bill.

Using credit wisely can also help you establish a good credit history, which can make it less expensive for you to use credit in the future. This is because people with a good record of using and paying for credit—people with good **credit histories**—may be able to borrow at lower interest rates. Nancy wishes she knew this before trying to buy her car. Her lack of a credit history meant that she was not eligible for the lowest available rates.

Figure 9.1 Cash versus Financing

Why do you think someone might choose to borrow money for 36 months rather than for a shorter period?

	Total paid	Interest paid
Cash purchase of car	$3,000.00	0
$3,000 financed for 12 months @ 12% 12 payments of $266.55 =	$3,198.60	$198.60
$3,000 financed for 24 months @ 12% 24 payments of $141.22 =	$3,389.29	$389.29
$3,000 financed for 36 months @ 12% 36 payments of $99.64 =	$3,587.04	$587.04

Disadvantages of Using Credit

Credit can be costly. And, using it badly can cause serious and long-lasting damage to your financial life. Consider these points:

It is often easier to get credit than it is to pay it back. If you borrow too much money, you may have difficulty making the payments, with disastrous results. Just as a good history can mean lower borrowing costs, a bad history can make borrowing more costly—or impossible. If you borrow money to buy a house or car and fail to make payments, you could lose your possessions and all the money you have invested in them. A representative of the bank or business from which you borrowed the money can literally take away the car or remove you from the house. Then, the lender can sell the car or house—and keep the money. Finally, failure to pay off loans can lead to bankruptcy. This is a legal process in which a court takes over certain aspects of a person's financial life. It is not a good situation.

Credit cards pose a special danger. They tempt us to purchase things *today* we would be wiser to save and pay for in full. And, credit card interest rates are usually very high, so it is extremely costly to carry a credit card balance from one month to the next. In most cases, it is wisest to use credit cards only for purchases you plan to pay off when the bill comes in—before interest charges add up. Bear in mind that if you borrow just $3,000 on a credit card that charges 21 percent interest annually and pay only the required minimum every month, it will take almost 23 years to pay off the balance.

What if you borrowed even more? At **www.chase.com**, there is a payment calculator where you can plug in different balances and interest rates. On the Web site, search for "credit card payment calculator."

Sabrina charged $800 at the local sporting goods store to buy some exercise equipment. The store offers no interest for 90 days if the balance is paid in full, or 24 percent annually if the balance is not paid in full prior to 90 days.

How much interest will she need to pay if she lets the account go for 91 days before paying the bill?

Solution: She will pay 2 percent—.02—a month, since the annual rate is 24 percent. At 91 days, she will owe for three months—3 × .02. Therefore, her interest will be $800 × .06 = $48.

You Do It

Activity #2

Credit Rights and Consumer Credit Laws

While credit can be dangerous to your financial health, it can also be invaluable. For that reason, federal law helps protect your access to credit. The **Equal Credit Opportunity Act** prohibits **creditors**—people who provide credit—from denying credit based on gender, age, race, national origin, religion, or marital status. This legislation also requires that creditors notify applicants within 30 days of whether or not they will receive credit and explain the reason for denial if credit is denied. Refer to Figure 9.2 for a list of other consumer credit laws.

✓ **CHECK Your Financial IQ**

What are the risks and benefits of consumer credit?

Figure 9.2 Major Consumer Credit Laws

The federal government has established many laws to help ensure fair and reasonable standards for consumer credit.

THE EQUAL CREDIT OPPORTUNITY ACT prohibits discrimination in the granting of credit on the basis of such factors as race, skin color, or sex.

THE FAIR CREDIT REPORTING ACT sets up a procedure for correcting mistakes on your credit record.

THE FAIR CREDIT BILLING ACT sets up procedures requiring creditors to promptly credit your payments and correct billing mistakes and allows you to withhold payments on defective goods.

TRUTH IN LENDING gives you three days to change your mind about certain credit transactions that use your home as collateral. It also limits your risk on lost or stolen credit cards.

Source: http://www.federalreserve.gov/pubs/consumerhdbk/

BUILDING GOOD CREDIT

Finance ONLINE

Just how important is your credit score? If you visit **www.myfico.com,** you can find information about how different credit scores affect different types of loans. Check out this site to see why it is worth your while to keep your credit scores up.

What was wrong with Nancy's credit? It's very likely that she had no credit history at all. You will sometimes read or hear about this or that person's "good credit" or "bad credit." This refers to a person's worthiness to receive credit. We all want to establish good credit. Nancy's situation helps illustrate the point. She wants to borrow money—that is, receive credit. She does not have bad credit, but she does not have good credit, either. She simply has no credit history. The result is that she may have to pay more for the credit she receives. Lenders often charge higher interest rates for people with less-than-good credit. That includes people with bad credit or people whose credit history is unproven. Therefore, it is vital that you know the process by which you build good credit and how that information is collected and reported to creditors.

Good credit scores save you money	About FICO® scores	myFICO® is the industry's most trusted source

The higher your FICO® credit score, the lower your payments!
See for yourself. Interest rates accurate as of November 24, 2008:

30 Yr fixed mortgage	15 Yr home equity loan	36 month auto loan
FICO® score	**APR**	**Monthly payment**
720-850	6.686%	$768
690-719	8.229%	$786
660-689	9.451%	$800
620-659	12.087%	$831
590-619	15.270%	$870
500-589	16.285%	$882

Location: National Avg.   Loan amount: $25,000   Recalculate

When you go to borrow money—for example, when you buy a car—the options available to you for borrowing and the interest rate you pay will depend in part on your credit history.

Your Credit History

Each person's credit history is collected in his or her individual credit report. How many times have you borrowed money? Did you pay it back on time? Were your payments late? This information is collected about everyone who borrows money. Lenders use this information every time you apply for credit. Every time you make a credit purchase, it will further establish your credit history, good or bad.

You can help or hurt your credit history in other ways, too. Whenever you sign up for and pay utilities, such as electricity, phone, and water service, you are building your credit history. Utility companies extend credit by allowing you to use services and then billing you for them. If you fail to pay your utility bills, that information becomes part of your credit history. It can affect your ability to get credit in the future.

Credit Bureaus and Credit Scoring

Who keeps track of your credit history? Organizations known as **credit bureaus** collect credit information on individual consumers. There are three main credit bureaus: Equifax, Experian, and TransUnion. Figure 9.7, which appears later in this chapter, contains contact information for these credit bureaus.

Credit bureaus provide credit reports to potential lenders, employers, and others upon request. Your **credit report** shows every time you have applied for credit of any kind, whether or not you have paid your bills on time, if you have paid your credit cards in full every month or carried a balance, and if you have paid late fees. Any other public information about personal bankruptcies, court judgments, and inquiries by various companies or potential employers also appears in your credit report.

Everyone can access his or her credit report once every 12 months free of charge. By providing some basic personal information, you will be able to see the types of records being maintained by these credit bureaus regarding your personal credit history.

Credit Reports

Figure 9.3 shows a sample credit report. Notice that there are six categories of information contained in the report. When you apply for credit, the potential creditor will study your report and make decisions about whether or not to extend additional credit. Also, employers often use this information to make decisions about job offers, and insurance companies may use this information to determine insurance rates. A federal law called the **Fair Credit Reporting Act** limits the sharing of your financial information only to firms that have a legal purpose to evaluate this information.

It is a good idea to review your credit report now and then to make sure that it contains accurate information. Sometimes, companies make mistakes in their record keeping—mistakes that can make it into your report and hurt your financial life. Examining your report can also help you know if someone has set up a credit account in your name. This is a growing problem, as you will read.

Finance ONLINE

An easy way to access your credit report is online via the following link: **www.annualcreditreport .com**. You can also phone or send mail requests for a credit report. These are processed and mailed within 15 days of receipt of your request.

Figure 9.3 What's in a Credit Report

Your credit report contains a brief record of all your past credit—and any problems that may have occurred. It's essential that your report be accurate and as free as possible of negative information.

Credit Bureau

Report Number 716-80
08/28/06

Please address all future correspondence to:

Credit Bureau
P.O. Box 0000
City, State, Zip Code
(888) 000–0000

Personal Information

Cynthia Zubicki
120 Greenmeadow Drive
Durham, NC 27704

Social Security Number: 000-00-0000

Previous Addresses:
264 Concord Road
Gilbert, AZ 85296

Last Reported Employment: Architect

401 Brownell Road
Chandler, AZ 85226

Public Record Information

Bankruptcy filed 04/04; Durham District Court; Case Number 873JM34; Liabilities: $56,987; Assets: $672

Collection Agency Account Information

North Shore Collection Agency (888) 000–0000

Collection Reported 11/02; Assigned 1/03 to North Shore Collection Agency; Client: Gilbert Medical Center; Amount: $1,267; Paid Collection Account

Credit Account Information

Company Name	Account Number	Date Opened	Individual or Joint	Months Review	Date of Last Activity	High Credit	Terms	Balance	Past Due	Status	Date Reported
Durham Savings Bank	8762096	02/05	I	6	11/05	$4,897		$2,958		Paid as Agreed	04/06
Macy's	109–82-43176	06/03	I	36	01/06	$2,000		$0		Paid as Agreed	02/06
Chester Auto Finance	873092851	03/04	I	27	02/06	$2,400	$50	$300	$200	Paid 120 days past due date	03/06

Previous Payment History: 2 times 30 days late; 2 times 60 days late

Inquiries

05/27/04 Citibank; 10/15/06 Bloomingdale's; 03/21/06 Home Depot

1. This information helps identify the report.
2. This section provides information that identifies the subject of the report.
3. Any public records related to the subject, such as bankruptcy information, appears here.
4. Unpaid accounts are turned over to so-called collection agencies. Information about such actions appear here.
5. Details about all open or closed credit accounts are listed.
6. Companies that have asked for credit information about the subject are listed here.

Credit Score

Credit bureaus use your credit history to create a **credit score** that is often used to assess your creditworthiness. Individuals with higher credit scores get better interest rates on loans since they are determined to have a lower risk of defaulting. A good credit score can save you thousands of dollars in finance costs and interest charges over your lifetime.

Credit scores are calculated based on a model created by **Fair Isaac Corporation**. So, they are very often called FICO scores. FICO scores will be between 300 and 850, with a higher score indicating better credit. In Figure 9.4, you can see that most people's credit scores fall in the 600–800 range.

In general, FICO scores are about 35 percent based on your credit history, 30 percent based on how much of your available credit you are using, and the rest based on other information contained in your credit report (see Figure 9.5). For 2008, FICO has modified the model slightly, and some factors now weigh lighter or heavier than in the past. It can be useful to know what aspects of your credit history are helping or hurting you the most in terms of your credit score.

Professor FIN

Here are just a few tips for improving your credit score:

- Pay your bills on time
- Keep credit cards and other "revolving credit" balances low
- Pay off debt rather than moving it around

For more tips go to www.myfico.com/CreditEducation/ImproveYourScore.aspx.

✓ CHECK Your Financial IQ

What are the elements of "good credit"?

Figure 9.4 Credit Score Distribution

Well over half of all consumers have a credit score that is 700 or above.

FICO Score	Percentage of Population
300–499	1 percent
500–549	5 percent
550–599	7 percent
600–649	11 percent
650–699	16 percent
700–749	20 percent
750–799	29 percent
800–850	11 percent

Source: www.scoretruth.com/basics/range.php

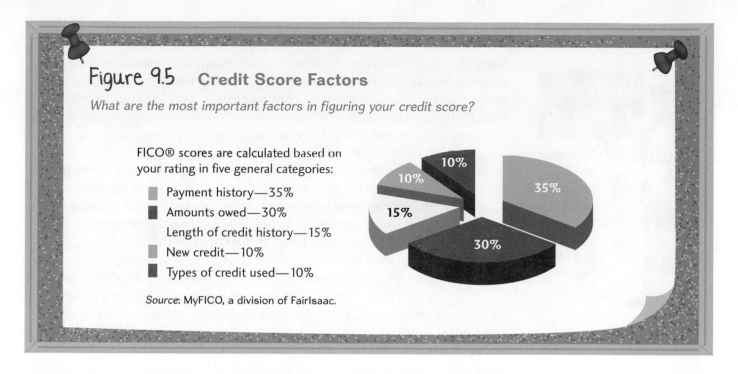

Figure 9.5 Credit Score Factors

What are the most important factors in figuring your credit score?

FICO® scores are calculated based on your rating in five general categories:

- Payment history—35%
- Amounts owed—30%
- Length of credit history—15%
- New credit—10%
- Types of credit used—10%

10%
10%
15%
30%
35%

Source: MyFICO, a division of FairIsaac.

THREATS TO YOUR CREDIT: IDENTITY THEFT

Identity theft occurs when someone uses your personal information without your permission for personal gain. For example, someone may use your personal information to open a department store credit account and buy furniture. This account will be reported to the credit bureau under your name. And when this dishonest person does not pay the bill, your credit score will suffer. In most cases, you will not even be aware that this event has occurred until you request a copy of your credit report and find out about the account.

Some criminals use your personal information to establish totally new identities and engage in criminal activity. In severe cases, people have had their credit completely destroyed to the point where they can no longer borrow money for anything. Obviously, identity theft is illegal; but it's very difficult to detect. Unfortunately, identity theft is increasing. The Federal Trade Commission estimates that 9 million people experience some type of identity theft each year.

Professor FIN

In a 2007 report, the Federal Trade Commission found that 3.7 percent of adults reported that they had discovered they were victims of identity theft. Many of these victims report that they had out-of-pocket expenses because of identity theft. In addition, they suffered problems such as being harassed by collections agents, being denied new credit, being prevented from using their existing credit cards, having their utilities cut off, being subjected to criminal investigation or civil suit, being arrested, or having difficulties obtaining a bank account or even accessing their own bank accounts.

For more information on this report, go to **www.ftc.gov** and click "identity theft" in the "quick finder" section.

Identity Theft Tactics

Professor FIN

To take a quiz to assess your level of preparedness to defend against identity theft, go to **www.privacyrights.org** and click the link for "identity theft."

Identify thieves use a variety of tactics. For example, **shoulder surfing** occurs when someone in a public place skims personal information to use against you by overhearing your conversation or viewing your personal information. Be cautious when someone seems to be standing too close to you when you're using a computer at a library, using a credit card at a store, and so on.

Identity thieves have been known to go through a person's trash to gather information. Credit card receipts, banking information, or even unsolicited offers for credit cards can enable someone to profit from your identity. Make sure to shred documents such as these prior to disposing of them.

Another common technique is called **skimming**. This involves simply copying your credit card or debit card numbers from your cards. Very often skimmers may be temporary employees of certain businesses. Highly advanced skimmers can even attach card reading devices to ATMs to get your bank account numbers and PIN.

Pretexting occurs when someone improperly accesses your personal information by posing as someone who needs data for one reason or another. The con artist may pose as a business or someone conducting a survey in order to get your information. When pretexting occurs online it is known as **phishing**. Common phishing techniques include e-mailing you and asking you to verify account information. **Pharming**, which is even more complex, uses e-mail viruses to redirect you from a legitimate Web site to an official-looking Web site designed to obtain your personal information.

Protecting against and Reacting to Identity Theft

Refer to Figure 9.6 for some methods that you should employ to prevent identity theft. These steps may seem time-consuming and some may cost money. But preventing the theft of your identity is well worth the simple investment. The purchase of identity theft insurance may also be worth considering.

Figure 9.6 Ways to Protect against Identity Theft

Preventing identity theft requires a little effort, but the benefits are significant.

1. Secure your wallet or purse by removing anything with Social Security number or PIN numbers for bank or credit cards.
2. Keep a list of all credit cards and bank accounts.
3. Use a document shredder for receipts and credit card offers
4. Don't print your Social Security number on checks.
5. Remove name and address from local phone directories.
6. Use a locked mailbox.
7. Shop online only on secure sites.
8. Don't verify any information over the phone or e-mail unless you initiate contact.
9. Mail all bills at the post office.
10. Monitor your bank and credit card statements.
11. Be cautious about giving credit card information over a cell phone.
12. Monitor your expected deliveries on credit card purchases.
13. Never have checks delivered to your home.
14. Install firewalls and virus software on your computer.
15. Have your mail held while on vacation.

If you detect a sign of identity theft, act quickly. Be sure to keep copies and notes about all correspondence. Figure 9.7 provides some helpful resources that you can use to prevent and respond to identity theft.

You can see that monitoring your credit report and protecting yourself from identity theft is critical to your long-term financial health. Good credit decisions and practices pay substantial benefits over your lifetime. Poor decisions cause increased cost and limit your options for just as long.

Monitor Your Credit Report

You should check your credit report periodically. Sometimes there will be simple mistakes that could harm your credit if left alone. When you find inaccurate information you need to contact the three main credit reporting bureaus and file a dispute related to the inaccurate information. The credit bureaus will then have to contact the creditor and verify the accuracy of the information. If the information is found to be inaccurate then the credit bureaus will make the change in your credit history. Inaccurate information is not that uncommon so monitor your credit closely.

 CHECK Your Financial IQ

What is identity theft?

Figure 9.7   Useful Sources of Information to Protect against Identity Theft

You have many allies in the fight to stop identity theft. These names and numbers can help you keep your personal information safe or limit damage if theft does occur.

How to Prevent Unsolicited Mail and Phone Calls
Stopping unwanted mail and phone calls helps block identity thieves from collecting valuable personal information.

To Opt Out of Pre-Approved Credit Card Offers
The following number can be used to notify all three major credit card bureaus that you wish to opt out of pre-approved credit card offers:
(888)5optout –or– (888)567–8688

To stop mail solicitations—write to:
Mail Preference Service, P.O. Box 7130, Boulder, CO 80306-7130

To stop telephone solicitations—write to:
Telephone Preference Service, Direct Marketing Association, P.O. Box 1559, Carmel, NY 10512

Contacts if You Are Subjected to Identity Theft
Major National Credit Bureaus
Equifax, Credit Information Services, Consumer Fraud Division, P.O. Box 740256, Atlanta, GA 30374 (800)525-6285, http://www.credit.equifax.com

Experian, National Consumer Assistance, P.O. Box 9530, Allen, TX 75013 (888)397-3742, http://www.experian.com

TransUnion, Fraud Victim Assistance Department, P.O. Box 6790, Fullerton, CA 92834 (800)680-7289, http://www.transunion.com

Governmental Agencies
Federal Trade Commission, Consumer Response Center, Room 130, 600 Pennsylvania Avenue, NW, Washington, DC 20580 (877)FTC-HELP

Social Security Administration (800)269-0271, TTY (800)325-0778, http://www.socialsecurity.gov

Internal Revenue Service (800)829-0433

U.S. State Department, Attn: Passport Services, 1111 19th Street, NW, Ste. 500, Washington, DC 20522 (To determine if a fraudulent passport has been issued in your name.)

U.S Postal Inspection Service (Contact your local Post Office)

United States Secret Service (Contact the local field office, a list of which can be found at http://www.secretservice.gov/field_offices.shtml)

Chapter Review

Summary

- Credit, or the ability to borrow funds that will be repaid in the future, comes in a number of different forms, including noninstallment, installment, and revolving open-end credit. Each of these has advantages and disadvantages. An advantage to credit is that it helps make large purchases easier. It also eliminates the need to carry cash or checks. A disadvantage is that credit can be costly. You can damage your financial life by borrowing more than you can afford to pay back.

- Building a good credit history is important to your financial future. Credit bureaus maintain a complete history of your credit transactions. They rate you numerically and determine your credit score and report this information to interested parties, who use this information to decide whether to extend credit and on what terms. You can obtain a free credit report from any one of the three credit bureaus to ensure that the report is accurate.

- Identity theft, which involves the use of your personal identifying information without your permission, is one of the fastest growing crimes in our country. Protecting your identity against actions such as shoulder surfing, skimming, pretexting, phishing, and pharming is vital to your good credit. Act quickly if you suspect identity theft and keep copies of all correspondence and credit transactions.

Key Terms and Vocabulary

Credit	Installment credit
Credit bureau	Interest
Credit history	Noninstallment credit
Credit limit	Pharming
Credit report	Phishing
Credit score	Pretexting
Creditor	Principal
Equal Credit Opportunity Act	Revolving open-end credit
Fair Credit Reporting Act	Shoulder surfing
Fair Isaac Corporation	Skimming
Identity theft	

What Do You Know?

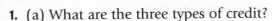
myFinLitlab

1. (a) What are the three types of credit?

   (b) Under what conditions might a consumer find each type useful?

2. (a) What is interest?

   (b) Why might someone be willing to pay interest on a purchase rather than pay it all in cash?

3. (a) What are some advantages and disadvantages of using credit?

   (b) Of the three types of credit, which do you think poses the greatest threat to your financial future, and why?

4. (a) The Equal Credit Opportunity Act prohibits creditors from denying credit for what reasons?

   (b) Why do you think it is important or helpful to know the reasons you have been denied credit?

5. (a) What three types of information do creditors use to determine a prospective borrower's creditworthiness?

   (b) Since lenders are careful who they loan to, why do you think so many people get into credit trouble?

6. (a) What are the six major areas of information that may be included on your credit report?

   (b) Why is it important to check the information on your credit report regularly?

7. (a) What factors determine your credit score?

   (b) What are some steps you might take to improve your credit score?

8. (a) What is identity theft?

   (b) How do you think technology has affected the problem of identity theft?

9. (a) Name and explain at least three tactics used by identity thieves to obtain information.

   (b) Discuss steps you can take to safeguard your personal information.

What Are Your Finance Math Skills?

myFinLitlab.

The first three questions correlate to *Math for Personal Finance* features located throughout the chapter.

1. Salinda bought a new television. The deal was attractive to her because she will be required to make monthly interest-only payments on the $1,200 purchase for the first year. How much interest will she pay each month and over the course of the first year assuming an 18 percent interest rate?

2. Hsui charged four items on his credit card in the past week. If his charges were $13.45, $62.49, $78.32, and $114.51 how much should he pay when his bill comes due?

3. Garvin bought skis that cost $500 at the new store opening. The store gave him 60 days free credit. However, if he does not pay within 60 days they will charge him a 12 percent annual interest rate. How much interest will Garvin pay if he lets the account go for 90 days?

4. Alan opened a $10,000 line of revolving credit at the bank. How much can he borrow if he has already borrowed $2,000 and paid back $500 of that amount?

5. Judy charged $800 worth of furniture using noninstallment credit since her tax refund is due shortly. If she intends to pay off the entire amount of her purchase, how much will she have to come up with if her refund is $535?

6. Jeremiah borrowed $1,500 from the bank to buy a home entertainment system. How much will he have to pay back in six months assuming the annual interest rate is 8 percent and he intends to pay the loan in full?

7. Sandy borrowed $1,600 from the bank that she will be making interest only payments on for the first year. Assuming the annual interest rate is 12 percent annually (1 percent monthly), how much will she need to pay every month?

8. Rayburn's dad offered to loan him $1,000 to buy a car with an annual interest rate of 7 percent. Assuming he pays his dad back at the end of one year, how much will he have paid for the car?

What Would You Do?

Joseph began applying for loans to go to vocational school to become an auto mechanic. He went to the bank to begin the process. While there, the loan officer saw that there were problems with Joseph's credit. It seems that the credit report showed that Joseph was behind by more than 60 days in payments on two credit cards.

The only credit that Joseph has is for his car, and he has been very good about payments. When he purchased the car, his parents said that if he ever got behind in payments they would take the car from him.

Joseph is now worried about what to do to correct what is on his credit report. Can you help him?

1. What steps should Joseph take to make corrections to his credit?

2. What could have happened if Joseph had not found the errors in his credit report so soon?

3. What if more time had passed before he did a credit check? What would happen then?

4. What would you do to make sure your credit is good at this time?

5. Do you think it is important for people over age 16 to check their credit reports?

What Are the Connections? Language Arts

In this cartoon, Zits is concerned about his father knowing a grade on a quiz. Zits feels it is an invasion of his privacy.

Write a paper taking a stand for Zits or for his father. Defend your position. In your defense, relate the concept of "gradesnoop" to the collection of credit information about individuals by credit reporting agencies. Determine whether or not the practice is fair. Identify three ways this process can hurt or help an individual.

Teamwork

In teams, develop a public service announcement about identity theft. This could be a video to show on the school's news network or at a Parent-Teacher meeting. You could also put together a skit to perform for a school assembly or for your class. Or, you could publish a newsletter to tell parents what to do to protect their identity or to tell classmates what to do to begin to protect their identity.

You can go online to research different Web sites that can provide information on protecting your identity, as well as statistics about identity theft.

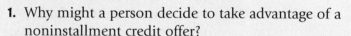

w!se | **Financial Literacy CERTIFICATION**

TEST PREP QUESTIONS

myFinLitlab.

1. Why might a person decide to take advantage of a noninstallment credit offer?
   a. Interest on this type of loan is much lower than interest on other types of loans.
   b. The loan can be paid back without interest charges any time within one year.
   c. The loan offered by Company A can be used to purchase items at Company B.
   d. There is no interest charged on the loan if it is paid back within a very short time.

2. A person finds the computer she needs on sale for $900. She can pay for the computer using her credit card and pay the amount borrowed over the course of many months; or, she can take advantage of the store's offer for her to pay for the computer within 30 days, which will be the same as buying the computer for cash. She knows that she will

receive her $1,200 salary bonus in her next paycheck. As a financially savvy consumer, she should

 a. take advantage of the store's noninstallment credit option so she does not have to pay any interest on the loan.

 b. buy the computer using her credit card so that she can take as long as she wants to pay back the loan.

 c. buy the computer using her credit card and then deposit her bonus in her savings account so it earns interest.

 d. take advantage of the store's offer but only pay back $500 the first month and then transfer the balance owed to her credit card.

3. Under what circumstance would it make financial sense for a person to make a purchase with an installment loan?

 a. He is currently paying off a large credit card balance and the installment loan will enable him to buy new furniture for his living room.

 b. He expects to receive a holiday bonus at the end of the year and he wants to buy a vacation package now while it is on sale.

 c. He has wanted to buy a boat for years and he does not have enough savings or revolving credit to make the purchase.

 d. He is offered a job that requires him to have a car, which he can only afford to buy with a loan.

4. If a person has a credit card with a limit of $2,000, it means that

 a. he will not be charged interest on purchases until he uses the credit card to make purchases over the $2,000 limit.

 b. he must pay the full credit card balance each month even if it is under $2,000.

 c. the credit card company is loaning him up to $2,000 to make purchases. He can pay the entire credit card balance each month or pay part of the bill and pay interest on the rest.

 d. he earns interest at the bank that issued the credit card on purchases made up to the $2,000 limit. That interest is subtracted from the balance owed each month.

5. The major purpose of the Equal Credit Opportunity Act is to

 a. make it easier for individuals to file for personal bankruptcy when they get into credit card debt.

 b. prohibit creditors from using age, religion, or race to deny credit to a person.

 c. make sure people are billed at least once a month for any outstanding debt.

 d. provide a way for people to correct mistakes that they believe have been made on their credit reports.

6. The information collected by credit bureaus such as Experian is accessible to

 a. only the person whose information has been collected.

 b. anyone who puts in a written request to the credit bureau.

 c. only banks and other financial institutions considering making a loan to the person.

 d. the person's potential employers, landlords, and lenders.

7. Everyone can obtain a free credit report once a year from each of the three main credit bureaus. It is
   a. not necessary to get a copy of the report since a person's bank reviews all depositors' credit reports for accuracy.
   b. a good idea to obtain the reports and review them for accuracy and file a written complaint if the report contains mistakes.
   c. a good idea to check your credit report each year, but nothing can be done to change the report until the information is seven years old.
   d. not necessary to review the report until a person applies for a large loan such as a mortgage or seeks employment.

8. FICO scores are based on a model created by the Fair Isaac Corporation and weight five major factors to determine the score. The action that would have the greatest negative impact on changing a person's FICO score is
   a. obtaining a new credit card.
   b. having a $5,000 line of credit and using all $5,000 but paying bills on time.
   c. paying most bills on time and paying the minimum required each month.
   d. obtaining a new car loan.

9. As protection from identity theft, many people do not want to receive mail or phone calls offering preapproved credit card offers because it
   a. prevents a thief from collecting valuable personal information.
   b. reduces the amount of mail coming to a person's house.
   c. keeps a person from accepting more credit cards and getting into greater personal debt.
   d. improves a person's credit score since there are not so many financial institutions contacting the person.

10. The best way to protect against identity theft is to
   a. give out personal information such as credit card numbers only to close friends and people calling to verify personal information.
   b. print a phone number on personal checks and shop online as much as possible.
   c. check credit bureau personal credit reports regularly and keep Social Security card or PIN information in a safe place.
   d. use the same PIN number for all accounts and keep a list of credit card and bank account numbers handy.

11. "Phishing" is the identity thief technique of
   a. spreading an online computer virus using a person's credit card information.
   b. getting information from a person online by asking her to complete a survey or provide certain information to win a free vacation or product.
   c. calling a person's place of employment saying that he has been arrested and needs someone to bail him out of jail and verify that he has a job.
   d. calling a person's home and telling the person who answers that she is one of five winners of an HDTV and only has to pay $100 for shipping and taxes to receive the television.

CHAPTER 10

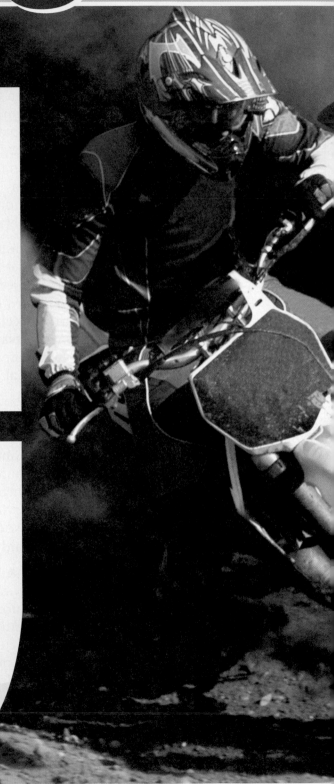

Learning Objectives

Describe the key features and qualities of personal loans.

Explain the unique issues and challenges of financing a home.

Explain the unique issues and challenges of financing an education.

Explain the unique issues and challenges of financing a car.

Key Terms

Annual percentage rate
Collateral
Cosigner
Down payment
Home equity loan
Lease
Mortgage
Personal loan
Policy rider
Secured loan
Unsecured loan

Personal Loans and Purchasing Decisions

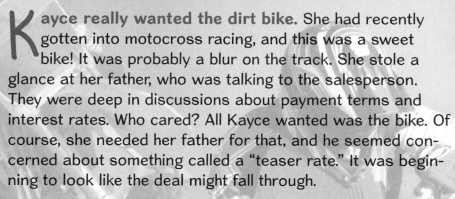

Kayce really wanted the dirt bike. She had recently gotten into motocross racing, and this was a sweet bike! It was probably a blur on the track. She stole a glance at her father, who was talking to the salesperson. They were deep in discussions about payment terms and interest rates. Who cared? All Kayce wanted was the bike. Of course, she needed her father for that, and he seemed concerned about something called a "teaser rate." It was beginning to look like the deal might fall through.

"Kayce, please come here," he said. Reluctantly, Kayce left the bike and walked over to her father.

"How badly do you want this bike?" Her father watched her intently.

"I think I could win some races with this one, Dad." Kayce's stomach turned flip flops. "I really want it."

"Do you want it enough to work extra at the shop to help make the payments?" asked her father.

"Sure," said Kayce. "How much will they be?"

"The bike's $5,000 and we can finance it for 48 months at 6 percent. That makes the monthly payment $117.42, or about 10 hours a week at the shop." He watched her expression. "Are you still in?"

Kayce looked back at the bike. "Of course I'm in."

"OK," said Kayce's father. "Let's sign the papers."

Kayce and her father have just agreed to obtain a personal loan to finance a dirt bike. **Personal loans** are a type of credit that is typically started at the time of purchase for a specific asset (car, boat, motorcycle, and so on).

Was it a good idea for Kayce and her father to take such a loan? We really do not have enough information to know for sure. We can say, though, that the use of personal loans is very common for the purchase of things that cost a few thousand dollars and more. You are likely to depend on personal loans for a variety of major purchases during your lifetime, and your knowledge of the process can mean the difference between smooth sailing and financial disaster.

PERSONAL LOANS

Can we reach a conclusion about the wisdom of Kayce and her father in taking a loan for the dirt bike? The details of this loan, such as the interest rate charged and the length of time over which the loan will be repaid might tell us whether or not the loan terms were good. Our goal, therefore, is to talk about the various features of personal loans. That way, when the time comes for you to make a decision about whether or not to take a loan, you will have the information you need to make a wise choice.

Why Take a Personal Loan?

Most of us do not have the money saved to pay cash for large purchases, such as cars and boats. Or, if we do have the cash, we may consider it wiser to invest it or use it for other needs. For this reason, typically we have to take out personal loans to cover the cost of the purchase. In most cases, such purchases also require the buyer to pay a portion of the purchase price with his or her own money—a so-called **down payment**. The money from the loan then makes up the difference between the down payment and the total purchase price.

For example, let's assume you have been saving for your first car for several years. You have set aside $2,000 for the purchase. What if you find a car you want that will cost $8,000? In this case, you might make a $2,000 down payment and take out a personal loan for the $6,000 shortfall. The lender would set up a repayment schedule that would spell out the details—called the terms of the loan. The terms include the amount of your payment, the interest rate charged, and the number of months you will need to make payments in order to repay the entire loan. At the end of that time period, assuming you have made all your payments on time, you will have paid off the loan.

Typical personal loans will have time periods of 24 to 72 months. A portion of the payment you make will pay the interest charges. The rest will be applied toward reducing the initial loan amount, which is called the principal. Your payment amount and terms of the loan will be calculated so that you will repay the entire loan with interest with your last payment.

You
Do It

Activity #1

The Personal Loan Process

Banks, credit unions, and other financial institutions are usual sources for personal loans. In addition, many of the major auto companies have

It is common to rely on credit for the purchase of expensive items, such as the boats being sold at this boat show.

financing divisions that make personal loans to people who buy their cars. People who sell costly items, such as appliances and recreational equipment, may also make financing available. Like Kayce and her father, when you are ready to make a major purchase, you may be able to get a loan at the same time.

The process of taking a personal loan begins with an application. Let's check out Kayce's application, shown in Figure 10.1. Note the section of the application headed Co-Borrower/Cosigner. A **cosigner** is someone who agrees to sign the loan document and to repay the loan if the other individual stops making payments. Be careful about cosigning loans for your friends or family.

Figure 10.1   Example of a Loan Application

When you seek a personal loan, you will fill out a detailed form that provides you and the lender with much information.

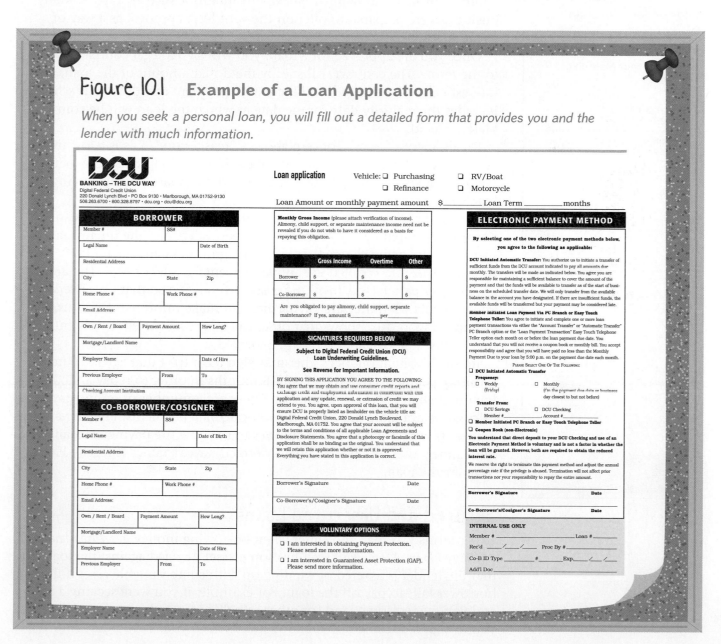

Kayce's father will serve as a cosigner on her loan since she has yet to establish a credit history. As you can see, a loan application will require you to provide information so that the potential lender can make a judgment about whether or not you will be able to pay back the loan. In almost every case, you will be required to list your income. Depending on the size of the loan and on factors such as your credit history, you may be asked to provide an income statement and balance sheet. These financial statements give the lender information about your current cash inflows and outflows. It also shows whether you have any assets that you might be able to sell in order to repay the loan. In most cases, the lender will contact the credit bureaus and access your credit score. Remember, your credit report contains a snapshot of your current and previous credit history.

Loan Contract

After you apply for a loan, you may be approved or unapproved. The approval process can happen quickly in situations such as Kayce's. Many businesses are prepared to offer on-the-spot loan approval as a way of encouraging people to make purchases.

Once you are approved for a loan, you will sign a legal contract agreeing to the terms. The contract will specify the dollar amount of the loan, the interest rate to be charged, and the loan repayment schedule. This schedule includes the **maturity date**, or the date at which the loan will be completely repaid.

Recall Kayce's father's concern about a "teaser rate." This is a low interest rate that may be offered at the start of the loan, to help make the loan seem like a great deal. But the teaser rate does not last, and eventually the loan's rate increases.

Indeed, lenders quote interest rates in a variety of ways. Lenders are, however, required by law to make sure you understand the interest rate you are really being charged—after all the gimmicks are taken into account. This rate is called the annual percentage rate, or APR. The **annual percentage rate** factors in all the costs of financing so that borrowers can know exactly what they are paying and can make informed decisions. For example, Figure 10.2 shows that other finance costs can effectively increase the interest rate you are paying on a loan.

In Kayce's situation, her father may sign a contract that agrees to make monthly payments of $117.42 for 48 months in order to repay a $5,000 loan that charges 6 percent interest. There are a number of online payment calculators available that will help you calculate payments. Plug in various amounts, interest rates, and maturities to see how the payments change. Remember, after he signs the loan contract, Kayce's father is legally liable to repay the loan.

Secured and Unsecured Loans

Other terms you may encounter when borrowing money is *secured loan* and *unsecured loan*. A **secured loan** has some asset pledged against the loan, so that the lender is assured of winding up with some valuable asset if the borrower fails to pay off the loan. For example, if you were seeking a loan and you owned some land (or other valuable asset), the lender might ask you to sign a document that allows them to sell your land if for some rea-

Figure 10.2 Measurement of the Annual Percentage Rate

Remember, the interest rate advertised for a particular loan may be considerably different from the APR.

	Interest Expenses	Other Finance Expenses	Total Finance Expenses	Number of Years	Average Annual Finance Expenses	Annual Percentage Rate (APR)*
Bank A	$200	0	$200	1	$200	$200/$2,000 = 10%
Bank B	160	$100	260	1	260	$260/$2,000 = 13%
Bank C	120	200	320	1	320	$320/$2,000 = 16%

*The APR is calculated by dividing the average annual finance expenses by the average annual loan balance.

MATH for Personal Finance

Assume Kayce's loan was for $5,000 and that she will make 48 monthly payments of $117.42 to repay the loan.

How much total interest will she pay over the life of the loan?

Solution: Kayce will pay a total of $117.42 × 48 months = $5,636.16 for the bike. The price of the bike is $5,000; therefore, the interest is equal to $5,636.16 − $5,000 = $636.16.

son you did not repay the loan. This process is commonly referred to as pledging the asset. The loan therefore is secured by the assets pledged that may be sold to repay the loan in the event of default. We call the assets that have been pledged against loan repayment **collateral**.

Often, the item purchased with a loan is used as collateral. For example, Kayce's dirt bike will be used as collateral for her loan. If Kayce's father stops making payments—that is, **defaults** on the loan—the lender will repossess the dirt bike, which means that the lender will physically remove the bike from Kayce's possession. The lender will then sell the bike to someone else to recover as much as possible of the outstanding loan. Whatever Kayce and her father have paid as a down payment and monthly payments will be lost. In addition, even if the lender gets all its money back by reselling the bike, Kayce's father will still be legally liable. The lender will report his default to the credit bureaus. This will show up on his credit history and could prevent him from being able to borrow again for some time.

Unsecured loans have no collateral pledged against the loan. Sometimes these loans are called signature loans, because they are made solely on the basis of someone's good name—that is, their good credit history.

 CHECK Your Financial IQ

What is the usual purpose of a personal loan?

FINANCING A HOME

If you're like most people, the biggest single purchase you will make in your life will be a home. Chances are also extremely good that you will finance the purchase with a loan. Knowing the unique issues surrounding the purchase of a home—and whether or not to make such a purchase—can play a big role in your financial life.

Mortgage Loans

You have probably heard a homeowner speak of his or her mortgage. **Mortgage** is the common term for the type of loan people take to obtain a

For millions of Americans, purchasing a home is only possible through the use of credit.

home. Technically, a mortgage is a legal instrument by which the home becomes collateral for the loan. But most people also use the word to refer to their home financing arrangement.

Mortgages come in two basic forms: fixed rate and adjustable rate. With a **fixed rate mortgage**, the interest rate remains the same for the life of the loan. This means the payment will never go up or down. An **adjustable rate mortgage** (ARM) is one where the rate may go up or down over time. The rate change occurs at some preset time—for example, after a year. The amount and direction of the rate changes depends on changes in the economy. Because the rate goes up or down, the monthly mortgage payment will go up or down, too. Such mortgages may also be called variable rate mortgages.

Why would someone choose an ARM? One reason is that the starting rate is often lower than available in fixed rate mortgages. This means lower mortgage payments—at least until the rate is reset. Remember, this reset occurs at times specified in the loan agreement. Another reason to choose an ARM is if you believe interest rates will go down in the foreseeable future. Of course, it is vital to consider the effects of an interest rate increase. On loans of $100,000 to $300,000—not uncommon for a mortgage—a change of a couple percentage points can raise monthly mortgage payments by hundreds of dollars.

Since many ARMs are fixed for the first three or five years they also appeal to someone who frequently moves because of job transfers. If you know you will be transferred in four years and you decide that buying a home is the best option, then an adjustable rate mortgage may be a good choice.

Many ARMs may also begin with very low teaser rates. Remember from Kayce's story: A **teaser rate** is an extremely low interest rate for a short period of time that is used as a deal sweetener. Teaser rates are designed to make your first payments as low as possible and encourage you to take out a loan. Teaser rates are used on all types of loans including vehicle and home loans.

You may have heard of something called a **subprime mortgage**. Subprime mortgages are higher interest rate mortgage loans made to people with poor credit scores. Subprimes made a lot of news in recent years due to their higher rate of mortgage default. Many mortgage companies encouraged high-risk borrowers to borrow too much money using these loans. Over time, many people found that they could not make the payments and then defaulted. These widespread defaults became known as the "subprime meltdown" or "subprime crisis." It affected not only homeowners, but also many companies that lost money when the mortgages failed. It also affected taxpayers across the country. In October 2008, the crisis spurred the passage of legislation popularly called "the bailout bill" that committed as much as $700 billion of taxpayer revenue to buy financial assets backed by these bad mortgages.

Of course, mortgages are also significant on an individual level. Often, people take mortgages for long periods of time—sometimes 30 years or more. For many, the monthly mortgage payment is the largest bill they have to pay. The consequences of defaulting on a mortgage can be huge. You could lose your home and tens of thousands of dollars or more. It is essential that you make wise and informed decisions about the benefits and drawbacks of each type of loan. That way, when it is time to purchase a home, you can make a wise decision. Make sure you don't buy a house that will demand a payment that is—or may become—more than you can afford. Remember, not all lenders have your best interest in mind.

Other Costs of Buying a Home

Home buyers also may incur certain costs when buying a home and taking out a mortgage. Common expenses include appraisal fees, home inspection fees, mortgage origination fees, loan application fees, filing fees, and title insurance to make sure that the home's title is not encumbered in some way. Some buyers may even pay "points" to buy down their interest rate. A point is equivalent to 1 percent of the loan amount. These costs—which are commonly referred to as "closing costs"—can total several thousands of dollars. When shopping for a mortgage, it is important to consider these fees. Some lenders waive many closing costs.

Home Equity Loans

Home equity loans and home equity lines of credit (HELOCs) have become a very popular source of personal loans for many homeowners. A **home equity loan** allows a homeowner to borrow against the equity in his or her home—that is, the difference between the home's value and the amount owed to a lender. For example, let's assume you own a home valued at $200,000 and you owe $110,000 on your mortgage. In this case, you have $90,000 equity in the home. A typical home equity loan would allow you to borrow against this equity using your home as collateral. In most cases, home equity lenders limit the total amount of your mortgages to 80 percent of the market value of the home. So, using the example above, you may be allowed to borrow up to another $50,000 using a home equity loan (.80 × $200,000 = $160,000, minus $110,000 already borrowed = $50,000). Be cautious about home equity loans. If you fail to pay, you could lose your home.

Many homeowners opt to establish a home equity line of credit rather than take out a loan. A **line of credit** is an agreement to allow borrowing as needed up to a certain amount of money. Let's say a homeowner is approved for a $25,000 line of credit. He or she may leave the line of credit untouched for a period of time—and so pay no interest charges. Then, one month, the homeowner may draw on the line of credit to do some home repairs. The next month, he or she may draw on the line of credit for something else. The homeowner can do this repeatedly—as long as the total amount outstanding—the principal—doesn't exceed the limit of the credit line. Each month, the homeowner pays off some of the principal, as well as the interest charged on the amount borrowed.

Home equity borrowing became very popular when home prices were rapidly increasing. People were said to draw on their growing home equity to make purchases. Home equity loans are generally a much cheaper source of personal loans, with interest rates typically tied to various market interest rates. In some cases, if the proceeds are used for home improvement, the interest paid may be tax deductible.

Of course, home equity borrowing has risks. As with a mortgage, the borrowing is secured by the home. Failure to pay can lead to the lender seizing the borrower's home—even though the amount borrowed may be a fraction of the home's full value. Also, getting home equity loans may involve closing costs.

Buying versus Renting a Home

Buying a home is generally a good investment and one that many people aspire to. But it is not always the right decision—renting is often a good option.

The decision to buy or rent a home can be quite complicated. To begin with, the selection of homes available for rent may be entirely different from those available for purchase. In addition, when trying to decide whether to rent or buy, you must consider the following:

- How long do you plan to live in this area? In general, you should not purchase a home unless you plan to live in the area for several years. Often, there are expenses associated with a home purchase that take a few years to recover. For example, you may have to pay sales commissions to a real estate agent and mortgage origination fees to a lender. These can total several thousands of dollars.

- Do you have money saved for a down payment? Most lenders require you to put some money down and finance the remainder. Even if you can find a lender who will make a loan with little or no down payment, you will likely have to pay more for it.

- What is the price of homes relative to the price of rent in this area? Sometimes rent is a better deal. Remember, if you rent, someone else is responsible for the property maintenance and upkeep, which can be costly. But also remember that owning a home can provide a tax deduction that can lower your taxes. And, of course, when you buy a home, remember that some of what you pay each month may be building equity and increasing your net worth. In fact, one of the primary ways that many Americans have created wealth over their lifetimes is by buying a home. All of these factors must be considered. Figure 10.3 illustrates how buying a home can create wealth—that is, increase your net worth—versus paying rent.

- Are houses increasing in value or decreasing in value in the area? Home prices often rise and fall significantly. Predicting the direction of any market is difficult. But if it seems as though housing prices are likely to fall rapidly, it might be a good idea to hold off on purchasing.

- Do you have enough knowledge of the area to buy? Sometimes you need to live in an area to find out enough information to buy a home. Where is the best shopping? How long does it take you to commute to work?

- Rentals usually require payment of a security deposit to protect the owners from property damage done by renters who move out without paying for the damage. This is a sum of money that the property owner holds until the renter moves out. At that time, the property owner returns the deposit to the renter, minus any money used to repair damage that the renter left behind. You need to factor in the cost of the security deposit when determining whether to rent. How much are typical security deposits in the area? Do you have a pet, and will you therefore need to put up an additional pet deposit?

Figure 10.3   Effect of Homeowning and Renting on Net Worth:

When deciding whether to own or rent, you must consider not only how much you can afford each month in payments, but also how those payments may affect your net worth.

	Marcos	Sonia
Housing Expense	$1,500 (Rent per month)	$1,500 (Mortgage per month)
Annual Federal Tax Benefit	$0	$350 (assuming 28% tax bracket × $1,250 in interest)
Effect on Net Worth	–$1,500	–$900 ($1,500 in payment – $250 increase in equity – $350 tax benefit)

It is always a good idea to consult with a realtor who is familiar with the area to help you make these decisions. Buying a house may be the largest purchase you ever make and you should proceed with caution.

The Importance of Homeowners and Renters Insurance

Homeowners insurance provides insurance protection for your house in the event of a tornado, fire, theft, or other property damage. It also provides financial protection if someone gets injured at your house and sues you. Homeowner policies vary greatly in the types of perils that are covered. Refer to Figure 10.4 for the various types. You can also add numerous additional coverages, called **policy riders**, to cover things such as jewelry or valuable heirlooms that are often not fully covered by a typical policy.

As they do when people buy a car, lenders require that homeowners purchase at least enough homeowners insurance to cover the amount of the mortgage on the home. That way, if the house is destroyed, the homeowner will not default on the loan. But homeowners insurance is also essential for your own protection. It should be an important component of your financial plan to protect your assets. Remember, with each mortgage payment, you build equity in your home and add to your net worth. If you have owned a home for many years, your equity might be in the tens or even hundreds of thousands of dollars. It may represent a major share of your net worth. If the house were destroyed, you would want enough coverage not only to pay off the loan, but also to pay you back for the loss of the asset.

Many people don't realize that their possessions are not protected when they rent. For example, if you live in an apartment complex that is destroyed by fire and you lose all of your possessions, you will not be reimbursed for that loss by the building owner. Your possessions are not insured by the building's owners. However, you can purchase renters insur-

Figure 10.4 Types of Perils Protected by Homeowner's (HO) Insurance Policies

Homeowners and renters insurance can provide invaluable protection against loss. Different policies, however, cover different things.

HO-1: Protects against fire, lightning, explosions, hail, riots, vehicles, aircraft, smoke, vandalism, theft, malicious mischief, glass breakage.

HO-2: Protects against the events identified in HO-1, along with falling objects, the weight of ice, snow, or sleet, the collapse of buildings, overflow of water or steam, power surges, and the explosion of steam or hot-water systems, frozen plumbing, heating units, air-conditioning systems, and domestic appliances.

HO-3: Protects the home and any other structures on the property against all events except those that are specifically excluded by the homeowner's policy. The events that are typically not covered by this insurance are earthquakes, floods, termites, war, and nuclear accidents. It may be possible to obtain additional insurance to protect against floods or earthquakes. This policy also protects personal assets against the events that are listed in HO-2.

HO-4: Renter's insurance. Protects personal assets from events such as theft, fire, vandalism, and smoke.

HO-5: Protects the home, other structures on the property, and personal assets against all events except those that are excluded by the specific homeowner's policy. This policy provides coverage of the home similar to that provided by HO-3, but slightly more coverage of personal assets.

HO-6: Condominium owner's insurance. Protects personal assets from events such as theft, fire, vandalism, and smoke (review the specific policy to determine which events are covered).

HO-8: Protects the home from the same events identified in HO-1, except that it is based on repairs or cash values, not replacement costs.

ance that will protect you. Renters insurance can also cover your living expenses if the property you rent is being repaired as the result of some covered event. Renters with valuable assets should consider buying renters insurance to protect them from loss.

 CHECK Your Financial IQ

By what means do most people finance the purchase of a home?

FINANCING YOUR EDUCATION

For many people, the expense of getting an education rivals the expense of buying a home. In many cases, getting the training you need for a successful career will require borrowing money.

Student loans are another type of personal loan. Students and their families use these loans to finance the expense of going to college or trade school. Some student loans go directly to the student while others go to the student's parents. In general, student loans allow the borrower to obtain money for education bills—and to delay making payments on the borrowed money until after graduation.

Federal student loans are the largest source of student loans. Because they are guaranteed by the federal government, they also have the best terms. The government essentially acts as the cosigner on these loans and pledges to repay them if the borrower defaults. The government does this to encourage education. Remember, if you earn a degree you will likely earn much more income over your lifetime. Higher incomes mean you pay more taxes over the long run and are less likely to need other forms of government assistance. Federal Stafford loans and Federal Perkins loans are the two primary education loans made to students.

Federal Stafford Loans

Federal Stafford loans are the most common type of federal education loans. They come in two forms: subsidized and unsubsidized.

Subsidized Stafford loans are need-based. That means applicants must show a certain level of financial need in order to qualify. Subsidized Stafford loans are highly desirable because interest charges do not build up on these loans while the student is in school. So, a student can take a $5,000 loan in 2008, and at graduation in 2012, he or she will still owe just $5,000. After leaving school, subsidized Stafford loan recipients get a six-month grace period during which time interest does not accrue and payments do not have to be made. All this time, the federal government essentially pays this interest for the student. Compare this to a normal loan. Even if you could arrange not to make payments for four to five years, interest charges would build up. So, the $5,000 borrowed in 2008 might have grown to some $7,000 or more by 2012.

Unsubsidized Stafford loans are not need-based, and interest accrues on these loans while you are in school. They still offer recipients the advantage of not having to make monthly payments until leaving school. But, as you have seen, the amount of interest that can build up over four to five years is considerable.

Since both types of Stafford loans are backed by the government, neither one requires a credit check. Both types have limits on the annual and total amounts you can borrow.

Federal Perkins Loans

Federal Perkins loans are similar to Stafford loans except they are for students with "exceptional" financial need. Perkins loans carry a lower interest rate and offer a longer grace period before students have to begin repayment. These loans go to students coming from extreme poverty who will likely not get any financial support from their parents to attend school.

The Reality of Student Loans

Keep in mind that both Perkins and Stafford loans are still loans, and you are required to repay them. Many students take out too much in student

loans and have difficulty making the payments upon graduation. Remember, when you graduate you will have many more expenses that will use your income. Rent or house payments, utilities, possibly a car payment, and groceries will all chomp through your initial income very rapidly. Student loans are a useful financial aid, but students should use them with caution.

Parents also have the ability to borrow from many sources to finance a college education. All these loans have varying interest rates, repayment schedules, and maturities. They all have to be repaid. A student loan is still debt. Learn everything you can about your options, and enter into these contracts with the knowledge that you will need to repay this money at some point. You can find out more information about student loans by going to www.salliemae.com.

✓ CHECK Your Financial IQ

Why are student loans different from other kinds of personal loans?

FINANCING YOUR CAR

Another major expense for people is the car they drive. Many people finance car purchases with loans from the car dealer or from a bank or other lending institution. Car loans typically run from three to six years for new cars. Longer loan periods generally mean lower payments—but also that the borrower will pay more in interest over the life of the loan. In

Professor FIN

When you are purchasing a car, you will often hear someone talk about its Blue Book® Value. The name refers to an actual book, but today you can find the Blue Book® Value of your car at Kelley Blue Book's **www.kbb.com**.

Did you ever wonder where the name "Kelley Blue Book" came from? It began in 1918, when young Les Kelley parked three Model T Fords in a lot and began the Kelley Kar Company. His company went on to become the largest dealership in the world.

As Les Kelley began selling one car after another, he needed more inventory, so he distributed to other dealers and banks a list of cars he wanted to buy with the prices he was willing to pay for them. As his company grew, so did the respect from others in the business. They too, wanted to use the list Kelley had compiled. In 1926, Les Kelley published the first *Blue Book of Motor Car Values*, with an expanded list of automobile values that included new and used models. The rest is history!

Copy of an original *Blue Book*

Consumer Edition of the *Blue Book* (1993)

Source: www.kbb .com/kbb/ CompanyInfo/History .aspx

Note: The Kelley Blue Book trademark and photos are used with permission of Kelley Blue Book Co., Inc.

addition, loans of five and six years may put a car owner in the position of owing more on the car in the final months of the loan than the car is actually worth. Consider, for example, a car owner who still owes $5,000 on a loan for a now-five-year-old vehicle that has a market value of only $4,000.This could cause problems if the person wanted to sell the car, or if it were destroyed in an accident. In that situation, the owner would receive just $4,000 from the buyer or insurance company, have no car, and still owe the lender $1,000.

Used cars are a good option for many people, but often they present financing issues that a potential buyer may not face with a new car. Many sources of used car financing will only loan money on newer models that are less than five years old. In addition, the amount of the loan is typically restricted by the market value of the vehicle as determined by Kelley Blue Book or some other reputable source.

Recently, the Internet has emerged as a great source for used vehicles. Ebay, AutoTrader.com, and other sites sell thousands of used vehicles annually. Potential buyers can evaluate the feedback of potential sellers to determine their reputation before buying. Buyers should also use a service such as Carfax to research a car's history prior to purchasing to see for example, if the car has been in an accident or a flood. There are a number of online financing options for people with good credit, and in many cases, these lenders will loan money on older vehicles based on the borrower's credit history. Don't forget that you need to factor in shipping costs or the cost of retrieving your vehicle from the seller. Many purchases may be in another state, but these long-distance vehicle purchases are becoming common since a buyer can often get a very good deal on a used car.

There are other options to buying a car with a loan. Here we will consider the benefits and drawbacks of leasing a vehicle.

Leasing versus Buying a Car

Leasing vehicles instead of buying them has become popular in the past several years. A **lease** is essentially a long-term rental agreement. Each month, you pay a lease payment, much as you would make a payment to pay off a loan. Leasing a car offers some advantages over purchasing one. It also has some disadvantages. Therefore, the lease-versus-buy decision will not be the same for everyone.

One advantage of leasing is that it requires only a small down payment—or none at all. Also, lease payments for a new car are generally lower than loan payments for that same car. This is because when you lease, you pay only for use of the car for a period of time—not for the value of the car itself. Finally, at the end of the lease, you return the vehicle to the dealer and do not have to worry about selling the car.

At the same time, you do not own the car, and it can never be listed as one of your assets. You cannot sell it and use the proceeds for something else. When you return it to the dealer at the end of the lease, you have nothing. Yet, while you lease the car you are responsible for keeping the car maintained in perfect condition and are liable for any damage to it.

In addition, many vehicle leases have mileage limits—12,000–15,000 miles a year is common. If you drive the vehicle more miles than specified, you may face additional charges. There are often penalties for ending the

You
Do It
Activity #2

lease early. Many consumers allege that there are many hidden fees in lease agreements. Read the agreement carefully prior to signing.

The easiest way to make a lease-versus-buy decision is to compare the total cost of leasing versus buying. Refer to Figure 10.5 for an example of a simple comparison. Note that the result of this comparison could vary significantly depending on the cost of the vehicle, the length of the loan or lease, and many other factors.

The Importance of Car Insurance

You have read about the need to insure your home against loss. It is also important to insure yourself against loss that involves your car.

Figure 10.5 Comparison of the Cost of Purchasing versus Leasing

Leasing and purchasing a car each have their benefits and drawbacks, but you can make a good comparison of the actual costs of each option.

Cost of Purchasing the Car	Cost
1. Down payment	$1,000
2. Down payment of $1,000 results in forgone interest income:	
Forgone Interest	
Income per Year = Down Payment × Annual Interest Rate	
= $1,000 × .04 = $40	
Forgone Interest over Four Years = $40 × 4 = $160	160
3. Total monthly payments are:	
Total Monthly Payments = Monthly Payment × Number of Months	
= $412 × 48 = $19,776	19,776
Total	$20,936
Minus: Expected amount to be received when car is sold in four years	– 10,000
Total cost	$10,936

Cost of Leasing the Car for Four Years	
1. Security deposit of $800 results in forgone interest income (although she will receive her deposit back in four years):	
Forgone Interest	
Income per Year = Down Payment × Annual Interest Rate	
= $800 × .04 = $32	
Forgone Interest over Four Years = $32 × 4 = $128	$128
2. Total monthly payments are:	
Total Monthly Payments = Monthly Payment × Number of Months	
= $300 × 48 = $14,400	14,400
Total cost	$14,528

Whether you lease or buy you will be required to maintain adequate insurance on your car. Insurance is a service you purchase that protects you from loss associated with unexpected events. For example, auto insurance will pay for vehicle repairs if you get in a wreck. If you destroy the car in a crash, insurance will write you a check for the value of the car before its destruction.

Lenders require that you keep sufficient auto insurance to protect their investment. Think about this: If you buy a car by borrowing $15,000 from a bank, what happens if you wreck the car? You will still be required to repay the loan. And, you will have no car. What will you drive? Will you buy another car and have two car payments? Lenders know that the likelihood of loan default goes up if you can no longer drive the car. Therefore, they require insurance that will pay off the loan in the event you have a wreck. Many states also require you to maintain automobile insurance.

Auto insurance can cover you against the loss of your property—your car. It can also cover you against any damage you do to other people or their property. This is called **liability coverage**. The two primary liability components are property damage liability and bodily injury liability. Bodily injury liability covers the costs you may be responsible for if you are deemed to be at fault in a wreck that injures or kills someone. Such bills can be extremely large, as you can imagine. The property damage liability will cover repairs to their vehicle if you are at fault.

Insurance can be very expensive for young drivers with limited experience. Data shows that young drivers tend to have more accidents, so their insurance is priced accordingly. Sometimes individuals find that they cannot even purchase vehicle insurance if they have too many accidents or even speeding tickets or other violations. Remember, your credit rating can also impact the amount that you pay for vehicle insurance: Poor credit translates to higher insurance rates. Be a good driver and save yourself some money.

There are a number of other factors, such as the value of your car and where you live, that impact your insurance premium. In addition, people who drive more miles every year are charged higher rates. Shop around when you buy car insurance. Premiums can vary substantially from one agency to the next.

 CHECK Your Financial IQ

What are two major options for paying for a new car?

Summary

- Loans allow people to buy things and pay for them over time. People often take out personal loans for large purchases, such as cars or houses. These sorts of loans are available from a variety of sources, including banks, credit unions, and other financial institutions. They also come in many forms, including secured and unsecured loans.

- Interest rate charges on personal loans are reported as the annual percentage rate, or APR.

- When purchasing a home, you should begin by evaluating your financial situation to determine how much you can afford. Renting may also be an option. If you decide to purchase a home, you will get a loan called a mortgage. Mortgages come in two basic forms: fixed rate and adjustable rate. You will also get homeowners insurance. Renters should purchase renters insurance coverage on their personal belongings.

- Student loans are also common personal loans used to finance education. Federal student loans are the largest source of student loans because they are guaranteed by the federal government and have the best terms. But, like all loans, student loans must be repaid and should be taken with great care.

- While financing a car for purchase is one widely used option, some people find leasing to be an attractive alternative. Each option has benefits and drawbacks. In all cases, though, car insurance is a must.

Key Terms and Vocabulary

Adjustable rate mortgage	Liability coverage
Annual percentage rate	Line of credit
Collateral	Maturity date
Cosigner	Mortgage
Default	Personal loan
Down payment	Policy rider
Federal Perkins loan	Secured loan
Federal Stafford loan	Subprime mortgage
Fixed rate mortgage	Teaser rate
Home equity loan	Unsecured loan
Lease	

What Do You Know?

myFinLitlab

1. (a) List possible sources of personal loans.

   (b) Why might a person prefer to take a loan rather than spending money he or she has saved?

2. (a) Why do lenders need to collect so much personal information about people who seek loans?

   (b) Why might someone who has very little credit history have trouble obtaining a loan?

3. (a) Explain how collateral works.

   (b) What would you expect to find in comparing interest rates of secured and unsecured loans?

4. (a) What are your responsibilities if you cosign a loan?

   (b) What are the potential consequences of failing to live up to your responsibilities as a cosigner?

5. (a) Describe the characteristics of a fixed-rate mortgage.

   (b) Why do you think some homeowners prefer a fixed rate mortgage to an adjustable rate mortgage?

6. (a) Describe some of the costs of buying a home.

   (b) Why do those costs affect the decision to buy or rent?

7. (a) What kinds of loss does homeowners insurance protect against?

   (b) What would you stand to lose if you maintained a homeowners policy that was designed only to pay off the amount you owed on a mortgage in the event of a fire or other disaster?

8. (a) Who makes possible most of the student loans in this country?

   (b) What is the government's interest in helping to make education affordable?

9. (a) What financial criteria should be considered when buying a car versus leasing?

   (b) Why might you be concerned about having a too-long auto loan?

10. (a) What are the advantages and disadvantages of leasing?

    (b) Give some examples of a person for whom leasing a car would not be a good idea.

What Are Your Finance Math Skills?   myFinLitlab.

The first three questions correlate to *Math for Personal Finance* features located throughout the chapter.

1. Mousa borrowed $6,000 to buy a car and he will make 36 monthly payments of $185.81 to repay the loan. How much total interest will he pay over the life of the loan?

2. Lidell bought renters insurance with a $500 deductible to cover his possessions. A fire destroyed his apartment complex and he lost all his possessions. If his insurance coverage maxed out at $5,000, how large was the check he received from the insurance company?

3. How much interest will Blaine owe when he graduates from college if he took out a $2,000 student loan during his last year of college? The interest rate was 4 percent and interest was deferred during that year.

4. How much do you have to save for a down payment on a car if the price of the vehicle is $8,000 and the dealer wants a 20 percent down payment?

5. In the previous problem, how much will you be financing if the same terms apply but the dealer drops the price of the car by 10 percent?

6. If the mortgage lender requires a minimum 5 percent down payment on a $260,000 house, how much will you be financing?

7. Which payment will be lower assuming an interest rate of 6 percent: a $200,000 mortgage financed for 15 years or a $200,000 mortgage financed for 30 years?

8. If you get a personal loan to attend college, how much interest will accrue in the first year on a $3,000 loan assuming market rates of interest are 6 percent? Assume payments are deferred until you graduate.

What Would You Do?

The agreement that Kayce had with her father was to work a few extra hours at the shop. This worked out well for Kayce at the beginning. But then the racing season got underway and Kayce was really doing great at the track. Each week it seemed that Kayce had another excuse for not being able to work the extra hours. When the next payment for the bike was due, Kayce did not have the money to pay because of all the missed hours at the shop. Kayce's father had to step in and pay for that month. As the months progressed, it seemed that Kayce's father had to pay often for the bike because Kayce did not have the money. This extra payment was beginning to impact the family finances because Kayce's father had not planned for the bike payments in his financial budget.

1. What are Kayce's responsibilities toward the payments on the bike?

2. Is Kayce's behavior toward her father ethical?

3. What advice would you give to a parent or another person before they cosigned a personal loan?

What Are the Connections?
Language Arts, Technology, and Math

Research three cars that you would like to buy. They may be new or used. Be sure to cite the source of your information. Make a chart that shows the following information for each car:

- Car's features (options available on the make, model, color, etc.)
- Year of the car
- Any down payment you will have for the purchase
- Monthly payments for the car
- Insurance for the car (you may need to gather this information from a local insurance representative)

Summarize your findings with a recommendation of which car to purchase. Be sure to defend your choice.

 Teamwork

In a team, develop an advertisement for a car of your team's choice. Present all the features, consumer safety factors, incentives, and financing for the car. You may develop a colorful poster, full-page newspaper advertisement, video ad, or brochure about the car.

 **Financial Literacy**
CERTIFICATION

TEST PREP QUESTIONS

 myFinLitlab

1. Which of the following people does not have a financially sound reason for taking a personal loan?
   a. Ramon has the money to buy a car but he can invest the money and make more than he will be charged for his car loan.
   b. Carrie needs to borrow money in order to pay for her last year of college.
   c. David needs to borrow $1,000 so that he can buy season tickets to see the Yankees play in their new stadium.
   d. Tanya has enough money to make a 20 percent down payment on a new bed, but she knows that she can pay the balance if she has a loan for two years.

2. Which of the following terms is *not* correctly matched with its definition?
   a. Principal: the amount borrowed.
   b. Terms of the loan: cost of the item if it is not being financed.
   c. Down payment: the amount of money the buyer gives toward the purchase.
   d. Repayment schedule: number of months needed to repay the entire loan along with the dollar amount of each payment and the interest rate.

3. Why does a lender want information about a person's current cash inflow and outflow?
   a. The information helps to determine the number of cosigners a person will need for the loan to be approved.

b. Most lenders do not make loans to anyone whose assets are not twice his liabilities.

c. The lender needs to know the person's credit score before making the loan.

d. The information helps the lender make a decision on the person's ability to pay back the loan.

4. Why should a person be concerned if she has been offered a "teaser rate" on a loan?

a. She will be forced to pay that same rate for the life of the loan.

b. After a short time the rate will most likely go up.

c. It is not a valid loan and the item being purchased with this loan will probably be repossessed.

d. She will be able to get a loan at a much better interest rate in just a few months.

5. What is the purpose of a loan contract?

a. It is an offer by the lender to sell something at a given price to another person.

b. It is a legally binding agreement that explains the charges to be paid by the buyer and the obligations of the seller.

c. It is a promise made to the credit bureaus that the lender will protect the buyer from bankruptcy until the loan is paid in full.

d. It is a legally binding agreement that guarantees that the buyer will pay the lender in full and on time.

6. Why is it possible that the interest rate advertised for a loan is very different from the annual percentage rate (APR) on that loan?

a. The APR includes fees associated with the application, credit report check, and closing costs in addition to the annual interest.

b. The APR provides for a 10 percent annual discount if all loan payments are made on time.

c. The advertised loan was not multiplied by 12 to figure out the annual percentage rate.

d. The advertised loan is a teaser rate and the APR is the interest rate after the teaser rate is over.

7. Why should a person be very careful before agreeing to cosign a loan?

a. The cosigner is required to deposit the amount of the loan into a special bank account until the loan is paid in full.

b. The cosigner is agreeing to pay half of the loan.

c. The cosigner's credit score will be changed to the score of the other borrower.

d. If the borrower defaults on the loan, the lender will expect to receive full payment from the cosigner.

8. A person learns that the interest rate on his $2,000, one year auto loan is 5 percent. He is about to apply for the loan when a friend says that he should first know the APR on the loan. He discovers that there is a $50 application fee, a $50 credit check fee, and a $100 charge related to other closing costs. What is the APR on this loan?

a. The APR is 5 percent.

b. The APR is 10 percent.

c. The APR is 15 percent.

d. The APR cannot be determined from the information given.

9. Which of the following terms is *not* correctly matched with its definition?

a. Unsecured loan: no collateral is given in support of the loan.

b. Mortgage loan: the home serves as the collateral for the loan.

c. Secured loan: the collateral for the loan is a person's good credit history and her signature on a loan agreement.

d. Adjustable rate mortgage: the mortgage rate can change several times over the life of the mortgage.

10. What is a sound financial reason for a person to choose an adjustable rate mortgage (ARM) over a fixed rate mortgage?

a. She expects to trade up to a larger house in three or four years as her career advances.

b. She wants to be sure that she will never have to pay more than her current mortgage amount.

c. She believes that interest rates will be going up in the near future.

d. She is planning to retire in this house in 30 years with the mortgage completely paid.

11. Subprime mortgages are

a. mortgages offered at interest rates below the national average to first time homeowners.

b. low interest rate mortgages awarded to people with excellent credit histories.

c. mortgages offered to people who already have at least one mortgage on their current home.

d. high interest rate mortgages usually made to people with low credit scores.

12. How is a $50,000 home equity loan different from a $50,000 home equity line of credit?

a. There are no interest charges on money used from the line of credit; the equity loan rate is the same as the person's mortgage interest rate.

b. Loans require a person to complete an application and go through a credit check; lines of credit are approved if the person has an account at the bank.

c. The person who takes the loan receives the full $50,000 at once; the person with the line of credit can borrow against the credit line for any amount up to $50,000 as money is needed.

d. The $50,000 home equity loan must be used to improve the home; the $50,000 line of credit can be used for anything the borrower chooses.

13. When we say that a person with a home that is valued at $300,000 and who has an outstanding mortgage of $100,000 has a lot of equity in her home, we mean that she

a. has a lot of debt.

b. owns a large fraction of her home.

c. will not be approved for additional loans until her mortgage is paid in full.

d. will be considered to be at risk of defaulting on her mortgage.

14. A person's bank will only make an equity loan if the loan and his current mortgage do not exceed 80 percent of the market value of the home. If he has a $200,000 mortgage and his home is appraised at $400,000, how large an equity loan can he hope to obtain?

a. He can expect to obtain a loan of $80,000.

b. He can expect to obtain a loan of $120,000.

c. He can expect to obtain a loan of $160,000.

d. He can expect to obtain a loan of $320,000.

15. If a person has homeowners or renters insurance, it will protect the person

a. if she loses her job and cannot pay her rent.

b. from having to file for bankruptcy.

c. if someone falls in her house and sues her.

d. from the bank foreclosing on her home for not making mortgage payments.

16. If a person does *not* have renters insurance and her laptop computer is stolen from her apartment, she

a. does not have to worry because the landlord has to pay for her loss.

b. can still buy renters insurance and make a claim to be reimbursed for the loss of the laptop.

c. can file a claim for the loss through her car insurance company.

d. will have to replace the laptop computer at her own expense.

17. A high school senior whose family is very poor wants to go to college, but the family cannot afford to pay. To help finance her education, she should try to obtain the type of loan where interest charges do not build up while she is in school and even during the first nine months after graduation. This type of financing is known as a(n)

a. bank loan.

b. Federal Perkins loan.

c. subsidized Federal Stafford loan.

d. unsubsidized Federal Stafford loan.

18. A person decides to lease a $20,000 car for three years instead of buying the car and financing it with a loan. At the end of three years the car is worth $11,000. How much will he receive when he returns the car to the dealership?

a. He will receive $0, and he will have to cover the cost of any damages that have been done to the car.

b. He will receive $11,000, less the cost of any damages that have been done to the car.

c. He will receive whatever amount of money the dealer is able to get selling the car as a used car.

d. He will receive half of what the dealer gets from the sale of the used car.

19. A disadvantage of paying for a car with a long-term loan is that

a. the monthly loan costs are higher than the same loan taken for a shorter time.

b. the person cannot take possession of the vehicle until at least half of the loan has been paid.

c. toward the end of the loan, it is possible to owe more on the car loan than what the car is worth.

d. the loan increases in size and the interest rate on the loan goes up.

CHAPTER 11

Learning Objectives

Explain how credit cards work.

Describe different credit card features.

Explain how to use a credit card correctly.

Describe other risky credit arrangements.

Key Terms

Credit card
Debt consolidation
Grace period
Overdraft protection
Pawnbroker
Payday lending

Credit Cards and Other Forms of Credit

"**Man, you have to find a way to come along,**" said Mario. "Spring break in Florida is awesome!"

Anil rolled his eyes. "You don't have to rub it in, Mario. You know I haven't got any money right now. So unless you've got the cash to lend me ..."

"Can't you borrow the money from your mother?" asked Mario. "Or what about that rich uncle you're always talking about?"

"No way. My mother is angry about my grades, and my uncle was just telling me about all the money he's lost in the stock market recently. I can't ask him now."

"Well ... sorry, dude," said Mario weakly. Anil and Mario fell silent. Anil picked absent-mindedly through the stack of mail on the table. Then, he saw it.

"Hey!" said Anil. "I've got an idea!" He showed Mario the envelope. "Enjoy the freedom to pay over time," it said, and "Low introductory rate with no annual fee!" "I can get a credit card and pay for the trip that way!" said Anil.

"But Anil," said Mario, "how are you going to pay a credit card bill if you haven't got any money?"

"Well, all I'd need to do is pay the minimum for a couple months," said Anil. "Then I'll pay the rest off when I get a job this summer."

"I don't know," said Mario. "My sister warned me about using credit cards for stuff like this. One of her good friends got into deep trouble that way."

Anil slumped back into his seat. "Who cares what happened to someone I don't even know? That would never happen to me."

The lure of easy access to credit—through credit cards and other sources—is attractive. In fact, credit cards can be a useful financial tool. Yet easy access to credit of the sort credit cards and certain other options offer can create serious financial difficulties. Your financial future depends on approaching this type of credit cautiously.

HOW CREDIT CARDS WORK

Credit cards provide people with revolving open-end credit, which they can draw from repeatedly up to some preset limit. A **credit provider**, such as a bank, agrees to make a certain amount of credit available to the cardholder. The cardholder can then use this credit as he or she wishes. Simply by presenting the card at a place of business that accepts the credit card, the cardholder can make a purchase without using any cash. He or she can continue to use the card until reaching the credit limit. Each month, the cardholder receives a bill listing all of the credit card purchases. Then, he or she pays off all or some of the borrowed money.

A credit card can be a very useful financial tool. However, it is also perhaps the easiest one to abuse. Often, people find themselves in financial trouble over the easy access to credit that credit cards afford them. Anil planned to pay for a spring break trip with a credit card—even though he had no money to pay off the debt. Does that seem wise? Let's take some time and evaluate the positive and negative of credit cards, as well as all the various features and options.

Ease of Availability and Use

Perhaps the easiest way to establish credit is to apply for a credit card. Offers abound. Many people receive credit card offers in the mail almost daily. And it isn't necessary to wait for someone to mail you an offer. You can apply for a card at banks, through Web sites, and in many other ways.

A credit card allows you to buy products and services wherever the card is honored. A wide variety of businesses honor credit cards. People typically use credit cards for lower-priced convenience purchases such as meals, gasoline, clothing, air travel, and groceries. Costly items such as houses and cars are not typical credit card purchases. As you can see in Figure 11.1, Anil used his credit card to eat at several restaurants over spring break.

Billing takes place monthly. At the end of each monthly billing cycle, you will receive a statement that identifies purchases you made during the period. The statement gives the total amount borrowed. It also gives a minimum payment you must pay. Look at Anil's statement again. You can see his minimum payment and the interest rate charged. Obviously he had fun on spring break.

Credit cards offer three advantages. First, you can purchase products and services without carrying a large amount of cash or checkbook. Second, as long as you pay the balance in full at the end of each billing cycle, you do not incur any interest charges. Third, you receive a monthly statement that contains a list of your purchases for that month. This list can help you keep track of spending. Some cards provide an annual statement that aids in preparing your taxes. These statements allow you to track annual spending in various categories and help with budgeting.

Today, consumers can use credit cards of all types at a wide range of businesses.

Figure 11.1   Sample Credit Card Statement

Notice that Anil does not have to pay off the entire balance of his account, although he will pay a high interest rate on the balance.

1 Your First Bank

CREDIT CARD STATEMENT

SEND PAYMENT TO
Box 1234
Anytown, USA

ACCOUNT NUMBER	NAME	DATE	PAYMENT DUE DATE
4125-239-412	Anil Doe	2/15/08	3/05/08

CREDIT LINE	CREDIT AVAILABLE	NEW BALANCE	MINUMUM PAYMENT DUE
$1200.00	$697.31	$502.69	$40.00

REFERENCE	SOLD	POSTED	ACTIVITY	AMOUNT
32F349ER3	1/12	1/15	Record Recycler, Anytown USA	14.83
89102DI8S2	1/13	1/15	Befforama Rest., Anytown USA	30.55
NX34VJS32	1/10	1/10	Great, Big City USA	27.50
84RT3293A	1/20	1/21	Dino-Gel Petrol, Anytown USA	12.26
873DWS321	2/09	2/09	Shirts 'N Such, Tinyville USA	40.10
12345AB56	2/10	2/10	Seaside Restaurant, Hotspot FL	25.00
789CD4567	2/10	2/10	Sunny's Restaurant, Hotspot FL	27.45
112345DE1	2/11	2/11	Beach's Motel, Hotspot FL	325.00

Previous Balance	(*)	Current Amount Due	
Purchases	(*) 502.69	Amount Past Due	
Cash Advances	(*)	Amount Over Credit Line	
Payments	(*)	Minimum Payment Due	40.00
Credits	(*)		
FINANCE CHARGES	(*)		
Late Charges	(*)		
NEW BALANCE	(*) 502.69		

Finance Charge Summary	Purchases	Advances	For Customer Service Call:
Periodic Rate	1.65%	2.50%	1-800-XXX-XXXX
Annual Percentage Rate	19.80%	30.00%	For Lost or Stolen Card, call:
			1-800-XXX-XXXX
			24-Hour Telephone Numbers

Please make check or money order payable to Your First Bank. Include account number on front.

Source: www.practicalmoneyskills.com/english/resources/tutor/statements/credit_state.php

Applying for a Credit Card

To get a credit card, you must apply for it. These days, as you have read, many people receive credit card offers in the mail, or through other sources. Figure 11.2 shows a sample credit card application.

Applying for a credit card is much like applying for a loan or other form of credit. Your potential creditor will obtain personal information from you. They will consider personal information, such as cash inflows or income, and current cash outflows, such as house payments or car payments. In addition, some creditors will also evaluate your assets, such as savings or other financial assets and real property.

Potential creditors will also perform a **credit check**—that is, they will access your credit report in order to examine your credit history and determine your ability to repay. Your credit report summarizes your existing lines of credit and past credit. Did you pay your bills on time or default on any loans? This information will show up on a credit check. In general, creditors will be more likely to extend credit to people with high levels of cash inflows, low levels of cash outflows, and a good credit history. Many also evaluate potential for high cash inflows. For example, college students are often bombarded with credit card offers in spite of having low cash inflows and limited credit history. That is clearly what was happening in the case of Anil, who has no cash inflow and few assets. Potential creditors are betting on the completion of a college degree and the higher level of income that results. Some credit card companies will offer free t-shirts or other teasers to encourage people to sign up. Just remember, there is no "free lunch." You have to pay the bill every month.

Creditors may also consider economic factors. Is the economy healthy or weak? Is a recession approaching? Are people losing their jobs in unusual numbers? Creditors are more reluctant to extend credit during a weak economy.

Figure 11.2 Sample Credit Card Application

These days, it can be relatively simple to obtain a credit card by providing only a small amount of personal information.

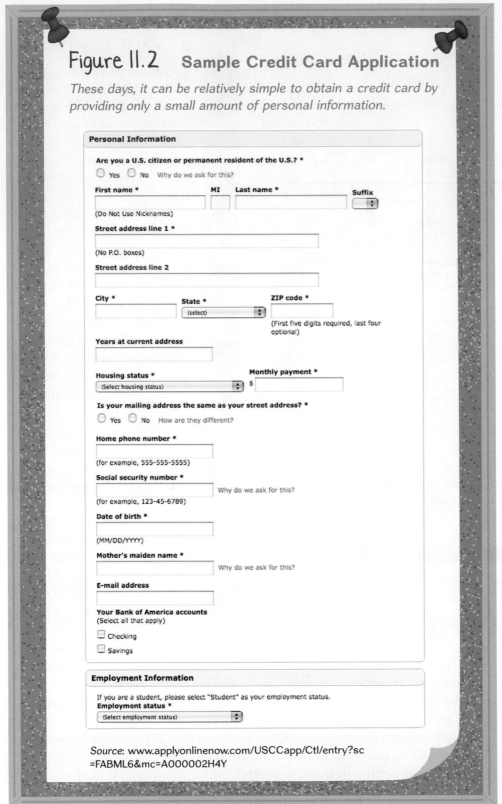

Personal Information

Are you a U.S. citizen or permanent resident of the U.S.? *
○ Yes ○ No   Why do we ask for this?

First name *   MI   Last name *   Suffix

(Do Not Use Nicknames)

Street address line 1 *

(No P.O. boxes)

Street address line 2

City *   State *   ZIP code *
              (select)
                             (First five digits required, last four optional)

Years at current address

Housing status *   Monthly payment *
(Select housing status) $

Is your mailing address the same as your street address? *
○ Yes ○ No   How are they different?

Home phone number *

(for example, 555-555-5555)

Social security number *
                        Why do we ask for this?
(for example, 123-45-6789)

Date of birth *

(MM/DD/YYYY)

Mother's maiden name *
                        Why do we ask for this?

E-mail address

Your Bank of America accounts
(Select all that apply)
☐ Checking
☐ Savings

Employment Information

If you are a student, please select "Student" as your employment status.
Employment status *
(Select employment status)

Source: www.applyonlinenow.com/USCCapp/Ctl/entry?sc =FABML6&mc=A000002H4Y

Types of Credit Cards

The most popular brands of credit card include MasterCard, Visa, American Express, and Discover. MasterCard, Visa, and Discover allow the financing of purchases over time. That is, if you buy items worth, say, $500 during a billing cycle, you have the option of paying for them all at once or over a period of several months—with interest added, of course. In the past, American Express did not offer this option, but now they offer this payment flexibility on some cards.

Credit cards are recognized and accepted by most merchants in the United States and globally. Merchants accept these cards because it helps them sell goods. They know that some consumers might not make a purchase at their place of business if they are unable to use a credit card.

While credit cards help merchants, they also cost them money. That's because credit card companies receive a percentage of the purchase price in return for their services. This way, the credit card company makes money on your use of the card even if you pay off your balance every month and never pay a nickel in interest. Most cards receive between 2 and 4 percent of the purchase price. For example, if you buy $100 worth of goods from a store and pay with a credit card, that store would pay the credit card company between $2 and $4 for this transaction. Thus, the store makes less on a credit card purchase than on a comparable cash purchase. Obviously, a large retailer such as Wal-Mart will be able to negotiate a better deal with the credit card companies than a small retailer.

Many financial institutions issue MasterCard and Visa credit cards to individuals. Each financial institution makes its own arrangements with the credit card companies with regard to billing and financing for individuals who opt not to pay the balance in full every month. Some universities and charities also sponsor credit cards and negotiate various arrangements.

In addition to the primary issuers mentioned, there are also numerous retail cards available. Target Stores Inc., Sears, and other retail stores issue cards. Oil companies, such as Shell and Exxon Mobil also issue credit cards to use at their retail outlets. However, in most cases, these types of specific cards cannot be used at other retail outlets. For example, your gasoline card will not be accepted at Wal-Mart. Visa and MasterCard credit cards can be used at almost any retail outlet.

 CHECK Your Financial IQ

What can a consumer do with a credit card?

CREDIT CARD FEATURES

As you shop for and use credit cards, you must become familiar with their different features and options available. Here are some of the more common ones.

Credit Limit

Credit card companies evaluate your creditworthiness not only to determine whether to extend credit but also to establish an individual credit limit. Recall, a credit limit is the maximum that you can borrow at any one time. In other words, the total amount of your outstanding debt to the credit card company cannot exceed the credit limit. So, if your credit limit is $5,000, you can buy up to $5,000 worth of goods or services—until you make a payment and reduce your outstanding balance to below $5,000. At that point, you can borrow the difference between that balance and $5,000.

Some low-income, high-risk individuals may begin with a credit limit as low as $300. Anil—who has little credit history but decent job prospects—has a limit of $1,200. Other individuals with good credit history and high incomes may have limits exceeding $25,000. A word of advice: Creditors monitor how much of your limit you keep charged up. If your card has a $5,000 limit and you keep it charged near the limit, it will negatively impact your credit score.

Overdraft Protection

 You Do It

Activity #1

Some credit cards have **overdraft protection**, which is a feature that allows you to "overdraw," or exceed your credit limit. (Note that overdraft protection is also a feature of checking accounts, where it protects you in the event you write a check for more money than you have in your account.)

With credit cards, overdraft protection prevents you from attempting to use your credit card and having the charge denied because you are over limit. Sounds great—but there is a catch. This feature should be used only in emergency situations, since the overdraft charge can be as high as $30 or

more for each overdraft. In addition, overdraft often triggers higher interest rates on any balances you are carrying.

Some individuals prefer overdraft protection to avoid the embarrassment of being denied a charge. Others would prefer not to have this feature in order to prevent them from charging too much.

Annual Fee

Many credit cards companies charge an **annual fee** of $20 to $70 for the privilege of using their card. In cases where people have good credit history and use their card frequently, companies often waive the fees. Other cards advertise charging no fee at all. Still others offer fee-free service for a period of time—for example, the first year or two. Read all offers carefully. All things being equal, it is better to avoid paying a fee.

Incentives to Use the Card

Some credit cards offer bonus incentives to encourage people to use their credit cards. Many offer cash-back bonuses, airline miles, donations to various charities, or the ability to cash-in accumulated points for gifts. Such incentives can be quite valuable for people who make frequent use of their credit cards—and who can manage the risk that comes with such use.

Prestige Cards

Financial institutions often issue prestige cards. These cards, often called platinum or gold cards, provide additional benefits to cardholders, such as special warranties on purchased products or insurance on travel.

Grace Periods

Credit cards typically allow a **grace period** in which you are not charged interest on your purchases. Typical grace periods are 20 days from the time the statement is "closed," or your bill is calculated and mailed. So, if you receive your bill and pay it within the grace period, you will pay no interest on the amount borrowed. This is, in effect, a short-term free line of credit (see Figure 11.3).

Professor FIN

Did you know that there are a variety of fees that your credit card company can charge you?

- *Annual fee* (sometimes billed monthly). Charged for having the card
- *Cash advance fee.* Charged when you use the card for a cash advance; may be a flat fee (for example, $3) or a percentage of the cash advance (for example, 3 percent)
- *Balance-transfer fee.* Charged when you transfer a balance from another card
- *Late-payment fee.* Charged if your payment is received after the due date
- *Over-the-credit-limit fee.* Charged if you go over your credit limit

- *Credit-limit-increase fee.* Charged if you ask for an increase in your credit limit
- *Set-up fee.* Charged when a new credit card account is opened
- *Return-item fee.* Charged if you pay your bill by check and the check is returned for insufficient funds
- *Other fees.* Some credit card companies charge a fee if you pay by telephone or to cover the costs of reporting to credit bureaus, reviewing your account, or providing other customer services.

Be sure you understand all the costs associated with your credit card!

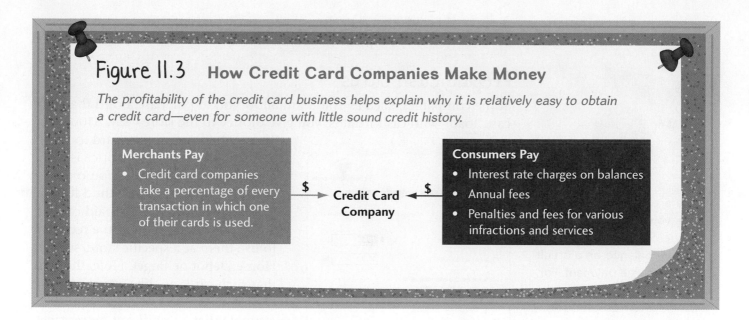

Figure 11.3 How Credit Card Companies Make Money

The profitability of the credit card business helps explain why it is relatively easy to obtain a credit card—even for someone with little sound credit history.

Merchants Pay
- Credit card companies take a percentage of every transaction in which one of their cards is used.

$ → **Credit Card Company** ← $

Consumers Pay
- Interest rate charges on balances
- Annual fees
- Penalties and fees for various infractions and services

MATH for Personal Finance

Twila used her credit card to get a $40 cash advance at a local ATM. She intended to pay the balance in full when the bill came in. Twila paid the $40 advance back and also paid $4 in fees ($2 for the ATM and $2 for the credit card company) when the credit card statement arrived 20 days later.

What is the approximate annual interest rate that Twila paid for this advance?

Solution: The $40 advance cost her $4 for 20 days. This amounts to 4/40 or 10 percent for 20 days use of the money. Assuming there are 18 twenty-day periods in a year, Twila would be paying 18 × 10 percent = 180 percent a year in interest if she did this same withdrawal every 20 days.

Cash Advances

Many credit cards allow **cash advances** at banks or automated teller machines (ATMs). That is, you can use your card to get cash rather than just purchasing a good or service. Anil had considered using this option to pay for much of his Florida adventure. Fortunately for him, he reconsidered. If his credit card was like most, he would have paid special transaction fees for this service, and he may also have had to pay a higher interest rate for cash advances. In addition, cash advances do not have grace periods. So, the cost of getting cash out of his credit card rather than using it for the individual purchases he made would certainly have been higher.

Financing or Interest Charges

As you know, many individuals make purchases with their credit card and then pay just a portion of the balance for several months or years. From a financial perspective, this is not a good decision. Most credit cards charge interest rates on carried balances that range between 15 and 22 percent. So, while using credit cards as a type of financing is convenient, it is also extremely expensive.

In addition, cardholders who make payments late may pay late fees *and* see rates increase more than 30 percent. Many credit card companies make more money from some consumers from late fees and other charges than they do from interest charges.

Note also that card companies will sometimes offer low teaser rates for a three- to six-month period to encourage people to make charges and carry balances. When the teaser rates expire, the cards revert to the typical high interest rates.

Credit cards typically change interest rates as market interest rates change. If interest rates increase, so do credit card rates.

All of these features, including annual fees, overdraft protection, acceptance by merchants, interest rates, and other incentives, should be evaluated when determining which card to apply for. Be cautious about accepting too many offers. Many consumers find themselves with 10 or more credit cards that they do not necessarily need or use—or, even worse, 10 cards that they keep charged to the maximum limit.

Prepaid Cash Cards

Some companies, such as Wal-Mart, allow you to purchase a card that you can "load" with cash. That is, you give money to the store—say, $100. Then, when you use the card to make a purchase, the purchase price is deducted from the $100. You can keep using the card until the $100 is gone. Other common prepaid cards are gift cards that require the recipient to use them at a specific store, such as Home Depot or Target. Note, though, that such cards are like actual cash—with the same sort of risks. Experts estimate that a significant percentage of these cards are lost or never used. In that case, the business issuing the card keeps the cash—and the consumer loses everything.

Finance ONLINE

There are many online calculators you can use that show the true cost of paying the minimum balance on a credit card or charge payment. For example, you can find one at **www.creditcards.com**. The calculator lets you change the amount of the purchase, the interest rate, and the minimum payment.

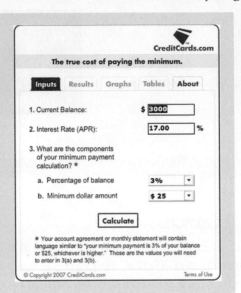

CreditCards.com

The true cost of paying the minimum.

| Inputs | Results | Graphs | Tables | About |

1. Current Balance: $ 3000

2. Interest Rate (APR): 17.00 %

3. What are the components of your minimum payment calculation? *

   a. Percentage of balance   3%

   b. Minimum dollar amount $ 25

[Calculate]

* Your account agreement or monthly statement will contain language similar to "your minimum payment is 3% of your balance or $25, whichever is higher." These are the values you will need to enter in 3(a) and 3(b).

© Copyright 2007 CreditCords.com   Terms of Use

✓ CHECK Your Financial IQ

Identify five key features of a credit card.

TIPS ON USING CREDIT CARDS

Credit cards are popular, widely available, and risky. The Federal Reserve has a lot of information on credit cards. Go to **www.federalreserve.gov**, and click "Consumer Help." In addition, here are some general rules you can follow so that you can enjoy the benefits of having a credit card without suffering the negative consequences.

Use a Credit Card Only If You Can Cover the Bill

Use a credit card only for convenience and not as a source of financing. In other words, before you charge something, be sure you will have enough cash to pay the bill in full at the end of the month. The cost of borrowing money beyond the grace period with a credit card is just too high. For example, let's look at the following. What if you charged a $2,000 item on your credit card that carried an 18 percent annual rate and paid a minimum payment equal to 2 percent of the balance each month? Over the course of the next 12 months you would make nearly $500 in payments but reduce the balance only by $123.56. It is much more prudent to save up for major purchases and make them when you have accumulated enough cash to cover the charge.

Impose a Tight Credit Limit on Yourself

While your credit card company will establish a credit limit, you may find it necessary to impose a stricter standard on your own spending. For example, a credit card company may establish your maximum limit at $5,000. However, you may examine your cash flows and realize there is no way you could pay a $5,000 charge every month. Your self-imposed maximum should correspond to the amount you can safely repay every month in order to prevent carrying high-interest balances on your card.

Pay Credit Card Bills First

If you do find yourself carrying credit card balances, pay them off as soon as possible. Remember—credit cards generally charge between 15 and 22 percent interest. This is very high. Pay credit card balances before paying off any other, less costly debt.

Indeed, it is generally a good idea to pay off credit card debt rather than putting money into savings or investments. These generally earn less interest than credit card companies charge.

Use Savings If Necessary

If your cash inflows are not sufficient to cover this month's credit card bill, pull savings out to pay the difference. You can replenish your savings later. (This, of course, is vital. You need a source of available liquid money.) Again, chances are your savings are earning just a few percentage points in interest. Credit card debt is costing you 15 to 22 percent. Your money is much more wisely used to reduce that debt (see Figure 11.4).

Professor FIN

Different credit cards charge different interest rates. The following chart is an example of different interest rates for a variety of credit cards:

Card Type	Today	Last Week
Balance Transfer	10.31%	10.03%
Low Interest	11.01%	10.97%
For Bad Credit	13.02%	13.12%
Cash Back	11.47%	11.46%
Business	11.10%	10.91%
Airline	12.75%	12.69%

These rates can change daily and can change if your credit rating goes down. It is your responsibility to keep track of the interest rate you are paying on credit cards. You can contact the credit card company to work toward getting a lower rate. You can do this more than once a year!

If You Experience Credit Card Debt Problems

It's good to avoid credit card debt problems if you can. But nobody is perfect. Sometimes, even money-savvy people miscalculate or find themselves in a tight spot. If you find yourself with high credit card debt, there are steps you can take to deal with the problem.

First, try to negotiate new terms. In some situations, when you find that you have overextended yourself financially, you may have the ability to negotiate better terms. Credit card companies will often lower interest rates or help work out more favorable repayment terms if you call them and request it. Credit card companies prefer this type of arrangement to bankruptcy or default where they may get little if any of their money back.

Credit counseling agencies are another source of help if you get into credit card debt. They can often help you negotiate better terms with your creditors.

Figure 11.4 Why It Pays to Pay off Credit Card Debt with Savings

Since savings accounts typically pay very low interest rates, you are certain to do better financially by using savings to pay down credit card debt.

Suppose you have $1,250 in a savings account and an existing credit card debt of $1,000. Should you use your savings to pay off the debt or let it be?

Leave savings alone:

$1,250 ⟶ 2 percent average annual return ⟶ Total interest earned by the end of one year: $25.00

Use $1,000 to pay off credit card debt:

$1,000 ⟶ Credit card balance at 22 percent interest ⟶ Money saved by the end of one year: $220

Finance ONLINE

There are numerous online debt consolidation companies. A quick search with a major search engine for nonprofit outfits will turn up many options. Be aware of sites that will help you only for a fee.

As you try to lower your rates, limit your spending. Remember, to pay off debt you will have to have greater cash inflow than cash outflow. Reduce your spending to necessities. Take steps to increase cash inflow. Work more hours or take a second job. You may be able to borrow money from a family member or friend.

Debt consolidation may be an option as well. **Debt consolidation** means combining several small accounts into one larger account that you may be able to finance at a lower rate at a bank. This option works best when you have assets you can pledge as collateral against the loan. For example, many people take a loan from a bank using the equity in their home as collateral. This is a so-called home equity loan. Such a loan may allow you to pay off your credit card debt, car loan, and other personal loans. You replace the three or four smaller loans with one larger loan. Rather than three or four monthly payments, you make one larger payment. If the larger loan is at a lower rate, this strategy can reduce the overall cost of your borrowing.

There are risks with debt consolidation. Too many people pay off their credit card debt with a home equity loan—and then run their credit card balances higher again. And of course, failure to pay off a home equity loan could have disastrous consequences—the loss of the home.

Personal bankruptcy is the last resort. **Bankruptcy** is a process in which the courts provide protection for a person who is unable to pay off his or her debts. The courts will help a bankrupt person propose a plan to repay at least a portion of his or her debts. Most bankruptcy debt workouts involve a three- to five-year repayment plan. However, bankruptcy is reported to the credit bureau and listed on the person's credit report for seven years. In most cases, this will prevent the person from borrowing money during that period or ensure that the interest rate will be extremely high. Bankruptcy is a costly option.

☑ CHECK Your Financial IQ

What is the main rule for using credit cards wisely?

The problem facing Anil at the start of this chapter is a familiar one. A person wants to buy something today for which he or she does not have ready cash. Credit cards are one way people address this dilemma. But not everyone has access to a credit card or wants to use one. Such people have a number of options. However, most of them are not good ones. Among them are payday lending, tax refund loans, and pawn shops. It is important to understand the characteristics—and possible drawbacks—of these expensive and risky credit options.

Payday Lending

Recent years have seen the development of a new form of credit called payday lending. With **payday lending**, a lender provides cash advances at a high cost to customers who provide a check dated for some time in the future.

For example, let's say Anil had finally broken down and asked his mother for some money for his Florida trip. She reluctantly agreed—but told him he would not receive the money until March 10, when she received her annual work bonus. Unfortunately, Anil and Mario were leaving for Florida on March 5. It seemed as if Anil would be out of luck—until a friend told him about a local payday lender.

Anil found that he could go to the payday lender on March 4 and write a $500 check to the lender dated March 11—a week into the future. The lender would then give Anil $400—$500 minus a $100 fee. The payday lender would then hold Anil's check until March 11. If all went as planned, Anil would have by then received the money his mother had sent. That is, he would have had a payday. With the money in Anil's bank account, the lender would be able to cash his check and get the $500. This would end the transaction.

Payday lending is an extremely costly form of credit that wise consumers avoid.

As you can see, payday lenders charge a very high fee for their service. Fees typically range between $15 and $30 for every $100 loaned. Loans are generally small—less than $1,000. They normally last for 7 to 14 days. This means that the fees amount to an interest rate that is equivalent to several hundred percent per year.

Payday lending has other dangers, too. If there is a delay in receiving the money you are counting on to cover your check, the check to the payday lender will bounce. The bounced check will result in additional fees. It may also damage your credit report. The following consumer Web site provides a wealth of information about the dangers of payday lending: www.paydayloaninfo.org/.

Why do people use payday lending? In general, it is easy and fast and does not require a credit check. Still, you should never rely on payday lending as a source of financing. Even high-interest credit cards are a better option than a payday loan. Establish good credit and protect it so that you are never forced into a situation where you need the services of a payday lender.

Tax Refund Loans

In recent years, many people have taken short-term loans with the idea that they will use their income tax refund to repay what they have borrowed. A number of income-tax preparers offer this option during tax season. These tax anticipation loans go by many names, such as "Rapid Refund" and a variety of others.

The process is relatively simple. When people use the services of a tax professional to prepare their taxes, the preparer may offer an instant refund based on the calculated income tax refund. Remember, most employers withhold federal taxes from their employees' paychecks and send that money to the government. Often, the amount withheld is greater than what the employee will actually owe in taxes when tax returns are filed after the conclusion of the year. If, in fact, the employer withheld too much in income tax, the employee will get an income tax refund. In addition, certain provisions in the tax code also allow tax "credits" to low income individuals who paid no taxes. They, too, may receive a check from the government at tax time.

You Do It
Activity #2

The typical fees for these loans are high. In fact, in some cases, they can be equal to an annual interest rate of over 100 percent. Another danger is that some people find their refunds to be lower than expected. In such a situation, the borrower would have a debt that is larger than the refund he or she receives.

Consumers need to be cautious of scams linked to tax refund advance lending. In one common scam, victims receive a call offering to speed up their tax refund for a fee charged to their credit card. Armed with the victim's credit card number, the con artist then uses the card to the available credit limit. The victim is left with a serious identity theft problem. And, of course, the victim does not receive the tax refund any earlier than he or she would have.

Pawn Shops

Before the development of the payday lending industry, pawn shops were a popular source of short-term loans. In many regions of the country, pawn shops still service this particular niche. A **pawnbroker**, or pawn shop representative, receives and holds items in exchange for loans that run for 30 days to as much as three months. Commonly pawned items are firearms, jewelry, vehicles, tools, electronic equipment, and musical instruments. These items serve as collateral for the loan. The customer signs an agreement that allows the pawnbroker to sell the item if the customer does not repay the loan within a certain time.

Of course, customers may redeem their item if they repay the loan prior to the due date. As with payday lenders and tax refund advance loans, the

Professor FIN

Did you know that pawnbrokers can be found as far back as ancient Greek and Roman empires? Their symbol is three spheres and is attributed to the Medici family of Florence, Italy. In the Italian province of Lombardy, medieval merchants hung the three spheres in front of their houses. Many think it is symbolic of three gold coins, but the spheres were more visible and therefore attracted more attention. Others attribute 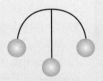 the symbol to Saint Nicholas, the patron saint of pawnbrokers, because of the story of Nicholas and the three bags of gold. The three bags of gold were supposed to have been secretly given to a poor man who had three daughters. Nicholas gave the three bags of gold, one for each daughter, so the father would have a dowry for them.

cost of a pawnshop loan can be very high. For example, if you pawn an item valued at $300 in return for $150 and do not redeem the item, you have paid several hundred percent in annual interest charges depending on the length of the loan.

Pawnbrokers often specialize in certain types of items. After all, their success depends on their ability to appraise objects being pawned.

Cell Phone Leases

If credit cards are a major source of financial difficulty, cell phone plans are not far behind. You may not think of your cell phone plan as a type of debt, but it is. Landline telephone service falls into the same category as other utilities: You pay a deposit and then you are billed monthly. If you cannot pay a bill, your service may be disconnected until the bill is paid. Cell phone plans, however, are different. Most cell phone service providers require that you sign a 12-month lease. This is a binding agreement to pay for one year's service. Plans typically charge a monthly fee ranging from $39.99 to $200 or more. These plans vary based on the number of minutes you are allowed to use, the services you have available, and on calling regions. In most cases, per-minute charges apply if you use the phone more than the plan allows. Some plans charge higher rates for other features such as data delivery via text messages and Internet access. Additional charges may apply for the downloading of ringtones and other data.

When obtaining cell phone service, always compare features and buy the plan that best suits your usage pattern. Remember: When you sign the lease agreement, you are entering into a contract. If you default, the service provider will report it to the credit bureaus. A cell phone lease is credit extended to you and should be treated as such. Early termination fees typically apply if you need to void the lease, and they can be $150 or more. Paying such a fee may be irritating. But it may prevent a negative mark on your credit report that could cost you more in the long run.

Cell phone companies also use tactics similar to credit card companies when courting new subscribers. They may use free t-shirts, phones, and other items to entice you to sign a lease. Be cautious and only sign up for what you need or want. Don't let a few dollars worth of "free" items entice you into a binding contract that obligates you for service you don't need.

☑ CHECK Your Financial IQ

What are some examples of other risky types of credit?

Summary

- Credit cards provide people with convenient and easy-to-use credit, and they can be a very useful financial tool. They are also easy to apply for and obtain. A disadvantage of credit is that it is easier to obtain than to repay. The major sponsors of credit cards are Visa, MasterCard, Discover, American Express, a proprietary merchant (such as JCPenney), or some other sponsor.

- Key credit card features include the credit limit, the annual fee, the interest rate charged on credit not paid by the due date, a grace period between the closing of the statement and the date when payment is due, and the availability of cash advances. Cards may offer "prestige" versions and also incentives. Some have overdraft protection.

- Credit cards should be used with discipline. You should impose your own credit limits rather than spend up to the limit granted by the card. You should attempt to avoid financing costs, either by using income to cover the amount due or by withdrawing money from savings if necessary. Deal with any problems quickly.

- There are several other examples of credit arrangements that meet a similar need to credit cards—and carry similar risks. These include payday lending, tax refund loans, and pawnbroking. Although many people don't realize it, cell phone leases can be a costly form of credit.

Key Terms and Vocabulary

Annual fee	Debt consolidation
Bankruptcy	Grace period
Cash advance	Overdraft protection
Credit card	Pawnbroker
Credit check	Payday lending
Credit provider	

What Do You Know?

myFinLitlab

1. (a) What are two advantages of using a credit card?

   (b) What is a disadvantage?

   (c) How does credit card credit differ from a personal loan?

2. (a) What kinds of information are creditors looking for?

   (b) Do you need to have all these attributes to get credit?

3. (a) What is credit limit?

   (b) How can you use the credit limit to determine how much credit you can safely use?

4. (a) What is the purpose of overdraft protection?

   (b) Explain how using this feature may both help and hurt you.

5. (a) What is the grace period?

   (b) How can this feature enable you to use a credit card at no direct cost to you?

6. (a) Are all credit cards the same in their use and features?

   (b) Explain which features you would find particularly useful.

7. (a) Why is paying your credit card balance in full important?

   (b) What should you do if you can't avoid credit card debt? Explain.

8. (a) What is payday lending?

   (b) If you had the option of using a standard credit card for a $500 purchase or a payday loan, which would you choose? Why?

9. (a) What is a tax refund loan?

   (b) How is it similar to and different from a payday loan?

10. (a) How does the financial obligation to consumers of cell phone plans differ from landline telephone service?

    (b) What, besides money, is the major threat from misuse of a cell phone plan?

What Are Your Finance Math Skills?   myFinLitlab.

The first three questions correlate to *Math for Personal Finance* features located throughout the chapter.

1. Paula's mom just sold a new prom dress in her shop for $675. However, the customer paid for the dress with a MasterCard. Assuming Paula's mom receives 97 percent of the sale after paying a 3 percent credit card fee, how much will she actually receive from the sale?

2. Reshawda used her Visa card to put $20 worth of gas in her car. However, when she got her bill she noticed the charge put her over her credit limit. Assuming the credit card company charges her a $25 over-limit charge, how much did the gas actually cost her?

3. Kari got a $50 cash advance at a local out-of-network ATM. She paid the $55 balance in full when the bill came in. Kari's bill included the $50 cash advance and $5 in fees. Approximate the annual interest rate that Kari paid for this advance. Remember that these charges represent only one month and to approximate annual rates you need to multiply by 12.

4. Assume you carry a $1,000 balance on your credit card that charges a 24 percent annual interest rate. How much interest will you pay for this account next month?

5. If a vendor makes a credit sale of $238.49, how much will the vendor receive after they pay the customary 3 percent fee to the credit card company?

6. Jim has four credit cards with limits of $4,000, $9,000, $3,600, and $11,300 respectively. If he has all of his cards charged up to 85 percent of his credit limit, how much does he owe?

7. In the previous question, assuming Jim pays the minimum payment next month on each card and that is 3 percent of the outstanding balance, how much will Jim's payments be?

8. Jerry pawned his power tools valued at $800 for $450 cash. Assuming he pays the pawnbroker $40 a month for three months and then pays the balance and retrieves his tools, what was the approximate annual interest rate for this loan?

What Would You Do?

Chen recently graduated from college and accepted a job in a new city. Furnishing his apartment had proven more costly than he anticipated. To assist him with making purchases, he applied for and received a credit card with a $5,000 credit limit. Chen planned to pay off the balance over six months.

Six months later, Chen found that there were other expenses incurred in starting a new career, which restricted him to making minimum payments only. Not only that, he had borrowed on his card to the full extent of its credit limit. Upon returning from work one day, Chen found a letter from the credit card company offering to increase his limit to $10,000 because he has been a good customer and has not missed a payment.

a. Discuss the ethics of credit card companies that offer to increase credit limits to individuals who make only minimum payments and who have maxed out their card.

b. Should Chen accept the credit card company's offer? Why or why not?

What Are the Connections? Math and Technology

Look at the following chart. It shows several situations for someone who has a $2,000 credit card balance and who charges $150 or $100 each month. You can use an online calculator to determine for each scenario how long it would take to pay off the balance and how much interest you would pay in the process.

Amount owed	Monthly charges	Monthly payments	Annual interest rate	Annual fee	Total interest expense	Time to pay off debt
$2,000	$150	$350	19%	0		
$2,000	$150	$350	7%	0		
$2,000	$150	$450	7%	0		
$2,000	$100	$350	7%	0		

Go to www.creditcards.com. Then, under Tools, click "Credit Card Calculators." Click "What will it take to pay off my current balance?"

a. Input the information from the first row, click "calculate." Note the total interest expenses and time to pay off the debt.

b. Click "inputs." Change the annual interest rate to 7 percent. Click "calculate." Note the total interest expenses and time to pay off the debt.

c. Click "inputs." Change the monthly payments to $450. Click "calculate." Note the total interest expenses and time to pay off the debt.

d. Click "inputs." Decrease the monthly payments to $350 and reduce the monthly charges to $100. Note the total interest expenses and time to pay off the debt.

What conclusions can be drawn from the information provided in the chart? How can such information benefit you when working on your financial plan?

Teamwork

In teams, look up the four leading cell phone providers in your surrounding area. Make a chart that compares the costs, features, services available, call area, and any other interesting facts. Present your information on a poster that can be displayed in the halls of your school for students to help them make a decision about purchasing one cell phone plan over another.

TEST PREP QUESTIONS

1. A financial tool that provides people with revolving open-end access to funds that they can draw from repeatedly up to some preset limit is known as a
   a. mortgage.
   b. certificate of deposit.
   c. credit card.
   d. checking account.

2. Which of the following is a true statement about a credit card?
   a. It must be accepted at any place of business that accepts cash.
   b. It most often is used to make large purchases such as a car.
   c. It cannot be used to make purchases under $10.
   d. It allows a person to make purchases wherever the card is accepted.

3. The greatest advantage of using a credit card is that it provides
   a. an easy way to establish a personal credit history.
   b. an easy way to avoid going into debt.
   c. a less expensive way to pay for college.
   d. a safe way to improve a person's credit score.

4. Which of the following is *not* an advantage of having and using a credit card?
   a. Credit card statements help a person keep track of spending.
   b. No interest is charged if a minimum payment is made on the account each month.
   c. A person who is making most purchases with credit cards can see if he is living within his budget.
   d. A cardholder does not have to carry a lot of cash when traveling.

5. Which of the following is a true statement?
   a. Creditors require a person to complete a credit application and will conduct a credit check before issuing a credit card.
   b. Creditors are more likely to loan money when the economy is in a recession.
   c. Creditors are likely to loan money to people who have high levels of cash outflow and low levels of cash inflow.
   d. Creditors charge all cardholders the same rate of interest on outstanding balances, purchases, and cash advances.

6. Why do credit card companies benefit when cardholders pay their bills in full each month and never have to pay interest on balances?
   a. Credit card companies charge a flat monthly 8 percent interest even if cardholders pay their bills in full.
   b. Credit card companies get a higher credit score if cardholders pay their bills in full.
   c. Credit card companies make most of their money by charging a monthly fee to use the company's card.
   d. Credit card companies receive 2–4 percent of the purchase price of every good or service that is sold to a cardholder.

7. Which of the following credit card fees is correctly matched with its description?
   a. Credit limit: the most that can be spent for a single item using a credit card.
   b. Overdraft protection: the number of purchases that can be made by a person over their credit limit.
   c. Annual fee: fee that is charged by the company for the privilege of using the company's card.
   d. Cash advance fee: fee that is charged by the company if the cardholder goes over the credit limit and has to borrow money.

8. Even though a person has overdraft protection on her credit card, she should avoid using this feature because
   a. the overdraft charge can be as high as $30 per transaction.
   b. each time a person uses overdraft protection, her credit score will drop by 50 points.
   c. using overdraft protection will cause the interest a person earns on other accounts to drop.
   d. using overdraft protection will cause the person's credit limit to be increased.

9. Which of the following credit card fees is *not* correctly matched with its description?
   a. Late-payment fee: charged if a person's payment is received after the due date.
   b. Credit-limit-increase fee: charged if a person asks for an increase in his credit limit.
   c. Balance-transfer fee: charged if a person transfers a balance from one credit card to another.
   d. Over the-credit-limit fee: charged if a person spends too much money on all his credit cards together.

10. Which of the following is a true statement about credit cards?
    a. If a person pays her total credit card bill within the grace period, interest on the account is charged at a lower rate.
    b. If a person uses his credit card to obtain cash advances, there is no interest charged.
    c. Some credit cards encourage people to use their credit by offering them cash back if they buy a certain amount of goods or services.
    d. Some credit cards, called prestige cards, do not charge interest if the cardholder makes only the minimum payment each month.

11. A person knows that she cannot afford to pay $400 for a coat that she really wants. The financially wise action for her to take is to
    a. buy the coat with a credit card and pay as much as she can each month until it is paid off.
    b. take a cash advance using her credit card and pay for the coat that way.
    c. buy a less expensive coat that she can pay off in full in a shorter time.
    d. apply for a credit limit increase to cover the cost of the coat.

12. Why would a credit card company offer a person the opportunity to open a credit card account that will charge 0 percent interest on purchases or balance transfers for 12 months?
    a. The credit card company expects that the person will continue to make purchases and carry a balance after the introductory period when interest charges go back to normal rates.
    b. Credit card companies get tax breaks based upon the number of people who use their cards.
    c. Late fees that are charged to all the people who take advantage of this offer make up for any money lost by not charging interest on the account.
    d. Companies that make this offer receive better ratings from consumer protection groups.

13. What is the advantage to a consumer of having a prepaid cash card?
    a. Many people never use the cards and the company gets to keep the money.
    b. The person can purchase items up to the limit on the cash card without paying any interest.
    c. Cash cards earn monthly interest.
    d. There is no credit limit when using cash cards.

14. A person with $5,000 in credit card debt with an 18.5 percent annual interest rate (APR) receives an end-of-year bonus of $2,000. It is generally considered a financially smart move for this person to
    a. invest the bonus money until he earns $5,000 and can pay off the credit card bill.
    b. put the money into savings so that he earns an equivalent rate of interest.
    c. pay off $2,000 of the credit card debt with the bonus so that he pays less in interest.
    d. buy the next $2,000 worth of items that he wants using the bonus money instead of credit cards.

15. If a person has mounting credit card debt and cannot pay it down, the first thing she should do is
    a. contact each credit card company with which she has an account and try to negotiate new terms such as a lower interest rate.
    b. pay one of the credit card bills each month.
    c. declare personal bankruptcy and start over with a clean slate.
    d. open a new credit card account, make all purchases using that account, and pay the minimum on the old accounts.

16. A person who has a total of $17,000 in credit card debt decides to use her house as collateral for a bank loan. She then uses her $30,000 home equity loan to pay off the credit card debt. She is now paying back one larger loan at a lower interest rate. What is the danger of using this method to pay back her debt?
    a. If she cannot pay back the equity loan, she is in danger of losing her home.
    b. There is no danger; this is a guaranteed way to get rid of debt.
    c. The credit card companies will cancel her accounts once they have been paid.
    d. Debt consolidation is the same as declaring bankruptcy and her credit score will be affected in the same way.

17. Why is a payday loan considered to be an unwise way to finance a purchase?
    a. Everyone in the company can go online to see the names of people who have had to take payday loans.
    b. The person who takes a payday loan will not be eligible for a raise for a year.
    c. Payday loans carry very high fees equivalent to more than a 100 percent annual interest rate (APR).
    d. The person's employer will probably give the employee who takes a payday loan a poor job evaluation.

18. If someone uses a ring worth $500 as collateral for a $200 loan, she has most likely obtained a loan from a
    a. pawnbroker.
    b. credit card company.
    c. tax preparer.
    d. payday lender.

UNIT

4

Saving &
Investing

CHAPTER 12

Learning Objectives

Explain the difference between different types of financial institutions.

Learn the basics of having a checking account, including how to balance an account.

Describe other available banking services.

Describe the two major federal insurers.

Explain the function and goals of the Federal Reserve.

Key Terms

Check
Checking account
Credit union
Debit card
Federal Deposit Insurance
    Corporation (FDIC)
Federal Reserve System
Fiat money
Monetary policy
National Credit Union Savings
    Insurance Fund

Banking Procedures and Services

Tamara was leafing though the mail when she saw an envelope addressed to her. It was from the bank where she had recently opened a checking account. Inside the envelope was a yellow slip with the words *insufficient funds* across the top. Below that were some numbers—it was hard to understand. As best as she could tell, the note was saying that the amount of money in her account was actually less than the amount of one of the checks she had written.

Just then, her mother walked in the room. "Mom," said Tamara, "I just got this from the bank—what does it mean?" Her mother looked at the slip, and she sighed.

"Oh, Tamara," she said. "You've bounced a check!"

Tamara had heard that term before. But she wasn't sure, really, what it meant. "What's going to happen?" she asked.

"Well," said Tamara's mother, "you're fortunate you have overdraft protection. The bank is going to cover the check and pay whomever you wrote the check to. But look here—they're charging you a $25 fee."

"Oh, great!" Said Tamara. "I write a lousy $9 check for some pizza, and it costs me $34!"

"It could have been worse, Tamara," said her mother. "If you didn't have overdraft protection, the bank would send the check back to the pizza place—unpaid. They would probably charge you a fee, too!"

Tamara didn't exactly feel lucky. But she was glad she had opted to go with the bank that offered overdraft protection. She was also anxious to find out how she had gotten into this situation. She wanted to be sure it never happened again.

Banks and other financial institutions offer individual services such as providing personal loans and accepting deposits. In most cases, they offer accounts that allow you to draft payments. Not only are these institutions a critical component of our personal financial plan, but also they are important to the overall economy.

Tamara is learning directly about the value of certain banking services—and about the importance of using banks properly. We will now discuss some of the basics of banking and the services they offer.

BANKS AND FINANCIAL INSTITUTIONS

There are probably several banks in your community. In addition, there may be a number of other kinds of financial institutions that offer financial services. What are the differences between these institutions? To begin, you should understand that there are two major types of financial institutions: depository institutions and nondepository institutions.

Depository Institutions

Depository institutions are financial institutions that provide traditional checking and saving accounts for individuals and businesses. They also provide loans. Depository institutions take in and secure people's money, and they loan it to people and businesses in the community. Types of depository institutions include commercial banks, savings banks, and credit unions. These institutions all serve a similar function. In general, they differ in terms of the government regulations under which they operate.

Depository institutions generally pay interest on the deposits people leave with them. Then, they use the deposits to make loans, on which they charge an even higher rate of interest. In this way, they earn a profit. They also make money by charging various fees for services. One example is the

Professor FIN

Did you know that in the banking industry, there is an expected growth of 4 percent in employment between 2006 and 2016? Many of the jobs that will result from this growth will be in the area of computer specialists as Internet banking services continue to grow. This does not mean that computer specialists are the only growing jobs within the banking industry. Customer service will grow also. Customer service representatives will be expected to have good people and communication skills. These skills are needed for face-to-face customer service. But with the advance of technology, a customer service representative must be able to handle customers on the telephone or Internet.

You can find more information about jobs in the banking industry at **www.bls.gov**.

214   **Chapter 12**   Banking Procedures and Services

one Tamara's bank charged her for overdraft protection. Another common fee is the monthly fee many people pay for their checking account.

Nondepository Institutions

Nondepository institutions consist of institutions that provide certain financial services but do not accept traditional deposits. Nondepository institutions include insurance companies, finance companies, and securities firms and investment companies. For now, we will confine our discussion to depository institutions, which we will refer to generally as banks.

Choosing a Bank

Banks and other depository institutions can differ significantly on fees charged, interest rates paid on deposits, and access to **automatic teller machines (ATMs)** and branches. Keep in mind that while you can usually access most accounts via any ATM, if the ATM is not in your bank's network, there can be significant fees charged per withdrawal. While some Internet banks pay a higher deposit rate, they also provide limited access. Everyone must weigh the pros and cons of various financial institutions when choosing a bank.

 CHECK Your Financial IQ

What are two types of financial institutions?

Finance ONLINE

One source of information about financial institutions and the services they offer is available online. Visit **dir.yahoo.com**, click "Business and Economy," then "Finance and Investment," and finally "Banking." You will gain access to a wide range of information about specific institutions, including the services they offer and the rates they pay on deposits or for loans.

BANKING BASICS: CHECKING ACCOUNTS

One of the more widely used banking services is the checking account. It is also a service that can lead to trouble if not managed carefully. Tamara discovered that when she wrote a bad check.

Most communities have a number of banks and other types of depository institutions available for the safe and secure storage of wealth.

How Checking Accounts Work

When you open a **checking account** at a bank, you create an account into which you deposit money and from which you gradually withdraw money by writing checks or using a debit card.

A **check** is a written order from you to your bank instructing it to pay money from your account to another party. When you write a check and someone accepts it for payment, that party eventually presents that check to your bank. That is, the party "cashes" the check. The bank takes money out of your account equivalent to the amount of the check. Then, it gives the money to the party presenting the check. Often, this process of presenting the check to the bank and receiving payment occurs electronically. See Figure 12.1 to see a sample check and an explanation of its parts.

Most of us open checking accounts because it allows us to have an accurate payment record. It also allows us to carry less cash. Checks also make it safer to send payment via the mail. Think about it like this. If you mail a cash payment to the electric company, someone could intercept that payment and pocket the cash. If you mail a check made out to the electric

Figure 12.1 Example of a Blank Check

Checks are a convenient way to allow the transfer of funds from one person to another—without the need for cash. Checks have several safeguards to prevent theft.

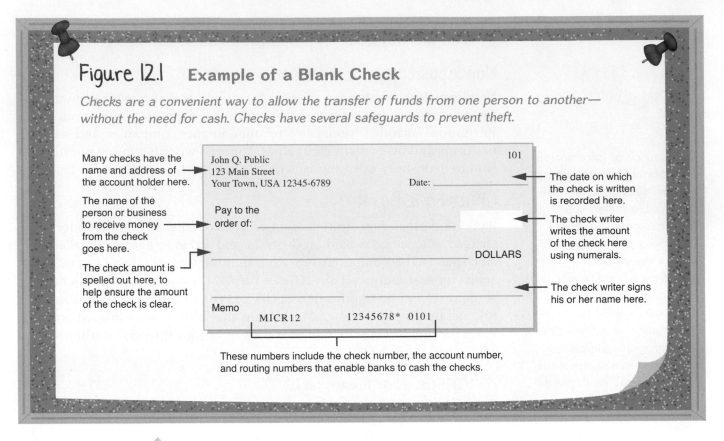

Many checks have the name and address of the account holder here.

The name of the person or business to receive money from the check goes here.

The check amount is spelled out here, to help ensure the amount of the check is clear.

John Q. Public
123 Main Street
Your Town, USA 12345-6789

101

Date: _____

Pay to the order of: _____

_____ DOLLARS

Memo _____   _____

MICR12   12345678* 0101

The date on which the check is written is recorded here.

The check writer writes the amount of the check here using numerals.

The check writer signs his or her name here.

These numbers include the check number, the account number, and routing numbers that enable banks to cash the checks.

You Do It

Activity #1

company, only the electric company can cash the check. If the check is lost or stolen, nobody can get your money.

NOW Accounts

Generally, you will not earn interest on money kept in ordinary checking accounts. **Negotiable order of withdrawal (NOW) accounts** function much like checking accounts except they pay a small amount of interest on money in the account. They require you to maintain some minimum balance in order to earn interest so they are not quite as liquid.

Debit Cards

Many banks provide debit cards to their account holders. A debit card looks like a credit card (which may also be available from your bank). But it works differently. A **debit card** enables you to withdraw cash from your account at ATMs, or to pay directly for goods or services at thousands of stores and restaurants. There is no credit involved—the amount of money is withdrawn immediately from your account.

Debit cards are convenient. But be cautious. Debit cards make it easy to spend money. It is also easy to forget to record ATM withdrawals or debit purchases. Make sure you record debit card withdrawals and purchases in your check register or you will find yourself overdrawn. Debit cards also require you to use a **personal identification number (PIN)**. PINs are usually four-digit numbers that you need to memorize in order to be able to use your debit card. Be careful with your PIN. No one should know it but you, since inputting this number along with your debit card will grant anyone access to your account and your cash.

MATH for Personal Finance

Jim's checking account balance was $541.39 at the beginning of the month. He deposited a $50 check he earned from mowing lawn and wrote a check for $28.32. His monthly service fee was $8.

What is Jim's new account balance?

Solution: $541.39 + $50 − $28.32 − $8 = $555.07.

MATH for
Personal
Finance

You
Do It

Activity #2

MATH for
Personal
Finance

Mary Beth's checking account balance on her bank statement shows $184.32. However, she wrote checks for $41.78 and $12.10 that have not cleared the bank yet.

How much do Mary Beth's outstanding checks total?

Solution: Outstanding checks are checks that have not cleared the bank so the total is $41.78 + $12.10 = $53.88.

Using Your Checking Account

Let's say you open an account with a deposit of $500. That amount is your balance. You should record that amount in your **check register**, a small ledger the bank will provide you for keeping track of your account balance. As you write checks or use your debit card, you will record those as well. For each check, you subtract the amount of the check from your balance, giving you a new balance. If you make another deposit, you add that amount and update your balance.

Keeping an accurate balance is essential. If you don't know how much money is in your account, you might wind up like Tamara. You might overdraw your account—that is, bounce a check or checks. Some checking accounts, such as Tamara's, come with overdraft protection. This means that the bank will cash checks up to a certain amount even if you do not have money in your account. (Of course, you must pay back the bank, and pay a fee). Overdraft fees can be as small as zero for very good customers and as high as $25 or $35 for others. Some checking accounts, however, do not have overdraft protection. If you overdraw such an account, the bank will not cash any checks. In fact, they will charge you a fee for overdrawing your account. Most businesses will also charge you a fee for writing them a bad check. So, each bounced check can cost you an additional $50 to $70 depending on the fees charged. You can pay this much even if—like Tamara—the check you wrote was for a small amount. And, if you bounce more than one check, you can pay that amount for each one.

Balancing Your Account

Even if you faithfully record deposits and checks, it is possible for errors—yours or the bank's—to occur. To discover these errors quickly, you should regularly compare your records to the bank's. Here's how you do it:

At the end of each month the bank will send you a bank statement. This lists the bank's records of all the deposits and checks written against your account. When you receive this statement you need to reconcile the bank's balance with your balance recorded in your ledger. It is helpful to use a separate sheet of paper, divided into two columns, for this exercise. One column represents the bank statement balance. The other represents your checkbook register balance.

1. In one column, write the balance given on the statement.
2. Add any deposits that you have made that do not appear on the bank statement.
3. From this total, subtract any ATM withdrawals you have made from your checking account and any checks that you have written that do not appear on the statement. These would include withdrawals and checks you wrote in the last few days, after the statement was prepared and mailed to your home. The amount represented by these outstanding checks is likely to be taken from your account at any moment, when the checks are presented for payment. If you fail to account for it, you may think that you have more money in your account than you really do.

The total you have after completing steps 1–3 is the reconciled balance.

Figure 12.2 Balancing a Checking Account

Reconciling what your check register says and what your bank says you have in your account is essential in preventing overdrafts. Mistakes—either by the bank or by the checking account holder—are not uncommon and can lead to confusion—and bounced checks.

Bank Statement Balance	$	Checkbook Register Balance	$
Plus Deposits in Transit *(Total of deposits that appear in your checkbook but do not appear on the bank statement)*	$	Plus Interest Earned	$
Minus Outstanding Checks ATM Withdrawals, or Debits *(Total of any checks that you have written or withdrawals you have made since the beginning of the statement period that do not appear on the bank statement)*	$	Minus Service Charges	$
Reconciled Balance	$	Reconciled Balance	$

Activity #3

4. Now, move to the other column on your sheet. There, record the balance listed in your checkbook register.

5. To this amount, add any interest earned, and deduct any fees your bank has charged you in the last month. These amounts should be listed in your bank statement.

6. Compare the final reconciled bank balance with the reconciled balance in your register. They should be the same. If the amounts are not equal, you need to track down the mistake. It may be a math error on your part or it could be an error on the bank's part. Look at Figure 12.2 for a sample of reconciling your checking account balance.

☑ CHECK Your Financial IQ

Why are checking accounts useful?

OTHER BANKING SERVICES

In addition to housing and maintaining your checking account, your bank will offer a variety of different services. A few of them are discussed here.

Safety Deposit Boxes

Safety deposit boxes are usually available for rent at most banks. **Safety deposit boxes** are small containers located inside the bank vault and are used to store valuable documents such as wills and small objects such as jewelry, rare coins, and legal documents.

Cashier's Checks, Money Orders, and Travelers Checks

Banks are also a source of cashier's checks. A **cashier's check** is a type of check that is written to a specific payee but charged against the bank instead of your account. When you buy a cashier's check, the bank takes the money for the check out of your account immediately. Why bother paying by cashier's check? They may be accepted in situations when a personal check from your own account would not. That's because the recipient of a cashier's check does not have to worry about whether you have enough money in your account. Since it is drawn against the bank's account, the recipient can be confident he or she will get the money.

People often use cashier's checks for larger purchases and when one party does not know the other well enough to accept a personal check. Cashier's checks may also be useful if you have bounced a check and the recipient will no longer accept your personal check.

Money orders function in a similar way to cashier's checks: They are purchased for cash so that the recipient can trust that they are worth what they say they are. The United States Postal Service sells money orders for a fee. If you've bought something in an online auction, you may have used a money order to mail payment so that the seller did not have to wait for your check to clear before mailing your item.

Travelers checks are checks written by a large financial institution with no payee specified. As with cashier's checks or money orders, people pay for them in advance. So, when a person presents a $50 travelers check as payment, the recipient can be confident that the check will be cashed. In fact, travelers checks are accepted around the world. Plus, travelers who lose travelers checks can usually replace them. For this reason, when on a trip, many people carry them instead of cash.

Arrangements for Credit Payment

By now, you know that paying off borrowed money in a timely way is vital to your financial life. Bank drafts can help you perform this duty faithfully.

Bank drafts occur when you authorize someone to take money out of your bank account automatically to satisfy some financial obligation. People commonly use bank drafts to make car payments and house payments, and to pay utility bills. People also use bank drafts to make contributions to retirement accounts or other investments.

Bank drafts are an example of electronic funds transfer. Whenever you authorize someone to access your bank account for payment or for deposit, you are utilizing **electronic funds transfer**.

A bank draft authorization will set a specific date on which the money is taken from your account. For example, you may set up a bank draft for your car payment that allows the finance company to withdraw $205.18 on the 21st of every month. The benefit of a bank draft is that you do not have to write a check to make the payment, and the car loan payment will be made every month on the exact date. This convenience saves time and, if you have an interest earning account, it allows you to earn interest on your money up until the due date. It also ensures you do not miss payments and suffer penalties. Bank drafts are also a good way to force you to make monthly contributions to your savings or retirement accounts.

You must be sure, of course, to account for bank drafts in your check register. Failing to do so can lead to confusion on your balance—and to bounced checks.

Other Online Services

Most banks now offer a variety of online services. You can opt to have payments drafted directly out of your account or utilize online bill payment services, transfer funds between checking and savings accounts, make loan applications, and check your bank statements. There is no doubt that in the future these online services will become more and more commonplace and more banking will be done electronically.

✓ CHECK Your Financial IQ

Besides checking accounts, what services are typically offered by banks?

DEPOSIT INSURANCE

One of the purposes of putting money in the bank is to keep it safe. You want to know that nobody can steal your cash. You also want to know that if the institution were to make a lot of bad loans and go bankrupt, your money would be protected. In order to offer this assurance to their customers, most financial institutions have deposit insurance on the first $250,000 you have on deposit. The major federal insurers are the **Federal Deposit Insurance Corporation (FDIC)** and the **National Credit Union Savings Insurance Fund (NCUSIF)**.

FDIC

The federal government created the FDIC in 1933 after a rash of bank failures during the Great Depression. In many cases, depositors went to the bank to withdraw their money, only to find that the bank had gone out of business. Their savings were gone.

The bank failures shattered people's confidence in the banks generally. People began taking money out of even healthy institutions. This reaction hurt the banks and reduced the amount of money available for borrowing. The government needed a way to restore faith in the banking system. After all, saving money is critical to economic growth. If there is no money deposited in the banks, businesses can't borrow. If they can't borrow, they won't build new factories, open new shops, and hire new workers. The entire economy will suffer.

The FDIC was meant to restore and maintain depositors' confidence in the banks by insuring people's deposits against loss. Currently, the FDIC provides deposit insurance on the first $250,000 of deposits at insured institutions. This amount was $100,000 per insured account until the passage of the Emergency Economic Stabilization Act of 2008. This law, passed in October 2008, increased the insurance coverage to $250,000 through

December 31, 2009. However, many experts believe this increase will become permanent at some point in the future.

FDIC insurance covers checking accounts, savings accounts, NOW accounts, and certificates of deposit. In addition, the FDIC will insure up to $250,000 per depositor for self-directed retirement accounts. Again, each financial institution can insure up to $250,000 for an individual. So, if you had $1,000,000 that was not in a retirement account and wanted to make sure you were protected, you would need to place $250,000 with four different financial institutions that are not branches of the same bank.

NCUSIF

The NCUSIF performs the same function for credit unions that the FDIC performs for other types of financial institutions. A **credit union** functions similarly to a bank. But, unlike a bank, a credit union has nonprofit status and is owned by its members. The National Credit Union Association (NCUA) charters and supervises credit unions and provides deposit insurance with the same limits as FDIC insured deposits. This program is also backed by the federal government to ensure that depositors have faith in the financial system.

 CHECK Your Financial IQ

Why is it important to give people confidence in the safety of their deposits?

THE FEDERAL RESERVE AND THE BANKING SYSTEM

The bank where you have your accounts is more than just your bank. It is part of a larger system that plays a central role in the nation's economy. At the heart of that banking system is the Federal Reserve System. The Fed, as it is known, helps regulate our banking system and, in fact, our whole economy.

Finance ONLINE

The following Web site contains a wealth of information about the Fed's history and current functions: www.federalreserveeducation.org.

Multiple Roles

The Federal Reserve Act of 1913 created the **Federal Reserve System**, which serves as the central bank of the United States. The Fed has several roles in our economy. The Fed regulates banks, making sure that they follow rules and practices designed to ensure a sound banking system. For example, the Fed ensures that banks always have cash on hand to meet the demand. Therefore, banks never have to turn away customers wishing to withdraw their money. The Fed also serves as the branch of government that clears checks.

In addition, the Fed is a major instrument for carrying out the nation's economic policies. The Fed's major economic goals are to create ongoing economic growth, encourage full employment, and promote price stability. The Fed uses monetary policy in order to achieve these goals.

Price Stability

A main goal of Fed policy is **price level stability**. In other words, the Fed focuses a lot on making sure that we don't have inflation (or deflation).

The Fed is the nation's bank, and it provides a variety of services that help regulate our nation's economy.

Inflation is defined as a sustained increase in the general level of prices. When we have inflation, prices of goods and services are generally going up. Inflation is considered problematic to the government and the Fed because it harms businesses and individuals in our economy.

Inflation can especially hurt individuals on fixed incomes, such as retirees. Think about this: What if your income remained the same but prices went up by 5 percent? You would not be able to buy as many products after that 5 percent inflation. Your standard of living would decline. What if you had money in the bank earning 3 percent? Your money at the end of the year would now buy fewer goods and services than it would have at the beginning of the year.

Monetary Policy

The Fed uses monetary policy as its primary tool to fight inflation and promote a healthy economy. **Monetary policy** involves the raising or lowering of the money supply to achieve some goal.

Think about money for a minute. We use money to make purchases and make our payments. We use money as a way to store wealth. The money we currently use in the United States is known as fiat money. **Fiat money** has value not because the coins and bills have some value in their own right, but because the government orders that it be accepted as payment. With fiat money, a five-dollar bill is worth five dollars because the government says it is.

Thanks to government fiat, or decree, little slips of paper and small coins have great value. For this reason, the government must carefully control how much of that paper and coin is circulating in the economy. The United States Treasury is in charge of printing money and minting coins, but it does so at the Fed's direction. The Fed is the agency in charge of determining how much money is in circulation.

While the physical money in circulation is the most visible part of the money supply, there is a lot of electronic money that we never see. For example, you or your parents may have their paychecks deposited electronically into their checking account. Then, they may pay bills electronically out of that account. Although they never see the money they've deposited and spent, it is still in circulation.

Recall that monetary policy involves changing the money supply. As the economy grows and more people need money to make purchases, the Fed expands the money supply. It takes steps to place more money in circulation. This includes more electronic money, paper money, and coins (see Figure 12.3).

The Fed also uses monetary policy to change interest rates and impact buying behavior. How does the Fed do this? When you borrow money, the lender charges you interest. In effect, you can think of the interest you pay as the price of money. You also know that interest rates—the price of money—go up and down. Why is that? The Fed is largely responsible. If the Fed wants to increase transactions and encourage people to spend more money, it increases the money supply. When more money is available, it drives interest rates down and encourages spending. And, when the Fed reduces the money supply, interest rates go up.

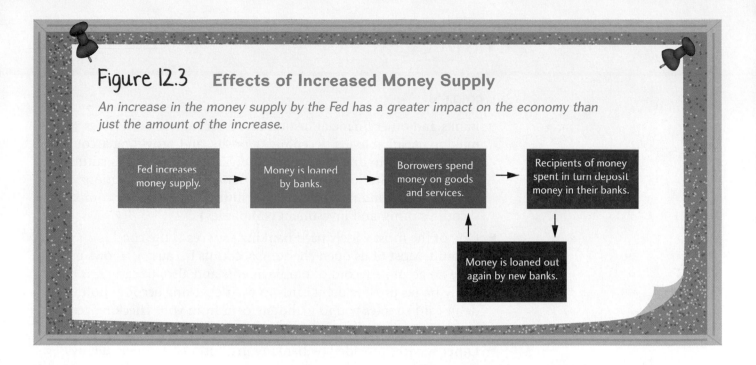

Figure 12.3 Effects of Increased Money Supply

An increase in the money supply by the Fed has a greater impact on the economy than just the amount of the increase.

Fed increases money supply. → Money is loaned by banks. → Borrowers spend money on goods and services. → Recipients of money spent in turn deposit money in their banks.

Money is loaned out again by new banks.

How does the money supply affect interest rates? Think about an online auction. If there are 100 buyers for one item, the buyers will compete and the price will go up. The same thing happens in our economy. If the Fed shrinks the money supply, lots of people will compete for an item—money—that's in limited supply. The price of that money—interest rates—will go up. So, when the Fed is concerned about inflation, it will shrink the money supply. This, in turn, will drive up the price of money (that is, raise interest rates) and discourage spending. This action should slow inflation.

Understand, the procedure of increasing or decreasing the money supply is actually much more complex than simply minting or printing more money. If you want to learn more about this, check out the Federal Reserve Web site at www.federalreserve.gov.

In most cases, the Fed uses the money supply to impact the interest rates. However, occasionally the Fed will change the interest rate it charges to banks when it loans them money. This interest rate is known as the **discount rate**, and banks use the option of borrowing money from the Fed only on occasion. Either of these actions, changing the money supply or changing the discount rate, are designed to slow the economy or stimulate the economy depending on what the Fed determines is needed at the time.

You can see that the Fed has to maintain a balance. It wants enough money in the economy to encourage economic growth, but not too much because that can spur inflation. And, it must understand that the actions it takes will take a while to produce the desired effect.

Pay attention to the news. You will see that the Fed is in the news a lot. Keep the Fed's overall goals in mind: stable prices, economic growth, and full employment. What is the Fed trying to do right now?

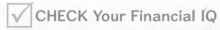 CHECK Your Financial IQ

What is the main tool the Fed uses to influence the economy?

Summary

- Banks and other financial institutions offer individual services such as making personal loans, accepting deposits, and providing accounts that allow you to draft payments. There are two types of institutions: depository institutions (commercial banks, savings institutions, and credit unions) and nondepository institutions (insurance companies, securities firms, and investment companies).

- One of the most widely used banking services is the checking account. Most of us open checking accounts because it allows us to have an accurate record of our payments and also, to carry less cash. Many banks provide debit cards to their checking account holders. A debit card enables you to withdraw cash from your checking account at an ATM or pay directly for goods or services at stores or restaurants.

- Other services provided by banking institutions are safety deposit boxes, cashier's checks, money orders, and travelers checks. Banks also offer services for credit payment.

- The Federal Deposit Insurance Corporation (FDIC) and the National Credit Union Savings Insurance Fund (NCUSIF) are two major insurers for most financial institutions. Most financial institutions have deposit insurance to protect your money up to some maximum amount.

- The Federal Reserve, also known as the Fed, is the heart of the banking system and helps regulate banking, as well as the whole economy. The Fed regulates banks, making sure they follow rules and practices designed to ensure a sound banking system. The Fed's major economic goals are to create ongoing economic growth, encourage full employment, and promote price stability. The Fed uses monetary policy to help accomplish these goals.

Key Terms and Vocabulary

Automatic teller machine (ATM)
Bank draft
Cashier's check
Check
Check register
Checking account
Credit union
Debit card
Depository institutions
Discount rate
Electronic funds transfer
Federal Deposit Insurance Corporation (FDIC)
Federal Reserve System

Fiat money
Inflation
Monetary policy
Money orders
National Credit Union Savings Insurance Fund (NCUSIF)
Negotiable order of withdrawal (NOW) accounts
Nondepository institutions
Personal identification number (PIN)
Price level stability
Safety deposit boxes
Travelers checks

What Do You Know?

1. (a) How do depository institutions differ from nondepository institutions?

    (b) Give an example of each.

2. (a) What are some of the benefits offered by depository institutions?

    (b) How might the economy suffer if there were no banks?

3. (a) Explain how a checking account works.

    (b) What makes a checking account useful compared to an ordinary savings account?

4. (a) Describe the steps to follow when balancing your checking account.

    (b) What might happen if you do not identify a difference between your balance and the bank's balance?

5. (a) Explain how a debit card differs from a credit card.

    (b) How might use of a debit card create problems in your checking account?

6. (a) What do cashier's checks, money orders, and travelers checks have in common?

    (b) What is a circumstance in which you might want to use one of these as opposed to a personal check?

7. (a) Explain the function(s) of the Federal Deposit Insurance Corporation (FDIC).

    (b) How does the FDIC differ from the National Credit Union Savings Insurance Fund (NCUSIF)?

    (c) What might happen if people did not have confidence in the banking system?

8. (a) What role does the Fed play in banking?

    (b) Why do you think it is important for banks across the country to follow similar rules?

9. (a) What does it mean to say our money is fiat money?

    (b) How does the existence of fiat money enable the Fed to exercise control over the money supply?

What Are Your Personal Finance Math Skills?

1. Jerry has $321,000 in a bank account at his local bank. How much does he stand to lose if the bank goes out of business?

2. Rashaun has $235 in his checking account but has written two checks that have not cleared for $23 and $67.50 respectively. Does

he have enough money in his account to make his car payment of $202?

3. Brandy made a withdrawal of $50 cash from an ATM that was not in her network. Assuming the bank charges $2 for out of network withdrawals, how much will her account be charged in total?

4. Marvin deposited $400 in his checking account but also wrote checks for $224.21 and $311.34. Assuming his original balance was $622.43, how much does he have in his account now?

5. Ben wrote a check for $52 that was more than his account balance. The bank charges $25 for bounced checks and the local business that accepted his check charges $20 for bounced checks. How much in total would Ben have to pay for that one check?

6. Gurinda's previous checking account balance was $532.14. Since then she has written a check for $46.19 and one for $138.32. She also made a $200 deposit into her account. Assuming her monthly service charge is $6, how much is her new balance?

7. Emily logged into her checking account from her computer. She had written three checks for $34.15, $45.98, and $121.15 respectively. Only the last check was posted to her account. How much are her outstanding checks?

8. Caleb withdrew $100 from his checking account. However, he used an ATM that was not in his bank's network. Assuming his bank charges $2 for that service and the bank he used charges $3, how much will his checking account be debited?

What Would You Do?

Susan, a recent college graduate, opened a checking account with a local bank. She asked numerous questions before deciding on this bank, including inquiring about checking account fees and annual credit card fees. When Susan returned from her first vacation in the Bahamas, she was surprised to see numerous fees on her credit card statement and her bank statement. When she called the bank, they informed her that they recently added service charges on international transactions involving their checking and credit card accounts. Susan began to protest; the bank stated that her last bank statement included a flyer detailing these changes. In looking back, Susan realized that she had, in fact, received the information, but had ignored it because it was included with considerable advertising information about purchasing CDs. The lengthy document was written in such small print that she did not bother to read it.

a. What do you think of banks and other financial institutions' efforts to notify their customers of fee changes? Should the bank have sent a letter to customers that specifically addressed the changes to international transactions? Do you think this would have ensured that their customers would read this information and feel informed about the changes?

b. What lesson do you think Susan has learned?

c. Would you change banking institutions if this had happened to you? Why or why not?

What Are the Connections? Math

Assume Charlene's checking balance and the bank's balance were reconciled last month. Using a separate sheet of paper, reconcile the following bank statement against Charlene's statement. Is there an error somewhere in Charlene's records?

Bank Statement		Charlene's Check Register	
Balance	**$1,504.00**	Charlene's Balance	$1,440.50
Interest earned	$ .07	Check #100	$60.00
Fees	$6.00	Check #101	$75.50
Check #100	$60	Check #102	$47.50
Check #101	$75.50	Check #103	$100.10
Check #103	$101.10	Check #104	$55.00
Check #104	$55.00	Check #105	$9.75
Check #105	$9.75	Check #106	$15.00

Teamwork

Work in teams to complete this activity. As a group, do the following:

1. List five important banking services to consider when deciding on a financial institution.

2. Rank them in order of importance.

3. Design a spreadsheet that includes the following:
   a. Column A: Banking services in order of rankings
   b. Columns B–D: Three financial institutions in your area
   c. Final row: Total score

4. Use the newspaper, Internet, phone book, or other resources to find information about each of the financial institutions your group listed. Gather data about each of your banking services listed. Grade each banking service on a scale of 1–4 (1 being the least desirable and 4 being the most desirable).

5. After gathering the information, total each banking institution's column.

6. Present your information to the class in a poster, slide presentation, written report, and so forth.

1. Banks do *not*
   a. take in and secure people's money.
   b. make loans to individuals and businesses.
   c. pay interest on the money on deposit with the bank.
   d. sell corporate stock to the public.

2. Which of the following statements about banks is true?
   a. All banks in a community charge the same fees for services.
   b. When one bank raises the interest rate it gives on deposits, all other banks will match that rate of interest.
   c. ATM fees are not charged when a person uses a bank near his home.
   d. All banks must follow state and federal government regulations.

3. An account into which a person deposits money and then can withdraw funds by making a written order to the bank instructing it to pay money from the account to another person or business is known as a
   a. savings account.
   b. checking account.
   c. cashier's account.
   d. credit account.

4. Why do banks require a person to have a PIN in order to use an ATM?
   a. They want to know that a person does not have accounts at a competing bank.
   b. They want to be sure that a person has enough money in the account before writing a check.
   c. They require the information to update the customer's account.
   d. They require the number to be used along with a debit card or ATM card to help protect the person from theft.

5. Why do many people prefer to use a debit card instead of a credit card?
   a. They can purchase items and have the money withdrawn directly from their account without having to pay interest on a credit card balance.
   b. They can earn interest on accounts equal to 5 percent of purchases made with the debit card.
   c. They do not have to worry about overdrawing on their checking accounts.
   d. There are no fees charged when a debit card is used to withdraw money from an out-of-network ATM.

6. Having overdraft protection on a checking account is a good idea but it can also be an expensive feature. Why?
   a. Banks charge a monthly fee for having overdraft protection on their checking accounts.
   b. A fee, which can be as high as $25–$30, is charged every time overdraft protection on the checking account is used.

    c. The bank charges 20 percent of the amount taken from the over-draft protection.

    d. The bank stops paying the person interest on savings accounts or CDs each time overdraft protection is used.

7. What is the purpose of a check register?
    a. It automatically balances a person's checking account.
    b. A person who balances his own checking account does not have to pay a bank fee for the service.
    c. A person can keep track of all deposits to and withdrawals from the checking account.
    d. It protects a person from identity theft.

8. What does it mean when a person says that she is "reconciling" her checking account?
    a. She is making sure that her checking account is not overdrawn.
    b. She is making sure that all deposits have been made to her savings account from her company's direct deposit program.
    c. She is comparing her checking account balance with her savings account balance.
    d. She is comparing recorded transactions in her checkbook register to the transactions that appear on the bank's monthly statement.

9. A person reconciling his checking account register with the bank's checking account statement sees that his record shows that he has $15.30 more than the bank says he has in the account. What should he do?
    a. He should make out a check to his bank for $15.30.
    b. He should use the balance shown on the bank's statement since it is a computer-tracked total.
    c. He should contact the bank if after checking the math and recording outstanding checks, interest, and fees, he still has a different balance.
    d. He should deposit $15.30 into his savings account until he is able to reconcile his account record with the bank.

10. Why do people sometimes have to use a cashier's check instead of a personal check?
    a. The person is buying a large item such as a car and the dealership will only accept a check that is charged against the bank's account.
    b. The person has a poor credit record and hopes to improve his credit score by using cashier's checks that are guaranteed by the bank.
    c. The person does not have enough money in her checking account so she borrows money from the bank in the form of a cashier's check.
    d. The person wants a safe way to transfer money from her CD that has just matured to her checking account at the bank.

11. Which of the following bank services is correctly matched with its function?
    a. Money order: a check from a personal checking account that is cosigned by the bank.

b. Cashier's check: a check that the bank draws on its account with the Federal Reserve System.

c. Travelers check: a check that a person is only able to buy in another country.

d. Bank draft: authorized withdrawal from a person's bank account to make payments such as a mortgage or car loan automatically.

12. Which of the following is *not* an advantage of having bills paid by electronic funds transfer (EFT)?

a. The person who has an interest-earning account earns interest until the date that the money is transferred out of the account.

b. EFT prevents a person from overdrawing on her bank account.

c. The person who has EFT does not have to worry about bills being paid on time.

d. EFT saves a person from paying for stamps to mail checks to pay bills.

13. Why did the government establish the Federal Deposit Insurance Corporation (FDIC)?

a. The government wanted to be sure that banks did not fail.

b. The government wanted to be sure that people who took bank loans would be charged a fair rate of interest.

c. The government wanted to protect people from losing their money if the banks failed.

d. The government wanted to protect the banks from being taken over by other businesses.

14. A person has $50,000 in certificates of deposit (CDs), $25,000 in a savings account, $35,000 in a NOW account, and $12,000 in a checking account all in the same bank. If the bank fails, the amount of his money that will be protected is

a. only the $25,000 in the savings account.

b. $100,000.

c. $122,000.

d. only the $50,000 in the certificates of deposit.

15. What is a credit union?

a. It is a nonprofit business that functions like a bank and is owned by its members.

b. It is a business that brings together a number of other businesses that offer credit to the public.

c. It is a bank that only makes loans to members of labor unions.

d. It is a business that is run by the federal government and whose job it is to make credit available to low-income people.

16. The Federal Reserve System *cannot*

a. make sure that banks follow the rules designed to create a strong banking system.

b. adjust the amount of money in circulation in the economy.

c. prevent the economy from entering a recession.

d. require banks to keep a certain amount of money on hand to meet customers' daily need for cash.

17. The Federal Reserve System tries to keep inflation under control by
    a. lowering interest rates on the money it loans out to member banks.
    b. providing more money to the federal government to spend on goods and services needed to fight a war.
    c. increasing bonuses given to workers at the end of the year.
    d. decreasing the supply of money that banks have available to make loans.

18. The Federal Reserve System uses monetary policy to
    a. create new businesses, close failing businesses, and loan money to consumers.
    b. create ongoing economic growth, encourage full employment, and promote price stability.
    c. keep the government from cutting federal jobs and increasing spending on the military.
    d. keep banks from increasing interest on savings accounts and charging for checking account overdraft protection.

19. Which of the following is a true statement about the supply of money in the United States?
    a. The total money supply of the United States is coin and currency.
    b. The money supply of the United States is backed by gold.
    c. The United States Treasury prints more money when the Federal Reserve System directs it to take this action.
    d. The United States Treasury does not consider money that is transferred electronically to be part of the money supply of the United States.

20. If the Federal Reserve System is concerned about inflation increasing, what action can it take?
    a. It can increase the discount rate, which is the interest rate it charges member banks to borrow money.
    b. It can make more money available to member banks by directing the United States Treasury to print more money.
    c. It can lower interest rates charged for loans to consumers.
    d. It can borrow more money from the banks that are members of the Federal Reserve System.

21. Why is it said that an increase in the money supply by the Federal Reserve System has a greater impact on the economy than just the dollar amount of the increase?
    a. Inflation increases the amount of money that is in circulation.
    b. The money that banks receive is loaned out to consumers who then spend the money or deposit it in bank accounts and it is loaned out again.
    c. The money is kept in the banks so that the banks are considered to be stronger businesses and more people will deposit their own money in these banks.
    d. The increase in the supply of money will keep interest rates rising.

CHAPTER 13

Explore the ways in which savings can earn interest.

Examine the different types of bank accounts that can aid in saving.

Describe retirement savings options.

Key Terms

401(k)/403(b)

Annuity

Certificate of deposit (CD)

Demand deposit

Individual Retirement Account (IRA)

Money market deposit account

Pension plan

Vesting

Methods of Saving

"LaTanya, I can't buy you everything you want." LaTanya's mother was irritated. "I'm not made of money."

"I know that, Mom, but I'll have to have a car someday." LaTanya stared at the car in the neighbor's driveway with a For Sale sign in the window. Their neighbor, Mr. Hawkins, was asking $2,200 for the car. "And that's a really good deal. You know Mr. Hawkins takes care of his cars."

"It doesn't matter, LaTanya. I don't have the money." Her mother sighed. "We have talked about this before. I told you a couple years ago: If you expected to have your own car, you would have to save for it yourself. I don't make enough to afford a second vehicle." With that, she walked away.

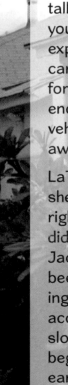

LaTanya hated to admit it, but she knew her mother was right. And, in fact, when she did all that babysitting for the Jacksons last year, she had been doing a good job of saving. She opened a bank account and deposited nearly $1,000. The babysitting had slowed down a lot since the Jacksons moved. But LaTanya began to wonder: How much interest has that account earned over the last few months? Excited, she decided to run down to the bank to find out. She knew she wouldn't have enough to buy the car. But maybe she was closer than she had thought!

While borrowing money can be a necessary and financially wise step, there is no escaping the need to save money. For much of the rest of your life, you will face the task of building up your wealth and managing your money. Placing money in various savings options will be key to your success. Here we will learn about some of the options for saving money.

INTEREST AND YOUR SAVINGS

LaTanya was wise to have opened a bank account for her savings. After all, banks are a great place to keep savings. They offer safety and security. In general, deposits up to $250,000 in bank accounts are guaranteed against loss. In addition, many types of bank accounts offer interest on deposits. So, while you are working to earn more money, your money is "working," too. It is making money and helping your savings grow. LaTanya is hopeful that this feature of her savings account has helped take her a few steps closer to buying the car she wants.

Interest Rates on Deposits

One of the ways that banks and similar financial institutions make money is by borrowing and lending money. They take in money from depositors. Then, they use that money to make loans, on which they charge interest. In other words, banks use depositors' money to make money. In fact, because depositors' money is so valuable to them, banks will often pay interest on deposits.

The amount of interest the financial institution is willing to pay depends on several factors. One factor is the length of time you are willing to commit to leaving the money on deposit. In general, the longer you are willing to leave the money, the higher the rate. In addition, deposits covered by FDIC or NCUSIF generally earn less than uninsured deposits. Other factors that determine interest rates paid on deposits include the policies of the financial institution and the market rates of interest—that is, the overall level of various interest rates charged by other banks and financial institutions doing business in the market.

Market Rates of Interest

The Federal Reserve has a significant impact on the market rate of interest. By manipulating the money supply—and therefore the price of money or interest rates—the Fed stimulates the economy or slows it down. The Fed

MATH for Personal Finance

Candace put $1,000 in a savings account that pays 2.5 percent in annual interest.

How much interest will she earn during the year?

Solution: $1,000 × .025 = $25.

also influences the interest rate market when it sets the discount rate, or the interest rate it charges banks for loans. The Fed does not control all interest rates, but interest rates tend to move up or down along with Fed-controlled rates.

Liquidity

Interest rates offered for deposits also differ depending on the level of liquidity the account offers. **Liquidity** refers to how quickly you can convert something to cash without significant loss of value. Accounts that offer a high degree of liquidity—that is, the ability to take money out on demand—usually offer the lowest interest rates. Why is this? Think about it from the bank's perspective. Offering people quick access to their money limits their ability to loan out that money and make money on it. Therefore, they offer these short-term depositors less. This fact will impact LaTanya, as you will see.

✓ CHECK Your Financial IQ

What is the relationship between liquidity and interest?

TYPES OF BANK ACCOUNTS

Banks offer a wide range of different accounts and services. As options for saving money, each type has benefits and drawbacks. You should understand the basic features of the different types of accounts available.

Checking and NOW Accounts

Many people open basic checking accounts. These are the most liquid type of bank account, since you can access your money instantly by writing a check or using an ATM. The money put into a checking account is sometimes referred to as a **demand deposit** because it can be withdrawn at any time—on demand. The liquidity of a checking account helps explain why traditional checking accounts do not pay interest. Because they do not pay interest, they are not a very good way to save money.

There is a type of withdrawal account that functions much like a checking account and that does pay interest. This type of interest-paying demand deposit account is often referred to as a negotiable order of withdrawal (NOW) account. NOW accounts function in the same manner as checking accounts in that you can write drafts (checks) on these accounts. But most NOW accounts require you to maintain a minimum monthly balance, or pay higher interest rates if you maintain a certain balance. This way, the bank is confident of having a certain amount of your money on hand to loan out and earn interest on. However, these accounts typically offer the lowest interest rates of any deposit account. And remember—there may be penalties if you fail to maintain a minimum balance. NOW accounts are insured.

Interest Bearing Savings Accounts

Savings accounts generally pay a little higher rate of interest on deposits than NOW accounts. These accounts are still very liquid in that you can withdraw money at any time. They do not, however, provide check-writing

services. For this reason, people tend to have less transaction activity in their savings accounts and generally do not access them frequently. In LaTanya's case, this lower liquidity made it easier for her to save money. Of course, she also earned a relatively low interest rate. She will find when she checks her balance that the $1,000 she had deposited has not grown enough to make a $2,200 purchase possible.

Individuals often use a savings account to save money for specific purposes. For example, LaTanya may have had a car in mind when she opened such an account to save money from her babysitting jobs. Others use savings accounts for an emergency fund, holiday gift fund, or vacation.

Certificates of Deposit (CDs)

Certificates of deposit are a financial product offered by many financial institutions. A **certificate of deposit (CD)** is essentially a contract between an individual and the financial institution that specifies some length of time that the individual will leave a certain amount of money deposited at the particular bank. CDs specify a minimum amount invested and have a specific maturity date—that is, a future date when you can cash in the CD. For example, you might buy a $5,000 or $10,000 CD that has a one-year maturity. Common CD maturities are one month, three months, six months, one year, three years, and five years. Of course, savers can find CDs with virtually any maturity and dollar amount.

Typically, CDs offer a higher interest rate than savings accounts because the bank can count on the money being there for them to loan out. Remember, a bank makes money by loaning out money that it has on deposit. If the money is likely to be withdrawn at any time, the bank cannot loan as much of it.

Again, the financial institution pays a higher interest rate for a CD because the money is locked up until maturity. You can access your money prior to maturity, but you will pay a penalty for early withdrawal. Therefore, you should consider CDs only when you know that you will not need the money until after the CD matures. Is a CD a viable option for LaTanya at this time?

Money Market Deposit Account (MMDA)

Money market deposit accounts have some of the features of checking accounts and some of the features of savings accounts. These accounts require you to maintain a minimum balance, have no maturity date, pay interest, and offer limited check-writing privileges. A typical MMDA might require you to keep a $2,500 minimum average monthly balance and allow you to write five checks a month. Most impose fees if your balance falls below the minimum or if you write more checks than allowed.

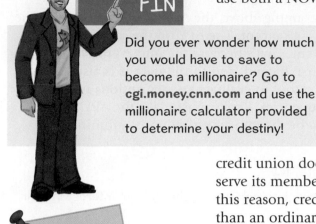

You Do It

Activity #1

MMDAs differ from NOW accounts in that they provide only very limited check-writing privileges and pay a higher rate of interest. Many people use both a NOW account for their typical monthly expenditures and an MMDA to maintain a larger balance that is still liquid yet earns a slightly higher interest rate. As you can see in Figure 13.1, various money market investments have unique advantages and disadvantages.

About Credit Unions

Credit unions differ from other depository financial institutions primarily due to their nonprofit status. A credit union does not exist to earn money for investors. Rather, it exists to serve its members—the people who deposit money in the institution. For this reason, credit unions can often pay higher interest rates on deposits than an ordinary bank can. Their expenses may be lower and any profits are redistributed to members. A credit union is a good place to check interest rates on deposits.

APY and Comparing Savings Options

Sometimes, you may find it necessary to compare savings options that have different compounding frequencies. The term compounding, or **compound interest**, refers to the way that interest added to an account earns interest. Compounding frequency, then, is how often the bank puts interest you have earned into your account—where it then can earn interest. More frequent compounding is better given the same interest rate. That's because when the interest is put in the account, it also begins to earn interest. The more frequently this happens, the more interest you earn.

When you shop for savings options, you may find the following situation: One bank advertises a 4 percent interest rate on a CD with annual compounding and another bank advertises a 3.95 percent interest rate and quarterly compounding. How do you compare those offers? Which would give you more money in the end? Without doing some math, you can find your answer by checking the annual percentage yield.

Figure 13.1 Comparison of Money Market Investments

As you can see, different accounts offer different levels of liquidity, which in turn affects the account's ability to earn interest.

Money Market Investment	Advantages	Disadvantages
Checking account	Very liquid	No interest
NOW account	Very liquid	Low interest rate; minimum balance required
MMDA	Liquid	Low interest rate
Savings account	Liquid	Low interest rate
Certificate of deposit (CD)	Relatively high interest rate	Less liquid

The **annual percentage yield**, or **APY**, is the interest rate that takes the compounding frequency into account. That is, it tells you what your account will really earn on an annual basis once compounding is taken into consideration. In the example above, the APY on the first offer is the same as the advertised rate—4 percent. The APY on the second offer is slightly higher—4.009 percent. That's because the interest placed in the account at the end of the first, second, and third quarters is also earning interest. Always use APY as a tool to evaluate savings options that have different compounding frequencies. Banks must make the APY available to you, although it may not be the rate advertised most prominently.

✓ CHECK Your Financial IQ

In general, how do people manage to achieve a higher rate of interest in their bank accounts?

RETIREMENT SAVINGS OPTIONS

Finance ONLINE

To learn more about retirement and which type might be best for you, you can visit **www.irs.gov** and click "retirement plans community."

Finance ONLINE

Do you want to see how your savings can grow with the power of compounding interest? There are many online calculators that can show you what can happen assuming various savings and interest rates. For example, visit: **www.lfg.com**. Then, click "Planning Tools," then "Financial Calculators."

Like LaTanya, you probably have some short- or intermediate-term savings goals. You might be saving for a car or simply putting money aside for a rainy day fund. For many of these goals, you would most likely use the savings options we've already discussed, such as CDs or savings accounts. But what about long-term goals? Do you know someone who has achieved a lifestyle you would like to have? How old are they? When did they begin thinking about financial security? Like LaTanya, your primary goal may be short-term in nature, but you don't want to neglect the future because time is your best friend when trying to accumulate wealth. If you begin early and use the large amount of time you have, even small but steady levels of saving can build to a large stockpile by retirement. Did you know that LaTanya could accumulate more than $1 million if she saved $100 a month for 40 years and averaged a 12 percent annual return? However, if she saves the same amount for 30 years she will have about $350,000. That extra 10 years makes a big difference, and it is because of compound interest. As your savings grows, like LaTanya's, the amount you have accumulated begins to earn far more than the amount you contribute each month. Your money begins working for you instead of you working for your money. Even if you invest a lump sum of $5,000 today, you can accumulate a tremendous amount of wealth with time on your side. Check out Figure 13.2 to see how much difference a few years makes.

To get an even bigger shock, check out Figure 13.3. See how much you would have if you put in $5,000 every year.

Saving for retirement is a critical, but often neglected part of a young person's financial plan. Fortunately, there are several investment and savings options designed to encourage and facilitate saving for retirement. We will briefly look at Individual Retirement Accounts (IRAs) and various pension plan options.

Individual Retirement Accounts (IRAs)

Individual Retirement Accounts (IRAs) are a type of savings account created by the government to encourage people to save for retirement. To

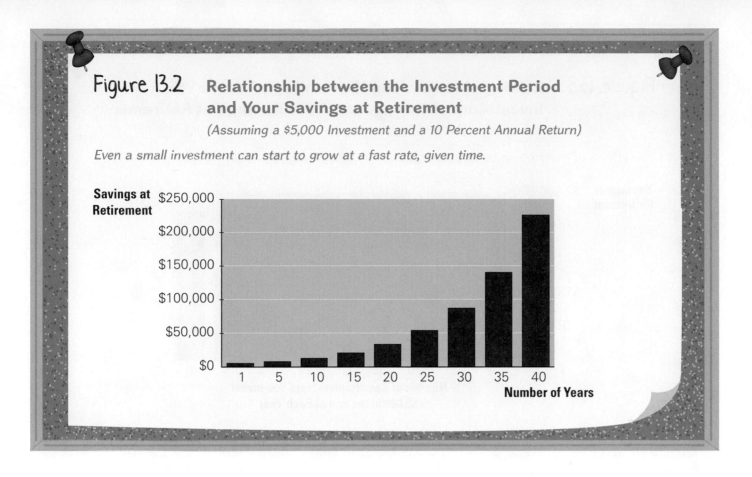

Figure 13.2 **Relationship between the Investment Period and Your Savings at Retirement**

(Assuming a $5,000 Investment and a 10 Percent Annual Return)

Even a small investment can start to grow at a fast rate, given time.

make saving in an IRA attractive, the government offers certain tax benefits that allow investors to reduce their income taxes. And, to ensure that people use IRAs only for retirement, the government put limits on when you can use IRA funds. You can withdraw IRA funds beginning at age 59.5. If you withdraw IRA funds prior to age 59.5, you will pay a penalty equal to 10 percent of the money withdrawn, in addition to income taxes on the amount withdrawn.

All IRAs can include a range of different types of investments. For example, you can have CDs, mutual funds, or both in your IRA account.

There are two main types of IRAs: traditional IRAs and Roth IRAs. They differ in the type of tax benefit they provide.

The key features of a **traditional IRA** are that many people can make tax deductible contributions, and all earnings are tax deferred. What does this mean? **Tax deductible** means that if you are eligible and contribute, say, $3,000 in a given year, you can deduct $3,000 from your taxable income and pay no federal tax on that amount. This feature allows you to reduce your income taxes for the year you made the contribution. **Tax deferred** means that the account's earnings, such as from interest, are not taxed until they are withdrawn after retirement. Tax deferral helps you in two ways. For one: A tax-deferred account will grow in value more quickly than one earning the same rate but in which earnings are taxed. For another: When you do withdraw monies, it may be at a lower tax rate because you will be retired and most likely earning less money.

The tax-deferred benefit of traditional IRAs is available to everyone. However, certain higher-income individuals are not allowed to deduct contributions from their taxes, and there are limits on how much a person can

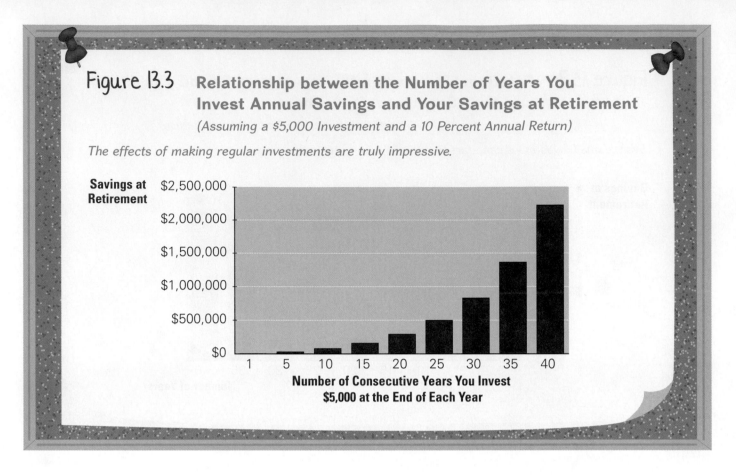

Figure 13.3 Relationship between the Number of Years You Invest Annual Savings and Your Savings at Retirement

(Assuming a $5,000 Investment and a 10 Percent Annual Return)

The effects of making regular investments are truly impressive.

Savings at Retirement

Number of Consecutive Years You Invest $5,000 at the End of Each Year

contribute to a traditional IRA. In 2008, the contribution limits were $5,000 per person unless you are 50 or older. Persons over age 50 are allowed to contribute an additional $1,000 to their accounts.

The Roth IRA has the same contribution limits as the traditional IRA. But, it has unique features. **Roth IRA** contributions are not tax deductible, but the earnings from an eligible account are never taxed, even after withdrawal. Eligibility to contribute to a Roth IRA phases out at high levels of income. Roth IRAs also have their own rules for how the money is distributed at retirement.

Which type of IRA is right for you? The answer depends on a number of factors. There are various online tools that can help you make the choice that best meets your needs. See Figure 13.4 for an example of one of these tools.

Self-employed people may be eligible for a Simplified Employee Plan IRA (**SEP-IRA**). These function much like traditional IRAs, but they have their own contribution limits.

You Do It

Activity #2

Employer-Sponsored Retirement Plans

One of the benefits you might receive when you begin working full time is an employer-sponsored retirement plan. **Employer-sponsored retirement plans** are set up by the employer, and the employer will generally make some contributions to the plan on your behalf. These plans are designed to help you save for retirement and are often used as an incentive to attract high-quality employees. It's important to note that employers are not bound to offer such plans.

Employer-sponsored plans come in two main forms: the defined-benefit plan and the defined-contribution plan. There are many variations within

Figure 13.4 Online IRA Calculator

The choice between Roth and traditional IRAs depends on a number of factors. Tools such as this can help you make the right decision.

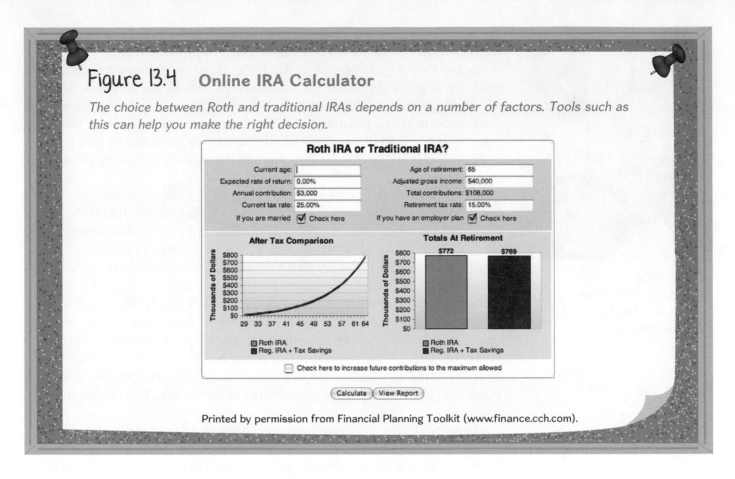

Printed by permission from Financial Planning Toolkit (www.finance.cch.com).

MATH for Personal Finance

Barton's employer has a 401k plan where they match $.50 of every $1 he contributes up to $3,000.

How much will the total contributions into his 401k be this year if he contributes $3,000?

Solution: His employer will contribute an additional $3,000 × $.50 = $1,500 so his total contributions will be $3,000 + $1,500 = $4,500.

each category. But, in both cases, you do not pay taxes on contributions or earnings until you retire and begin making withdrawals.

Defined-benefit plans guarantee you a specific amount of income when you retire. The benefit is often based on factors such as the number of years worked and the average salary earned during your peak earning years. Such defined-benefit plans are popularly referred to as **pension plans**. Under them, the employer makes contributions to the plan on the employee's behalf. The money generally goes into a large fund and professional managers then invest and manage the fund. The employer establishes guidelines regarding the number of years a person must work before becoming eligible to withdraw money from the fund. Note that many of the restrictions and requirements of employer-sponsored retirement plans are governed by federal law.

When an eligible person retires, he or she receives the agreed-to benefit from the fund. If the retiree lives five years, he or she gets benefits for five years. If the retiree lives 25 years, he or she receives benefits for 25 years.

This process of earning eligibility for an employer benefit is known as **vesting**. For example, a worker might have to work for an employer for five years before being fully vested and eligible to withdraw full benefits.

Defined-benefit plans are less common than in the past. This may be because people are living longer and so employers providing these plans are assuming more financial risk. In contrast, defined-contribution plans shift this risk to the retiree.

In **defined-contribution plans**, the employer contributes to the employee's retirement account but does not guarantee a specific retirement benefit. Such plans often offer the employee some control over where

Today, more and more Americans' retirements are funded with the help of defined contribution plans.

contributions are invested. Defined-contribution plans limit the employer's liability to the individual. The employer agrees to make regular contributions, but they are not bound to pay benefits for an unknown period of time. These plans shift more of the retirement risk to the employee since the employee is primarily responsible for building and funding his or her own account. When an individual's funds are gone, the employer has no other obligation to that individual. The flexibility in investing and the shifting of risk to the employee has made these plans extremely popular in recent years.

401(k) and 403(b) plans are popular types of defined-contribution plans named after the sections of the IRS code that established these plans. For-profit companies can establish 401(k) plans for their employees. Nonprofit and charitable institutions can offer employees a similar type of plan, called a 403(b). **401(k)/403(b) plans** allow employees to make contributions into their own accounts, which may feature a range of investment options. The money employees contribute reduces their taxable income and therefore lowers the taxes withheld from their checks. So, for example, imagine you were contributing $500 per paycheck to a 401(k). This money would be taken from your pay before your tax was withheld. Your tax, therefore, would be lower. The taxes on this money are deferred. When you take money from your 401(k) at retirement, you pay income taxes on it.

Many employers offer employer matching on plan contributions. So, for example, a company may offer a $.50 contribution for each $1 contributed by the employee. Most companies that elect to match employee contributions cap the amount that they are willing to match.

401(k) and other defined-contribution plans often offer you a choice about how much to contribute. Unfortunately, this decision often causes people to postpone saving for retirement. It can be hard for a young person who has many needs and wants and a relatively low salary to have the discipline to put away money for several decades down the road. But the decision not to contribute can be costly, particularly if the employer has a program where employee contributions are matched up to some level.

Annuities

Annuities are a type of financial product that guarantees annual payments to the owner for a fixed period of time or for a person's lifetime. They generally require a minimum investment—typically at least $5,000. The amount invested grows tax free and will not be taxed until disbursed to the investor/retiree.

Annuities come in two forms: fixed and variable. With a **fixed annuity**, the return and ultimate payment is a guaranteed amount. With a **variable annuity**, the return and ultimate payment depend on the performance of the investments. One word of caution: Most annuities have very high fees associated with the initial sale that goes to pay the people who sell them. Also, annuities have fees, known as surrender charges, for early withdrawal.

 CHECK Your Financial IQ

What role do employers play in the retirement savings of many people?

Summary

- Banks are a great place to keep savings. They offer safety and security, and in many cases, a chance to earn interest. Banks offer a wide range of different accounts and services. An understanding of the basic features of different types of accounts for saving money is an important part of your financial plan.

- Popular short-term saving accounts include checking accounts, NOW accounts, savings accounts, CDs, and MMDAs. Checking accounts and NOW accounts offer the most liquidity—but also, the lowest rates.

- Retirement should be a key savings goal. Individual Retirement Accounts, which come in several forms, help promote retirement savings by offering some valuable tax advantages. Employers often offer retirement savings plans, normally classified as defined-benefit plans or defined-contribution plans. Today, many employers encourage employees to contribute to 401(k) or 403(b) plans. Self-employed people may be able to set up a Simplified Employee Plan IRA (SEP-IRA). Annuities are also commonly used for retirement savings.

Key Terms and Vocabulary

401(k)/403(b) plan	Liquidity
Annual percentage yield (APY)	Money market deposit account
Annuity	Pension plan
Certificate of deposit (CD)	Roth IRA
Compound interest	Savings account
Defined-benefit plan	SEP-IRA
Defined-contribution plan	Tax deductible
Demand deposit	Tax deferred
Employer-sponsored retirement plan	Traditional IRA
	Variable annuity
Fixed annuity	Vesting
Individual retirement account (IRA)	

What Do You Know?

myFinLitlab.

1. (a) What is liquidity?

   (b) What is the relationship between the concept of liquidity and interest rates?

2. (a) What is a NOW account?

   (b) What feature of a NOW account makes it possible for a financial institution to offer interest on the account?

3. (a) Why is knowing the APY of a CD so important?

   (b) Why are rates on CDs higher than those on savings accounts?

   (c) What factor would most affect your choice of maturity date on a CD?

4. (a) What are the key features of a money market deposit account?

   (b) How does a money market deposit account (MMDA) differ from a NOW account?

5. (a) Define an Individual Retirement Account (IRA).

   (b) How has the government provided people with an incentive to use IRAs?

6. (a) What is the difference between tax deductible and tax deferred?

   (b) Compare the benefits of each.

7. (a) What are the two major types of IRA?

   (b) How might the size of a person's income affect the decision to choose a Roth or a traditional IRA?

8. (a) What are two categories of employer-sponsored retirement plans?

   (b) Compare a defined-benefit plan to a defined-contribution plan offered by an employer.

9. (a) Discuss the general characteristics of a 401(k)/403(b) plan.

   (b) If an employer is matching $.50 for each $1 you contribute, what kind of return are you earning on your initial investment to a 401(k)/403(b) plan?

10. (a) What is an annuity?

    (b) What is the difference between a fixed annuity and a variable annuity?

 What Are Your Finance Math Skills?   myFinLitlab.

1. How much interest will you earn on a two-year $6,000 CD that will pay annual interest of 5 percent? The first year's interest will remain in the CD and also earn interest during the second year.

2. If your employer matches your retirement contributions on a dollar-for-dollar basis up to $4,000, how much will be contributed to your account by the end of the first year if you take advantage of the entire match?

3. If you put $2,000 a year for three years into an IRA that earns 3 percent a year, how much will you have saved at the end of the third year?

4. Anita earned 2 percent on the $1,200 she had in savings and 3.5 percent on a one-year $4,000 CD. How much did she earn in interest during the year?

5. If you withdraw $10,000 from your IRA at age 35 to buy a car, how much penalty will you pay for this withdrawal?

6. How much money will Jerod earn in interest this year on a $3,000 CD that pays 5 percent in annual interest assuming annual compounding?

7. Assuming Brenda earns annual interest of 6 percent on her two-year $5,000 CD, how much will she earn in interest during the second year? Remember that her first year's interest will be added to the original principal and will earn interest during the second year.

8. If Nathaniel's employer matches 50 percent of the first $2,000 he contributes to his annual retirement account, how much will he have in his account assuming he takes full advantage of his employer match?

What Would You Do?

Suzanne received holiday money from a relative. But, the relative told Suzanne that the gift came with a catch: She must save the money for college, which was three years away. After a discussion with her parents and the local banker, she decided to place the money in a money market account.

Three years pass and Suzanne is making decisions about college, such as what she will need to bring, whether or not to buy a computer, how to buy books, and so forth. Fortunately for Suzanne, and as a result of her hard work, she received a number of scholarships that will go a long way toward meeting these expenses. Then she remembers the money market account. This money was for college. She is about to go to college but would really like to have a car. She knows she doesn't need a car at college, but the idea of being on her own and having her own car is very exciting. Her parents argue that it would be more in keeping with the intention of the gift to use it to start an IRA. But they leave the decision up to her.

Suzanne has come to you for help making her decision. What would you tell her?

a. Is she bound to use the money for college needs only?

b. Is a car really a college need or just something she wants?

c. Has she earned the right to use the money as she wishes by working hard and earning scholarships to help pay for college?

What Are the Connections? Language Arts and Technology

Gather information from one banking or financial institution on the different savings options available. Collect information on rates for all kinds of savings products. Put this information in a poster for your fellow students that would help them quickly analyze the information and make a decision about the type of savings plan that is best for them.

Be sure to make a list of each type of account, how much it costs to open the account, the interest rate on the account (including APY), and other pertinent information.

Teamwork

Bart is a college student who has never invested his funds. He has saved $1,000. Now he wants to invest this money but he will need the $1,000 to help get into an apartment when he graduates in a year.

In a group, help Bart make a decision of where to put his money so that he will get the most return on his investment.

a. Make a chart of various types of investments Bart can make with his $1,000.

b. Be sure to look at what it will cost him when he takes the money out in a year. Will he make enough to leave some in the account or investment at the end of the year to not withdraw everything?

c. Write your group's decision on how Bart should invest. Use the information gathered in your chart. Be sure to give support for your group's decision.

d. Prepare a presentation for Bart about your group's decision.

TEST PREP QUESTIONS

1. Banks use their depositors' money to make money. What is meant by this statement?
   a. The Federal Reserve System pays member banks based on the amount of money they have on deposit.
   b. Banks loan out money that they have received from depositors at a higher rate of interest than the interest they pay to their depositors.
   c. Depositors often forget how much money they have in their accounts and the banks can use that money to invest for the bank.
   d. Banks are able to print additional money based on the amount of money they have on deposit.

2. Which of the following is *not* an explanation for why accounts in banks earn different rates of interest?
   a. The Federal Reserve System is trying to stimulate the economy by lowering the discount rate.
   b. The bank gives people a higher rate of interest when the person is willing to leave money on deposit with the bank for a longer period of time.
   c. A person with a low credit score will *not* earn as high a rate of interest on a savings account as a person with a high credit score.
   d. The Federal Reserve System has directed the United States Treasury to make more money available.

3. Which of the following is a true statement about liquidity?
   a. The more liquid an account, the higher the rate of interest offered by the bank.
   b. The only liquid account at a bank is a savings account.
   c. If an account has a high degree of liquidity, it means that the account owner can easily and quickly access the funds in the account.
   d. If someone needs to have money available for payment of monthly bills, the person should keep that money in an account that has low liquidity.

4. Which of the following is *not* a true statement about checking accounts?
   a. A checking account is considered to be the most liquid type of bank account.
   b. Checking accounts are sometimes called "demand deposits" because the account owner can withdraw funds at any time from the account.
   c. Checking accounts usually do not pay interest because the banks cannot loan out money in the accounts for a long time.
   d. Checking accounts are good for a young person to use when saving for a large purchase such as a car.

5. The sequence of accounts in order from the most liquid to the least liquid is
   a. NOW account, CD, checking account, savings account.
   b. checking account, three-month CD, savings account, NOW account.
   c. checking account, NOW account, savings account, one-year CD.
   d. six-month CD, checking account, savings account, NOW account.

6. A person receives gifts for her 18th birthday totaling $750. She also saved $1,500 from her summer job and keeps the money at home in a safe place. She wants to buy a car when she turns 21. She has a part time job and plans to work full time next summer and save most of that money. She has a monthly cell phone bill and a credit card that she uses for emergencies and then pays the bill in full each month. Which of the following is the most financially wise recommendation for her when it comes to opening bank accounts at this time?

a. She should open a checking account with $1,000 and keep the rest of the money in cash at home for emergencies.

b. She should put $1,500 in a two-year CD, $600 in a checking or NOW account, and keep $150 in cash.

c. She should put $2,000 in a five-year CD and open a checking account with the $250 left.

d. She should put $750 into a savings account, $1,000 into a checking account, and keep $500 in cash at home for emergencies.

7. The difference between a money market account and other types of checking and savings accounts is that money market accounts

a. pay a higher rate of interest and require depositors to maintain a larger minimum balance than other types of checking accounts.

b. pay interest on deposits after six months and permit the account owner to write an unlimited number of checks.

c. charge a fee every time a check is written and offer higher rates of interest than CDs.

d. are the same as savings accounts with the additional feature of daily compounding.

8. How does the annual percentage yield (APY) help a person decide whether to put his money in bank A or bank B if both are offering 24-month CDs at 4.25 percent interest?

a. The APY will tell the person which bank has earned the highest profits in the past year.

b. The APY is able to determine whether the earnings on the CD will keep ahead of the rate of inflation.

c. If bank A has a higher credit rating than bank B, bank A will have a higher APY.

d. The APY will show the actual interest rate earned as opposed to the stated rate after the frequency of compounding is taken into effect.

9. It is said that "time is a person's best friend when it comes to planning for retirement." What does this statement mean?

a. A person who is young has plenty of time before having to think about saving money for retirement.

b. A young person can take advantage of the benefits of compounding by starting to invest a small amount of money regularly from an early age.

c. By the time today's young people are ready to retire, the economy will have grown and Social Security will pay for their retirement needs.

d. Young people tend to be healthier than old people and therefore have plenty of time before needing to spend money on health insurance.

10. Person A is age 40 and planning to retire in 25 years. Person B is age 25 and planning to retire in 40 years. Both invest $5,000 in an IRA with a guaranteed 10 percent annual rate of return on the investment and neither one adds to the account again. At retirement, person A has about $53,000 in his account and Person B has about $230,000

in her account. Why is there such a huge difference in the value of their IRAs?

a. Person A's account lost money during a recession.

b. Person B's account earned a higher rate of interest during periods of prosperity.

c. Person A was penalized for not keeping money in the account for at least 30 years.

d. Person B's account had longer to benefit from the compounding of interest.

11. Which of the following is a true statement about IRAs?

a. If withdrawals are made from an IRA before the age of 59.5, the person has to pay a 10 percent penalty plus taxes on the amount of money withdrawn.

b. IRAs are designed to help rich people make more money and avoid paying taxes on that money while working or after retirement.

c. An IRA account is made up of the stock from the bank where the person has the account.

d. By encouraging people to save for retirement through IRAs, the government is saving millions of dollars in Social Security payments.

12. What is the major difference between a traditional IRA and a Roth IRA?

a. Contributions to a Roth IRA are only tax deductible if a person earns under $50,000 a year; contributions to a traditional IRA are completely tax deductible.

b. Earnings from a Roth IRA are never taxed whereas withdrawals from a traditional IRA are taxed.

c. Roth IRAs do not start earning income until the person retires; traditional IRAs start earning tax-deferred income after a person reaches the age of 59.5.

d. Roth IRAs are made up of mutual funds; traditional IRAs are made up of CDs.

13. Why are fewer employers offering defined-benefit retirement plans?

a. As people are living longer in retirement, employers have greater financial risk as they must keep paying the retirees their pensions as long as they live.

b. Most employees do not want to have their money kept in the same account for so many years and would rather invest their money on their own.

c. Employers are no longer permitted to take their contribution to an employee's pension plan as a tax deduction.

d. Employees can earn more money by investing the employer's contribution in a bank CD.

14. How does a person who is planning to retire in 30 years benefit now from making contributions to her employer's retirement plan?

a. Her contributions to the company's retirement plan now means that she will not have to contribute to Social Security in the future.

b. Employers return employees' pension contributions in the form of annual bonuses.

c. Her yearly contributions to the plan are tax deductible; therefore, they reduce the amount of income on which she has to pay taxes.

d. The sooner she starts contributing to the plan, the sooner she can start withdrawing the money without having to pay a penalty.

15. Why is an employer-sponsored retirement plan that includes an employer matching feature considered an important benefit offered to attract top employees?

a. In this type of defined-contribution plan, employees are guaranteed to have enough money to live on when they retire.

b. This benefit is like getting a raise or free money since the employer is giving the person extra money in the form of contributions to the person's retirement account.

c. The employee benefits from the employer's financial expertise regarding the best investment products.

d. The employer will continue to contribute to the employee's retirement plan after the employee retires to help employees keep up with cost-of-living increases.

16. What does vesting mean?

a. It is the amount of time that an employee has to work before he is fully eligible for an employer benefit such as a retirement plan.

b. It is the number of years that a person receives pension benefits after retirement.

c. It is a guarantee of employment by the employer after a person works for the company for a certain number of years.

d. It is the period of time that a person has to wait after retiring to collect both a pension and Social Security benefits.

17. A person earning $50,000 a year contributes 10 percent of his income to his retirement plan. As a result, his employer matches up to 5 percent of his salary as a contribution. What will be the total contribution to his retirement plan account for one year?

a. It will be $5,000.

b. It will be $5,250.

c. It will be $7,500.

d. It will be $10,500.

18. Which of the following terms is *not* correctly matched with its description?

a. Employer-sponsored retirement plans: set up by a company to help the employees save for retirement; money is usually contributed by both the employee and the employer and the fund is managed by professional financial managers.

b. Defined-benefit retirement plan: guarantees a person a certain amount of income when the person retires based upon the number of years worked, salary, and contributions to the plan; these plans are also known as pensions.

c. 401(k) and 403(b) plans: defined-contribution retirement accounts that permit employees to contribute to plans that reduce their taxable income while they are working; employers often match at least part of employees' contributions.

d. Annuities: a financial product that guarantees an employee the same income in retirement as she earned during the last three years that she worked at the company.

CHAPTER 14

Learning Objectives

Explore the reasons for investing.

Describe the process of investing in stock.

Describe the process of investing in bonds.

Describe the process of investing in mutual funds.

Explore other options for investing.

Key Terms

Brokerage

Commission

Diversification

Dividend

Securities and Exchange Commission (SEC)

Shareholder

Treasury bonds

14.56

Methods of Investing

7855

7810

7765

Kari stifled a sob. She had always been close to her grandfather, and the memories of the good times were still fresh even though he had passed away several years ago. It was still hard to think about his passing, but when she looked at her stock account she couldn't help it.

Gramps had given each one of his grandchildren an account that contained $10,000 worth of stock. He also gave specific instructions on what they were supposed to do with it. Kari was 18 now, and according to those instructions, she could begin to make some limited decisions with the consent of her father. Gramps wanted his grandchildren to learn about investing, and Kari vowed she would.

The few years had been good to her account. Today, it was worth nearly $14,000. However, one stock had not performed well. Part of her thought she should just leave well enough alone. But she could still hear her grandfather telling her to "sell the dogs"—that is, get rid of the bad stocks. Kari was thinking about asking her father if they could sell the poorly performing stock and invest the money in another one. She had even done some research about the company she wanted to invest in. The stock price seemed low compared to the earnings, and a recent change in management offered promise for the future.

Even though her grandfather had insisted that Kari could not use the money until she turned 30, she felt a responsibility to manage the fund carefully. She knew that making wise decisions would please her grandfather. But she could also see that it might pay off for her in a big way in the future.

An **investment** is something that you acquire with the goal of making money. Not everyone is as fortunate as Kari and will inherit money to invest. But if you carefully build a solid financial plan, you should find that after meeting all your obligations you may have some money available for investing. Then, you will need some knowledge about the many options available to you. Here, you will read about those options.

WHY INVEST?

As you build your financial plan, your first priority should be to save a cash reserve that is placed in liquid investments. These include the kinds of insured bank accounts such as checking accounts, certificates of deposit (CDs), and savings accounts. This is money you will use to deal with emergencies or unexpected expenses that pop up. Experts suggest building a cash reserve large enough to pay for three to six months' worth of your regular bills.

So, why not just choose these guaranteed and liquid options for all the money you set aside? Unfortunately, highly liquid, lower-risk investments generally offer very low interest rates. Often, these kinds of accounts barely keep pace with normal levels of inflation—or actually lag behind. Not keeping pace with inflation means that if you put $5,000 in one of these accounts and left it for several years, it would actually buy less than it did when you started. You should strive to make some investments that offer the hope of higher returns. There are certain types of investments that, historically, offer a reasonable hope of outpacing inflation *over time.* In this chapter, we will focus on such investments, including stocks, bonds, and mutual funds.

Of course, with the promise of higher returns comes higher risk. While these types of investments are more fun to watch and trade, they often do not produce steady, even results. Investments may go up and down in value unpredictably. The stock market, for example, has generally produced much higher long-term returns than more liquid investments. It also tends to have major up and down price swings. Trends in either direction may last for months, even years. Sharp increases or decreases are also possible. Value built up over a period of months can be lost in a matter of hours. For this reason, you should consider riskier investments to be long-term investments. You should avoid—or get out of—such investments if you expect to need the money in the near future. You don't want to be in a situation where you need your money at a time when your investments are doing poorly. You want to be able to pick and choose when you sell them to your greatest advantage.

Think about Kari's case. She can't access her inheritance investments until age 30, so those funds could stay in longer-term investments. In the meantime, she needs to begin saving other monies that are more liquid.

It is also important to understand that a risk of many of these longer-term investments is the total loss of the investment. If, for instance, you buy stock or bonds in a company that goes bankrupt, you may lose all the money you invested. There is no insurance to protect you.

✓ CHECK Your Financial IQ

Why is it a good idea to invest money in something like stocks or bonds?

INVESTING IN STOCKS

Professor FIN

Did you know that stock certificates can be traced back to 1606? The Dutch East India Company was the first company known to issue shares of stock after the Middle Ages. See **www.stockmarketstory.com** to learn more.

Finance ONLINE

You can learn about firms that are about to engage in an IPO and about the performance of recent IPOs by logging on to **www.ipohome.com**.

Stocks are certificates that represent pieces of ownership in a company. For example, if a company has issued 100 shares of stock that represents the entire ownership of the firm, then each share of stock would be equivalent to 1 percent of the firm's value. In this example, each share of stock represents one share of ownership worth 1/100th of the firm's value. Most recognizable companies, such as Microsoft or Apple, have issued millions of shares, so each share represents a much smaller fraction of the firm's ownership. In general, stock ownership also carries voting rights, so each share of stock also has one vote attached to it that allows the owner to vote on the firm's board members, who in turn oversee the firm's management.

Stock Exchanges

Companies issue and sell stock as a way to raise money for business operations, expansion, and other needs. But not all companies offer shares of their stock for public sale. When a company chooses to "go public," the first sale of stock is called an **initial public offering (IPO)**. The IPO occurs in what is called the **primary market**. This initial sale is when the company receives money. That is, if the company has an IPO of a million shares, which sell for $10 a share, the company receives $10,000,000 in cash— $10 × 1 million shares. Later, the shares may be bought and sold by many different investors. But those later transactions involving those same shares of stock do not provide the company with any more money.

The transactions that take place after the IPO are the ones we are more familiar with. They are the ones reported in the newspapers, such as the *Wall Street Journal* or on the financial news on television. These occur in the so-called **secondary market**, which includes the organized stock exchanges such as the **New York Stock Exchange (NYSE)** or **the National Association of Security Dealers Automated Quotation** system **(NASDAQ)**.

Traders on the floor of the New York Stock Exchange buy and sell stocks, creating profits—and sometimes losses—for stockholders.

When a company begins trading on one of the organized stock exchanges, it is said to be "**publicly traded**." Many investors buy and sell stocks on these exchanges through stock brokers such as Merrill Lynch or through Internet accounts such as E*TRADE.

You may recognize the New York Stock Exchange from the common scene on television, where someone rings the bell and everything looks like chaos, with people yelling and shouting. What's happening is actually an auction in which a lot of auctioneers are all yelling at the same time. In spite of the seeming chaos, it works remarkably well as a system for buying and selling stocks. When you place an order to buy stock in a company that is "listed"—bought and sold—on the New York Stock Exchange (NYSE), that order eventually flows through that chaotic market, and your order is carried out.

The NASDAQ is also a stock exchange, but it does not have a central location where dealers gather. Rather, it is an electronic network of dealers who buy and sell stocks.

Each day that trading occurs, the stock exchanges publish the prices at which stocks trade. Many major newspapers carry this information. It is also available online. In this way, investors can follow the value of their investment.

You Do It

Activity #1

The Behavior of Investors

Professor FIN

Stocks may be listed on one exchange and bought or sold on several other exchanges. One type of exchange is relatively new in the United States. They are called ECNs (Electronic Communication Networks). ECNs focus on trading stocks—for example, allowing people to buy and sell after the larger main exchanges are closed—and also foreign currencies. Two of these ECNs are Archipelago and Instinet. To learn more about these ECNs, go to **www.sec.gov**.

There are many types of investors who trade—buy and sell—stocks. They include **institutional investors**, who trade large volumes of stocks on behalf of large institutions. An example of such an institution is a huge pension fund. Mutual funds, which we will discuss later in the chapter, are another good example of institutional investors. Individual investors, such as Kari and you, are also well represented in the stock market.

Investors trade stocks to make a profit. While there are many ways to try to make money in the stock market, most investors attempt first and foremost to buy a stock at a low price with the expectation of selling it later at a higher price.

Share prices for a company tend to go up when the company succeeds at its business. For example check out Figure 14.1 to see what factors drive stock prices up or down. So, investors are looking for good companies that seem ready to enjoy increased success in the marketplace. Skilled investors carefully research the companies and industries they want to invest in. They learn to evaluate a range of factors that can hint at future success—or failure. Kari has begun to gain these skills. With them, she has identified an investment she feels will perform better than a stock she currently owns.

Keep in mind that the stock market can go up or down. Perhaps you've heard the term "bull market" for markets that are trending upward and "bear market" for markets that are trending down. *Bull* and *bear* are examples of some of the common jargon you hear investors use. For those of

Jennifer bought 900 shares of stock for $45 a share in a company's IPO.

Not counting commissions, what was her dollar return if she sold the stock two weeks later for $56 a share?

Solution: 900 × $45 = $40,500 that Jennifer paid for the stock. She sold the stock for $56 × 900 = $50,400. Her return is the difference or $50,400 − $40,500 = $9,900.

you who get more involved in the stock market, you will soon see it is akin to learning a new language.

Many companies also regularly distribute cash to **shareholders**, the people who own stock in the company. These distributions of cash are known as **dividends**. Companies pay dividends in cash, or sometimes, in additional stock. Dividends are another way some stockholders make money in the stock market.

Not all companies give out dividends. For example, a company that is trying to grow rapidly may opt to use all profits to expand the business. By not paying dividends, the company may hope to be more successful in the future and reward investors then with a higher stock price. Whether a company pays dividends or seeks to maximize growth is one factor an investor should consider when purchasing a stock. Both types

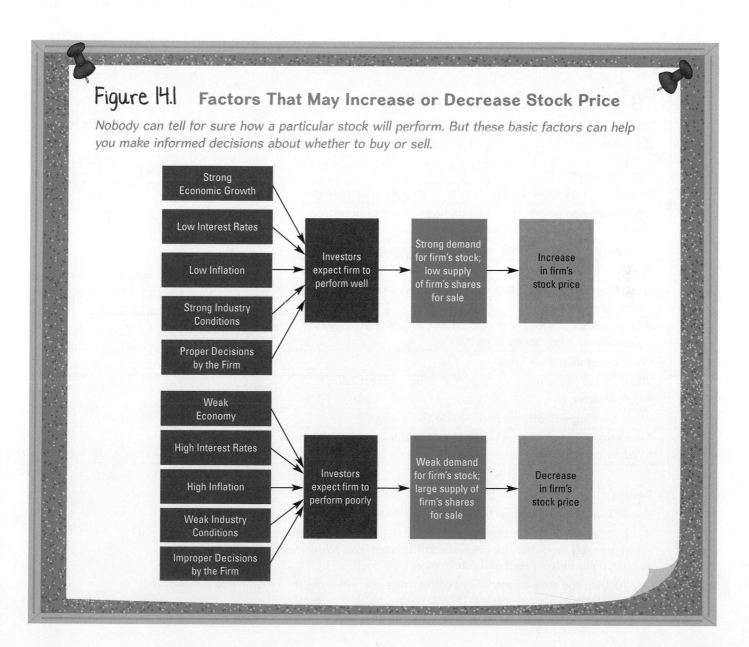

Figure 14.1 Factors That May Increase or Decrease Stock Price

Nobody can tell for sure how a particular stock will perform. But these basic factors can help you make informed decisions about whether to buy or sell.

Strong Economic Growth

Low Interest Rates

Low Inflation

Strong Industry Conditions

Proper Decisions by the Firm

→ Investors expect firm to perform well → Strong demand for firm's stock; low supply of firm's shares for sale → Increase in firm's stock price

Weak Economy

High Interest Rates

High Inflation

Weak Industry Conditions

Improper Decisions by the Firm

→ Investors expect firm to perform poorly → Weak demand for firm's stock; large supply of firm's shares for sale → Decrease in firm's stock price

can be good investments, but only if they match the investor's goals for either short-term income or long-term growth.

The stock markets, unlike the banks, do not have insurance on your money. The FDIC insures your money up to $250,000 if you deposit it in a bank. The stock market has no such guarantee so it is much riskier. Check your own tolerance for the kind of risk investing in stocks involves (see Figure 14.2).

You Do It
Activity #2

While your stock investment is not insured, there is a government agency that regulates and monitors the stock market. This agency is the **Securities and Exchange Commission (SEC)**. The word **security** is a widely used term for investments issued by corporations or governments in which the investor receives proof of ownership.

The main purpose of the SEC is to make sure that companies that offer stock for public sale provide accurate information to investors and obey established rules designed to make the stock market a "fair" game for everyone. The government needs the economy to have an active stock market. The stock market provides investors who buy the stock in the primary

Figure 14.2 Risk Tolerance Quiz

Stocks are a good investment, but some people think that they involve too much risk. To determine your risk tolerance, say whether the following statements are true or false and then check the results.

Risk Tolerance	True	False	
If I own stock, I will check its price at least daily if not more often.			
When driving on an interstate, and traffic and weather permit, I never drive in excess of the posted speed limit.			
If the price of my stock declines, my first reaction is to sell.			
Another stock market crash similar to 1929 could occur very unexpectedly.			
When I fly in less than perfect weather, I get nervous and concerned about my safety.			
If I sold a stock at a loss of more than 25 percent, it would greatly shake my confidence in my ability to invest.			
I intensely dislike blind dates.			
When I travel I write down a packing list to be sure that I don't forget anything.			
When traveling with others I prefer to do the driving.			
Before buying a bond I would want to talk to at least two other people to confirm my choice.			

Results

0 – 3 True: You have the risk tolerance to invest in individual common stocks.

4 – 6 True: You would be a nervous investor, but with more knowledge and a few successes, you could probably raise your risk tolerance to a suitable level. Mutual funds might prove a good starting point for your level of risk tolerance.

7 – 10 True: You are probably a very conservative and risk-intolerant investor who is probably better suited to a bond portfolio.

market with a way to sell their ownership shares at a later date. Without the liquidity that active stock markets offer, few investors would buy the initial public offerings (IPOs). This, in turn, would cut off a major source of funding that companies need to start and grow their business.

Example of a Stock Transaction

Buying or selling stocks will require you to open an account at a **brokerage**, a firm that provides you access to the stock markets. (Not just anyone can walk onto the floor of the New York Stock Exchange and start yelling out orders!) You can open such an account at one of many **full-service brokerage** firms that provide advice and execute your trades for you. Examples include firms such as Merrill Lynch and Edward Jones. Such firms offer a high level of service—for which you pay. Typically, firms charge customers a **commission**, or a fee for carrying out a transaction.

Some investors decide to go with a **discount brokerage**, which offers a reduced level of service, lower costs, and often the ability to make your trades yourself online. Examples of discount brokerages you may recognize are Scottrade and E*TRADE.

Let's go back to Kari's case. Assume she wants to sell 100 shares of ICA Corporation at the market price. First, she might check the newspapers or online to learn the price at which the stock traded at the last session. If she's satisfied that the price is acceptable, she can submit that order to sell "at the market." Her broker, whether full-service or discount, will route the order to one of the stock exchanges. The order will be executed almost instantly at the current market price. Other investors who have submitted orders to buy that stock will purchase the shares. One word of caution—the market price at the time of execution can be different than the last price the stock traded.

Assume that when Kari sold her stock, she received $12 a share, or a total of $1,200. From that total, she must pay her broker's commission. Many discount commissions are less than $10 for this kind of transaction. A full-service broker's commission can be several times more. Kari's profit or loss on this transaction depends on what she paid for the stock and what dividends, if any, she received while she owned the stock. Figure 14.3 contains a flowchart outlining the process.

Let's say Kari's grandfather originally bought the stock for $11 a share. Then Kari would have made a return of about $1 per share. This works out to a return of 9.09

Figure 14.3   Selling Stock

The buying and selling of stock happens quickly and smoothly on today's stock exchanges.

Kari submits order to sell stock through online broker

Online broker contacts representative at organized exchange

Exchange matches Kari's "sell" order with someone else's "buy" order for same stock

Exchange remits confirmation of sale back to online broker

Kari receives confirmation of sale

Evelyn paid $32 a share and later received $38 a share.

What percentage return did Evelyn make on the stock?

Solution: ($38 − $32) / 32 = .1875 or 18.75 percent. Keep in mind this return is not an annualized return and may be good or bad depending on how long Evelyn held the stock.

percent—($12 − $11)/$11. Since we know she held the stock for several years, and we know that the investment carried real risk, this would not be a good return. In fact, she could have gotten a better annual return investing in CDs—and enjoyed a safer investment at the same time. This example illustrates the uncertainty associated with investing in the stock market. It also explains why even a stock that increases in value may be considered a "dog." In fact, there are many stocks that actually lose value.

Of course, neither Kari nor her grandfather could have known for sure how the stock would perform. Stock investors must be prepared to evaluate their holdings regularly. They may opt to sell poor performing stocks in hopes of finding a better investment. In addition, investors are generally wise to own a number of different stocks. As risky as stocks can be, it is even riskier to depend on a single stock.

 CHECK Your Financial IQ

Why do companies sell shares of stock to investors?

INVESTING IN BONDS

Many investors place some of their money in bonds. A **bond** is basically a promissory note, or a promise to repay a certain amount of money at some point in the future. Companies, nonprofit organizations, and government agencies issue bonds as a way of basically taking a loan. Investors buy the bonds, effectively lending money to the bond issuer. In return, the investor earns interest.

How Bonds Work

Each bond has a face value (typically $1,000) and a stated rate of interest that will be paid annually to the bondholder until the bond expires. This expiration date is known as the bond's maturity, or **maturity date**. Bonds typically have maturity dates ranging from five to thirty years. The term **face value** comes from the fact that a bond's maturity value is printed on the front of the bond, also known as the bond's face. A bond's interest rate is often called its **coupon rate** because bonds originally came with booklets of prewritten coupons for the interest due on the bond. Each coupon had a date listed on which the bondholder could tear it from the booklet and take it to a bank for payment.

So, consider the example of a bond issued by Company X with a face value of $1,000 at a coupon rate of 9 percent and a maturity date of five years. This means that every year for five years, Company X will pay each bondholder 9 percent of $1,000 ($90). At the end of five years, Company X will return the $1,000 face value to the bondholder. The bondholders are loaning Company X money at that stated rate of interest. Check out Figure 14.4 for a flowchart of the process.

Kenneth held a bond for five years that had an 8.5 percent coupon rate and a $1,000 face value.

How much did Kenneth receive in interest from the bond?

Solution: $1,000 × .085 = $85 per year × 5 years = $425.

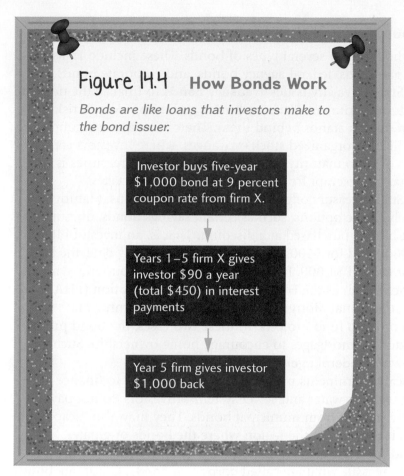

Figure 14.4 How Bonds Work

Bonds are like loans that investors make to the bond issuer.

Investor buys five-year $1,000 bond at 9 percent coupon rate from firm X.

Years 1–5 firm X gives investor $90 a year (total $450) in interest payments

Year 5 firm gives investor $1,000 back

Like stocks, bonds offer investors more than one way to make money. You have just read about the regular interest payments, or **coupon payments**. In addition, bondholders can look to trade their bonds at a value higher than their face value. A bond's value moves up and down due to a number of factors, such as interest rate changes or changes in investors' beliefs in the bond issuer's ability to repay a bond. Some investors may elect to sell their bonds prior to the bond's maturity date. If the bond's sale price is more than its face value, the investor will make a profit. If the price is lower, the investor will have a loss on the sale of this bond.

Also, like stocks, most bonds carry some risk. Remember, when you purchase a bond you are basically lending the bond issuer money. If the bond issuer has financial problems, you may not get the interest you are due or your money back. Corporations can go bankrupt and leave bondholders with nothing. There are rating services that rate bonds and help investors evaluate their risk. In general, the lower the rating, the higher the interest rate the bond pays. After all, a lower-rated issuer has to find some way to attract buyers. Check out Figure 14.5 for a sample of how bonds are rated.

Figure 14.5 Bond Rating Classes

Ratings help investors understand some measure of the risk they are taking, although they do not guarantee the bond's performance.

Risk Class	Standard & Poor's	Moody's
Highest quality (least risk)	AAA	Aaa
High quality	AA	Aa
High-medium quality	A	A
Medium quality	BBB	Baa
Medium-low quality	BB	Ba
Low quality	B	B
Poor quality	CCC	Caa
Very poor quality	CC	Ca
Lowest quality	DDD	C

Bonds are a type of investment in which the investor lends money to a bond issuer in hopes of earning interest and getting the original investment back.

Types of Bonds

Investors can choose from several types of bonds. These include Treasury bonds, municipal bonds, federal agency bonds, and corporate bonds.

The United States Treasury issues **Treasury bonds** to finance the debt of the United States government. Treasury bonds present no default risk since the federal government stands behind them. There is an active secondary market, much like the organized stock exchanges, where investors can sell Treasury bonds prior to maturity. The interest earned on Treasuries is subject to federal tax but exempt from state and local income taxes.

The United States Treasury offers a variety of bond options. Maturity dates vary widely. Some options, such as certain savings bonds, do not pay regular interest but are purchased at a discount. That is, an investor buys a face value $1,000 bond for $500. At the end of the maturity date, the bond is redeemed for the full $1,000. In between, there are no coupon payments.

Federal agencies such as the Federal Housing Administration (FHA) and the Government National Mortgage Association (called Ginnie Mae) may issue bonds in order to fund projects. In these two cases, the bond proceeds are used to buy mortgages to encourage home ownership. Such bonds are known as **federal agency bonds**.

State and local governments may issue **municipal bonds** to finance large public projects, such as water and sewer systems. Investors do not pay federal taxes on the interest from municipal bonds. They may also escape state and local taxes if they live in the region where the bonds originate. Municipal bonds do have a slight default risk.

Large firms may issue what are called **corporate bonds**. Corporate bonds have all degrees of risk depending on company strength. Companies with a solid financial position will have a low risk of default. Other companies may have a high risk of default. Bonds from companies with the highest risk are called **junk bonds**. In any case, corporate bonds have a greater likelihood of default than a government-backed bond. The top four categories of bonds shown in Figure 14.5 are considered investment grade bonds and are reasonably safe. Everything below that is considered junk.

You Do It

Activity #3

Buying Bonds

Investors can buy and trade bonds in much the same way they buy stocks. They may use a broker, including discount brokers, to arrange transactions. Investors can also buy Treasury bonds directly from www.treasurydirect.gov.

 CHECK Your Financial IQ

What is supposed to happen at the end of a bond's maturity date?

MUTUAL FUNDS

Mutual funds are another investment option. **Mutual funds** sell shares to investors in order to collect a pool of money that is then used to buy various investments. A team of professional fund managers oversee these investments. The shareholders see an increase or decrease in the value of their shares based on the overall performance of the fund's investments.

Mutual funds are attractive to some investors for several reasons. Since mutual funds pool large amounts of money, the fund will typically own a wide range of investments. This process of investing in multiple investments is called **diversification**. Diversifying investments reduces risk because failure of one company (or even one industry) will not significantly impact the entire amount invested. A mutual fund will lose the amount invested in the failed company, but investments in a number of companies that are doing well should offset this loss.

Investors who buy individual stocks and bonds can achieve diversification on their own, but it takes many purchases—and a considerable amount of money. So investors with limited funds who want to diversify may choose a mutual fund. It is possible to make a mutual fund investment with as little as $500. Yet this small investment in a well-managed fund will be diversified.

Another advantage of mutual funds is that they are managed by experienced people. Such people *may* be better at picking good investments than a newcomer to the game of buying and selling stocks and bonds. Of course, not all mutual fund managers are successful, and some funds clearly have a better record than others.

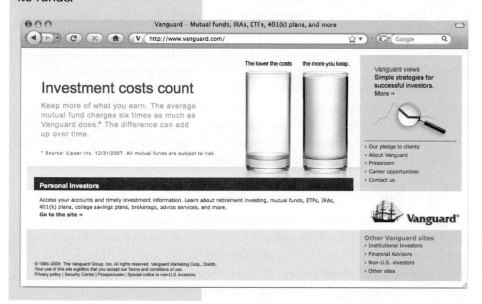

There are thousands of mutual funds that invest in stocks and bonds, with many specializing in certain types of securities. For example, you can purchase shares in a mutual fund that only invests in Japanese companies or one that invests in gold mining stocks. Mutual fund companies and rating services categorize their funds by level of risk or whether the fund goals are producing long-term growth in share value or providing steady income for shareholders. (This is basically the same distinction as the one between stocks that pay dividends to stockholders and those that do not.) Indeed, there are several services that rate different funds based on their performance. It is relatively easy to see how funds compare with each other.

Investors can purchase mutual funds through a brokerage. They can also buy funds directly from the companies that sell them. Funds vary widely in the fees they charge. It pays to research any purchase carefully.

Remember that one of your primary reasons to invest is for retirement. For those long-term monies, you need to make sure you take advantage of the current tax laws that allow you to grow investments in a tax sheltered retirement account such as a 401(k) or Individual Retirement Account (IRA). These accounts provide the benefit of allowing your money to grow tax free until you retire and accumulate a much larger sum of money as a result.

 **CHECK Your Financial IQ**

What is a major benefit of investing in mutual funds?

OTHER WAYS OF INVESTING

When you think of investments, you may first think of stocks, bonds, and mutual funds. But there are other ways to invest your money.

Real Estate

Many people have used real estate as an investment. In fact, one way millions of people invest in real estate is to buy a home. Housing values move up and down over time depending on the supply and demand for homes in an area. Think about it like this. If a factory suddenly closes in your area and a lot of people are forced to move to find work, you will see a lot of houses for sale. Sellers of those houses may lower their prices in order to sell faster. More sellers than buyers will tend to push home prices down.

The reverse is true if you have a growing region where a lot of people are moving into an area. More buyers than sellers will create a market where housing prices will be going up.

In general, home prices have increased over the very long run and created wealth for long-term homeowners. In addition, investing in real estate offers tax benefits, or the ability to take advantage of rules in the tax code that may reduce your tax liability. And, of course, you need a place to live. These factors make buying a home a good investment for most people.

Some people invest in real estate by buying rental property. You may know someone who owns apartments that he or she rents out on a monthly basis. Or you may know someone who owns and rents commercial property. Very often, real estate investors find that the rent they receive covers the payments on the loan they took to buy the property. Profits will come from the real estate increasing in value over time.

Owning a Business

Many people have a dream of owning their own business. In fact, we know from sources such as *The Millionaire Next Door,* by Stanley and Danko, that a large number of millionaires in the United States are small business owners. Restaurants, retail stores, and services all provide opportunities for someone who works hard to generate wealth.

You may also have opportunities to invest in someone else's small business at some point. Be careful, though, since many small ventures fail. The potential rewards are very high, but the risk is very high, too.

 CHECK Your Financial IQ

What are some investment options besides stocks, bonds, and mutual funds?

Chapter Review

Summary

- While liquid investments are important, it is important to aim for a return that will beat inflation. This generally involves making riskier investments with a more long-term goal.

- Stock is partial ownership in a company and is a good way to seek a profit. While the behavior of stocks cannot be predicted precisely, research can provide clues about which companies provide good opportunities. Brokerages, both full-service and discount, make it possible to trade stocks.

- Bonds are promissory notes from an issuer to an investor. The bond issuer generally pays interest on a regular basis, and agrees to pay back the face value at the maturity date. There are many types of bonds, including Treasury bonds, federal agency bonds, municipal bonds, and corporate bonds. The highest risk bonds are known as junk bonds. Bonds can be sold at a profit or loss before their maturity date.

- Mutual funds are another investment option. They provide diversification and professional management for a relatively low initial investment. They also allow investors to target their investments in certain industries or sectors. Investors can purchase shares in mutual funds through a brokerage or directly from the companies that sell them.

- People can also invest in real estate and in small businesses. As with any investment, there are clear risks involved, as well as the possibility for great reward.

Key Terms and Vocabulary

Bond	Maturity date
Brokerage	Municipal bond
Commission	Mutual fund
Corporate bond	National Association of Security
Coupon payment	Dealers Automated Quotation
Coupon rate	(NASDAQ)
Discount brokerage	New York Stock Exchange (NYSE)
Diversification	Primary market
Dividend	Publicly traded
Face value	Secondary market
Federal agency bonds	Securities and Exchange
Full-service brokerage	Commission (SEC)
Initial public offering (IPO)	Security
Institutional investor	Shareholder
Investment	Stock
Junk bond	Treasury bonds

What Do You Know?

myFinLitlab.

1. (a) What are stocks?

   (b) Why do investors invest in stocks?

   (c) Why are companies willing to give up a share of ownership in their enterprise?

2. (a) Distinguish between the primary and secondary stock markets.

   (b) Why do you think the price of a stock changes each day in the secondary market?

3. (a) Explain the difference between the New York Stock Exchange (NYSE) and the National Association of Security Dealers Automated Quotation system (NASDAQ).

   (b) Why is it necessary to use a broker to make a trade on the NYSE?

4. (a) What is the difference between an individual and an institutional investor?

   (b) Would these two types of investors likely apply similar or different standards for choosing a stock? Explain.

5. (a) Who are shareholders?

   (b) In what ways do shareholders earn returns from investing in stock?

6. (a) What are dividends?

   (b) In what circumstance might an investor prefer stocks that do not pay dividends?

7. (a) What are the basic steps of a stock transaction?

   (b) What role does the brokerage play in the process?

8. (a) What is the face value of a bond?

   (b) What are two ways bondholders can make money on bonds they own?

9. (a) What are mutual funds?

   (b) Why would it take a lot more money to achieve the diversification of a mutual fund when buying individual stocks and bonds?

10. (a) What kind of investment have millions of homeowners made?

    (b) Explain why owning a home must be considered a long-term investment.

What Are Your Finance Math Skills?

myFinLitlab

1. If you own 500 shares of stock in a company that has 100,000 shares of stock outstanding, what fraction of the firm do you own?

2. What is your profit on the sale of 250 shares of stock for $38 a share if you paid $26 a share two years ago (not counting commission)?

3. What is the total value of your stock holdings if you own 50 shares of XYZ valued at $32.50 a share, 90 shares of ABC valued at $54.25 a share, and 125 shares of DEF valued at $112.12 a share?

4. How much interest will you receive annually on a 7 percent coupon rate bond with a $1,000 face value?

5. What is the total dollar amount you would make on a 9 percent coupon rate bond with a face value of $1,000 but for which you paid $1,035 and that you held for one year before maturity?

6. Castille sold 35 shares of stock for $47.50 a share. She bought the stock for $51 a share last year. What was her dollar return (loss), not counting commission?

7. Breanne paid $11.75 a share for stock Y last year. Today, she sold the stock for $14.25 a share. What was her percentage return, not counting commission?

8. How much money did Jeremy receive in interest on a $1,000 face value bond that he held for two years and that had a 7 percent coupon rate?

What Would You Do?

Juanita just celebrated her 16th birthday. Her parents realized they have accumulated only half the money needed for Juanita's college education. With college only two years away, they became concerned about how they will save the remaining amount in such a short time.

June, Juanita's mother, was discussing the dilemma of financing her daughter's education with her boss, Mr. Rodriquez. Mr. Rodriquez told June of an investment his broker told him about that has doubled his money in just over one year. Mr. Rodriquez assured June that this would be a sound investment that would continue to grow and that had very little risk.

June went home to tell Juan, Juanita's father, about the information given to her by her boss. Juan thought she should ask her boss if there were any other tips he could give her from his broker to help them increase their daughter's college savings.

The next day, June asked Mr. Rodriquez if his broker had any other tips. Mr. Rodriquez told June of a small startup company that his broker believed would double within the next two years with virtually no risk. June and Juan immediately invested their daughter's college fund into the stock of this company. One year later, June and Juan received a letter from the company announcing they were out of business and closing their doors. Upon calling their broker, June found the stock was now worthless.

a. Comment on Mr. Rodriquez's ethics of assuring his employee that the investments he was recommending upon the advice of his broker could produce major rewards with virtually no risk.

b. What basic investing principle did June and Juan forget in their desire to fund their daughter's college education?

c. With less than a year to go until Juanita leaves for college, what can be done to begin saving for college?

What Are the Connections? Language Arts

Determine whether investments in stocks, bonds, or mutual funds will help you achieve some short-, intermediate-, and long-term goals. Remember that a short-term goal should be achievable within one year, an intermediate-term goal should be achievable in one to five years, and a long-term goal will take five years or more. Create a worksheet to display your goals. Have column headings as follows:

- Goals
- Yes or No
- Type of Investment
- Justification

List one or two short-, intermediate-, and long-term goals. Be sure to separate each type of goal as you are putting the information in the columns. In the Yes or No column, you will need to determine whether investing in stocks, bonds, or mutual funds is suitable for that particular goal. If the answer is no, do not complete the rest of the row for that goal. If the answer is yes, be sure to determine the type of investment you will choose, and provide a justification for that investment.

Refer to the following example when designing your worksheet:

Goals	Yes or No	Type of Investment	Justification
Short-Term			
Buying an IPod	No		
Intermediate			
Buying a car	Yes	Bonds	Short-term high-grade bonds will provide a higher return than bank accounts.
Long-Term			
Buying a house in 10 years	Yes	Diversified stock mutual funds	Mutual funds allow immediate diversification and should maximize return over a 10 year period.

Questions to answer after you have created your worksheet:

1. Summarize your reasoning for either investing or not investing to meet your goals.

2. If you decide to invest, how much will you invest each month? How will you determine how much you will invest each month? What types of investments will you purchase? Why?

Teamwork

Each team will have an imaginary $5,000 to invest. Teams choose five stocks to watch for one week. Make a chart to collect data for each of the stocks. At the end of the week, present your stocks to the class. Provide the following information:

a. Explain why your team chose each company. Show how much stock you purchased in each company you choose.

b. Decide which stocks your team will sell and which stocks you will reinvest in. Explain your decisions to the class.

w!se Financial Literacy
CERTIFICATION

TEST PREP QUESTIONS

myFinLitlab.

1. A person should include an emergency fund in his financial plan to
   a. have money available in case he wants to go on an unplanned vacation with friends.
   b. have money to pay living expenses if he loses his job or has a serious illness or injury.
   c. have money available for daily spending during retirement.
   d. have at least two months of salary in cash for current daily expenses.

2. Financial products in an emergency fund should include
   a. stocks that can make a quick profit for a person to make up for any loss in income.
   b. two-year CDs that offer higher interest rates instead of short-term CDs.
   c. government bonds that are very low risk and offer a guaranteed rate of return.
   d. liquid accounts such as checking and savings accounts so that money is quickly available.

3. A person wants to use a gift of $2,000 to buy a new car when he graduates next year. He decides to purchase stock in a new, alternative energy company with the money. Is this a good idea?
   a. No, because he needs the money in a year and it may take much longer for this company to earn a profit.

b. Yes, because alternative energy companies will guarantee investors a minimum yearly profit.

c. Yes, because the government wants energy companies to succeed so they will protect this company from failure.

d. No, because he would be much better off investing in the auto industry.

4. What is meant by the statement: "With the promise of higher returns comes higher risk?"

a. When a company promises a person that investing in the company's new product will make her rich, she needs to know that it may take years for the company to produce a profit for its investors.

b. The reason that long-term CDs provide owners with greater return on their investments is because these CDs are riskier than three-month CDs.

c. When a person buys stock during a recession, the company has to pay the shareholder a higher dividend since the whole economy is weak.

d. A person expects a higher return on an investment in stocks to compensate for the higher risk that a stock carries relative to a CD or savings account.

5. Which of the following is a true statement about investing in stock?

a. A person who invests in stock can lose all of her invested money.

b. The SEC protects a person's investments so that he always makes a minimum profit.

c. If a stock price does not increase, the company will give the investor a share of the company's profits in the form of a dividend.

d. If the stock is listed on one of the exchanges, it means that the company is expected to be profitable.

6. Which of the following investment products is *not* correctly paired with its description?

a. Stock: a person has pieces of ownership in a public company.

b. Bond: how a company or government agency takes a loan from the public.

c. Mutual fund: a company offers the public the chance to own part of the company or to give the company a loan.

d. Treasury bond: how the government finances federal debt.

7. Which of the following financial terms associated with the trading of stock is correctly paired with its explanation?

a. Primary market: the place where the country's largest companies buy the securities of other large companies.

b. Secondary market: the place where small companies access funding for expansion.

c. Publicly traded: the method used to reach people who want to buy government securities.

d. Institutional investment: the trading of large amounts of a security by a mutual fund or a pension fund.

8. An initial public offering (IPO) is
a. the trading of securities of large companies on a stock exchange.
b. the first time a company offers stock to the investing public in order to raise capital for the company.
c. when an investor purchases a company's stock that is listed on the New York Stock Exchange.
d. the bundling of a number of securities to create a mutual fund.

9. The sequence of actions that correctly names the steps involved in executing a stock trade is as follows:
a. exchange confirms sale to broker; sell order is matched with buy order; person contacts broker; person receives confirmation of sale.
b. person submits order to buy stock to broker; broker contacts stock's representative at exchange; sell order is matched with buy order; person receives confirmation of sale.
c. exchange confirms order with purchaser of securities; sell order is matched with buy order; person contacts broker; confirmation of trade is made with broker.
d. person submits order to sell to broker; confirmation of trade is made with broker; sell order is matched with buy order; broker contacts stock's representative at exchange.

10. Which of the following is a true statement about the stock exchanges?
a. A person can buy the stock of any publicly traded share on any of the exchanges.
b. A person can only buy technology stock using an Internet account such as E*TRADE.
c. The stock exchanges operate very much like large auctions with many people bidding on the same securities.
d. The public needs to contact a stock broker in order to get the price on a particular security.

11. What causes the price of a share of stock to increase?
a. More people want to buy the stock of a given company at a certain price than there are people willing to sell it at that price.
b. The SEC agrees to insure the company issuing the new stock.
c. The company has decided to take loans in the form of bonds to make up for the losses in sales for the year.
d. The national rate of inflation has gone up less than the price of the products the company is making.

12. Generally, the price of a company's stock will *not* decrease because of
a. a weak overall economy.
b. a high interest rate.
c. a low rate of inflation.
d. weak sales in the industry.

13. Even if the price of company A's stock does not go up and the person holds on to his shares, the person can make money on his investment. How is this possible?

   a. The person buys more shares of the stock of companies that are in competition with company A.

   b. The amount of the drop in company A's stock price can be taken as a tax deduction.

   c. Company A may declare a dividend that benefits the company's shareholders.

   d. Company A can change how the company operates, which saves the company a lot of money.

14. Why is investing in the stock market, even in very solid stocks, considered riskier than putting money in a savings account or CD?

   a. Savings accounts provide the depositor interest on his savings even when the economy is in recession.

   b. Companies may decide to put their profits into corporate growth or replace outdated equipment instead of giving dividends to their shareholders.

   c. The price of the stock may not go up but the CD will increase in value over time.

   d. The FDIC protects money in savings accounts and CDs, but money invested in the stock market is not insured by any organization.

15. What is the purpose of the Securities and Exchange Commission (SEC)?

   a. The SEC keeps the prices of stocks from falling below a certain point during a deep recession.

   b. The SEC makes sure that companies issuing stock to the public provide accurate information to investors before they purchase securities.

   c. The SEC provides advice to individual investors on which securities are appropriate to purchase at a given point in life.

   d. The SEC makes money available to companies when they initially issue shares of stock to the public.

16. Which of the following is *not* a true statement about bonds?

   a. In most cases, a bondholder will receive interest on a bond until the bond's maturity date.

   b. A bond can be issued by a nonprofit organization as well as a corporation.

   c. A bond is always a safer investment than a stock.

   d. A person can also make money on a bond by selling it before maturity if the price is higher than its purchase price.

17. Which of the following is a true statement about mutual funds?

   a. A person needs to have at least $10,000 before being able to invest in a mutual fund.

   b. The holdings of a mutual fund are determined by the Securities and Exchange Commission (SEC)

   c. Mutual funds can provide a way for a small investor to have diversified holdings in some of the country's wealthiest companies.

   d. The person who invests in a mutual fund can decide which stocks or bonds the person wants to have in the mutual fund.

CHAPTER 15

Learning Objectives

Explain the concept of time value of money, including factors that influence it and ways to calculate it.

Explain the role of diversification in managing an investment portfolio.

Describe how time value concepts affect retirement planning.

Describe how time value concepts affect estate planning.

Key Terms

Asset allocation

Compounding

Estate planning

Future value

Portfolio

Present value

Simple interest

Time value of money

Will

Planning for the Future

Mark fumbled through his notes on today's lecture. He was sure he'd missed something, because the guest speaker had told them they could all be millionaires when they retired. How could that be? As far as he was aware, he'd never known a millionaire, and he wasn't going to medical school.

Mark planned on going to the career and technical school near his home to study diesel mechanics. His father worked at a trucking company and said they were always short-handed with mechanics. From Mark's perspective, they made good money. But probably not enough, he thought, to become a millionaire.

Still, Mark was sure he heard correctly when his friend Frank told the guy that he was planning to fix air conditioners for a living, and the man assured Frank he could still become a millionaire. It was there in his notes: All Frank had to do, the lecturer said, was to live on less than what he made and begin making investments while he was very young. In fact, the man told Frank that if he would open an account immediately after he got out of school at age 19 and deposit $2,000 a year, he could become a millionaire. According to the numbers he'd shown the class, if Frank invested in a mutual fund that averaged a 12 percent annual return, he would have over $1.5 million before he turned 60. Mark still could not be sure he had heard right, but after the lecture, he had gotten the man's card. He would call him in a few days to ask about it.

The speaker in Mark's class was right. What experts call the "time value of money" can work what seems like major miracles if you begin investing at an early age. What happens is that you begin earning a return—for example, interest—on your original investment plus any returns that you have earned in the past. Your money begins working for you instead of you working for your money. In the next few sections, we will spend some time looking at the financial math behind these miracles.

TIME VALUE OF MONEY

The **time value of money** refers to the fact that money received today is worth more than money received next year or the year after. The reason is that we can put that money to work for us in various investments. This concept is so powerful that Albert Einstein stated it was one of the strongest forces on earth. And, from all accounts, Einstein was a pretty sharp guy.

Let's look at a couple of examples:

- Armin, who is 18, has pledged not to smoke. This decision could make him a millionaire by the time he retires at age 67. After all, let's assume he will save about $6.00 a day—the amount, on average, he spends on cigarettes. Each year for 49 years Armin will have available $2,190 to invest ($6.00 × 365 days). Assuming a rate of return of 8 percent per year, Armin would accumulate $1,161,450 by age 67!

- Suppose your ancestors settled in the American colonies in 1693. At that time, one of them invested $20 at a local bank earning 5 percent interest annually. Also assume that this ancestor never informed his family of this transaction and that the money remained in the account accumulating interest until the year 2009, when the bank locates you and informs you of the account. Over this time, the $20 would have grown to $87 million.

You can see that the time value of money can be put to work for you to begin saving for any number of goals, such as a new home, a vacation, or retirement. The possibilities are endless if you make the decision to postpone certain purchases now and save the money instead. Do you really need those new shoes? Couldn't you bring lunch from home rather than ordering out every day? Give some thought to your spending habits as you study the time value of money.

With time on your side, even the small amount of money you save by emptying your pockets each day can be turned into a huge fortune over a period of years.

MATH for Personal Finance

Assume that Jenise invested $1,000 in the stock market and earned an average annual return of 12 percent.

How much would she have after 50 years?

Solution: The formula solution is future value = present value $\times$ (1 + interest rate)^n, where n = number of years. Jenise will have $1,000(1.12)^{50}$ = $289,002.19.

You Do It

Activity #1

Future Value versus Present Value

Future value is the projected value of a sum of money at some point in the future. Calculating future value, or the process of seeing how much you can accumulate by some point in the future, is perhaps the most important time value concept when focusing on wealth accumulation. You can use this time value of money tool to calculate how much you can save by the time you reach age 40 or 60 or whatever age you choose.

Let's look at an example of how your money can work for you when trying to accumulate wealth. What happens when you put $2,000 in an account that averages a 10 percent annual return? At the end of the first year you will have your original $2,000 plus the 10 percent you earned on that investment for a total of $2,200.

The next year you will have a total of $2,200 invested that you will now earn interest on. So at the end of the second year you will have $2,420 ($2,200 $\times$ .10 = $220 + $2,200 = $2,420). A quick way to do this calculation is to multiply $2,200 by 1.10. This process of **compounding**, or earning interest on the principal and the interest earned in the past, will continue as long as you leave the money untouched. In fact, if you keep this original $2,000 amount invested earning 10 percent compounded for 40 years, you will accumulate $90,518. Imagine how much you could accumulate if you invested $2,000 every year for those 40 years! Obviously, the higher the interest rate you can earn, the more money you will accumulate for a given number of years. Figure 15.1 illustrates this point.

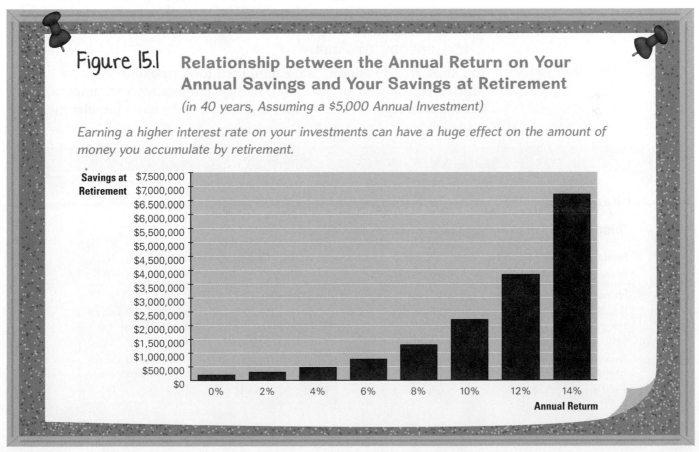

Figure 15.1   Relationship between the Annual Return on Your Annual Savings and Your Savings at Retirement

(in 40 years, Assuming a $5,000 Annual Investment)

Earning a higher interest rate on your investments can have a huge effect on the amount of money you accumulate by retirement.

MATH for Personal Finance

Shane's uncle promised to give him $10,000 when he graduates college in one year.

What equivalent amount could Shane receive today assuming he could put the money in a CD earning 4 percent?

Solution: This question is asking for the present value of $10,000. So, $10,000/(1.04)^1 = $9,615.38. In other words, Shane could put $9,615.38 in a CD earning 4 percent and have $10,000 at the end of next year.

Present value is the value of a sum of money—for example, the million dollars you hope to have at retirement—at the present time. Present value techniques are just the opposite of future value. Instead of trying to take some amount today (present value) and seeing what it will grow to in the future (future value), you are taking some future value and bringing it back to the present.

For example, you may know that you will receive a $5,000 gift when you turn 21. How much is that amount worth today—what is its present value—assuming you are 20 years old? It depends on the interest rate you could earn, but assuming a 5 percent rate, the $5,000 you will receive in the future has a present value of $4,762. In other words, you could invest $4,762 at 5 percent and end up with $5,000 at the end of one year.

Doing a present value calculation is the exact opposite of figuring a future value. Instead of multiplying by 1 plus the interest rate, you divide by 1 plus the interest rate. So, $5,000/1.05 = $4,762. If the future value is two years into the future you would divide by $(1.05)^2$. The present value of $5,000 to be received four years in the future would be $5,000/(1.05)^4 = $4,114 (see Figure 15.2).

Compound Interest versus Simple Interest

In contrast to compound interest we just discussed, **simple interest** earns interest only on the original amount or principal. In our example in which we had an initial deposit of $2,000 earning 10 percent interest, we would earn $200 in interest the first year. With simple interest, we would also earn only $200 the second year because, unlike with compound interest, we would not earn interest on interest. Compounding will always create wealth faster for any given interest rate.

The Concept of Annuity

You know that an annuity is the term used for a type of investment in which a person pays an amount of money and receives a set amount of income on a regular basis. In fact, the word *annuity* has a broader meaning.

Figure 15.2   Formulas for Future Value and Present Value

These formulas can help you calculate future and present values.

Formula for Calculating Future Value

Principal × (1 + Interest Rate)^Number of Years into the Future

For example:
To calculate the 2010 future value of $400 you have in 2009 assuming a 10 percent interest rate:
$400 × 1.10 = $440
To calculate the 2013 future value of $400 you have in 2009 assuming 10 percent interest rate:
$400 × 1.10^4 = $585.64

Formula for Calculating Present Value

Principal ÷ (1 + Interest Rate)^Number of Years into the Past

For example:
To calculate the 2009 present value of $400 you will receive in 2010 assuming a 10 percent interest rate:
$400 ÷ 1.10 = $363.64
To calculate the 2009 present value of $400 you will receive in 2013 assuming a 10 percent interest rate:
$400 ÷ 1.10^4 = $273.21

An annuity is defined as any situation in which you have equal cash flows occurring at equal intervals for a fixed period of time. Good examples of annuities are all around us. For example, a car payment is an annuity. In most cases, you make equal payments every month for some fixed number of years. House payments, or any other loan payments set up on a similar schedule are examples of annuities.

Our previous example of $2,000 invested every year for 40 years earning 10 percent a year is also an annuity. We can also solve for the future value or present value of an annuity. This is very useful to us when we are trying to determine how much to save every year to achieve a certain goal or also how much a particular payment would be for a house, car, or any asset. Review Figure 15.1 to see an example of how saving an annuity of $5,000 a year with a 10 percent annual return can generate a vast sum of money.

Using Financial Calculators

The concept of present and future value can seem confusing. Fortunately, you can perform both present value and future value calculations easily on a financial calculator. After you learn the appropriate keys to use, you can solve any present value or future value problem, including annuities. Online versions of these calculators are available (for example, see Figure 15.3). By following the instructions, you can figure the future value for an initial investment given a certain interest rate and period of time. You can also figure the future value of an annuity—for example, what you would wind up with if you made the same deposit each year for a period of time.

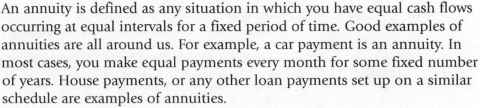

Finance ONLINE

Go to **www.moneychimp.com**. Search for "rule of 72," and you will find an explanation for the rule and a calculator. Plug in some figures to see what would be needed for you to have the money you hope to have when you reach retirement age.

Figure 15.3   Financial Calculators

Financial calculators can perform the complicated mathematics involved in figuring future values and present values.

Input	Function
12	N
10	I
-5687	PV
0	PMT
?=17848.24	FV

Suppose you have $5,687 to invest in the stock market today. You like to invest for the long term and plan to choose your stocks carefully. You will invest your money for 12 years in certain stocks on which you expect a return of 10 percent annually. Although financial calculators can vary slightly in their setup, most would require inputs as shown at left.

Where:

N	=	number of periods
I	=	interest rate
PV	=	present value, which is the initial amount deposited
PMT	=	payment, which is not applicable in this problem
FV	=	future value of the deposit you make today, which is computed by the calculator

The PV is a negative number here, reflecting the outflow of cash to make the investment. The calculator computes the future value to be $17,848.24, which indicates that you will have $17,848.24 in your brokerage account in 12 years if you achieve a return of 10 percent annually on your $5,687 investment.

MATH for Personal Finance

Using future value techniques for a lump sum amount, calculate the value of a three-year annuity of $1,000 invested at 5 percent.

Assume you invest the first $1,000 today, the second $1,000 in one year, and the last amount in two years.

Solution: The annuity formula in a financial calculator will generate the same solution as this, but understanding the process is important. In this problem, you will simply calculate the value of each $1,000 amount and add them up. The value of the annuity equals:

$1,000 × (1.05)^3 = $1,157.62
+ $1,000 × (1.05)^2 = $1,102.50
+ $1,000 × (1.05)^1 = $1,050.00
$3,310.12

Rule of 72

One simple rule of thumb that we can often use in figuring future values is known as the **rule of 72**. This rule allows us to see how long it would take to double our money for a given interest rate. For example, if you assume a 12 percent return, you can divide 72 by 12 to find out it would take roughly 6 years to double your money.

You can also use this technique to see what kind of return someone is promising you. If someone tells you that he or she can double your money in 8 years, you know that the person is expecting an annual return of about 9 percent since 72/8 = 9. While its applications are limited, the rule of 72 can be a handy tool to make quick approximations in some cases.

Professor FIN

A fun fact about the rule of 72: In 1494, the rule is referenced in the *Summa De Arithmetica* by Fra Luca Pacioli. Pacioli brought the rule into a discussion of estimating the doubling time of an investment. Although he discusses the rule, he is not credited with its discovery. Thus, there are those who think the rule predates Pacioli.

 CHECK Your Financial IQ

What does the time value of money mean?

MANAGING YOUR INVESTMENTS

While many of you may opt to use a financial professional to manage your investments, you will be in charge of what strategy the professional follows. And, you should always monitor your investments—your **portfolio**—to make sure the people you have hired are following your guidelines. Every individual will have a different set of investment goals and objectives. These goals and objectives should dictate your investment guidelines or instructions you have set up with the professional for investing your money. There are two important factors to consider: You should keep your portfolio diversified, and you must understand that there is a risk/return tradeoff in the investment arena. We will discuss both of these factors in the next sections.

Diversification

Diversification is the application of the old saying "Don't put all your eggs in one basket." That is, you should not rely on any single type of investment to achieve your financial goals. The kinds of investments you need to make in order to achieve your long-term goals, including stocks, bonds, and real estate, have a lot of uncertainty regarding their future performance. Each of these types of investments is called an **asset class**, and each carries a different level of uncertainty or risk. Each responds differently to specific events or market conditions. For these reasons, it is wise to diversify, or invest in a lot of different types of assets or asset classes. **Asset allocation** is the process of spreading your investments among asset classes—diversifying your investments. Your objective is achieving some desired return with an acceptable level of risk.

A diversified portfolio of assets will over time reduce your risk. For example, suppose you have a portion of your wealth in stocks, bonds, and real estate. When one asset class is down, you can reasonably hope that the others will offset the decline and increase in value. Different asset classes perform better during different economic periods.

Since you don't have the ability to tell in advance which assets will perform better next year, it is wise to maintain diversification. That way you should always have some assets that are doing really well to offset those that perform poorly. Make sure you are properly diversified and don't get caught with all your money in stocks in a declining stock market.

Risk and Return Tradeoff

When you make an investment, you are making a tradeoff between risk and return. If you want low risk, generally you must be willing to accept lower returns. Higher-risk investments will have to give a reasonable hope of higher returns to attract investors. For example, why would anyone accept the risks of investing in the stock market if the expected return were only 3 percent? Most of the time you could earn that return with no risk by investing in FDIC-insured bank CDs. Using the same reasoning, no one would invest in start-up companies with a high risk of failure unless the potential return were much greater than investing in established, blue-chip companies. Every market investment carries a different level of risk and therefore should hold a reasonable hope of a different potential return. Never forget, of course, that no return is guaranteed.

The overall return you should seek for your portfolio obviously depends on your tolerance for risk. And, your age should also dictate to some extent the level of risk you can assume. Younger people have more time to recover from a financial misstep than someone nearing retirement.

Too Good to Be True?

You Do It
Activity #2

If someone promises you something that seems too good to be true, it probably is. What does this mean? Whenever you are talking about investing money, you will find that someone is out there trying to separate you from your cash. You may have someone that promises a 20 percent return without any risk. Those types of promises are not reasonable, so be very

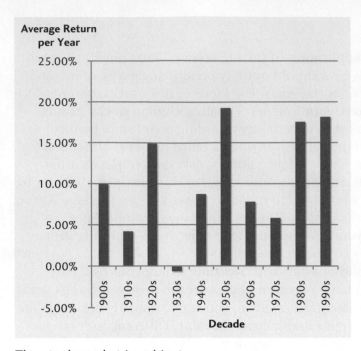

Average Return per Year

The stock market is subject to sharp ups—and downs. But over time, stocks tend to outperform less risky asset classes.

cautious about jumping into an investment like that. Do you really want to trust your money to someone who is trying that hard to lure you in?

In fact, anything that is presented as a promise or as a sure thing ought to make you think twice. There are very few promises you can rely on in the financial world. You can rely on FDIC insurance. You can rely on the ability of the federal government to pay off its bonds. But beyond that, there is some risk involved in any decision you make.

There really are no get rich quick schemes. There are a number of get rich slow-but-steady schemes. Don't allow anyone to rush you into a financial commitment or trick you into thinking you can beat the system. It always pays to think about it and do some investigating on your own. Don't take anyone's word for something unless you know and trust that person 100 percent. It's your hard-earned money. Don't let anyone cheat you out of it.

 CHECK Your Financial IQ

Why is diversification an important part of managing your portfolio?

RETIREMENT PLANNING AND TIME VALUE CONCEPTS

Mark, like you, is a long way from retirement. For that reason, both of you may find it strange to be thinking about retirement planning. But there is really no better time to start the process. Why? As you can see from the time value concepts we covered in this chapter, you can accumulate wealth much more easily if you have time to put your money to work for you. You now have the ability to see how much difference it makes if you wait until you are 30 years old to begin saving for retirement. Starting at age 20 makes much more sense.

Once you have established some financial goals, you can begin taking steps to accomplish them. For example, if you want to retire at age 55 with $2 million in the bank, you can use the time value tools to see how much you need to save every year and how much risk to take with your investments. Use a financial calculator to figure what you'd need to save to reach that or some other goal.

Think about your long-term goals. What do you want out of life? While we know that money does not buy happi-

Professor FIN

You may have heard of AARP, but do you know what they do to help with your retirement?

AARP provides a wide range of services and information for people over age 50. Many times you will see discounts for AARP members at hotels, restaurants, grocery stores, and such. One day you may be interested in joining AARP not only for the discounts but also for the support this organization provides to its members. For more information go to **www.aarp.org**.

ness, financial worries complicate life. Financial security is not a bad thing and can be achieved with some careful planning followed by action. If all goes well, you will have income from a number of sources (but you must be careful about counting too heavily on the Social Security system to provide a significant piece of your retirement pie). You have the ability to provide your own retirement income, and if you receive any Social Security income it will be a bonus.

 CHECK Your Financial IQ

Why is it better to begin planning for retirement at age 20 than at age 30?

ESTATE PLANNING

Estate planning is even further into the future than retirement but is something you should be aware of. **Estate planning** is the process of determining how your wealth will be allocated on or before your death. In other words, what happens to your assets when you die? Do you want them to go to the state, to a particular charity, or to your children and grandchildren? If you resolve these questions prior to your death, you are more likely to have your wishes honored. It will also make it easier on your loved ones.

Your Will

One of the most critical tasks in estate planning is the creation of a will. A **will** is a legal request for how your estate (everything you have accumulated during your life) should be distributed upon your death. If you have any surviving minor children, a will can also determine who will be their legal guardian.

In your will you can specify who will receive your estate—your **beneficiaries**, or heirs. If you die without a will (known as being **intestate**) the court will appoint an administrator who will distribute your estate according to the laws of the state. Dying intestate can result in someone getting more than you would have wanted and others getting less than you would have wanted. Figure 15.4 shows an example of a simple will.

Many people make the mistake of thinking they do not have enough assets or that they are too young to have a will. It is important to understand that you will quickly build net worth if you develop a sound financial plan, and that it is always a good idea to plan for the unexpected.

Estate Taxes

Your estate may be subject to taxes before it can be distributed to your heirs. For example, as of 2009, you can distribute up to $3.5 million of your estate to your children or others tax-free. However, you should be aware that these laws will change in the next 40 years. As you begin to accumulate wealth, you should review the current law on estate taxes and take the steps necessary to minimize the tax liability for your heirs.

Finance ONLINE

Go to the following site for Free Estate Planning Forms and more on estate planning: **resources.lawinfo.com**. Search on "Estate Planning" for a wide range of estate planning forms.

Figure 15.4   A Sample Will

A will is a necessary part of estate planning for people of all ages.

WILL of James T. Smith

I, James T. Smith of the City of Denver, Colorado, declare this to be my will.

ARTICLE 1
My wife, Karen A. Smith, and I have one child, Cheryl D. Smith.

ARTICLE 2 Payment of Debt and Taxes
I direct my Executor to pay my funeral expenses, my medical expenses, the costs of administration, and my debts.

ARTICLE 3 Distribution of the Estate
I direct that my estate be distributed to my wife, Karen A. Smith. If my wife predeceases me, my estate shall be distributed to my Trustee, to be managed as explained in Article 4.

ARTICLE 4 Trust for Children
4A. Purpose. This trust provides for the support of my daughter, Cheryl D. Smith, and any other children born to me.
4B. Use of Funds. The Trustee shall use as much of the trust income and principal as necessary to care for my child (or children). When the youngest of my children reaches the age of 25, the assets of this trust shall be split equally among the children.
4C. No Survivors. If no child of mine survives until age 25, assets of the trust shall be liquidated and 100 percent of the proceeds shall be donated to the San Diego Humane Society.
4D. Nomination of Trustee. I appoint my brother, Edward J. Smith, to serve as Trustee. If he is unable or unwilling to serve, I appoint my sister, Marie S. Smith, to serve as Trustee.

ARTICLE 5 Executor
I appoint my wife, Karen A. Smith, to serve as Executor. If she is unable or unwilling to serve, I appoint my brother, Edward J. Smith, to serve as Executor.

ARTICLE 6 Guardian
If my spouse does not survive me, I appoint my brother, Edward J. Smith, to serve as Guardian of my children. If he is unable to serve as Guardian, I appoint my sister, Marie S. Smith, to serve as Guardian.

ARTICLE 7 Power of Executor
My Executor has the right to receive payments, reinvest payments received, pay debts owed, pay taxes owed, and liquidate assets.

ARTICLE 8 Power of Trustee
My Trustee has the right to receive income generated by the trust, reinvest income received by the trust, sell assets in the trust, and use the proceeds to invest in other assets.
IN WITNESS WHEREOF, I hereby sign and declare this document to be my Will.

_____   _____

James T. Smith   Date

The above-named person signed in our presence, and in our opinion is mentally competent.

Signatures of Witnesses   Addresses of Witnesses

_____

Kenneth Tagan   44241 Lemon Street
Denver, Colorado 80208

_____

Barbara Russell   101 Courtney Street
Denver, Colorado 80208

Trusts

Estate planning often involves establishing a trust to transfer assets in a manner that avoids taxes. There are a number of types of trusts defined by law but all are essentially legal mechanisms that help reduce tax liability as assets are transferred from one person to another. **Trusts** place assets in the custody of a third party known as a trustee. The trustee manages those assets for the designated beneficiaries. These types of arrangements can be very complex and require expert legal advice to establish properly.

✓ CHECK Your Financial IQ

Why is it worthwhile to engage in estate planning today?

Chapter Review

Summary

- Understanding the time value of money concept can help you see vividly the importance of planning for the future. Planning for the future is easier if you know how much money you need to save and invest every month or year to achieve your goals. Seeing the power of compound interest can demonstrate how your dreams can come true. Future value calculations can help you make those determinations. Present value calculations can help you determine how much house you can afford or car payments you can handle.

- You can also use this financial math to help you evaluate different investment options and manage your portfolio. You know that a risk/return tradeoff exists in which you must assume more risk to get a higher return. However, you also know that proper diversification can help you reduce risk in your investment portfolio.

- Sound investing will allow you accumulate wealth for retirement and pass some of this wealth to your heirs.

- Estate planning and the creation of a will can help you reduce the tax liability when you pass wealth to subsequent generations.

Key Terms and Vocabulary

Asset allocation	Estate planning	Rule of 72
Asset class	Future value	Simple interest
Beneficiary	Intestate	Time value of money
Compounding	Portfolio	Trust
Diversification	Present value	Will

What Do You Know?

myFinLitlab

1. (a) What is the time value of money?

   (b) How is it related to the concept of opportunity cost?

2. (a) What is a present value?

   (b) How can present values be used in financial planning?

3. (a) Define compounding.

   (b) How is it used in financial planning?

4. (a) What is simple interest?

   (b) Compare compound interest to simple interest.

5. (a) What is an annuity?

   (b) Give examples of annuities.

6. (a) What are future values?

   (b) How can future values be used in financial planning?

7. (a) Explain what a portfolio is in terms of investments.

   (b) What do you need to do to achieve a diversified portfolio?

8. (a) Explain the risk and return tradeoff faced by investors.

   (b) What should you do with an investment that is not achieving a return that is appropriate for the level of risk involved?

9. (a) What is an estate?

   (b) What is estate planning?

   (c) Who benefits most from estate planning?

10. (a) What is a will?

    (b) Why is a will important?

    (c) What is an example of a bad outcome from not having a will?

What Are Your Finance Math Skills?   myFinLitlab.

1. How much would you accumulate if you invested $4,000 for 30 years at 8 percent?

2. Assuming you could earn 5 percent interest, what amount could you receive today that would be equal to receiving $6,000 in two years?

3. How much could you accumulate over a 30-year period if you invested $3,000 a year and earned an 11 percent annual return?

4. How much interest will you earn on $2,500 invested for 5 years at 7 percent assuming simple interest?

5. How much interest will you earn on $2,500 invested for 5 years at 7 percent using compound interest?

6. Niko invested $3,000 in the stock market and expects to earn 10 percent a year. Assuming annual compounding, how much money will Niko have in 30 years?

7. Jenny will receive $4,000 at the end of next year. Assuming she could invest the money and earn 5 percent, what is the present value of that gift?

8. How much will Skyler earn in simple interest on a deposit of $2,000 for two years earning 6.5 percent annually?

What Would You Do?

After college graduation, Amanda and George were married. They had been high school sweethearts. Both remembered a class where the teacher discussed the need to begin planning for retirement early in their lives. With this in mind, they began planning.

In their 30s, Amanda and George became once again concerned about retirement. Their family had grown and now included two children. They continued to follow the lessons learned in school about saving for retirement, but now they also needed to include saving for college educations for their two children. With other bills, saving for retirement became a lower priority for them. In a discussion with Amanda's Aunt Shea about how to handle retirement investing, Aunt Shea told them not to worry. She had provided well for them in her will. After this discussion, Amanda and George felt better about having a comfortable retirement with this inheritance to help.

Fifteen years later, Aunt Shea passed away. At the reading of her will, Amanda was surprised to learn that Aunt Shea had made the same promise to her cousins. As all four sat listening to the reading, they found that $800,000 was to be divided between them after $400,000 was donated to the university where Aunt Shea had taught for 20 years.

a. Discuss your views on the ethics of Aunt Shea's decision.

b. What do you think should be done with the inheritance for Amanda and George?

c. Looking at Amanda and George's experience, what lessons about retirement planning can be learned?

What Are the Connections? Language Arts and Mathematics

Each of you is given $1,000 in cash as graduation gifts from various relatives and family friends. You would like to invest this in a certificate of deposit (CD) so that you will have a down payment on a car when you graduate from college in five years.

1. Work in teams to find the best buy for a CD.
  a. Look at what is being offered by three different banks.
  b. Provide data on the interest being paid by each bank.

2. Write a recommendation for purchasing the CD that will return the most money to you at the end of the five years.
  a. Determine how much you will have in five years to put down on a car.
  b. Does this amount surprise you in any way?

Teamwork

As a team, develop a Public Service Announcement (PSA) about planning for the future. Your audience for this PSA is your fellow students. Think about what you have learned in this chapter about planning for the future. What would you tell them about investing, putting together a portfolio, when they need to begin planning, and retirement. You can develop your PSA as a brochure, newsletter, video, skit, or other type of announcement that is interesting, captures their attention, and teaches them the facts.

1. Financial experts say "the time value of money" can make a person a million-aire in retirement. Which example illustrates this statement?
   a. A person deposits $50,000 into her retirement account five years before her planned retirement. The account returns an average of 10 percent a year.
   b. A person planning to retire at age 68 begins investing $3,000 a year into his retirement account as soon as he graduates from college and gets a job. The account's average annual return is 8 percent.
   c. A person, planning to retire at age 70 puts $10,000 a year into a retirement account starting at age 60. The account has an annual return of 10 percent.
   d. A person age 50, planning to retire at age 75, deposits $100,000 into a savings account returning 2.5 percent annually.

2. Which of the following terms is *not* correctly defined?
   a. The time value of money: money received today is worth more than money received in the future because the money can be put to work earning more money.
   b. Future value: an amount of money earned in the future based on inflation.
   c. Compounding: earning money on both the principal deposited in the account and interest earned on that principal in the past.
   d. Present value: the value of some future sum of money in the present.

3. A person who spends $5 every day for coffee and soft drinks decides to give up this habit and invest the money instead. Assuming the average annual rate of return on his investment is 10 percent, how much money will he have after five years?
   a. He will have $2,007.50.
   b. He will have $9,125.
   c. He will have $10,037.50.
   d. He will have $12,255.98.

4. A person has a choice of receiving $3,000 now or $4,000 after she graduates from college in five years. She decides to take the $3,000 and invest it at an expected 10 percent annual rate of return. Did she make a wise decision?
   a. No, because the time value of money shows that money received in the future has more purchasing power than money received today.
   b. No, because the annual rate of inflation of 5 percent will cancel out any money earned on the $3,000.
   c. Yes, because $3,000 received today and invested for five years at 10 percent will be worth more than $4,000 received after five years.
   d. Yes, because she will have over $4,000 in her investment account after only two years of investing the money, which is three years ahead of schedule.

5. Based on the rule of 72, the time it will take for a $5,000 investment to double in value at an annual 6 percent rate of interest is
   a. 7.2 years.
   b. 12 years.
   c. 36 years.
   d. impossible to know because not enough information is provided.

6. Which of the following terms is correctly matched with its definition?
   a. Diversification: the method for determining the value of a person's assets.
   b. Simple interest: the amount of money that an investment earns on a daily basis.

c. Annuity: an insurance program such as the FDIC designed to protect a person's investments in case a company goes bankrupt.

d. Portfolio: a complete picture of all of a person's investments and savings assets.

7. Which of the following statements about diversification is *not* accurate?

a. Asset allocation is the process of dividing investment among several different asset classes.

b. Having a diversified portfolio is a way to reduce risk.

c. If a person has 90 percent of her investments in the stock of a company that produces a variety of consumer goods, her portfolio is considered diversified.

d. The benefit of having a diversified portfolio is that if the stocks in the portfolio are falling in value, the value of the bonds or real estate in the portfolio may be going up.

8. Which of the following is a true statement about the relationship between risk and return?

a. A young person can take bigger risks in hopes of earning higher returns compared to an older person because the younger person has more time to recover in the event the risky investments decline in value.

b. A low risk stock investment promises a guaranteed rate of return on the investment.

c. A young person with a high degree of risk tolerance should put all of her investment money in corporate bonds and United States Treasury bonds.

d. An older person should have riskier investments in her portfolio than a younger person because an older person needs a greater rate of return on her investments because she is close to retirement.

9. When it comes to retirement planning, it is a good idea

a. to hire a financial planner who promises that she can invest a person's money so that the person can retire at age 50.

b. if someone age 25 wants to retire at age 55 with a $2,000,000 retirement account to figure out how much money needs to be saved and invested for the next 30 years using the time value of money and a financial calculator.

c. if people in their 20s today plan on most of their retirement income coming from Social Security.

d. not to spend the time and money to have a will prepared unless assets are above $1.5 million.

10. Estate planning is

a. naming a person to be the beneficiary of a person's assets.

b. something people should begin to work on after they retire and begin collecting retirement benefits.

c. the process of determining how a person's assets will be divided before or after a person dies.

d. the division of real estate between a person's family and the state.

11. A person should have a will to

a. guarantee that her financial portfolio remains diversified after her death.

b. protect investments in a retirement portfolio from losing value.

c. make sure that her heirs never have to pay estate taxes on the money they inherit.

d. give a person the opportunity to determine how she wants her assets to be divided after her death.

Glossary

401(k)/403(b) plans Popular types of defined-contribution retirement plans. They allow employees to contribute into their accounts, which may feature a range of investment options.

Accreditation An official recognition that a school or program meets a certain standard.

Adjustable rate mortgage Mortgage with a rate that may go up or down. The rate change occurs at some preset time—for example, after one year.

Adjusted gross income Total income minus certain allowable amounts such as contributions to some retirement accounts, alimony payments, and interest paid on student loans.

Annual fee Charged by credit card companies for the privilege of using their card.

Annual percentage rate (APR) The interest rate that shows what a borrower is actually paying with all the costs of financing factored in.

Annual percentage yield (APY) The interest rate that shows what an account will earn annually with compounding factored in.

Annuity A situation in which there are equal cash flows occurring at equal intervals for a fixed period of time.

Apprenticeship On-the-job program in which a person may receive formal training.

Asset Something owned.

Asset allocation The process of spreading investments among asset classes—diversifying investments.

Asset classes Investments, such as stocks, bonds, and real estate, that one makes to reach long-term goals.

Automatic Teller Machine (ATM) Provides banking customers with access to financial transactions in a public space without the need for a bank teller.

Baby boom A period of very high birthrates that occurred between 1946 and 1964.

Bank draft Used to authorize someone to withdraw money from a bank account automatically to satisfy some financial obligation.

Bankruptcy A legal process in which a court takes over some of the finances of a person who is unable to pay his or her bills.

Beneficiary A person who receives payment from a life insurance provider when the policyholder dies.

Bond A promissory note to repay a certain amount of money at some future point.

Brokerage A firm that provides access to the stock markets.

Budget A list of planned expenses and revenues.

Budgeting The process of forecasting future expenses and income.

Business cycle The economic pattern of alternating periods of shrinking and expanding.

Capital gain Taxable income that occurs when an asset is sold for more than it originally cost.

Cash advance The ability to use a credit card to withdraw cash from a bank or ATM (rather than just purchasing a good or a service).

Cash inflow Money received.

Cash outflow Money spent.

Cashier's check A type of check that is written to a specific payee but charged against a bank instead of an individual account.

Certificate of deposit (CD) A contract between an individual and a financial institution that specifies the time that the individual will leave a certain amount of money deposited in the account and the interest rate earned.

Certification An official document or record that states that a person has met some standard for training or knowledge.

Check A written order from an individual to a bank that instructs the bank to pay money to another party.

Check register A small ledger provided by a bank for keeping track of an account balance.

Checking account An account into which a person deposits money and from which a person withdraws money by writing checks or using a debit card.

COBRA The Consolidated Omnibus Budget Reconciliation Act. It allows an individual temporarily to continue health insurance coverage at group rates.

Coinsurance The share of costs for covered insurance services that an individual is required to pay out of pocket. Often called a co-pay.

Collateral Assets that have been pledged against a loan repayment.

Commission Fee charged by a brokerage firm for carrying out a transaction.

Compensation Money earned and benefits given by employers.

Compound interest Interest earned on interest added to an account.

Compounding The process of earning interest on interest previously added to an account.

Consumer price index (CPI) The formal measure of prices used to calculate inflation that tells us whether things overall are more expensive now than in the past.

Corporate bonds Bonds issued by a large company—they have all degrees of risk depending on the strength of the corporation.

Cosigner A person, other than the principal borrower, who signs for a loan and assumes equal liability for it.

Coupon payment Regular interest payments on bonds.

Coupon rate A bond's interest rate, so-called because originally bonds came with booklets of prewritten coupons for the interest due.

Credit Money that a lender makes available to a borrower with the understanding that the borrower will repay the money.

Credit bureau Organization that collects credit information about individual consumers.

Credit card Provides individuals with revolving open-end credit, which they can draw from repeatedly up to some preset limit.

Credit check Performed by potential creditors to access a person's credit report to examine the individual's credit history and the ability to repay.

Credit history Record of credit use and payments.

Credit limit A person may borrow up to this amount based on his or her income level, debt level, and overall credit record.

Credit management Decision making about getting and using credit.

Credit provider An entity, such as a bank, that agrees to make a certain amount of credit available to a cardholder.

Credit report Summarizes an individual's existing and past lines of credit.

Credit score Created by credit bureaus to assess an individual's creditworthiness.

Credit union Functions similarly to a bank, but has nonprofit status and is owned by its members.

Creditor Someone who provides credit.

Current liability Debt that is due within one year.

Debit card Enables one to withdraw cash from an ATM or to pay directly for goods or services at stores and restaurants.

Debt consolidation Combining several small accounts into one larger account that may be able to be financed at a lower rate.

Deductible The amount of money that a policyholder must pay before an insurance policy will begin to cover a claim.

Default When a person stops making payments on a loan.

Defined-benefit plan An employer-sponsored retirement plan in which an employer guarantees an employee a specific amount of income at retirement. The benefit is often based on factors such as the number of years worked and the average salary earned during peak earning years.

Defined-contribution plan An employer-sponsored retirement plan in which an employer contributes to an employee's retirement account but does not guarantee a specific retirement benefit.

Demand deposit Money put into a checkable account that can be withdrawn at any time.

Demographics The study of human populations.

Depository institution A financial institution, such as a savings bank, that is legally allowed to accept monetary deposits from consumers.

Depression A severe recession.

Disability insurance Insures the beneficiary's earned income against the risk that sickness or injury will make working (and therefore earning) impossible.

Discount brokerage Offers a reduced level of service, lower costs, and often the ability to trade online.

Discount rate The interest rate the Fed charges to banks when it loans them money.

Diversification The process of investing in multiple investments.

Dividend The distribution of cash to shareholders.

Down payment The initial upfront portion of the total amount due on a purchase.

Economics The production, distribution, and consumption of goods and services. Economists seek to understand ways that individuals and businesses make decisions, the factors that influence their choices, and the impact these decisions have on others.

Economy The system related to the production, distribution, exchange, and consumption of goods and services in which individuals, businesses, governments, and the world interact.

Electronic funds transfer Authorization for someone to access a bank account for payment or deposit.

Employer-sponsored retirement plan Set up by an employer and designed to help employees save for retirement. The employer generally contributes to the plan.

Equal Credit Opportunity Act Prohibits creditors from denying credit based on gender, age, race, national origin, religion, or marital status.

Equity Ownership in something.

Estate planning The process of determining how wealth will be allocated on or before a person's death.

Expense Anything on which money is spent.

Face value A bond's maturity value, which is printed on the front of the bond.

Fair Credit Reporting Act A federal law that limits the sharing of an individual's financial information to firms that have a legal purpose to evaluate it.

Fair Isaac Corporation Created a model on which credit scores (FICO scores) are calculated.

Federal agency bonds Issued by federal agencies whose proceeds are used to buy mortgages to encourage home ownership.

Federal Deposit Insurance Corporation (FDIC) A major federal insurer that provides deposit insurance on the first $250,000 deposited in a bank account.

Federal Perkins loan Similar to a Stafford loan, but for students with "exceptional" financial need. This loan carries a lower interest rate and offers a longer grace period before repayment must begin.

Federal Reserve System The central bank of the United States.

Federal Stafford loan The most common type of federal education loan; it is available in two forms: subsidized and unsubsidized.

Fiat money The money currently used in the United States. It has value because the government orders that it must be accepted as payment.

Finance To pay a portion of the cost of a major purchase such as a house or a car by taking a loan.

Fixed annuity A type of financial product that guarantees annual payments to the owner for a fixed period of time or for a person's lifetime. The return and ultimate payment is a guaranteed amount.

Fixed expense An expense that remains the same from period to period.

Fixed rate mortgage A mortgage in which the interest rate remains the same for the life of the loan.

Forecast A projection about future cash flows.

Forecast error The difference between the actual value and the predicted value for the corresponding period.

Fraud Occurs when someone submits false information to get a financial benefit.

Full-service brokerage Provides advice and executes trades for a price; for example, Merrill Lynch and Edward Jones.

Future value What money is "worth" at a specified time in the future assuming a certain interest rate.

Global economy The world in which economies of all countries interact and depend on each other.

Grace period Time in which credit card companies do not charge interest on purchases. Typical grace periods are 20 days from the time the statement is "closed," or the bill is calculated and mailed.

Gross domestic product (GDP) The total dollar amount of all final goods and services purchased domestically in a given year.

Gross income The total amount of a person's income.

Gross pay Hourly wage multiplied by hours worked.

Group plan Insurance plans that cover a large group of individuals, such as employees of a particular company or local government. Within a group plan, an individual's high risk or loss is spread across the entire pool of group members.

Health insurance Provides payment to people who suffer a financial loss as a result of illness or injury.

HIPAA The Health Insurance Portability and Accounting Act ensures that workers can continue their health insurance coverage if they switch jobs. The act prohibits insurance companies from denying new employees access to coverage based on their health or preexisting conditions.

Home equity loan Allows a homeowner to borrow against the equity in his or her home—that is, the difference between the home's value and the amount owed to a lender.

Household asset Tangible possessions owned by a household. Furniture is one example.

Identity theft When someone uses an individual's personal information without permission for personal gain.

Income Money coming in through wages earned, allowance, or other sources.

Individual retirement account (IRA) A type of savings account created by the government to encourage people to save for retirement.

Inflation A sustained increase in the general level of prices. During a time of inflation, most things become more expensive and the purchasing power of money decreases.

Initial public offering (IPO) The first sale of stock issued by a company to raise money for business operations, expansion, and other needs.

Installment credit Used for specific purchases; allows the borrower more time to repay.

Institutional investor One who trades large volumes of stocks on behalf of large institutions; for example, for a huge pension fund.

Insurance A financial product that when purchased provides reimbursement paid to a person in the event of certain types of financial loss.

Interest Fee charged by a lender on money borrowed.

Internal Revenue Service A branch of the United States Treasury Department that carries out the federal tax system.

Internship A temporary, short-term position designed to provide exposure to and training for a particular job.

Intestate When an individual dies without having a will.

Investment Something acquired with the goal of making money.

Itemized deduction A specific expense that, under tax law, can be deducted from income to reduce the amount of income subject to income tax.

Junk bonds Corporate bonds issued by companies with the highest risk.

Lease A long-term rental agreement.

Liability What is owed (debt).

Liability coverage Auto insurance that covers damage to an individual's car or damage caused to other people or their property.

Life insurance Provides payment to a specific person or persons when the policyholder dies.

Line of credit An agreement to allow borrowing as needed up to a certain amount of money.

Liquid asset Something owned that can be rapidly converted to cash without a risk of significant loss.

Liquidity Available cash on hand for meeting immediate wants and needs.

Long-term goal A goal that will take more than five years to accomplish.

Long-term liability Liabilities that will take more than one year to pay off.

Macroeconomics The study of broad economic issues that impact the economy as a whole.

Market value The current quoted price at which investors buy or sell a share of common stock or a bond at a given time.

Maturity date The date at which a loan will be completely repaid.

Medicaid A government-sponsored program that provides health insurance for low-income individuals.

Medicare Funded by payroll taxes. Provides health care coverage to older Americans and some younger disabled people.

Microeconomics The study of individual choices or decisions made by small units.

Middle-term goal A goal an individual aims to meet within the next one to five years.

Monetary policy The raising or lowering of the money supply to achieve some goal.

Money management Making decisions about how much cash or liquid assets to keep in reserve and how much to invest.

Money market deposit account Has some features of a checking account or a savings account. These accounts require an individual to maintain a minimum balance, have no maturity date, pay interest, and offer limited check-writing privileges.

Money order Functions similarly to a cashier's check. It is purchased for cash so that the recipient can trust its worth.

Mortgage The common term for the type of loan people take to purchase a home.

Municipal bond Issued by state and local governments to finance large public projects such as water and sewer systems.

Mutual fund Sells shares to investors in order to collect a pool of money that is then used to buy various investments.

National Association of Security Dealers Automated Quotation (NASDAQ) An organized stock exchange in the secondary market in which stock sales occur.

National Credit Union Savings Insurance Fund (NCUSIF) A major federal insurer that provides deposit insurance on the first $250,000 deposited in a credit union account.

Negotiable order of withdrawal (NOW) Functions like a checking account but pays a small amount of interest on money in the account. NOW accounts require the user to maintain a minimum balance in order to earn interest.

Net pay Wages that remain after taxes are withheld (take-home pay).

Net worth Assets minus liabilities.

New York Stock Exchange (NYSE) An organized stock exchange in the secondary market in which stock sales occur.

Nondepository institutions Insurance companies, finance companies, and securities firms and investment companies that provide certain financial services but do not accept traditional deposits.

Noninstallment credit The simplest form of consumer credit. It is usually for a very short term, such as 30 days.

Opportunity cost The opportunity lost to do something with money when an individual uses that money to do something else.

Overdraft protection A feature that allows a person to "overdraw," or exceed the credit limit. (Overdraft protection is also a feature of checking accounts, where it protects someone in the event that a check is written for more money than is in the account.)

Pawnbroker Holds items in exchange for loans that run for 30 days to as much as three months.

Payday lending A lender provides cash advances at a high cost to customers who provide a check dated for some time in the future.

Payment terms Specific information about the interest rate and the time period for paying back a loan.

Payroll tax Tax withheld from paychecks and sent to the government by employers.

Pension plan A defined-benefit plan under which an employer makes contributions to the plan on the employee's behalf.

Personal balance sheet Lists current assets such as cash in checking accounts and savings accounts, long-term assets such as common stock and real estate, current liabilities such as loan debt and mortgage debt due or overdue, and long-term liabilities such as mortgage and other loan debt.

Personal finance Financial issues that can affect an individual.

Personal financial plan Specifies financial goals and describes in detail the spending, financing, and investing plans needed to reach those goals.

Personal financial planning The process of planning every aspect of personal finances.

Personal identification number (PIN) Typically a four-digit number needed to access a bank account or debit card.

Personal income tax A tax levied on the financial income of individuals.

Personal loan A loan that is not backed by collateral. Also known as an unsecured loan, it is based solely upon the borrower's credit rating.

Pharming Identity theft technique that uses e-mail viruses to redirect someone from a legitimate Web site to an official looking Web site designed to obtain personal information.

Phishing Pretexting that occurs online.

Policy rider Additional insurance coverage to cover things such as jewelry or valuable heirlooms that are often not fully covered by a typical insurance policy.

Policyholder A person who buys a health insurance policy or subscribes to it through an employer.

Portfolio An individual's investments.

Preexisting condition A health condition that existed before an individual's policy was granted.

Premium Regular payments paid to an insurance company in return for coverage.

Present value The value of a cost or benefit computed in terms of cash today.

Pretexting Occurs when someone improperly accesses an individual's personal information by posing as someone seeking data.

Price level stability A goal of the Fed to ensure that inflation or deflation does not occur.

Primary market The initial sale of financial assets in which a company receives money during an IPO.

Principal The total amount of money outstanding on a loan.

Publicly traded When a company begins trading on one of the organized stock exchanges.

Real estate Buildings and land.

Recession A period of time in which the economy is shrinking.

Résumé A snapshot of an individual's qualifications including background, education, and previous work history.

Revolving open-end credit Allows consumers to borrow up to some preset maximum amount.

Risk The possibility of a financial loss.

Roth IRA Similar to a traditional IRA, but contributions are not tax deductible. Earnings from an eligible account are never taxed, even after withdrawal.

Rule of 72 Shows how long it would take to double an amount of money for a given interest rate.

Safety deposit boxes Small containers located inside a bank vault used to store valuable documents such as wills and small objects such as jewelry, rare coins, and legal documents.

Sales tax Tax collected by a merchant when a purchase is made and then sent to the government.

Savings account Bank account that generally pays a low rate of interest on deposits.

Secondary market Transactions that take place after an IPO.

Secured loan Has an asset pledged against the loan. The lender is assured of ending up with some valuable asset if the borrower fails to pay off the loan.

Securities and Exchange Commission (SEC) A government agency that regulates and monitors the stock market.

Security Investment issued by a corporation or government in which the investor receives proof of ownership.

SEP-IRA An IRA for self-employed people.

Shareholders People who own stock in a company.

Short-term goal A goal to be accomplished within the next year.

Shoulder surfing An identity theft technique that involves someone in a public place accessing personal information by listening to a conversation or viewing personal information.

Simple interest Interest earned only on the original amount or principal.

Skimming Identity theft technique that involves copying credit card or debit card numbers from credit or debit cards.

Social Security Funded by payroll taxes. It provides payments to eligible retirees and disabled people.

Standard deduction A fixed amount individuals are allowed to deduct from their adjusted gross income to reduce their tax liability.

Stock A fractional share of ownership in a company.

Subprime mortgage High interest rate mortgage loan made to people with poor credit scores.

Take-home pay Wages that remain after taxes are withheld (net pay).

Tax Money collected by a government from its citizens and businesses in order to operate the government.

Tax deductible A feature that allows people to reduce their income taxes by reducing taxable income for the year in which they make a contribution (for example, to an IRA).

Tax deferred When account earnings, such as from interest, are not taxed until they are withdrawn after retirement.

Tax return A report submitted to the IRS that includes all the information relative to an individual's income taxes.

Teaser rate An extremely low interest rate for a short period of time that is used to entice a borrower into a deal.

Term insurance Life insurance provided over a specific period of time.

Time value of money Refers to the fact that money received today is worth more than money received next year or the year after.

Traditional IRA An account in which people can make tax deductible contributions and all earnings are tax deferred.

Travelers checks Checks paid for in advance and written by a large financial institution with no payee specified.

Treasury bond Issued by the United States Treasury to finance the debt of the government.

Trust Legal mechanism that helps to reduce tax liability when assets are transferred from one person to another.

Universal life insurance Provides coverage for a specified term and builds savings for the policyholder.

Unsecured loan A loan in which there is no collateral pledged.

Variable annuity A type of financial product that guarantees annual payments to the owner for a fixed time or for a lifetime. The return and ultimate payment depend on the performance of the investments.

Variable expense An expense that changes from one period to the next.

Vesting The process of earning eligibility for an employer benefit.

Whole life insurance Provides coverage for as long as the policyholder continues to pay the premium.

Will A legal request for how an individual's estate (everything accumulated during a lifetime) should be distributed upon death.

Index

V

Variable annuities, 242
Variable expenses, 43
Vesting, defined-benefit plans and, 241
Visa cards, 194–195

W

W-2 forms, 102
Wages
  cash inflows, 54
  choosing career and, 74
  gross income and, 102–103
Wal-Mart
  ability to get better deal with credit card companies, 194
  prepaid cash cards, 198
Wall Street Journal, 255
Walton, Alice, 58
Web site resources. *See* www
Whole life insurance, 120–121
Will, estate planning and, 283–284
www.aarp.org (senior support), 282
www.acinet.org (job training), 78
www.bls.gov
  Bureau of Labor Statistics, 78
  job salary information, 75
  jobs in banking industry, 214
  Occupational Outlook Handbook, 70, 75
  on service-related occupations, 74
www.capitalone.com (auto loan calculator), 170

www.careerbuilder.com (job availability), 75
www.careerjournal.com (job salary information), 75
www.careers-in-finance.com/fpskill.htm (careers in finance), 12
www.careers.com (career options), 75
www.census.gov (health insurance information), 116
www.cfp.net (careers in finance), 12
www.chase.com (payment calculator), 152
www.collegeboard.com (career profiles by college major), 78
www.federalreserve.gov
  Consumer Help, 198
  information on Fed role in money supply, 223
www.forbes.com (researching wealthy people), 58
www.ftc.gov (identity theft information), 157
www.ifg.com (financial calculators), 238
www.ipohome.com (IPO information), 255
www.irs.gov
  income tax information, 94–95
  tax forms available from, 98
www.kbb.com (Kelley Blue Book), 59, 179
www.medicare.gov (Medicare information), 114
www.moneychimp.com (rule of 72), 279
www.MonsterTrak.com (employment site), 82
www.myfico.com (credit score information), 153
www.mymoneyanswer.com/goals.htm (financial goal setting), 41
www.paydayloaninfo.org (payday lending information), 201
www.salliemae.com (student loan information), 178
www.sec.gov (ECN information), 256
www.stockmarketstory.com (history of stock market), 255
www.treasurydirect.gov (Treasury bonds from), 262
www.vanguard.com (mutual fund information), 263